CHRONICLES

OF THE

TUDOR QUEENS

DAVID LOADES

SUTTON PUBLISHING

First published in the United Kingdom in 2002 by
Sutton Publishing Limited · Phoenix Mill
Thrupp · Stroud · Gloucestershire · GL5 2BU

British Library Cataloguing in Publication Data
A catalogue record for this book is available from the British Library.

ISBN 0-7509-2742-9

Typeset in 11/13pt Sabon.
Typesetting and origination by
Sutton Publishing Limited.
Printed and bound in England by
J.H. Haynes & Co. Ltd, Sparkford.

Contents

Preface

Mary was England's first ruling Queen. To a generation accustomed to fifty years of Elizabeth II, and at least aware of Victoria, Anne and Elizabeth I, it is hard to realise what an unnerving experience that was. The notional nine-day reign of Queen Jane does not count; and the Empress Matilda who had claimed the crown in 1135, and fought for it, had never been accepted. Henry VIII had moved heaven and earth to avoid such a contingency, and Edward VI, before death overtook him, had been equally emphatic. Had he been able to find a man with a remotely plausible claim to the Crown, Mary might well have failed to secure the right that her father had (eventually) bequeathed her. However, in spite of his determination, he was reduced to using another woman in an attempt to block her claim, and that ensured his failure.

From whatever angle she is viewed, Mary was in most respects unsuccessful. Her marriage was ill-fated; her war against France failed; and her religious settlement was frustrated both by opposition and by lack of time. But in one specific respect she succeeded. She established the legal precedent that a woman could exercise the royal office, without limitation, and even after marriage. Philip was King, not Prince Consort, but his power was extremely limited, and his right ended with her life. This was more important than it is now easy to imagine. A monarch no longer needed to be (even theoretically) a warrior. Consequently, although there must have been many in 1558 who wondered whether England could survive another female, Elizabeth had no difficulty either in asserting her right or exercising her own power. She was to reign for forty-five years, remain unmarried and preside over one of the most creative and formative periods in English history. Her debt to her father is well known; her debt to her brother rather less so; but her debt to her sister is hardly ever mentioned.

What follows in this book is a collection of documents that treats the years from 1553 to 1603 as a unit; the England of the Queens. The Salic law prevented France from undergoing a similar experience, and in fact no other European country was to provide a parallel until the Russia of Catherine the Great. Both Mary and Elizabeth governed in a specifically female way; but whereas Mary depended for her strength principally upon inflexibility of conscience, Elizabeth deployed a full range of artifice and device. The men who served her were beguiled, fascinated and intimidated; they were also, on occasion, driven to apoplectic fury. I hope that the texture of both Marian and Elizabethan politics will emerge from the selection that I have made. The range of potential material is vast, particularly for the well-documented years after 1558, but I have tried to avoid the obvious tactic of skipping from one salient event to the next. The balance, it will be immediately observed, is not strictly proportional; the five years of Mary's reign occupying nearly a third of the whole, instead of just over the tenth to which they should be strictly entitled. The reasons for this are: partly that these were very disturbed years, particularly in respect of the religious settlement and persecution; partly because of Mary's ambivalent attitude to the policies of her father, and even her grandfather; and partly because they were the pioneering days of female rule. In terms of high-profile achievement, there can be no comparison between the two women; but that is another reason for placing slightly more emphasis upon Mary. No one would have dreamed of dubbing her Gloriana. Instead the epitaph of John Foxe has lingered in the national subconscious: '. . . we shall find never no reign of any prince in this land or any other, which had ever to shew in it (for the proportion of time) so many arguments of God's great wrath and displeasure, as was to be seen in the reign of this Queen Mary . . .'. In fact, without Mary Elizabeth would not only have been diminished; she might never have come to the throne at all.

Acknowledgements for reproductions, both of documents and of illustrations, are separately listed. Apart from that, I accept full responsibility, both for the selection of documents and for the brief commentaries that accompany them. My major debt of gratitude, as always, is to my wife, guide and mentor, Judith, to whom this work is affectionately dedicated.

David Loades
Burford, January 2002

List of Plates

Plates 1 to 8 are between pp. 70 and 71; plates 9 to 15 are between pp. 134 and 135; plates 16 to 22 are between pp. 198 and 199; and plates 23 to 29 are between pp. 262 and 263.

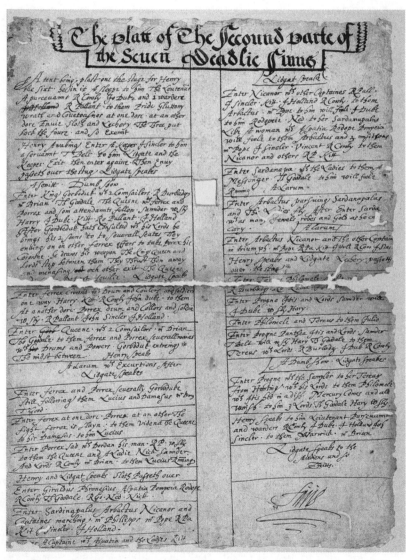

'The platt of the Seconnd parte of the Seven Deadlie Sinnes', Dulwich College
MS XIX. (By permission of Dulwich College)

Introduction

The second half of the sixteenth century was for England a period of dramatic contrasts and immense creativity. When Edward VI died on 6 July 1553, the country was faced with a choice of great significance. Edward, preoccupied with male legitimacy, and overtaken by his own declining health, tried to bar both his half-sisters from the succession. In the case of Elizabeth, this was partly on the grounds of bastardy, and partly that her unmarried condition posed a threat to national autonomy and security. In the case of Mary, there was the additional problem of her religious conservatism. She had defied all her brother's religious reforms to the best of her ability, and there was no doubt that, if she succeeded to the Crown, she would undo the Protestant settlement by which he had set such store. Edward, therefore, with the active assistance of his mentor, John Dudley, Duke of Northumberland, decreed that the Crown should pass to his cousin, Jane Dudley. She was the daughter of Frances Grey, Duchess of Suffolk, and granddaughter of Henry VIII's younger sister, Mary. Jane was legitimate, she was a Protestant, and she was already married to Northumberland's youngest son, Guildford.

Unfortunately, Henry's last succession act of 1543, and his will of January 1547, both decreed that in the event of his son dying without lawful heirs, the Crown was to pass first to Mary, and then to Elizabeth, provided only that neither had married without the consent of the council. The choice in the summer of 1553 was therefore stark: either support the lawful heir, Mary, and take a chance on where her marriage might lead; or support Jane, and gamble on what implications that might have for the authority of statute law. At first it appeared that Northumberland, who immediately caused Jane to be proclaimed, held all the cards: support of the council, and control of such military power as was available. Most outside observers thought that he would prevail. However, the political nation of England supported Mary. She proclaimed herself and mobilised her own affinity, which formed the nucleus of a rapidly growing power at Framlingham in Suffolk. Even the majority of Protestants, who had the most reason to doubt her religious intentions, supported her at this juncture. As a result, Queen Jane reigned for just nine days, the shortest reign in English history. By 19 July the council had split, and

Northumberland's military force had melted away. He was already unpopular, and after this defeat was demonised by Mary's supporters, particularly those who shared her religious views.

Although Mary thus came to the throne with the wind of popular and aristocratic support behind her, she immediately began to encounter problems. Her withdrawal from active political life during her brother's reign meant that her personal affinity contained no men with significant political experience. Consequently her council came to be made up partly of personal servants, whom she trusted but who had never held office, and partly of experienced politicians who had served her father or brother (or both), and who she did not entirely trust. Self-interest alone was sufficient to guarantee that the latter served her loyally, but relationships within the council continued to be uneasy, and Mary never found a way to resolve or control them. Furthermore, she immediately informed her council of her intention to restore the papal jurisdiction in England. This came as a surprise to many (if not most), because her declared position for nearly twenty years had been to support and protect her father's settlement. The 'old religion' which she was known to stand for was understood to mean the mass, and the traditional ceremonies of the Catholic Church as her father had left them. This was a generally popular position, but the papacy was something else, and attitudes both among the nobility and the people at large were much more equivocal. There was a general feeling that papal jurisdiction was 'foreign' and intrusive, and a more particular anxiety existed among all those who had purchased former ecclesiastical land, about the security of their investment.

Finally, there was the problem of her marriage. Everybody, including Mary herself, believed that this should happen as quickly as possible. She was thirty-seven, and would not be capable of childbearing for much longer; moreover, a female ruler was unprecedented, and there was general agreement that she needed a husband to carry out those functions of government not 'pertinent to women'. The prevailing sentiment, both at court and in parliament, was in favour of a domestic marriage. However, there was no suitable candidate. The front-runner, Edward Courtenay, Earl of Devon, was a dissolute youth, incapable of sustaining the role; and if the queen married within the realm, there was bound to be faction and destructive tensions. At the same time, Mary was emotionally committed to her cousin, the Emperor Charles V, looking to him for advice and support as she had done for over twenty years. Charles seized the opportunity created by her accession to put forward the name of his widower son, Philip of Spain. The emperor had his own agenda, which had everything to do with securing Philip's inheritance in the Low Countries, and nothing at all to do with the interests of England. But Mary was programmed to do what her cousin wanted, and immediately accepted the suggestion.

These early decisions dictated the course of the reign. The council remained divided, and feuds between the Lord Chancellor, Stephen Gardiner and Lord Paget, and later between Paget and Cardinal Reginald Pole, confused policy and drove the queen to distraction. The council functioned efficiently as an executive, directed largely by Paget, and its unwieldy size was less of a problem than many claimed at the time, but as an advisory body it did not function well. Mary's own inexperience and lack of self-confidence caused her to seek unanimous (or at least consensual) counsel, but for obvious reasons that was not forthcoming. The queen expected to make up her own mind on matters of importance, but was constantly troubled by the diversity of voices close to her. Her religious policy at first worked satisfactorily. The opposition to her early conservative moves was strident but very limited. She sensibly (and crucially) decided to proceed by means of parliamentary repeal, and within six months had dismantled the whole of her brother's Protestant settlement.

After that, it became more difficult. Mary's own advisers, particularly Gardiner, were anxious to complete the reconciliation with Rome before Philip arrived in England. Charles, who wanted his son to get the credit for such a coup, countermined them, and made sure that Reginald Pole did not get anywhere near the homeland to which Pope Julius III had hopefully sent him. Gardiner in any case had no mandate to negotiate on the crucial issue of Church lands, and his feud with Paget ensured that the latter could block his initiative, with general support, in April 1554. Consequently, it was left to Philip, who had all the necessary influence in Rome, to force the pope to back down on this issue, and enable a deal to be struck. This was embodied in the second repeal act of January 1555, but it also meant that the restored Catholic Church became indissolubly linked with the unique experience of a foreign king. Foreignness thus linked the pope and the king together in a way which was potentially very destructive.

This might not have mattered had Mary not decided in January 1555 that the dissident Protestant minority within her realm must be forced into line by whatever means necessary. One reason for this was the common assumption that religious dissent and political sedition inevitably went together. There is very little evidence that English Protestants harboured seditious intentions towards the queen, until she began to provoke them by persecution. However, Mary can hardly be condemned for sharing the prevailing view. At the same time, she was motivated by what can only be described as hatred. She blamed the Protestants in general, and leaders such as Cranmer in particular, for her own troubled early life. On the one hand, so-called Protestants must be hypocrites and time-servers, because no one could possibly believe their proclaimed doctrines; on the other hand, heresy was a lethal virus which devoured the immortal souls of anyone whom it attacked. Severe punishment for those spreading such infection was therefore not an option, or a policy, but a solemn duty.

In this way a woman who was by general consent a gentle and humane person, was driven to become the most ferocious persecutor in English history. In about three and a half years she burned alive nearly 300 people, and left thousands of others exiled, dead, in prison, or scarred in life and conscience. This toll was greater than that of the French *chambre ardente* and the Spanish Inquisition combined over a similar period. The victims included some senior clergy, and a few minor gentlemen, but were mostly artisans, labourers and servants. Many were women: wives, widows and maids. John Foxe later blamed a satanic clerical conspiracy for this carnage, but the driving force was undoubtedly the queen. Neither Gardiner nor Philip (both of whom tried in different ways) could deflect her relentless sense of purpose.

In other respects, the restored Catholic Church was more in the mode of the humanist reform movement of the 1530s than of the contemporary Counter-Reformation. Its worship was carefully and conscientiously restored, and it was well administered. Pole was not a great evangelist, and certainly not a popular one, but some efforts were made to reinstruct the laity in doctrines which were long out of mind. It is difficult to say how successful this low-key campaign might have been in the long run, because it was destroyed, partly by politics, and partly by the lethal legacy of the persecution, which left the Catholic Church a byword for ferocious cruelty in the popular culture of England for nearly three centuries.

Mary's emotions did not serve her well in guiding her political judgement. Pragmatically, there were good reasons for a Habsburg marriage in 1553. It provided the queen with a powerful and well-connected consort of unimpeachable religious orthodoxy; it represented a useful traditional alliance; and it avoided domestic faction and dissent. However, there were equally valid reasons for not choosing Philip: he was eleven years younger than the queen; he was unpopular everywhere outside Spain; and most important, he was the immediate heir to more than half his father's vast dominions. Mary was 'bounced' into her decision by Charles's ambassador, Simon Renard, a crafty and self-serving diplomat with a strong personal agenda. Renard convinced the queen (if she needed convincing) that her council was unreliable, and that only he, speaking for the emperor, could give her sound advice. The marriage agreement was the great coup which was intended to make his career, and his comments on English politics at that time have to be seen in that light.

Knowing perfectly well what had happened, Charles allowed the English council to negotiate a very favourable treaty, giving Philip little power in England, and exempting the country from his ongoing war with France. Realising how unpopular the marriage was going to be in England, he judged these concessions to be necessary to secure acceptance. Philip was not amused, and declared that he would not be bound by the restrictions, but his declaration remained secret, and the treaty largely achieved its objectives in England. Before it could be proclaimed, there was conspiracy in London and rebellion in Kent. Both were briefly dangerous, but collapsed as news of the treaty became public. Opposition continued to cause alarm, particularly to Renard, and the French threatened forceful intervention; but Philip was undeterred, and his arrival in July 1554 was uneventful, even welcoming.

Philip and Mary were married at Winchester, and although there were problems over his household, and the instinctive antagonism between the two nationalities, there was no significant dissension. The king busied himself with securing the reconciliation of the Church, in which his role was crucial, but otherwise kept out of the political limelight. This was partly because of his ignorance of the realities of the English situation, but more because his main attention was focused on the continent, where his father was preparing to abdicate.

In November, Mary announced that she was pregnant; and for about three months it appeared that her judgement, and tenacity of purpose, were being vindicated on all fronts. Thereafter, however, everything began to go wrong. Philip was increasingly anxious to leave as his father's plans matured, and was kept in England mainly by the prospect of Mary's forthcoming confinement. A select group of Protestant leaders, who were supposed to collapse in abject penitence, in fact proved defiant and had to be burned, thus triggering the persecution noted above. Finally, and most important, the queen's 'pregnancy' fizzled out in May and June, an embarrassing fiasco which left her physically and emotionally shattered, and the credibility of her regime undermined. There would be no child, and Mary's health was obviously suspect.

With no prospect of an heir, Philip at first tried to secure his position in England by obtaining a coronation, and when that did not work began to lose interest. By January 1556 he was King of Spain as well as Archduke of Burgundy; and Mary, as a barren wife, was more a liability than an asset. As Charles went into retirement at San Yuste, he could congratulate himself on his English treaty. However unproductive it had been for Mary, it had brought Philip two significant advantages. It had ensured a peaceful and secure handover of power in the Low Countries, and it had set him up as the chief lay protector of the Counter-Reformation. But by 1556 there was little long-term future for Philip in England, and the need to rid himself of an unfruitful wife was looming uncomfortably.

Before that situation could be resolved, though, there were two further important consequences of the marriage. The king's influence in Rome lasted only as long as the life of Pope Julius III. When the latter died in

March 1555, Charles and Philip mismanaged the conclave, with the result that the violently anti-Habsburg Cardinal Carafa was elected as Pope Paul IV. Paul deliberately provoked the King of Spain into war in the autumn of 1556, and summoned Cardinal Pole to return from England to face charges of heresy. Mary refused to allow Pole to go, and when his legateship was withdrawn, refused to accept his designated successor. Anglo-papal relations became cold and formal at precisely the point where active papal leadership was required to counter English suspicions. Instead those suspicions were strengthened, and England remained semi-detached from the main body of the Church.

The other important consequence was that England declared war on France in May 1557. The pope was no longer a belligerent by that time, so one embarrassment was spared, but Philip had been pressing Mary for such a declaration since Christmas. Although in some respects she was disillusioned with her husband, and disinclined to gratify him, either over his coronation or over his marriage plans for Elizabeth, on this issue she was willing and anxious to please. The majority of her council (including Pole) pointed out reasonably enough that England had no interest in such a war, and could not afford it anyway. After a titanic struggle, the queen's finances were gradually improving, and the last thing the country needed was an expensive and unnecessary war. However, the council did not make such decisions. In March 1557 Philip visited England a second time to add his weight to Mary's voice, and a mysterious little raid on the Yorkshire coast was deemed to be a provocation; so war was declared. At first the result was positive. An English force took part with credit in the siege of St Quentin in August, but after that poverty, and the debilitating effects of an influenza epidemic, sapped what fighting spirit there was.

In January 1558 the Duke of Guise overran the Calais Pale, and England's last remaining continental possession was lost. The blow was more symbolic than real, but it was keenly felt and Philip (most unreasonably) was blamed. What little enthusiasm he had for the English alliance was virtually destroyed by this contretemps. By the autumn of 1558 he needed peace, and was negotiating with Henry II, but Mary's somewhat desperate attempts to insist on the return of Calais were a handicap he could have done without. Although he maintained a correct facade, her death in November was a relief in more ways than one.

In the last two and a half years of her reign, Mary had more than her fair share of misfortune. The harvests of 1555 and 1556 were among the worst of the century, and were followed by malnutrition and disease. The influenza epidemic of 1557–8 caused great mortality, and was the only significant check on demographic growth between 1450 and the English Civil War. The war with France produced only humiliation, and the quarrel with the papacy reduced Pole to a shadow of his former self before the influenza carried him off. Philip's relations with the critically important city of London declined from suspicion to acrimony as he backed first the Portuguese and then the Flemings against London interests.

Above all, the failure of Mary's pregnancy left her exposed. Her own refusal to accept the logic of such an event was pathetic, and regarded in Europe as ludicrous. For Philip to have pressed a claim to the succession would have meant civil war, and he knew that, even if she did not. As her life drew to a close, there was no real alternative to Elizabeth, who was her heir by the law which she herself had upheld. Mary disliked her half-sister for a variety of understandable reasons, and justifiably did not trust her professions of religious conformity. However, neither Mary Stuart nor Margaret Douglas were realistic alternatives, and Mary chose not to suffer the kind of posthumous humiliation which had overtaken Edward.

At the end of her life, her warmest supporters were left wondering why the God she had so devotedly served had chosen to burden her with childlessness, and her realm with disease, hunger and defeat. Of course, to John Foxe and his fellow Protestants, this presented no mystery. Anyone who chose to persecute the saints of God was inviting Divine retribution. Mary became an affliction imposed by God to test the vocation of the English to (Protestant) greatness and godliness, hence her unenviable place in the pantheon of popular historiography.

However, before she is classifed as the victim of appalling bad luck, and her sister's posthumous vendetta, it should be remembered that her marriage, her insistence on submission to the papacy, and above all the religious persecution, were serious mistakes in the contemporary English context. Up to a point, Mary was the author of her own misfortunes. It should also be noted that the legacy of her reign was by no means entirely negative. She established the right of a woman to succeed and freed the Crown from gender disability, both enormous advantages later to Elizabeth. She confirmed the right of parliament to determine the succession and, equally important, the settlement of religion. She also governed well, or perhaps her council did, so in spite of all the pressures and misfortunes, there was little social unrest, and the realm which Elizabeth inherited was much less distracted than had been the case ten years before.

Consequently, Elizabeth succeeded in reasonably auspicious circumstances. There was no challenge to her succession, and although England was theoretically at war, no hostilities were in prospect. Above all, Philip needed her friendship. The French made no secret of their support for the Queen of Scotland, who was currently also married to the dauphin. The last thing Philip needed was a Franco-Scottish takeover in England, so although the idea that he fancied his attractive young sister-in-law belongs to the realms of romantic fiction, he dutifully offered to marry her. He

probably did not expect (or want) to be accepted, but he had confirmed
that he intended to be at least her 'good brother'. This suited both of them,
and probably confirmed an understanding which they had already reached
before Mary's death. Elizabeth was popular in England, and it was better
for him to have a secure friend than an insecure wife. Besides, one Tudor
woman was enough for any God-fearing man! So the pessimistic talk about
the country's weakness, and the fact that 'the king of France bestrides the
realm', was exaggeration, if not downright invention. Elizabeth had a
major problem, but it was only marginally to do with Philip. England was
deeply divided over religion, and feelings were running high. The safest
course for the new queen would have been to maintain the status quo,
while ending the persecution and seeking some kind of accommodation
with the Protestant minority. This, however, would have been to ignore
Elizabeth's chief priority, and her deepest point of empathy with her
subjects.

Her first policy objective was to restore English autonomy, to be 'mere
English' as she put it. The image of a lover and his lass, expressing her
relationship with the country, occurred spontaneously to the ballad writers
celebrating her accession, and was never far from her own mind.
Theoretically, it should have been possible to achieve that by returning to
her father's settlement. It had, after all, been Henry's 'Englishness' above
everything which had persuaded his divided subjects to support his
proceedings. However, the Marian clergy had poisoned that particular
pool. Once the old religion had been firmly reconnected to the papal
authority, there could be no uncoupling them again. Whatever Elizabeth
may have wanted, the surviving Marian bishops and other senior clergy
made it clear in early 1559 that they would accept no return to the Royal
Supremacy. Only among the Protestants, many of them returning from
exile, could a bench of bishops be found who would support and promote
a renewed break with Rome.

Elizabeth's personal vision of the Church was probably as idiosyncratic
as her father's, if somewhat different. Doctrinally, she was a convinced
Protestant; that much is clear from her personal prayers and meditations.
But ecclesiastically she was conservative. She liked both music and
ornament (up to a point), disliked married clergy, and preferred the
jurisdictional structure of the Church the way it was, with convocations,
consistories and archdeacons' courts.

However, she was also realistic enough to know that she could not
simply invent a Church to please herself. She had to build with the bricks
that were already in place, and in early 1559 this meant a return to her
brother's settlement. That had not been generally popular, but it had
attracted some enthusiastic support, and at least everyone knew what it
was. So the acts of Supremacy and Uniformity of 1559 recreated the

Edwardian Church (more or less), and a process of deprivation and appointment created a Protestant Bench, under the Royal Supremacy. Such a settlement gave hostages to fortune. Not only did it declare a position in the increasingly ideological conflicts of European politics, it also exposed the queen and her Church to the hostile indifference of most of her own subjects. If there was a 'general opinion', it was probably one of grudging acceptance tempered with the desire to hold on to as many of the old ways as possible, for as long as possible. As a religious statement, it satisfied no one. Most of those who accepted the Royal Supremacy deplored the Protestantism which went with it, while most Protestants deplored the 'dregs of popery' which remained in the liturgy and government. What no one quite realised at the time was that Elizabeth had nailed her colours to this particular mast, and for the rest of her reign would use the powers of the Act of Supremacy to resist both Catholic encroachment and Protestant pressure for further reform.

The queen's pragmatic approach to a Church settlement was paralleled in the structure of her government. All Mary's most trusted familiars disappeared both from the council and the court. Elizabeth's confidence was given first and foremost to men whom Philip's emissary, the Count of Feria, unhesitatingly described as 'heretics': William Cecil, Nicholas Bacon, Robert Dudley and the Earl of Bedford. The privy chamber was restocked with the wives and sisters of these same courtiers and councillors, and with the queen's Boleyn kindred. On the other hand many senior offices remained in the hands of such cautious conservatives as the Marquis of Winchester and the Earl of Arundel, and her Privy Council (much smaller than Mary's) was a judicious mixture. Elizabeth preferred to surround herself with educated laymen, but had no objection to noblemen of the old religion, provided they accepted the Supremacy. Unlike her sister, she did not favour clergy of any persuasion, outside their proper spiritual functions. Elizabeth's relationship with her council, like her defence of her Church settlement, is one of the ongoing themes of the reign. Francis Naunton claimed that she 'ruled much by faction', playing off antagonistic groups and individuals against each other in order to maintain her own freedom of action.

However, this was probably a rationalisation of a process which was in fact much more subtle. Unlike Mary, Elizabeth was a consummate actress, and enjoyed playing her royal role – the rules of which she made up as she went along. Her royal rages, her fits of sexual jealousy and coquettish dalliance, her notorious indecisiveness; all of this added up to a unique style of government which no man could have emulated, and Mary had not even dreamed of. Her contemporaries did not know, and historians now cannot firmly decide, when she was in earnest, and when play-acting. Even men who knew her very well, like Robert Dudley and William Cecil, were frequently baffled and driven close to despair by her apparently irrational behaviour. There is so much evidence of this bewilderment and anger that some scholars have concluded that she was just blundering around in an emotional fog, and was lucky enough to have ministers and advisers who were able to force sensible decisions out of her in the nick of time.

Yet she was far too consistently lucky for this to be plausible, and even if it were true she would have to be given the credit for choosing the ministers. It has to be concluded that Elizabeth was actually far more in control of herself, and of her policies, than she appeared to be, even to those close to her. At the same time, she had no control over her own mortality, and many of England's problems were solved as much by her longevity as by any decisions she made. Her ambiguous attitude towards the Church was only partly the result of her own idiosyncratic tastes. She knew that a period of settling and healing was required after the violent upheavals of the previous decade. To the fury of evangelicals, she at first appeared tolerant of conservative dissent, and intolerant of the 'godly', in flat contradiction of what her settlement seemed to promise. However, the absence of a 'Catholic' party to defend the Marian Church in the early years of the reign, and the dangers implicit in the Protestant doctrine of *sola scriptura* (which logically prevented any secular authority from determining doctrine or worship), made such behaviour perfectly rational in the circumstances. It was only when a Catholic rebellion in the north of England in 1569, and the papal bull of excommunication (*Regnans in Excelsis*) in 1570 altered the political landscape, that her policy changed. Pope Pius V's declaration of war forced the issue. From then on it was logically impossible to be both a good Catholic and a good subject of the English Crown, a choice which Elizabeth had tried very hard to avoid forcing upon her subjects. How many might have supported such an initiative from Rome in 1559 it is impossible to say, but by 1570 most English conservatives were settling in to a grudging conformity. What Pius's action did was to create recusancy. Recusants varied considerably in numbers and social status from one part of the country to another, but overall were a small minority, who could be identified if and when the pressure was on. Quite illogically, even after 1570, most of them claimed to be loyal to Elizabeth in all temporal matters, but the government for good reason did not trust them.

It was from the recusant community and its foreign supporters that the regular plots to assassinate or overthrow the queen came, or appeared to come. The undercover battle which these plots engendered provides some of the first great espionage stories, but the result was to complete the assimilation between national sentiment and the Protestant settlement which Elizabeth had always hoped for. In attempting to do his duty, and overthrow the heretic queen, Pius turned England into a solidly Protestant country far more effectively than its evangelical bishops could ever have done. But that would not have happened if Elizabeth had not created a workable settlement in the first place. The pope's action also enabled Elizabeth to forswear explicit religious persecution, and to execute Catholic activists for treason. This may have seemed a hypocritical distinction to the victims, but it was not to the onlookers, who saw their government fighting at least as much for national self-determination as for religious orthodoxy. The tragedy was that the law inevitably caught Edmund Campion as well as Anthony Babington.

Genuine dissenters on the Protestant side were rare; a nuisance rather than a danger. The godly campaigned strenuously and unremittingly for further reform from the 1560s to the 1580s, but always by pressure from within the system. They were supported not only by leading bishops like Edmund Grindal, but by powerful voices within the Privy Council. The argument for distancing the English Church as obviously as possible from Rome was a strong one, particularly after 1570, but the queen's instinct for keeping as many conservatives 'on side' as possible was sound. Moreover, when the so-called Puritans began to campaign for a Presbyterian system of Church government, they went seriously off the rails. Not only was this a direct challenge to the royal prerogative, it also forfeited the episcopal support which the godly had previously enjoyed. Their campaign was noisy, and at times scurrilous, but the *Marprelate Tracts* also rang alarm bells within the secular elite. The Presbyterians never transcended the bounds of political loyalty, but after 1585 they lost momentum and credibility. The totally unrelated defeat of the Spanish Armada in 1588 was also widely interpreted as evidence that God approved of the English Church, and opposition declined significantly in the last decade of the reign.

Although the formation of Elizabeth's council and the religious settlement dominated the first year of her reign, both were quickly overtaken as political and popular concerns by the related issues of the queen's marriage and the succession. That Elizabeth would marry soon, if not immediately, was taken for granted. At twenty-five, it was not quite as urgent as it had been for her sister, but mortality was uncertain, and the sooner the better. Mary had professed her personal reluctance, but willingness to heed the call of duty. Elizabeth used similar language, but not with the same meaning. Her real views baffled her contemporaries, and have remained opaque to interpretation. As the most eligible bride in Europe, there were soon suitors who had to be taken seriously; not only Philip but Eric of Sweden and the Archduke Charles. Only Philip was fairly rapidly dismissed, and with Charles the negotiations were long and earnest. It is impossible to say that they were not genuine, but in retrospect they look suspiciously like defensive diplomacy, and the queen seems to have had little true enthusiasm.

With Lord Robert Dudley the situation was completely different. Here, the political implications were domestic rather than foreign, but were none the less compelling. That Elizabeth loved Dudley in the ordinary sense of that word seems clear. That she ever slept with him, in spite of popular report, is much less evident. She denied it when she believed herself to be on the point of death, and was certainly never pregnant by him. When their relationship began he was a married man, and when his wife died in suspicious circumstances, the scandal was immense. Eventually it appears that Elizabeth's political common sense, and the urgent representations of some of her most trusted advisers, such as William Cecil, overcame her natural instincts. The most telling proof of how real her infatuation was lies not in the evidence of their indiscreet dalliance, but in the fact that when she believed herself to be fatally ill in 1562, she tried to make him protector of the realm. When she recovered, Elizabeth 'normalised' Dudley by making him Earl of Leicester and a member of the Privy Council. He subsequently married again, but their tempestuous and unique relationship continued until his death in 1588.

There were several other negotiations later; briefly with Henry, Duke of Anjou in 1570–1, and much more protractedly with his brother, Francis Duke of Alençon between 1572 and 1578. When Anjou became King Henry III in 1579, Francis became Duke of Anjou in his turn, and the marriage negotiation was revived, apparently on the queen's initiative, between 1579 and 1581. It is tempting to dismiss all these efforts as diplomatic ploys; aspects of a foreign policy which were never intended to come to fruition. This is particularly true of the last attempt, when Elizabeth was approaching fifty and even the most optimistic were looking to the Old Testament for precedents of childbearing. However, it is precisely in this case, and with this singularly unprepossessing man, that the evidence of the queen's personal involvement is most clear. Her subjects were outraged; her councillors were (once again) in despair. At length she drew back, and a crisis was averted, but no one at the time or since has ever really understood what she thought she was doing.

It is tempting to accept the romantic thesis, that when Elizabeth was reluctantly convinced that she could not have the man she wanted (Dudley), she then eschewed marriage in the interests of her country, and decided to become the Virgin Queen instead. In truth we have no idea what Elizabeth's attitude to marriage really was, and it is quite possible that she did not know herself. In spite of the sensible provisions of statute, Mary had never quite reconciled the roles of queen and wife, sovereignty and dutiful submission, and that drama had been worked out in front of Elizabeth's eyes. Elizabeth knew perfectly well that marriage would compromise her independence. The sixteenth century could not envisage an Albert, or a George of Denmark. On the other hand, without marriage there could be no children, and without children the succession would remain uncertain, with dangerous consequences.

It is possible that Elizabeth believed herself to be incapable of childbearing; she described herself in 1566 as 'a barren stock'. However, if that was the case there would, from her point of view, have been nothing to gain from marriage, and everything to lose. Yet the evidence seems clear that she seriously considered marriage on at least three occasions. But there was another side to Elizabeth. Unlike Mary, she did not believe that there were 'matters impertinent to women'. She was the queen, and the men around her were her servants, not her equals, an attitude aptly summed up in the phrase attributed to her 'I will have one mistress – and no master'. Elizabeth, in other words, was never tempted to marriage in order to have a man's support.

In this she was very unusual, almost unique; and it is this aspect which makes decoding her utterances so interesting, and ultimately unrewarding. It may well have been that time foreclosed her options without any conscious decision on her part; but it looks as though she deliberately risked the succession for the intangible advantages of being Gloriana. She may also have considered that after 1570 no child she might bear would be considered legitimate outside England, or deflect the purposes of those who saw Mary Stuart as the rightful Queen of England. Perhaps it was better to exploit the imagery of her symbolic marriage to the realm, and to play the godly maiden, than to take major political risks for uncertain gain. It was not until the late 1570s that she began to be spoken of regularly as the Virgin Queen, and the iconography usually associated with her began to be used. It is not clear whether any of this was her idea, but if it wasn't, she accepted it gratefully enough.

Perhaps it was good luck which eventually solved the succession problem, but it was good luck for which she had worked hard. Perhaps it was Cecil who pushed her into that crucial intervention in Scotland in 1560, but the final decision could only have been hers. Perhaps she would not have succeeded if the French had not become embroiled in their own troubles, but it could equally be argued that that was astute opportunism on her part. To contemporaries it appeared that the treaty of Edinburgh was no more than a temporary advantage. Mary's return to Scotland from France in 1561, her marriage to Lord Darnley and the birth of her son in June 1566, could all have been disasters for Elizabeth. However, her rival's capacity for self-destruction, and the vigilance of her own servants, ensured that the Protestant party remained in power in Scotland. Once Mary had been deposed and exiled in 1568, her son was brought up as a Protestant, and it was that circumstance which eventually made him an acceptable heir to Englishmen. Ironically, he became the son which Elizabeth never had. It was also Elizabeth who neutralised Mary, keeping her alive when most of the council wanted her dead, and allowing her to transform herself by degrees from a legitimate heir into a Catholic claimant. As Protestantism became more firmly established, Mary became increasingly unacceptable to the English; and when she was eventually snared into explicit conspiracy, her execution was a rite of passage for the English monarchy. Whether Elizabeth was really as distressed by this necessity as she claimed is anyone's guess. Whichever way it is looked at, her victory was complete.

Elizabeth is always said to have been paralysingly cautious, and unable to make up her mind about anything, but this seems to have been a male view of a woman's way of doing business. Whatever she may have said about her heart and stomach, no one would ever have taken her for a king. In fact she took risks all the time, sometimes successfully, sometimes less so. Her religious settlement, as has been seen, was very far from being the line of least resistance. Intervention in Scotland was a gamble which came off; intervention in France in 1562 was one which did not. Her subtle promotion of Darnley's bid for Mary's hand eventually brought great rewards, but allowing Cecil to impound the Duke of Alba's Genoese pay ships in 1568 merely provoked a crisis which led nowhere and had to be resolved with concessions.

Elizabeth never faced up to the realities of the English fiscal system; she allowed subsidy assessments to decline, and was never frank with parliament about her real needs. This left an intractable problem to her successors, but eventually guaranteed that the Lords and Commons did not go the same way as the Estates General. More positively, it forced her to innovate and improvise. She picked up the Duke of Northumberland's alliance with the City of London and ran with it, supporting the increasingly adventurous search for new markets, and earning invaluable credit facilities in return. Tough seamen like Hawkins, Drake and Frobisher served her with the devotion of knights errant, taking all sorts of risks, both physical and political. They earned the wary respect of their adversaries, and brought occasional windfalls to the royal coffers.

Elizabeth was wise enough to realise that government was not a matter of *arcana imperii*, but of partnership. In return for unrealistically lenient taxation, she expected her nobles and gentlemen to govern England in her name, and in her interests. In return for a free hand with the plunder, she expected her merchants and seamen to promote the defence of the realm at sea. Even her most loyal and efficient servants were no more than moderately rewarded, but they were allowed to reward themselves – up to a point. This was partly made possible by her native shrewdness, but partly also by her sex. Courtiers, councillors, officials and pirates, all were required to play the game of courtly love. She, the unattainable lady, smiled upon them and bestowed small favours, while they were required to do her bidding with humble devotion. As Sir John Davies remarked towards the end of her life, all the solemn business of the state was conducted like a courtly dance or charade. Whether this was carefully calculated or more or less instinctive, it worked brilliantly most of the time. Even the most pragmatic and experienced politicians did not know quite how to handle it, or how to react when they suspected they were being deceived or exploited. It was this game which lay behind the myth of faction. Councillors and courtiers quarrelled, and competed for favours or to have their policies accepted, and the queen often appeared supine when these quarrels got out of hand. Unlike her father, however, she bestowed her confidence consistently, and for known reasons. Her partnership with Sir William Cecil lasted almost the entire reign, and both in its storms and in its enduring quality, was more like the relationship between a father and daughter than that between a sovereign and a minister. Elizabeth did not promote faction; she did not need to. What she did do was to encourage emulation, and to maintain control by the most intangible means. It was, as James was to discover, an impossible act to follow.

There were, however, political realities which were not amenable to the queen's subtle arts of manipulation. Philip II admired her act as it developed, but he could not afford to be impressed by it. From being a useful friend, Elizabeth became first a nuisance and then an enemy. Civil war in both France and the Netherlands altered the political landscape between 1565 and 1570. In 1560 France still looked like the main threat to Spanish power, so Philip was quite happy to see her grip on Scotland disappear. But by 1570 France was no longer a threat, and English friendship was therefore expendable. On the other hand, there had been revolt in the Low Countries, which he had found necessary to suppress by force, and England was offering sanctuary and covert support to the rebels. At the same time English pirates, masquerading as traders, were plundering his colonies in the New World, which had not been designed to withstand attacks by European rivals. Elizabeth continued to profess friendship, but her actions, and those of her subjects, spoke otherwise.

For her part, the queen's concerns were defensive. In 1559 the threat had seemed to come from France, but ten years later it clearly came from Spain. Spain was by then the only major power in western Europe, and it was also the standard bearer of the Counter-Reformation. In the spring of 1572 Elizabeth signed the treaty of Blois with the government of Charles IX, providing mutual defensive guarantees; but Philip's allies, the Guises, promptly destroyed that safeguard by engineering the St Bartholomew's Day massacre in August.

Elizabeth was as frightened of diplomatic isolation as her father had been, but by 1572 there was not even a semblance of a balance of power to provide protection. England's best defence was the revolt in the Low Countries, which sprang into renewed life in that year. As long as that revolt could be kept alive, and Philip continued to be distracted by the Turks and the Barbary Corsairs, he was unlikely to carry out the papal sentence against Elizabeth. The queen dreaded the prospect of war. Not only was it expensive, but it also meant conceding far more power than she wished to the men who would have to wage it. Whether she liked it or not, war was not a woman's business; and in spite of a few Amazonian posturings, she knew that perfectly well. Unlike her father, she could not lead an army royal to France. Small forces and small commands, such as a Leith or Newhaven, were manageable, but a major war would have to mean powerful commanders, to whose judgement she would have to defer, and that was not an attractive prospect.

For about twelve years Elizabeth was able to gamble on Philip's preoccupations; now encouraging the depredations of her seamen, now drawing back; now allowing vounteers to serve in the Low Countries, now recalling them. This could have gone on indefinitely, but two developments forced the issue. In 1580 Philip became both stronger and richer by securing the throne of Portugal; and in 1584 William of Orange, the leader and inspirer of the Dutch rebels, was assassinated, leaving the revolt on the verge of collapse. As had happened over a number of issues, and was to happen again, Elizabeth's council was convinced that she would dither until all was lost. However, in spite of making a very visible display of reluctance and reservation, the queen nevertheless signed the treaty of Nonsuch in 1585, committing both men and money to preserving the cause of Dutch independence.

The well-displayed reluctance was of course for Philip's benefit, but he was understandably unimpressed. He regarded the treaty of Nonsuch as a declaration of war, and acted accordingly. England remained at war with Spain for the remaining eighteen years of Elizabeth's reign, which was by far the longest period of continuous hostilities conducted by any Tudor. In theory, the country should have been bankrupt within about two years, but it was not, and there were a number of reasons for that. The most important was the nature of the war itself. The English expeditionary force in the Low Countries was never very large, or very effective. It became embroiled in local politics, and its commander, the Earl of Leicester, was recalled in disgrace; it fought well in some engagements, disastrously in others. What it did do was to boost Dutch morale when it was at a very low point, and help them to hang on until their own fortunes turned.

The military and financial resilience of the Dutch was remarkable, and once Maurice of Nassau (William's son) had become established as commander, and particularly when Philip's great commander, the Duke of Parma, died in 1592, English aid became little more than symbolic.

The only other continental campaigns were even smaller in scale, and were fought in Normandy and Brittany in support of Henry IV against the

Spanish-backed Catholic League. Although war was never cheap, and Elizabeth was not entirely successful in trying to get Henry to pay for the French campaigns, these low-key hostilities were as economical as such operations come. There was no army royal, no Calais to defend, and the Scottish borders hardly needed a thought.

With Scotland a non-combatant, England was effectively an island, and the war was mainly fought at sea. Elizabeth's navy was not large, but it was highly professional: good ships, well equipped, well manned and well managed. More importantly, the seafaring community supported the war absolutely, and scores of privately owned ships attacked Spanish commerce, and supported the navy in its various operations. Although the English never succeeded in capturing Philip's treasure fleet from the Americas, they virtually destroyed normal Spanish trade.

Not all partnership operations were successful, because of confused priorities and command. The Lisbon expedition of 1589 was a disaster, as was Drake's last raid on the Caribbean in 1595, and the Islands Voyage of 1597. On the other hand Cadiz was successfully raided in 1587, and captured with immense destruction in 1596. Above all, the great Spanish Armada of 1588 was defeated. Philip intended this to be the knockout blow, not to conquer England, but to take it out of the war, and hopefully to get rid of Elizabeth. So convinced was he that he was doing God's work that he ignored warnings from his commanders that his plans were unrealistic. His forces in the Low Countries controlled no deep-water harbour; the problems of rendezvous between the fleet and the army of Flanders had been left to providence; the Armada had insufficient guns, ammunition of the wrong calibre, and inexperienced crews. In the event, the Armada did well to get as far as it did, but it never looked like defeating the English fleet, and ended by being scattered and humiliated. The campaign cost Elizabeth about £200,000; Philip about £2,000,000.

In military terms the defeat of the Armada was not decisive. Within five years Spain's Atlantic fleet was stronger than ever, and a second armada in 1596 was frustrated by the weather rather than the English. However, psychologically it was a turning point. Philip was left to agonise over how he could possibly have offended God so radically as to attract such punishment. When Cadiz was sacked at enormous cost eight years later, the Duke of Medina Sidonia drew the same conclusion. God was deeply displeased with a people who had always regarded themselves as His especial champions. Conversely, the English, who had fretted endlessly over whether they were doing the right thing by the Almighty, were reassured. John Foxe, who had died the year before, would have been gratified. Although he had the gravest doubts over the real godliness of his fellow countrymen (or their queen), He clearly approved of the 'English way'. The sacrifices of the Marian persecution had not been in vain.

Altogether, in the 1590s the English were feeling pleased with themselves, and the fact that plenty went wrong in that decade did not dent their confidence. Disastrous harvests caused hardship, and soaring prices; the queen became increasingly paranoid about spending money; and the integrity of government went into serious decline. Clumsy and insensitive plantation policies in Ireland caused a major revolt, which offered opportunities to Spain and cost a great deal to suppress. The Spanish war ran into stalemate after 1596, and attempts to establish colonies in North America came to nothing. Nevertheless, by 1600 the English knew who they were, and believed that their Church, and their laws, were good and acceptable to God. The latter part of Elizabeth's long reign saw great achievements in literature, art and music. English navigation, mathematics and cosmography, so long lagging behind the Iberians, were now ahead and servicing a commercial expansion which was spreading around the world.

The problems that had afflicted Elizabeth in the early part of her reign had either been solved, or had solved themselves. The queen's marriage was no longer an issue, and the succession was effectively resolved as James grew to manhood and secured control of Scotland. Religious divisions remained, but no longer threatened either the stability or the identity of the realm. In a sense the country was grateful to its long-lived queen, who had enabled all this to happen.

However, in her last years she had to some extent lost her touch. Her parsimony virtually forced her courtiers and officials into corruption; Admiralty salaries, for instance, had not been increased since 1557, a period which had seen 250 per cent inflation. Even her judgement of men, which had always been her great strength, became uncertain. She seriously mishandled the maverick Earl of Essex, and he ended on the block. It took her years to appoint Robert Cecil as principal secretary, a position for which he was the only realistic candidate, and far too long to send the highly professional Lord Mountjoy to sort out the mess which aristocratic amateurs had made in Ireland. Above all, perhaps, her failure to tackle England's inadequate financial system, and her refusal to allow important jurisdictional issues to be clarified, left problems which waylaid her successor with damaging consequences. When she died in 1603 there was loud and theatrical mourning, as became so theatrical a sovereign, but there was also great relief, and a sense that the time had come to deal frankly with the new king, in ways it had been impossible to do with such a unique and incomprehensible old lady.

PART I

Queen Jane and Queen Mary

ONE

The Suffolk Line

I

Extract from the Letters Patent of Edward VI for the limitation of the Crown; taken from the transcript by Ralph Starkey in BL Harley MS 35. Although it is described as '. . . a true coppie of Edward the Sixte his will, taken out of the originall under the Greate Seale, which sir Robart Cotton delyvred to the kinges majestie the xiith of Aprill 1611 . . .' no original seems to have survived. It was printed in 1850 by John Gough Nichols as an appendix to *The Chronicle of Queen Jane* (Camden Society, 48).

'. . . We therefore, upon good deliberation and advise herein had and taken, and haveinge also (thankes be to the livinge God), our full, whole and perfect memory, doe by these presents declare, order, assigne, limett, and appointe that yf it shall fortune us to decease haveinge no issue of our body lawefully begotten, that then the said imperiall crowne of this our realmes of England and Ireland, and of the confynes of the same, and our tytle to the crowne and realme of Fraunce, and all and singular honnores, castelles, prerogatyves, privelyges, preheminences, authorities, jurisdictions, dominions, possessions, hereditaments to us and our said imperiall crowne belonginge, or in anywise appertaininge, shall for lacke of such issue of our bodye, remayne, come and be unto (1) THE ELDEST SONNE OF THE BODYE OF THE SAID LADY FRAUNCIS, LAWFULLY BEGOTTEN, BEINGE BORNE INTO THE WORLD IN OUR LYFETIME, and to the heires males of the bodye of the said eldeste sonne lawfully begotten, and so from sonne to sonne as he shalbe by auncientry in birth, of the bodye of the said lady Francis lawfully begotten, beinge borne into the world in our lyfetyme, and to the heires males of the bodye of every such sonne lawfully begotten: And for defaulte of such sonne borne into the world in our lyfetime of the body of the said lady Frauncis lawfully begotten, and for lacke of the heires males of the bodie of every such sonne lawfully begotten, that then the said imperiall crowne, and all and singular other the premisses, shall remayne, come and be (2) TO THE LADIE JANE, eldeste daughter of the said ladie Frauncis, and to the heires males of the said bodye of the said ladie Jane, lawfully begotten: And for lacke of such heires males of the bodie of the said lady Jane lawfully begotten that then the imperiall crowne and all and singular other the premyses shall remaine, come, and be unto (3) THE LADY KATHERINE, second daughter of the said ladie Frauncis . . . (and to her heirs male lawfully begotten) (4) TO THE LADIE MARYE, thirde daughter of the saide ladie Frauncis . . . (and to her heirs male lawfully begotten) (5) THE ELDESTE SONNE OF THE BODIE OF THE FOURTH DAUGHTER OF THE SAID LADY FRAUNCIS . . . (and the heirs male of the body of the said eldest son) (6) THE ELDESTE SONNE OF THE BODYE OF THE LADY MARGARETE, daughter to the ladie Eleanore, sistere to the said ladie Fraunces, lawfully begotten . . . (7) THE ELDESTE SONNE OF THE BODY OF THE ELDESTE DAUGHTER OF THE SAID LADY JANE, lawfully begotten . . . (8) THE ELDESTE SONNE OF THE BODY OF THE ELDEST DAUGHTER OF THE SAID LADY KATHERINE lawfully begotten . . . (9) TO THE ELDESTE SONNE OF THE BODY OF THE ELDESTE DAUGHTER OF THE SAID LADY MARYE, sister to the saide ladie Katherine, and to the heires males of the body of the same eldeste sonne lawfully begotten . . . (10) TO THE ELDESTE SONNE OF THE BODY OF THE ELDEST DAUGHTER OF THE SAID FOURTH DAUGHTER OF THE SAID LADY FRAUNCIS, lawfully begotten . . . (11) TO THE ELDESTE SONNE OF THE BODY OF THE ELDEST DAUGHTER OF THE BODY OF THE SAID LADY MARGARETE, lawfully begotten . . . AND OUR MYNDE, DETERMINACION, AND PLEASURE IS that if after our decease any such heir male as is before declared, and being kinge of theis realme, be entered into eighteen yeares of age, that then he shall have the whole rule and governaunce of the said imperiall crowne, and other the premisses; but yf after the decease of the said lady Jane, lady Katherine and lady Marye, to whom as appertaineth the estat of the crowne, such heire male lymyted and appoynted as aforesaid be under the age of seventeene yeares complete, that then his mother to be the GOVERNOR of the said imperiall crowne, and other the premysses, untyll the said heire male shall enter his age of eighteene yeares, and that she shall doe nothinge without the advise of sixe persons, parcell of a COUNSELL to the numbere of xxx persons, to be appointed by us in oure laste wille . . . [further detailed provisons follow, and the document is signed by the Privy Council, and by the Lord Mayor and Aldermen of London].'

II

Extract from a despatch by the imperial ambassador in London, Jehan Scheyfve, to the Emperor Charles V, dated 4 July 1553. The original is in the State Archive in Vienna, and is reproduced here from the translation in the *Calendar of State Papers, Spanish*, vol. XIII, p. 69.

'Sire: I hear for a fact that the King of England has made a will, appointing as true heir to the Crown, after his death, [the Duke of] Suffolk's eldest daughter, who has married my Lord Guilford [Dudley], son of the Duke of Northumberland. The Princess [Mary] has been expressly excluded on religious grounds, and because she is asserted to have disobeyed the King and his Council, and infringed the decrees of Parliament. Some folk say that the Duke of Suffolk is to succeed, and that the Princess is to be declared a bastard, others that this is not to be done, partly out of fear of your Majesty and partly in order to be able to declare the Lady Elizabeth a bastard, as the King is said to have done in his will. This instrument, with its clauses of exclusion, was written by the King's own hand, and he requested the Council to sign his last will and testament, which they signed and swore to observe rather out of fear than for any other reason. Lord Shrewsbury, the Lord Treasurer [the Marquis of Winchester], the Lord Warden [of the Cinque Ports, Sir Thomas Cheyney], the Privy Seal [Earl of Bedford] and other members of the government demurred and made many difficulties before consenting, especially the Earl of Arundel who was made a councillor on the same day. Several gentlemen of the King's Bedchamber, certain lords who had been summoned to court, and some of the judges and other legal authorities who were consulted on the preparation of the will, affixed their signatures to the instrument. . . . It is still said that Parliament is to meet on September 18th. to satisfy the people, confirm and approve the measures that have been adopted, and perhaps, if all goes well, to take steps against the person of the Princess. There are some folk who assert that the execution of the will is to be subject to the authority of Parliament; but it is to be feared that as soon as the King is dead, they will attempt to seize the Princess, as I said in former letters. She was warned by a friend yesterday that she had better go further away into the country; and it has been decided that it will be wiser for her to retire to her house of Framlingham in Norfolk [*recte* Suffolk], sixty miles from London. She is at present at Hunsdon, twenty miles from London, where it would be much easier to seize her. She has confidence in her friends in Norfolk. . . .'

III

Henry Machyn, a citizen of London, recorded the king's death and subsequent events, as they were perceived in the capital. The original is BL Cottonian MS Vitellius F.v., and this extract is taken from the edition by John Gough Nichols for the Camden Society (vol. 42, 1848), p. 35.

'The vi day of July, as they say, dessessyd the nobull Kyng Edward the vi, and the vii yere of ys rayne, and sune and here to the nobull kyng Henry the viii; and he was poyssoned, as evere body says, wher nowe, thanke be unto God, ther be mony of the false trayturs browt to ther end, and j trust in God that mor shall folow as thay may be spyd owt. . . .

[The same day (7th July) there came to the Tower the Lord Treasurer, the Earl of Shrewsbury, the Lord Admiral (Lord Clinton), with others; and there they discharged Sir James Croft of the] constabullshype of the Towre, and ther thay put [in the said Lord] Admerall, and toke ys othe and charge of the Towre, and [the morrow] after he convayd in-to all plasys of the Towre and . . . grett gunnes, as the Whyt Towre on hee.

The ix day of July was sworne unto the qwen Jane alle the hed offesers and the gard as qwen of England . . . doythur of the duke of Suffolke, and servyd as qwen of . . .

The x day of July was reseyvyd in to the Towre [the Queen Jane] with a grett compeny of lords and nobulls of . . . after the qwen, and the duches of Suffoke her mother, bering her trayn, with mony lades, and ther was a shot of gunnes and chamburs has nott be sene oft be-tweyn iiii and v [of the clock]; by vi of the cloke be-gane the proclamasyon the same [after-] non [of] qwen Jane with ii harold[s] and a trompet blohyng, [declaring] that my lade Mare was unlafully be-gotten, and so [went through] chepe to Fletstrett, proclamyng qwen Jane; and ther was a yong man taken that tym for spykyng of serten wordes of qwen Mare, that she had the ryght tytle. . . .

The xix day of July was qwene Mare proclamyd qwene of England, France and Yrland, and alle domyn[ni]ons, [as the] syster of the late kyng Edward the vi and doythur unto the nobull kyng Henry the viii be-twyn v and vi of the cloke at nyght and ther wher at proclamasyon iiii trumpeters and ii harold[s] of armes, and the erle of Arundell, the erle of Shrossbery, th'erle Penbroke, my lord Tressorer, my lord Preveselle, my lord Cobham, my lord Warden, master Masun, and my lord Mare, and dyvers odur nobull men; and thys was done at the crosse in Chepe, and from that plasse thay whent unto Powlls and ther was Te Deum Laudamus, wyth song, and the organes playhyng, and all the belles ryngyng thrugh London, and bone-fyres, and tabuls in evere strett, and wyne and bere and alle, and evre strett full of bon-fyres, and ther was money cast a-way.'

Jane was the daughter of Henry Grey, Duke of Suffolk, and Frances, his wife. Frances had been born Frances Brandon, and was the daughter of Charles Brandon, Duke of Suffolk, and Mary (known as the French Queen, from her first marriage to Louis XII), the younger sister of King Henry VIII. The Lady Eleanor referred to was Frances's younger sister, who had married Henry Clifford, later Earl of Cumberland. Eleanor had died in 1543. Henry's last succession act of 1543, confirming the will which he subsequently made in 1546, settled the succession on Frances only in default of heirs from each of his three surviving children: Edward, Mary and Elizabeth. No mention was made of Mary Stuart, daughter and heir of James V of Scotland, and the granddaughter of Margaret

Tudor, Henry's elder sister, from her marriage with James IV. The document referred to as Edward's will was apparently the Letters Patent, based upon his 'Device', which was the instrument drawn up in his own hand. Scheyfve was not in the confidence of Edward's council, and his information is a mixture of reliable intelligence and hearsay; Machyn merely reported what was rumoured and seen on the streets of London. The contrast between the reporting of the two proclamations makes it clear where the sympathies of the citizens (including Machyn) really lay.

TWO

The Crisis of July 1553

I

Extract from a despatch written on 7 July 1553 to the Emperor Charles V by his special ambassadors to England: Jehan de Montmorency, Sieur de Courrières; Jacques de Marnix, Sieur de Thoulouse; and Simon Renard; and the resident ambassador, Jehan Scheyfve. The original is in the Vienna State Archive; this extract is taken from the *Calendar of State Papers, Spanish*, vol. XI, ed. M.A.S. Hulme, pp. 73–4.

'We have been in perplexity as to the decision we had best take in order to put your Majesty's instructions into effect, since it now seems that the Lady Mary's person will be in danger, and her promotion to the Crown so difficult as to be well-nigh impossible in the absence of a force large enough to counterbalance that of her enemies. Before our arrival here, and before my Lady knew your Majesty was sending us, she deliberated with her most confidential advisers on the course she had better adopt in case the king were to die. She came to the conclusion that, as soon as the king's death should be announced, she had better proclaim herself Queen by her letters, for thus she would encourage her supporters to declare for and support her. Also there is some custom here that the man or woman who is called to the Crown must immediately declare him or herself king or queen; and my Lady decided to do this in order to avail herself of her right and call upon her friends and all those who might wish to support her, either because of her reasonable and just claim, out of hatred for the Duke [of Northumberland], who is considered to be an unworthy tyrant, or merely because the people desire a change in government. My Lady has firmly made up her mind that she must act in this manner, and that otherwise she will fall into still greater danger and lose all hope of coming to the throne. We consider this resolution strange, full of difficulties and danger for the abovementioned reasons. All the forces of the country are in the Duke's hands, and my Lady has no hope of raising enough men to face him, nor means of assisting those who may espouse her cause. If she proclaims herself queen, the King and Queen appointed by the King's will – although that instrument be null – will certainly send troops against my Lady, who will have no means of resisting unless your Majesty supplies her with them; and it seems to us inadvisable to stir up the English against your Majesty now that you are engaged in a war with the French, and are obliged to defend various parts of your dominions. The hope that my Lady builds upon English supporters of her claim is vain, because of religion; and to proclaim herself without hope of (immediate) success would only jeopardise those chances that remain of her coming to the throne. . . .'

II

Extract from a contemporary chronicle, written anonymously by a resident of the Tower of London, and sometimes called 'the Tower Chronicle'. The original is BL Harleian MS 194, and this extract is taken from the version edited for the Camden Society in 1850 by J.G. Nichols, under the title *The Chronicle of Queen Jane, and of Two Years of Mary*, pp. 8–10.

'About this tyme [13 July 1553] or therabouts the vi shippes that were sent to lie befor Yarmothe, that if she [Mary] had fled to have taken hir, was by force of wether dreven into the haven, w[h]er about that quarters one maister Gerningham was raysing power on quene Maryes behalfe, and hering therof came thether. Wherupon the captaynes toke a bote and went to their shipes. Then the marynours axed maister Gernyngham what he wolde have, and wether he wolde have their captaynes or no; and he said, "Yea, mary". Saide they, "Ye shall have theym, or els we shall throwe theym to the bottom of the sea". The captaynes, seing this perplexity, saide furthwith they wolde serve quene Mary gladlie; and so cam fourthe with their men, and convayed certayn great ordenaunce; of the which comyng in of the shipes the lady Mary and hir company were wonderfull joyous, and then afterwarde doubted smaly the duke's puisance. And as the comyng of the shipes moche rejoyced quene Mary's party, even so was it as great a hart-sore to the duke, and all his campe, whose hartes wer allredy bent agaynst him. But after once the submysyon of the shipes was knowne in the Tower eche man then began to pluck in his hornes; and over that, worde of a greater mischief was brought to the Tower – the noblemen's tenauntes refused to serve their lordes agaynst quene Mary. The duke he thought long for his succours, and writ somewhat sharplie to the counsayll here in that behalfe, aswell for lacke of men as of munytion; but slender answer he had agayn.

By this tyme newes was brought that sir John Williams was also proclamyng quene Mary in Oxfordeshire. From that tyme forwarde certayne of the counsayll, that is, the erle of Penbroke and the lorde warden [Sir Thomas Cheney] sought to go out of the Tower to consult in London, but could not as yet.

The xvith daye of July the lorde highe treasurer [the Marquis of Winchester] was going to his howse in London at night, and about vii of the clocke the gates of the Tower upon a sudden was shut, and the keyes caryed upp to the quene Jane; but what the cause was I knowe not. The noyes in the Tower was that ther was a seale lackinge; but many men thought they surmysed that but the truthe was she feared some packinge in the lorde treasurer, and so they dyd fetch him at xii of the clocke in the night from his house in London into the Tower.

The xviii daye the duke, perceavinge howe their succours came not, and also receyving from some of the counsell at the Tower lettres of discomfort, retourned from Bury, and came back agayn to Cambridge.

Note here, the xixth day at night he harde howe that quene Mary was proclaymed in London. And the next morning he called for a herolde and proclaymed hir himself. Within an hower after he had lettres from the counsell here that he should forthwith dismysse his armye, and not to come within x myles of London, or els they wolde fight with him. The rumour hereof was no sooner abrode but every man departyd. Then was the duke arrested, by the mayre of the towne of Cambridge, as some say, some say by mr. Thomas Myldemay at the quenes commandement. . . .'

III

Extracts from the 'Vita Mariae Reginae' of Robert Wingfield of Brantham. The original is BL Add. MS 48093, and these extracts are taken from the translation made by Diarmaid MacCulloch, and published in the *Camden Miscellany*, vol. XXVIII (1984), pp. 251–67. The original, written in Latin, was presented to Sir Edward Waldegrave.

'Having first taken counsel with her advisers, she caused her whole household to be summoned, and told them of the death of her brother, Edward VI; the right to the Crown of England had therefore descended to her by divine and human law after her brother's death, through God's high providence, and she was most anxious to inaugurate her reign with the aid of her most faithful servants, as partners in her fortunes. Roused by their mistress's words, everyone, both gently-born and the humbler servants, cheered her to the rafters and hailed and proclaimed their dearest princess Mary as queen of England. However, this attempt should have been judged and considered one of Herculean rather than womanly daring, since to claim and secure her hereditary right, the princess was being so bold as to tackle a powerful and well-prepared enemy, thoroughly provisioned with everything necessary to end or to prolong a war, while she was entirely unprepared for warfare and had insignificant forces. . . . While the queen was thus passionately exhorting her followers at Kenninghall to try the hazard of death if need be (for as they say it was by taking risks that the Greeks came to Troy) rumours both of the king's death and of her bid for the throne were spreading far and wide through Norfolk and Suffolk with incredible speed, and it is remarkable to relate how much excitement there was among the countryfolk of the two counties; every day they flocked to their rightful queen ready to lay out for her in this worthy cause their wealth, their effort, and life itself, more dear by far than wealth and effort. . . .

Now that fortune was beginning to smile on sacred Mary's righteous undertaking, Sir Richard Southwell arrived, amply provided with money, provisions and armed men, to make the most humble submission that he could to the queen, repeatedly recalling in his petition the many favours heaped on him by Henry VIII; to the end that his submission might be more welcome to the tender-hearted queen, he is said to have contributed a respectable sum of money towards the prosecution of a campaign. Nothing at that time could have been more opportune or desirable than the arrival of this knight, the wealthiest of his rank in all Norfolk, for he brought reinforcements of men, a store of provisions and moreover money, the sinews of war, as they call it, not to mention his own skill in counsel and long experience; reinforcements which could alleviate her troubles and oppose her misfortunes. [On 12 July Mary moved from Kenninghall to Framlingham castle.] . . . To this castle Henry Radcliffe, earl of Sussex, a man much honoured for his descent and himself of great courage and readiness in dangerous situations, brought his support, as he had already promised, with a cohort of both horsemen and foot soldiers. He was followed by John, earl of Bath, himself also sprung from a noble stock, and a strong supporter of the queen, with a large band of soldiers. This most faithful nobleman had already met the queen as she was making for Norfolk from Hunsdon, and had offered his entire allegiance to her Highness.

. . . This exceedingly bold and courageous plan did not lack a happy and excellent outcome, so that ancient piece of proverbial wisdom, that fortune helps those who help themselves, did not seem entirely false. Once Mary was indeed proclaimed undoubted queen of England, one would not believe how rapidly and in what large numbers both gentlemen and ordinary folk gathered from the shires mentioned above, and I would not wish the leading names to remain hidden.'

These three extracts encapsulate the events of these extraordinary days. The despatch of the imperial ambassadors reflects partly Scheyfve's perception and partly received wisdom at the imperial court. The other envoys had been in London less than twenty-four hours. Charles V, although very sympathetic to Mary, had no opinion of either her judgement or her nerve. The ambassadors had been instructed to offer her only the most discreet encouragement, and to back off immediately if she seemed likely to lose. As they realised, the diplomatic consequences of overtly supporting a losing cause could have been serious. The emperor's objective was not to put Mary on the throne, welcome though that would be, but to prevent England from entering into an alliance with France. Neither he, nor any of his representatives, understood the religious situation in England. On the one hand they believed the Protestants to be much stronger and more numerous than they were; and on the other they failed to appreciate that there was a difference between 'Catholic' in the English sense (which might be called 'Henrician') and Catholic in the sense in which they understood it.

Robert Wingfield's somewhat cloying and repetitive rhetoric was a bit like a bardic 'praise song', and was intended to curry favour with the newly victorious queen. What it reveals very clearly is the manner and speed of Mary's mobilisation, and the fact that both she and her supporters were fully prepared for the crisis when it came, a circumstance which the author never openly admits, because his agenda is to describe a Divinely inspired miracle. He has a much fuller and more circumstantial account of the defection of the ships, a narrative full of miraculous coincidences. The most objective account is that provided by the 'Tower chronicler', who has no particular agenda, and who makes it clear that Northumberland's position was never as strong as less-well-informed observers believed. Many of the council were equivocal, quickly seeking to defect. Most significant of all is his observation that men would not follow their lords against Mary, a statement confirmed by several stories in Wingfield's somewhat rambling narrative. The capacity of gentlemen and yeomen to act independently of their superiors, and even directly against their wishes, was unexpected even to those knowledgeable about English politics, and quite amazing to outsiders. It marks the beginning of an extremely important, and distinctive, tendency.

THREE

Mary is Received and Established

I

Extracts from a despatch written by the imperial ambassadors to the emperor from London on 27 August. The original is in the Vienna State Archive, and these extracts are taken from the *Calendar of State Papers, Spanish*, vol. XI, pp. 183–93.

'Sire: The commissioners left in London by the Queen on her departure to Richmond have proceeded so well in the matter of the Duke of Northumberland and his accomplices' trial, that on the 18th of this month the Duke, the Marquis of Northampton, and the earl of Warwick, the Duke's eldest son, were brought by water to Westminster Hall, where the Parliaments are usually held. The old Duke of Norfolk, the earl Marshal of England, stood to represent the Queen as President of the Court.

. . . Four heralds assisted at the proceedings, and one whom they name the recorder; the whole body representing the criminal court of England. Before the Duke appeared one of the heralds cried "silence!" and the commission of the judges, in latin, was read out. The herald cited the Duke and adjured him to appear at the hour before the commissioners; and at the same time a citation and adjuration was addressed to the Captains of the Tower and of the castle to bring forth the person of the Duke, who was in their keeping and charge. The Duke was then brought in under safe escort, preceded by one carrying the axe of justice, and stood before his judges. The recorder read out his deposition and confession from among the documents of the trial, and asked if he maintained all that was stated therein, so that judgement might be given according to custom. The Duke raised his hand in sign of taking the oath; then he fell on his knees and appealed to the Queen for mercy, saying that all he had done was by the advice, consent and command of the Council; he confessed the occasion of it, and reiterated his confession. He proffered three requests: one that the Queen's Councillors and judges should intercede with her to obtain grace and pardon for him; the second that certain Councillors might be deputed to hear certain matters he wished to declare; the third that time might be granted to him to reconcile himself with God, and the execution of the sentence be deferred for a few days. Thereupon the Duke of Norfolk, without consulting the judges or commissioners, or taking their votes or advice – as indeed there was no need, as the Duke made a full confession – pronounced sentence against him. . . . The Duke recanted . . . confessed and received the holy sacrament . . . declaring loudly before those who were in the Tower that since he had forsaken God and the Church to follow the new religion he had done no good, and his actions had been unfortunate. He confessed publicly that he had continued in error for three or four years, and went so far as to approve the authority of the Roman church, using words that avowed the said authority, as we have been told. He did not merely declare what is said above in the Tower, but repeated the same words on the scaffold, loudly before the people. He recommended them to obey the Queen, whom he called good and virtuous, saying that she had attained the throne miraculously, by reason of her true right by inheritance, and that therein he acknowledged the hand of God. He exhorted noblemen and people to obedience; and declared that he had received no instigation or persuasion to make the profession, but was moved thereto by his own desire, calling to witness God and his confessor, who had ever heard the same from him. He added that a warning should be taken from the condition of Germany, where rebellion and troubles had followed upon the loss of faith and true religion. He made the sign of the cross, and kissed it [the crucifix] before his death. . . . The Duke's Christian death has been misinterpreted and denounced by the heretics, who say he did as he did out of hypocrisy, in the belief that he might incline the Queen to show him mercy. But small attention is paid to the sayings of heretics and misguided men, and the truth is generally accepted and recognised. . . . There is some talk here that Cardinal Pole might nourish the ambition of wedding the Queen, being of mature years and of the blood royal; and he might prove acceptable to the kingdom, especially as he is not in holy orders. This is the third name put forward as a possible match for the Queen, counting Courtenay. The earl of Arundel's son is too young, and cannot be counted among the candidates. The Earl of Derby is of the Queen's Council; and the Bishop of Winchester is Lord Chancellor of the kingdom. . . . It is said that the Queen found the kingdom in debt for 500,000 pounds sterling. . . .'

II

Extract from *A Summarie of our Englyshe Chronicles; Diligently collected by Iohn Stowe, Citizen of London, in the Yeare of our Lorde 1566*, ff. 246v–48.

'. . . after ward, beyng accompanied with a goodly band of noble men, gentlemen, and commoners gathered out of all partes of the realme came to London, and entered the Tower the iii day of August Queen Mary having to the number of 30,000 men, the Earl of Sussex beynge lieutenant of the army, when she disolved her camp at Framlingham, victuals was of such plentith that a barrell of biere was sold for vi*d*, with the caske, and iiii greate loaves of breade for a peny. In her fathers tyme and brothers tyme dyvers noble men, bysshoppes, and other, were caste into the Tower, as the Duke of Norffolke, the Lord Courtney, sonne to the Marques of Excester, Doctoure Gardener, bishop of Winchester, D. Tonstal bishop of Durham, and divers other; which continued there prisoners at the Quenes comyng to the Tower, to whom she grau[n]ted pardon, and restored them to theyr former dignitie. Doctour Gardener byshop of Winchester she dyd not only set hym at libertie, but also made hym hygh chancellour of Englande. For the great favoure that she shewed to the Lord Courtney, whom she made Earle of Devonshire, many men were in opinion that she purposed to have married hym; but in the ende it proved other wyse. . . . The xiii day of August, master Bourn canon of Paules, preachyng at Paules crosse sayd as followeth: This same day v yeares the reverende father in God, Edmunde, byshop of London, our diocesan, preachynge in thys place, and thys same Gospell whyche I now preache, for the same he was caste in prison & hathe there remayned tyll this tyme, that the quenes moste excellent maiestie hath delivered and set hym at libertie; whyche saying of the preacher so offended the audience, that they breakyng silence, sayd, the byshop had preached abhomination: other some cried (meanyng the preacher) pull hym out, pulle hym out; and some beyng nere the pulpyt, began to clymbe towarde the preacher, to have pulled hym out, wherwyth the preacher stepped backe, and one mayster Bradford, a preacher of Kynge Edwardes tyme, stepped fouthe into the preachers place, most myldely and gently persuadyng the audience to quietnes and obedience, whose presence lyked the people well: but nevertheless Bourne standyng by Bradford one threw a dagger at him whiche hytte one of the syde poastes of the pulpet, and rebounded backe agayne a great way; wherapon mayster Bradford was faine to breake of his speache & formed hymself with the helpe of John Rogers, an other preacher, to conveye Mayster Bourne oute of the audience, whiche with great labour they brought into Paules schoole. . . .'

III

Extracts from Nichols, *Chronicle of Queen Jane* (1850), pp. 27–32.

'Note that the xxvii of september, the quenes majestye cam to the Tower by water towarde hir coronatione, and with hir the lady Elizabeth hir sister, with diverse other ladyes of name, and the hole counsayll. The lord Paiget bare the sworde before hir that daye. Before hir aryvall was shott of a peale of gonnes.

Note the last daie of September 1553, the quene came thoroughe London towardes hir coronation, sytting in a charret of tyssue, drawne with vi horses, all betrapped with redd velvett. She sat in a gown of blew velvet, furred with powdered armyen, hangyng [*sic*] on hir heade a call of clothe of tynsell besett with perle and ston, and about the same apon her hed a rond circlet of gold, moche like a hooped garlande, besett so richely with many precyouse stones that the value therof was inestymable; the said call and circle being so massy and ponderous that she was fayn to beare uppe hir hedd with hir handes; and a canopy was borne over the char. Before hir rydd a nomber of gentlemen and knightes, and then dyverse judges, then dyverse doctours of dyvynity; then followed certeyn bushopes; after theym came certayn lordes; then followed moste parte of hir counsaille; after whom followed xiii knights of the bathe, every one in thir order, the names wherof were theis, the erle of Devonshire, the lorde of Cardyf, son to the erle of Pembroke, the erle of Arundell's son, being lorde Mountryvers [etc.]. Then followed the lorde of Winchester, being lorde chauncellor, the marques of Winchester, lorde highe treasurer, having the seale and mace before them; next came the duke of Norfolk, and after him the erle of Oxforde, who bare the sworde before hir; sir Edward Hastings led hir horse in his hande. After the quenes chariott cam another chariott, having canapie all of one covering, with cloth of sillver all whitt, and vi horses betrapped with the same, bearing the said charyat; and therin sat at the ende, with hir face forwarde, the lady Elizabeth; and at the other ende, with hir backe forwarde, the lady Anne of Cleves. Then cam theyre sondry gentyllwomen rydyng on horses traped with redd vellvet, after that charyet, and their gownes and kertelles of red vellvet likewise. Then rid sir Thomas Stradlyng after theym; then followed ii other charyots rydyng in chrymseyn satteyn, ther horses betraped with the same. The nomber of the gentillwomen that rydd were xlvi in nomber, besides theym that wer in the charyots. . . .

. . . Memorandum, the first daie of October, 1553, was quene Mary crowned; that daie she cam first by water to the old palice and ther tarryed tyll about xi of the clocke, and then went to the churche on foot apon blew clothe being rayled on every syde; she was in a gown of blew velvett, lyned with poudreyd armyn, having the same cyrclet on hir hedd with the whiche she cam thorough London the daye before. She was ledd betwen one bushope and [. . .] and many bishopes in their myters and crosiars before hir.

In the churche, before she was anoynted, the lorde chauncellour went to the foure corners of the no[. . .] and cried, "Yf eny man will or can alledge eny cause whie quene Mary shoulde not be crowned, let theym speke now": and then the people in every place of the churche cryed "Quene Mary! Quene Mary!". Then the bushope of Winchester, being lorde chauncellour, proclaymed the quenes pardon, wherin was excepted all prysoners in the Tower, the Flete, certayn in the Marshallsey, and suche as had eny comandement to kepe the house, and certayn other.

Note, she was ledde iiii or v tymes on the alter, with so many and sondery cerymonyes in anoynting, crowning, and other olde customes, that it was past iii almost iiii of the clocke at night or ever she cam from the church agayn.

And as she cam homeward ther was borne before her iii swordes shethed and one naked. She was ledd likewise betwen the old bushope of Dyrom and [. . .], having in hir hande a cepter of golde, and in hir other hande a ball of golde, which she twirled and tourned in hir hande as she came homewarde. She wore a chrymesyn vellvet gown, and a crown on hir hedd, every rely [erle?] and contesse following in crymseyn vellvet with crownets on ther hedds of gold. When she was enteryd in Westminster hall ther was ill scramble for the cloth and rayles; then was ther the wast meat cast out of the ketchen made under the pallaice wall with bordes, which was very muche of all kinde of meat. And when they had don casting out meat ther was no lesse scarambling for the ketchyn yt self, every man that wolde plucking downe the bordes therof, and carying yt away, that yt might welbe callyd a wast indedde.'

The observers who wrote these accounts were none of them privy to the queen's earliest intentions, and apart from Gardiner's appointment as Lord Chancellor, references to the dispositions of officers can only be recovered from the administrative records. The ambassadors were particularly concerned with the trial and execution of the Duke of Northumberland, knowing that Charles had advised Mary strongly to show him no mercy. The somewhat gloating account of his recantation is matched by several other narratives, and by a contemporary published version, *The Saying of John, Late Duke of Northumberland, upon the Scaffolde*. Most modern observers think that the despised heretics and men of 'little account' were correct in their deductions. Dudley's plea, that he had acted only on the orders of the council, reflects the fact (not mentioned) that he was only charged with acts committed after Edward's death. His plea was disallowed on the grounds that a usurper's council had no status. It was this sort of situation that John Harrington had in mind when he wrote 'Treason doth never prosper; whats the reason? Why, if it prosper none dare call it treason.'

The ambassadors were misinformed of the true state of England's finances. Edward's debt at the end of his life was about £180,000. Stow has picked up, perhaps from an oral tradition, the size of the force that Mary had assembled at Framlingham which, even if it is approximately accurate, explains why Northumberland was unable to face it. The cheapness of the victuals disposed of had probably lodged deep in rural memories! The Tower chronicler is clearly interested in Mary's early use of 'magnificence' to establish herself, both at her initial entry into London and also at her coronation, although his description of the crowning itself is curiously perfunctory. The slightly sardonic description of the queen twiddling the orb on her way back from the abbey, and the disgusted account of the mayhem which followed the coronation banquet, suggest that he was not very favourably impressed.

FOUR

The Old Religion

I

Proclamation concerning religious policy, issued from Richmond, 18 August 1553. A draft survives in the Domestic State Papers (PRO SP11/1/7), and it was printed by the queen's printer, John Cawood (STC 7849). This text is taken from P.L. Hughes and J.F. Larkin, *Tudor Royal Proclamations* (New Haven/London, 1969), vol. II, no. 390.

'The Queen's Highness, well remembering what great inconveniences and dangers have grown to this her highness's realm in time past through the diversity of opinions in questions of religion; and hearing also that now of late sithen the beginning of her most gracious reign the same contentions be again much renewed through certain false and untrue reports and rumours spread by some light and evil disposed persons, hath thought good to do to understand to all her highness's most loving and obedient subjects her most gracious pleasure, in manner and form following:

First, her majesty, being presently by the only goodness of God settled in her just possession of the imperial crown of this realm and other dominions therrunto belonging, cannot now hide that religion which God and the world knoweth she hath ever professed from her infancy hitherto, which as her majesty is minded to observe and maintain for herself by God's grace during her time, so doth her highnes much desire and would be glad the same were of all her subjects quietly and charitably embraced. And yet she doth signify unto all her majesty's said loving subjects that of her most gracious disposition and clemency her highness mindeth not to compel any her said subjects thereunto unto such time as further order by common assent may be taken therein; forbidding nevertheless all her subjects of all degrees at their perils to move seditions or to stir unquietness in her people by interpreting the laws of this realm after their brains and fancies, but quietly to continue for the time till, as before is said, further order may be taken; and therefore willeth and straightly chargeth and commandeth all her said good loving subjects to live together in quiet sort and Christian charity, leaving those new fangled devilish terms of papist or heretic, and such like; and applying their whole cares, study, and travail, to live in the fear of God, exercising their conversations in such charitable and godly doing as their lives may indeed express that great hunger and thirst of

God's glory and holy word which, by rash talk and words, many have pretended. And in so doing, as they shall best please God and live without danger of the laws and maintain the tranquility of the realm, whereof her highness shall be most glad; so if any man shall rashly presume to make any assemblies of people, or at any public assemblies or otherwise shall go about to stir the people to disorder or disquiet, she mindeth according to her duty to see the same most severely reformed and punished according to her highness's laws.

And furthermore, forasmuch as it is well known that sedition and false rumours have been nourished and maintained in this realm by the subtlety and malice of some evil-disposed persons which take upon them without sufficient authority to preach and to interpret the word of God after their own brain in churches and other places both public and private; and also by playing of interludes and printing of false fond books, ballades, rhymes and other lewd treatises in the English tongue concerning doctrine in matters now in question and controversy touching the high points and mysteries of Christian religion; which books, ballads, rhymes and treatises are chiefly by the printers and stationers set out to sale to her graces subjects of an evil zeal for lucre and covetousness of vile gain:

Her highness therefore straightly chargeth and commandeth all and every her said subjects, of whatsoever state, condition, or degree they be, that none of them presume from henceforth to preach, or by way of reading in churches or other public or private places (except in the schools of the universities) to interpret or teach any Scriptures or any manner points of doctrine concerning religion; neither also to print any books, matter, ballad, rhyme, interlude, process or treatise, not play any interlude except they have her grace's special licence in writing for the same; upon pain to incur her highness's indignation and displeasure.

And her highness also further straightly chargeth and commandeth all and every her said subjects that none of them of their own private authority do presume to punish or to rise against any offender in the causes abovesaid, or any other offender in words or deeds in the late rebellion committed by the Duke of Northumberland or his accomplices, or to seize any of their goods, or violently to use any such offender by striking or imprisoning or threatening the same, but wholly to refer the punishment of all such offenders unto her highness and her public authority, whereof her majesty mindeth to see due punishment according to the order of her highness's laws.

Nevertheless as her highness mindeth not hereby to restrain and discourage any of her loving subjects to give from time to time true information against any such offenders in the causes abovesaid unto her grace or her council for the punishment of every such offender according to the effect of her highness's laws provided in that part, so her said highness exhorteth and straightly chargeth her said subjects to observe her commandments and pleasure in every part aforesaid, as they will avoid her highness's said indignation and most grievous displeasure; the severity and rigour whereof, as her highness shall be most sorry to have cause to put the same in execution, so doth she utterly determine not to permit such unlawful and rebellious doings of her subjects (whereof may ensue the danger of her royal estate) to remain unpunished, but to see her said laws touching these points to be thoroughly executed; which extremities she trusteth all her said loving subjects will forsee, dread, and avoid accordingly.

Her said highness straightly charging and commanding all mayors, sheriffs, justices of peace, bailiffs, constables, and all other public officers and ministers diligently to see to the observing and executing of her said commandments and pleasure, and to apprehend all such as shall willfully offend in this part; committing the same to the next gaol, there to remain without bail or mainprize till, upon certificate made to her highness or her Privy Council of their names and doings, and upon examination had of their offences, some further order shall be taken for their punishment, to the example of others according to the effect and tenor of the laws aforesaid.'

II

Extracts from *The Diary of Henry Machyn*, citizen of London, p. 49.

'The xxv day of November was sa[int Katharine's] day, and at nyght they of Powlles whent a prossessyon abowt Powlles stepull with gret lyghtes, and [before them] sant Kateryn, and syngyng, with a vC lyghtes allmost halffe a noure, and when all was don thay rong all the belles of Powlles at vi of the cloke. . . .

The xxvi day of November dyd pryche master Whyt, warden at Powlles, mad a goodly sermon that we shuld have prossessyons.
[On the same day was a goodly herse for the late King Edward, hung with cloth of tissue, and a cross and a pax, silver] candyllstykes and xiii bedmen holdyng of tapurs, and the durge song in Laten, and the masse on the morowe. . . .

The viii day of December was prossessyon at Powlles. When all was don, my lord of London [Bishop Bonner] commondyd that every parryche chyrche shuld provyd for a crosse and a staffe and cope for to go of prossessyon evere Sonday and Wednysday and fryday, and pray unto God for fayre wether thrugh London. . . .

The [. . .] day was a proclamasyon thrugh London and all England that noman shuld syng no Englys serves nor communion after the xx day of Desember, nor no prest that has a wyff shall not menyster nor say masse, and that evere parryche to make a auter and to have a crosse and staff, and all othur thingeis in all parryches all in Laten, as hale-bred, hale-water, as palme and assesse. . . .'

III

Extract from John Foxe, *Actes and Monuments of Matters Most Speciall and Memorable* . . . (London, 1583), pp. 1497–8.

'August 1553
The 5. of August, an. 1553 was one William Rutler committed (by the Counsaile) to the Marshalsey, for uttering certayne wordes agaynst Maister Bourne Preacher, for hys Sermon at Paules Crosse on Sonday last before.

The 16. of August was Humfrey Halden committed to the Counter for wordes agaynst the sayd Bournes sermon at Paules Crosse.

A letter to the Shiriffe of Buckingham and Bedford for the apprehending of one Fisher person of Ammersham a preacher.

Another letter to the B. of Norwich, not to suffer any preacher or other to preach or expound the scriptures openly without speciall licence from the Queene.

The same day was M. Bradford, M. Vernon and M. Beacon preachers committed to the charge of the Lieutenant of the Tower.

The same day also was M. John Rogers Preacher commanded to keepe himselfe prisoner in his owne house at Paules, without having conference with any other the[n] those of his owne houshold.

The 22. of August, there was two letters directed to M. Coverdall B. of Exceter, & M. Hooper B. of Gloucester, for their indelayed repayre to the Court, and there to attend the Counsailes pleasure.

The same day Fisher person of Ammersham made his appearance before the Counsaile, according to their letter of 16. of August, and was appointed next day to bring in a note of hys sermon.

The 24. of August was one John Melvin a Scotte and and [sic] Preacher, sente to Newgate in London by the Counsaile.

The 26. of August there was a letter sent to the Mayor of Coventry and his brethren, for the apprehesion of one Symonds of Worcester preacher, and then Vicare of S. Michaels in Coventry, and for the sendyng of hym up to the counsaile with his examinations and other matters they could charge hym with, with a Commission to them to punish all such as had by meanes of his preachyng used any talke against the Queenes proceedings.

The 29. of August M. Hooper B. of Worcester made his personall appearance before the Counsaile, according to their letters of 22. of August.

The 31. of August M. Coverdall B. of Exceter, made hys appearaunce before the Counsaile, according to theyr letters of 22. of August. . . .

This being done in November, the people, and especially the Churchmen, perceiving the Queene so eagerlye set upon her olde religion, they likewise for theyr partes, to shewe themselves no lesse forwarde to serve the Queenes appetite (as the manner of the multitude, commonlye to frame themselves after the humour of the Prince and time present) began in their Quieres to set up the pageants of s. Katherine, and S. Nicholas, and of their processions in Latine, after all their olde solemnitie with their gaye gardeniance and gray amices. . . .'

IV

Extract from Robert Parkyn's narrative of the Reformation, ed. A.G. Dickens, in the *English Historical Review*, 62 (1947), pp. 58–83.

'. . . Then began holy Church to rejoice in God singing both with heart and tongue Te Deum Laudamus, but heretical persons (as there were many) rejoiced nothing thereat. Oh it was joy to hear and see how these carnal priests (which had led their lives in fornication with their whores and harlots) did lour and look down when they were commanded to leave and forsake the concubines and harlots and to do open penance according to the Canon Law . . . so to be brief, all old ceremonies laudably used beforetime in the holy Church was then revived, daily frequented and used. . . .'

The restoration of traditional worship was generally welcomed, although Henry Machyn's fairly low-key pleasure was probably more typical than Robert Parkyn's gloat. Like Mary herself, he had been particularly offended by the Edwardian permission for clergy to marry. The 'whores and concubines' were actually the lawful wives of Protestant ministers. As Foxe makes clear, the Privy Council immediately swung into action to arrest and silence Protestant preachers. His summary of the events of August was actually taken from the Council Register, although the first entry should refer to 15 August, not the 5th. The queen's proclamation, although honest in respect of her own position, was thoroughly misleading in its apparent disavowal of coercion. As the earlier extract from Stow demonstrates, not everyone was happy with 'the Queen's proceedings', and Parkyn shows a similar awareness. The council had some justification for its concern about public order. It also emerges clearly that 'ceremonies', rather than doctrine or authority, were the council's first concern.

FIVE

The First Ruling Queen

I

Extract from the statute of 1 Mary, st. 2, c. 1. *Statutes of the Realm*, 4, i, p. 201.

'And be it allso enacted by thaucthoritie aforesaid, That aswell the sayd Acte of P[ar]liament, entitled, An Acte declaring thestablishment of the Succession of the Kinges most Roiall Majestie of Thimperiall Crowne of this Realme, made in the xxvth yere of the raigne of the King yor Father, bee repealed, and be voide and of none effecte [25 Henry VIII, c. 22]. As also all and every suche Clauses articles braunches and matters conteined and expressed in the foresayd Acte of P[ar]liament made in the said xxviiith yere of the reigne of the seyd late King yor Father, or in any other Acte or Actes of P[ar]liament, As whereby yor Highnes is named or declared to bee Illegitimate, or the said marriage betwen the said King yor Father and the said Quene yor Mother is declared to be against the woorde of God or by any meanes unlawfull, shalbe and bee repealed, and bee void and of no force nor effecte, to all intentes construccons and purposes as if the same Sentence or Actes of P[ar]liament hadd never bee hadd ne made: And that the said Mariage, hadd and solempnised betwen yor said most noble father King Henrie and yor said most noble Mother Quene Katherin, shall bee definitivelye clerely and absolutlie declared demed and adiudged to bee and stande withe Goddes Lawe and his most Holy woorde, and be accepted reported and taken of good effecte and validitee to all intentes and pourposes.'

II

The statute of 1 Mary, st. 3, c. 1. *Statutes of the Realm*, 4, i, p. 222.

'An Acte declaring that the Royall Power of this Realme is in the Queenes Ma[jes]tie as fully and absolutely as ever it was in any of her moste noble Progenitours Kinges of this Realme.

Forasmuche as the Imperiall Crowne of this Realm, with all Dignities Honours Prerogatives Aucthorities Jurisdictions and Preheminences thereunto annexed united and belonging, by the Divine Providence of

Almighty God, ys most lawfully, justly and rightfully descended and come unto the Quenes Highnes that now ys, being the verye true and undoubted heire and inheritrix therof, and invested in her most Royall Person, according unto the Lawes of this Realme; and for by force and venture of the same all Regall Power Dignitie Honour Aucthoritie Prerogative Preheminence and Jurisdiction dothe apperteine, and of right ought to apperteine and belong unto her Highnes, as to the Sovereine supreme Governour and Quene of this Realme and the Dominions thereof, in as full large and ample maner as it hathe done heretofore to any other her most noble Progenitours, Kinges of this Realme: Nevertheles the most auncient Statutes of this Realme being made by Kinges then reigning, doo not only attribute and referre all Prerogative Preheminence Power and Jurisdiction Roiall unto the name of King, but also doo gyve assigne and appointe the Correccon and Punishment of all Offendours agaynst the Regalitie and Dignitie of the Crowne and the Lawes of the Realme unto the Kinge; By occasion wherof the malitious and ignorant persones may bee hereafter induced and perswaded into this errour and folly, to thinck that her Highnes coulde ne shoulde have enjoye and use suche lyke Royall Aucthoritie Power Preheminence Prerogative and Jurisdiction, not doo ne execute and use all thinges concerning the sayd Statutes, and take the benefitt and privilege of the same, nor correct and punishe Offendours against her most Royall Person and the Regalitie and Dignitie of the Crowne of this Realme and the Dominions thereof, as the Kinges of this Realm her most noble Progenitours have heretofore doon enioyed and exersised: For thavoiding and clere extinguishment of which sayd errour or doubtes, and for a playn declaraccon of the Lawes of this realme in that behalf: Be it declared and enacted by thaucthoritie of this p[re]sente P[ar]liament, that the Lawe of this Realme is and ever hathe been, and ought to bee understoode, that the Kinglye or Regall Office of the Realme, and all the Dignities Prerogative Royall Power Preheminences Privilegies Aucthorities and Jurisdiccons thereunto annexed united or belonging, being invested in either Male or Female, are and bee and ought to bee as fully wholly absolutely and enteerly demed judged accepted invested and taken in thone as in thother; so that what or whansoever Statute or Lawe doothe lymitte and appointe that the King of this Realme may or shall have execute and doo any thing as King, or dothe geve any profitt or comoditie to the King, or dothe lymitte or appointe any powers or punishment for the Correccon of Offendours or Transgressours against the Regalitie and Dignitie of the King, or of the Crown, The same the Quene (being supreme Governesse possessour and inheritour to the Imperiall Crowne of this Realme as our sayd Sovereigne Ladye the Quene most justlie presently is,) may by the same aucthoritie and power likewise have exercise execute punishe correcte and doo, to all intentes construccons and purposes without Doubte Ambiguitie Scruple or Question: Any Custome Use or Scruple or any other thing whatsoever to be made to the contrary notwithstanding.'

Mary's position was absolutely unprecedented. The only woman previously to claim the English Crown had been Matilda in the twelfth century, and she had failed to establish herself. It was therefore necessary to clarify the position of a ruling queen. Mary had been declared illegitimate by statute, although her right to succeed had been recognised. It was also a normal custom of inheritance that a woman's property passed in full ownership to her husband on marriage, and remained his property until his death, irrespective of her own fate, although he was not free to dispose of it. Mary used the recently extended authority of statute to tackle these problems in two stages. Firstly, she had her parents' marriage declared lawful, which avoided making her legitimacy dependent upon a papal dispensation which could be (and had been) challenged. To make assurance even more secure, parliament then additionally confirmed her right to the throne. The second stage was required by her forthcoming marriage. The marriage treaty declared that, in the event of Mary's death without heirs, her husband was to have no further rights in the kingdom; however, many did not trust the security of this safeguard, and as Philip secretly repudiated the limitations imposed by the treaty, they were entirely justified. A statute was therefore used to declare that the queen's authority was the same as that of previous kings; in other words that the traditional gender limitations of inheritance did not apply to the Crown. By 'ungendering' the Crown in this way, parliament thus both reinforced the provisions of the treaty, and made them unnecessary.

SIX

Negotiations for Marriage

I

Letter from Simon Renard to Antoine de Perronet, Bishop of Arras, the chief minister of Charles V, dated from London on 9 September. The original (written in French) is in the municipal archive at Besançon. This is taken from the *Calendar of State Papers, Spanish*, XI, pp. 227–9.

'My Lord: I have noted the contents of your last letters, and even before I received them was of the opinion I see you have adopted, because it is said that the marriage negotiations of his Highness [Philip, with the Infanta Maria of Portugal] are so far advanced that it will be impossible to withdraw, in which case to mention him might disincline the Queen from following his Majesty's advice, which she is at present very anxious to know, desiring to hear what aspirant he will propose. When she sees Scheyfve's secretary, she asks him whether we have received letters from his Majesty, and whether we have anything to say to her. As far as I am able to gather from certain remarks made by Scheyfve, it seems that she and certain of her council aspire to an alliance with the King of the Romans [Charles's brother, Ferdinand]. When we were talking over the matter, and some one said that if his Highness were unmarried he would make an excellent match from the point of view of both countries, Scheyfve said that he knew that the English did not at all want his Majesty or his Highness, but would prefer the King of the Romans or the Archduke [Ferdinand's younger son, also Ferdinand], partly because they dreaded the rule of Spaniards and partly for religious reasons; and he probably would not have said that had he not heard it from certain members of the council. Moreover, it has been certified to me that it has been represented to the Queen that his Highness will have great difficulty in keeping possession of the Low Countries after his Majesty's death, for the King of Bohemia [Maximilian] is loved there and his Highness and the Spaniards hated. These are warnings about which you ought to think more carefully than about anything else in the world, in order to forestall such designs and take measures to ensure his Majesty's succession. I feel sure you are doing so, and striving to reconcile these two princes if you believe there is real enmity between them and the Flemish and Spanish peoples; for success in this would be the masterpiece of all your labours.

However that may be, I know the Queen to be good, easily influenced, inexpert in worldly matters and a novice all round; and the English so grasping that if one cares to try them with presents and promises one may do what one likes with them by very simple means: namely to tell them that four out of their number will be chosen to govern the country in the Queen's absence. And although she asserts that she wishes to see the aspirant, she will not insist when she hears his Majesty's message. To tell you between ourselves what I think of her, I believe that if God does not preserve her she will be deceived and lost either by the machinations of the French, the conspiracies of the English, by poison or otherwise. The lady Elizabeth is greatly to be feared, for she has a power of enchantment, and I hear that she already has an eye on Courtenay as a possible husband, because she knows Courtenay's mother [Gertrude, Marchioness of Exeter] is always welcome with the Queen, and usually sleeps with her. This is very dangerous; and I foresee that Courtenay's friends, who include most of the nobility, are hatching some design that may later menace the Queen. M. de Gye was not sent to Courtenay with letters from the King of France for nothing; and I have suspicions of the Earl of Pembroke's departure for a house he has in the country, and it is said that Paget intends to retire from the court, and that [Sir John] Mason is of the same mind. All this, together with the hostility and jealousy prevalent in the council will throw her off the throne one fine morning; and she has no thought but to restore the mass and religion, which will also provoke attacks if God does not remedy it.

I am going into these details, so that you may understand the state of mind prevalent over here and the present aspect of the Queen's affairs, and communicate them to his Majesty if you see fit. And now that I know your views, I will keep the marriage question pending by means which you will not disapprove, and will contrive to persuade the Queen that I spoke to her entirely of my own accord. As soon as I get the chance I intend, if you approve, to tell her that I hear more rumours of his Highness's Portuguese match, and I have been able to obtain no news from Spain to settle my doubts. And I will devise means of dissuading her from wishing to see the aspirant, so as to prepare things as his Majesty desires.

The only difficulty is that I cannot have access to her when I wish and Master Scheyfve has grown jealous because I had private audience of her twice, was spokesman in our public and private audiences, and because my colleagues commanded me to do the writing. The said Scheyfve thinks I am trying to get hold of his post, which ambition has never crossed my mind, as my only wish is to do my duty towards his Majesty, and fulfil the obligation I owe you. I call you to witness of this fact, and beg you, my Lord, to justify me by recalling me soon, as my commission is at an end. . . .'

II

Extracts from a further despatch by Simon Renard (who had been entrusted with the negotiation) to the emperor, dated 5 October; from the *Calendar of State Papers, Spanish*, XI, pp. 227–9.

'Sire; I have learned from the private letters it has pleased your Majesty to write to me on the 20th of last month, your Majesty's resolve concerning the marriage. I considered that the negotiation could not well be opened or conducted without the knowledge and participation of the councillors; and having heard from the Queen that Paget was in favour of a foreign alliance, and knowing, moreover, that Paget wished to make good the loss and damage he suffered at the hands of his enemies and those who wished him ill; that he was a man of wit, and stood well among those who governed and administered the affairs of the country; and especially as he had questioned us several times as to the respective ages of his Highness, Don Luis of Portugal, and my Lord the Duke of Savoy, I addressed myself to him. . . .

. . . Some of the councillors, he said, had weighed the great burdens resting on the Queen, the trouble it cost her to administer the kingdom; on the other hand, they saw the condition to which the kingdom was brought, the lack of a true heir to the throne in the direct line, there being a stain of bastardy on the Lady Elizabeth; and so as to restore the succession and continue the line, they considered it necessary for the good of the kingdom that the Queen should enter into an alliance and marry; and the sooner the better, because of the state of her affairs and her years. Some astonishment had been felt that your Majesty, who had always favoured and protected her affairs as if they had been your own, had overlooked this question of her marriage. . . . The Queen had been approached in general terms, with the object of discovering her private inclinations, no names being mentioned; nor would it have been meet for any subject to presume to advance so far or take so much upon himself. Her answers seemed to imply that she would accept a marriage for the good of her people, and in the hope of begetting heirs, rather than from any private inclination or amourousness of disposition. I was to assure your Majesty that the Queen would not engage herself or her word to anyone without your Majesty's knowledge, and without communicating the matter to you before doing anything. . . .

The English must ponder the fact [the French ambassador] said, that if an alliance with his Highness were decided upon the good understanding between France and England would be at an end. . . . He painted the Spaniards in the darkest colours that he could devise; he impressed upon [the English] that if the alliance were to take place the Spaniards would try to dominate in England; said they were hated by the whole world, that they were unbearable, and much more in the same strain to decry the Spanish nation. He went so far as to dwell upon his Highness's parts, and said that his first progress on this side of the sea proved the nature of the hopes that were to be founded upon him for the future, his own subjects having been dissatisfied. . . .

[Paget] replied that he was happy to hear there was a good understanding between your Majesty and the King of the Romans and his sons; he for his part paid no attention to the talk of the French, and he knew very well what they could say and do. He then brought the conversation back again to the marriage, and said he thought the Queen's happiness ought to be taken into consideration, as well as her age and comfort; that a husband should be proposed to her suitable in these respects with whom she could live in happiness and content, and who would remain at her side. He himself had considered that even if his Highness were not already married to the Infanta of Portugal, he had so many kingdoms and countries, divided from one another, that his marriage, were it to take place, would not keep him in England, and this the people desired above all things. The Prince's age was but 26; he had heard that he was no linguist, and spoke no other language except Spanish. If the marriage were to come off, it would be expedient for him to learn to speak and understand English, otherwise it would prove a dumb marriage, and he could hold no communication with the Council or with the people. Although the marriage could make him no more than governor of the kingdom, yet he should be able to understand various things to save the Queen trouble. . . .

He repeated again that he knew for certain that the Queen would not marry without your Majesty's advice, and this fact encouraged him to speak to me more boldly and with greater confidence. He asked me to tell him if his Highness's marriage had taken place; to describe his character and parts, for he was already well aware of his exalted rank and descent. I replied that I had no news, either from Spain or from your Majesty's Court. He was a prince possessed of natural gifts as great as his acquired qualities, as prudent and discreet in his negotiations as one could wish, and he understood both French and Italian. . . .'

III

Extract from Nichols, *Chronicle of Queen Jane* (1850), pp. 33–5.

'Note that the morrowe after Newe yere's day [1554], being the second of Janyver, the embassadors called the erle of Englemod [Count of Egmont], the erle of Lane [Charles, Count de Laing], and Coryurs [the sieur de Courrières] came in for the knytting upp of the marryage of the quene to the kinge of Spayne, before whose landing ther was lett of a great peale of guns in the Tower. He landed at Tower wharf, and ther was met by sir Anthony Browne, he being clothed in a very gorgeouse apparell. At the Tower hill the erle of Devonshire, with the lorde Garret, and dyver other, receyved [him] in most honorable and famylier wise; and so the lorde of Devonshire gevyng him the right hand brought him thoroughte Chepsyde and so fourthe to Westminster; the people, nothing rejoysing, helde downe their heddes sorowfully.

The day befor his coming in, as his retynew and harbengers came ryding thorugh London, the boyes pelted at theym with snowballes; so hatfull was the sight of ther coming in to theym. The morrow following, being wenysday, the lord chancellour sent for the churchewardens and substancyllest of xxx parishes of London, to come before him, apon whose appearence he enquired of diverse of theym whie they had not the masse and servyse in Latten in their churches, as some of theym had not, as St. [. . .] in Mylke stret, and others; and they answered that they had don what lay in theym.

The xiii of Januarie, anno 1553 [1554], the bushope of Winchester, lorde chancellor of Inglonde, in the chamber of presence at Westminster, made to the lordes, nobilytye, and gentyllmen, an oration, very eloquentlie, wherin he declared that the quenes majesty, partely for the welthe and enryching of the realme, and partely for frendeship and other waighty considerations, hathe determyned, by the consent of hir counsaille and nobylyty, to matche herselfe with him in most godly and lawfull matrymonye; and he said further that she should have for her joynter xxxml ducketes by the yere, with all the Lowe Country of Flanders; and that the issue betwene theym two lawfully begotten shoulde, yf there were any, be heir as well to the kingdome of Spayne, as also of the saide Lowe Country. And he declared further, that we were moche bounden to thanck God that so noble, worthy and famouse a prince would vouchsaff so to humble himself, as in this marryadge to take apon him rather as a subject then otherwise; and that the quene shoulde rule all thinges as she dothe nowe; and that ther should be of the counsell no Spanyard, nether should have the custody of any fortes or castelles; nether bere rule or offyce in the quenes house, or elsewhere in all Inglonde; with divers other things which he then rehersed; when he sayde the quenes pleasure and request was, that like humble subjectes, for her sake they would receyve him with all reverence, joye, honnour etc.

Theis newes, althoughe before they were not unknown to many, and very moche mysliked, yit being nowe in this wise pronounced, was not onely credyted, but also hevely taken of sondery men, yea and therat allmost eche man was abashed, loking daylie for worse mattiers to growe shortly after.

On the morrowe following, being monday, the mayre, sheryfes, and diverse of the best commoners, wer sent for before the counsell, where the said lord chancellour made the like oration to theym, desyring theym to behave themselve like subjectes with all humblenes and rejoycing.'

In spite of Renard's extremely circumspect language, Mary had decided almost as soon as she reached London that marriage must be a priority. This was partly because of the needs of the succession, and partly because she believed that effective government required a man's hand, even if it was not strictly on the rudder. This was hinted at, rather than directly stated, by both sides.

Mary's long-standing commitment not to marry without the emperor's advice and consent is frequently mentioned, although again circumspectly, because the ambassadors were aware that this was an improper attitude for a sovereign prince, although it served their purposes. Charles did not at first know whether Philip was committed in Portugal or not, and it took some time to unravel that negotiation, hence the extremely cautious language in which he is referred to. The emperor did not want to push his advantage too hard, for fear of alienating the English council, and at first authorised Renard only to mention the prince casually, as though of his own thought. Paget, who, as Renard realised, was busy recovering lost ground politically, was therefore an extremely valuable and astute ally. In spite of the sensible reservations which he apparently voiced, Renard was soon able to persuade him that his interests would be best served by endorsing Philip's candidature, which he did.

Many of the council, who were known to be opposed to such a match, were kept in the dark. Scheyfve, who was much more sceptical than Renard, was quickly replaced by the latter as the principal negotiator, and by the end of October had a unique place in the queen's confidence. Early in November Mary decided to marry Philip, without consulting her whole council. Charles and Renard were both pleased and relieved, but then had to address the probable hostility of the English people to the match. This hostility is reflected very clearly in the account by the Tower chronicler of the reception accorded the formal embassy sent to conclude the treaty. If his report of Gardiner's oration is accurate, the chancellor was mistaken on a number of points. Mary's jointure was actually the much larger sum of £60,000 a year, but she was given no rights in the Low Countries, other than fiscal ones. It was specifically provided that any child of the marriage should not inherit Spain, protecting the rights of Philip's existing son, Don Carlos. It is highly unlikely that Gardiner got these important points wrong, as the treaty was newly signed; it seems that the writer's informant was not hearing straight. But his description of the public mood is authentic.

SEVEN

Mary and the Papacy

I

Extract from Cardinal Pole's letter to Mary, 13 August 1553, taken from the *Calendar of State Papers, Venetian*, vol. V, pp. 384–7. The manuscript, which is an Italian translation of the original English, is in St Mark's library, Venice. The following is a paraphrase rather than a verbatim re-translation.

'[He] is certain that her Majesty rejoices more at the proof thus afforded [of God's approval] than at the royal Crown itself; and if ever woman had merciful grace for which to praise God in the words of his blessed mother, whose name the Queen bears . . . when, replete with the Holy Spirit, she sang, saying "Magnificat anima mea Dominum". . . .

. . . hopes this effect of the Almighty's providence with regard to her Majesty will become daily more manifest by her governnment, with such increase of joy and contentment as desired, to the honour and praise of his Divine Majesty, for whose church and for the sake of the Queen herself, Pole is bound to warn her of one single thing at the commencement of her reign, which is, that having received such especial favour from the Divine goodness she be pleased well to consider from what root the great disorders in matters relating to justice and the true religion proceeded; the which disorders in England have for many years been seen to increase daily; greatly to the ruin both of private and public interests.

By doing so, her Majesty will perceive that the beginning and cause of all the evil, commenced at the time when the perpetual adversary of the human race placed in the heart of the king her father the perverse desire to make the divorce from the blessed queen her mother. To this great injustice towards God, towards her and Queen Mary, and towards himself at the same time he added another, much greater, that of divorcing himself from Queen Mary's spiritual mother, and from all faithful Christians, that is from the Holy Catholic Church, from which he departed by departing from the obedience of the Apostolic See. From this iniquitous and impious seed there subsequently sprang up those pestiferous fruits which have so corrupted every part of the kingdom, that since many years scarce any vestige has been seen of justice or religion, as if both one and the other had been banished the realm when reverence and obedience towards the Church were abolished; and I venture to make this prophecy, that they will never return, be the government whatever it may, until this divine obedience be again received into the mind of the ruler. . . .'

II

Extract from Henry Penning's report to Pope Julius III; taken from the *Calendar of State Papers, Venetian*, vol. V, pp. 429–32. The undated original, in Italian, is in St Mark's library, Venice.

'. . . the reply of the Queen, who said that she had always been most obedient and most affectionate towards the Apostolic See, and that [in her heart] his Holiness had no more loving daughter than herself, and that within a few days she hoped to be able to shew it openly to the whole world; and that thus far, she thanked our Lord God that she had never consented in any way to the heresies and impious laws made and published in England of late years, but had always been, and would continue, firm in that same religion in which she had been educated from her girlhood, as she hoped in a few days to shew his Holiness and the whole world; but it was first necessary to repeal and annul by Act of Parliament many perverse laws made by those who ruled before her. . . .

And speaking about the Bishop of Winchester who was to crown her, and of the few other catholics now there, her Majesty wished them also to be absolved, that they might be able to say mass and administer the sacraments without sin, until able to have the general absolution.

To this I answered her Majesty as God inspired me . . . that the Holy Mother Church absolved and pardoned those alone who repented of their errors, and resolved no longer to commit them; but not that his Holiness would absolve those who persevered in their errors. In reply to this her Majesty said to me that Sig. Commendone had well nigh promised it her; and this her Majesty charged me to keep secret.

. . . there [are] also many of the new religion in the government, who foresee that it is her Majesty's intention utterly to extirpate this pestiferous contagion; so they do not fail forming all possible evil designs, though, with God's assistance, they will not accomplish anything. . . .

. . . On the following Saturday, the 7th October, her Majesty informed me that matters had proceeded well; as in the Parliament she had found many of the chief personages of the kingdom who encouraged her to push the affairs of religion and of the union; whilst others were of the opinion that she had greater need of curb than spur. . . . Her Majesty also shewed me the holy oil, which she had sent to obtain at Brussels from the Emperor [for her coronation].'

III

Extract from Pole's letter to the Cardinal of Imola, Geronimo Dandino, 9 September 1553; taken from the *Calendar of State Papers, Venetian*, vol. V, pp. 409–10. The original, in Italian, is in St Mark's library, Venice.

'. . . to pass over in silence this point of the union of the church, could not but be very injurious to the cause, for the same reasons which the Legate will have heard from Pole's secretary, Fiordibello. Although it might seem imprudent for a Papal Legate or Nuncio to go to England at present, yet it does not seem to him by any means imprudent to approach that neighbourhood, and commence treating the matter. Pole will await such orders as the Pope may be pleased to give him after hearing Commendone. With regard to the fitting and necessary caution to be taken in this matter, Pole will agree with the Legate, provided it do not exclude the commencement of negotiation, and the subsequent discussion in the first parliament of this point, on which he is perfectly convinced there depends not only the advantage of the Apostolic See, but the salvation of that entire kingdom. . . .'

Almost as soon as the news of Mary's success reached him in Italy, Pole requested from his friend Julius III the mission to reconcile the English Church, and on 13 August he wrote to Mary informing her of this mission. The letter was carried by his chamberlain, Henry Penning. Mary had already informed her council of her intention to restore the Roman jurisdiction. The queen's reception of the letter, however, and of Penning, although friendly, was far more cautious than Pole liked. Shortly afterwards the papal legate in Germany, Geronimo Dandino, also sent a personal envoy to England, with instructions to report directly to the pope. Commendone also urged caution, and the postponement of Pole's mission for the time being, to the latter's great indignation. Peter Vannes, Mary's representative in Rome, reported on 23 September that Commendone had told the consistory that 'the schismatics are greater in number than the heretics [in England], and all enemies to the church of Rome', which was a realistic assessment of the situation. Pole's zeal was a very questionable asset in what was bound to be a tricky negotiation, and he knew England much less well than he thought he did.

EIGHT

The Wyatt Rebellion

I

Extracts from Nichols, *Chronicle of Queen Jane* (1850), pp. 36–51.

'Note that the xxvth of January the counsell was certyfyed that ther was uppe in Kent sir Thomas Wyat, mr. Cullpepper, the lorde Cobham, who had taken his castell of Coulyng, and the lord warden [Sir Thomas Cheney] who had taken the castell of Dover, and sir Herry Isley in Meddeston, sir James Croftes, mr. Harper, mr. Newton, mr. Knevet, for the said quarrell, in resystyng the said king of Spayne, as they said, ther pretence was this only and non other, and partely for moving certayn counsellours from about the quene. And about this time sir James Croftes departed to walles, as yt is thought to rayse his powre there.

The xxvith day ther was [brought] into the Tower as prysoners the lord marques [of Northampton] and sir Edward Warner knight, in the mornyng. And the same nyght there went out certeyn of the garde and other agaynste the Kentish men. Item the same day, in the mornyng, the cytey began to be kept with harnessyd men.

The day afore, the lorde treasurer being at the yeld hall, with the mayre and aldermen, declared that yt was goode to have a nombre of ii ml, or ther aboutes, in a redynes for the savegarde of the cyte &c with his [. . .].

Note, that the xxvth daie of Januarie the duke of Suffolk, the lord John Graie, and the lord Leonarde Gray, fledd. . . . The same day the duke of Norfolke wente down towardes Gravesende.

The xxvith day yt was noysed that Rochester bridge was taken by the rebelles.

About this tyme the lord of Bergenny by chance encounteryd with sir Herry Isely, and slew ii or iii of his men, he fleeing to the camp of Wyat.

The same day ther was made redy, by vi of the clock at nyght, about vC of harnessed men, and came together at Leaden hall; and the sonday followinge they went towardes Gravesende against the Kentyshe men. Note that the erle of Huntingdon went down to take the duke of Suffolk.

The duke of Norfolk was levtenant of the army, and with him the erle of Ormonde, master Gernyngham captayn of the garde, with a great nombre of the garde with him, and a great number of other soldyars. Apon the [. . .] they were sett in array towardes Rochester bridge, which was kept by

Wyat's company, and furnyshed with iii or four doble-cannons. One Tutton [. . .] FeWilliams and Bret, was captaynes of the said company . . .

. . . and even as the company was sett in a redynes, and marched forwarde toward the bridge, the said Bret, beinge captaine of the vC Londoners, of which the more parte were in the forwarde, turned himself aboute, and drawinge out his sworde, said, by reaporte, thes or moche like wordes: "Masters, we goe about to fight agaynst our natyve countreymen of Ingland and our friendes in a quarrell unrightfull and partely wicked, for they, consydering the great and manyfold myseries which are like to fall apon us if we shalbe under the rule of the proude Spanyardes or strangers, are here assemblyed to make resystance of the cominge in of him or his favourers; and for that they knowe right well, that yf we should be under their subjection they wolde, as slaves and villaynes, spoyle us of our goodes and landes, ravyshe our wyfes before our faces, and deflowre our daughters in our presence, have nowe, for the avoydinge of so great mysschefes and inconveynences likely to light not only apon theymselves but on every of us and the hole realme, have taken apon theym now, in tyme before his comyng, this their enterprise, agaynst which I thinck no Inglysshe hart ought to say, moche lesse by fyghting to withstande theym. Wherfore I and theis (meanyng by such as were in that rank with him,) will spende our bloode in the quarrell of this wourthy captain, maister Wyat, and other gentyllmen here assemblyd." Which wordes once pronounced, eche man turned their ordenance against their fellowe. The Londoners thereupon cryed, A Wyat! A Wyat! of which sudden noyse the duke, the erle of Ormonde, and captayne of the garde, being abashed, fledd forthwith. Immedyately came in maister Wyat and his company on horseback, rushing in emongst theym, saying, aswell to the garde, Londoners, as to all the rest, "So many as will come and tarry with us shalbe welcome; and so many as will depart, good leave have they." And so all the Londoners, part of the garde, and more than iii partes of the retynue, went into the campe of the Kentyshmen, where they styl remayne. At this discomfyture the duke lost viii peces of brasse, with all other munytyon and ordenance, and himselfe, with the erle of Ormonde and Gernyngham and other fledd to London. Ye shoulde have sene some of the garde com home, ther cotes tourned, all ruyned, without arowes or stringe in their bowe, or sworde, in very strange wyse; which dyscomfiture, lyke as yt was hart-sore and very dyspleasing to the quene and counsayll, even so yt was almost no lesse joyous to the Londoners, and the most part of all others.'

II

Extract from John Procter's *The Historie of Wiats Rebellion* (1554), ed. and repr. A.F. Pollard in *Tudor Tracts* (London, 1903), pp. 239–40.

'But her Highness doubting that London, being her Chamber and a city holden of dear price in her princely heart, might by WYAT and such ruffens as were with him, be in danger of spoil, to the utter ruin of the same: her Highness therfore, as a most tender and loving Governess, went the same day [31 January] in her royal person to the Guild Hall to foresee those perils.

Where, among other matter proceeding from her incomparable wisdom her grace declared how she had sent that day two of her Privy Council to the traitor WYAT: desirous rather to quiet tumult by mercy rather than by the justice of the sword to vanquish: whose most godly heart fraight[ed] with all mercy and clemency, abhorred from all effusion of blood.

Her Highness also there shewed the insolent and proud answer returned from WYAT: whereat the faithful citizens were much offended; and in plain terms defied him as a most rank traitor, with all his conjurates.

And touching the Marriage, her Highness affirmed that nothing was done herein by herself alone, but with the consent and advisement of the whole Council, upon deliberate consultation, that this conjunction and Second Marriage should greatly advance this realm (whereunto she was first married) to much honour, quiet and gain.

"For", quod her Grace, "I am already married to this Common Weal and the faithful members of the same; the spousal ring whereof I have on my finger: which never hitherto was, nor hereafter shall be, left off. Protesting unto you nothing to more acceptable to my heart, nor more answerable to my will, then your advancement in wealth and welfare, with the furtherance of GOD's glory." And to declare her tender and princely heart towards them, she promised constantly not to depart from them, although by her Council she had been much moved to the contrary: but she would remain near and prest to adventure the spense [shedding] of her royal blood in defence of them.

Such matter passed from her besides as did so wonderfully enamour the hearts of the hearers as it was world to hear with what shouts they exalted the honour and magnanimity of Queen MARY.

This done her Grace returned towards Whitehall, and passing through the streets, being full of people pressing to behold her Grace wherein they had singular delight and pleasure, one amongst all, most impudent of all others, stepped forward saying, "Your Grace may do well to make your Foreward in battle of your Bishops and Priests: for they be trusty, and will not deceive you!"

For which words he was commanded to Newgate: who deserved to be hanged at the next bough, for example to all others, . . .'

III

A further extract from Nichols, *Chronicle of Queen Jane* (1850).

'Here was no small a-dowe in London, and likewise the Tower made great preparation of defence. By x of the clocke, or somewhat more, the erle of Penbroke had set his troopp of horsemen on the hill in the higheway above the new brige over against saynct James; his footemen was sett in ii battailles somewhat lower and nerer Charing crosse. At the lane turning downe by the brike wall from Islington-warde he had sett also certayn other horsemen and he had planted his ordenance apon the hill side. In the meane season Wyat and his company planted his ordenance apon the hill beyonde sainct James, almost over agaynst the park corner; and himself, after a fewe words spoken to his soldears, came downe the olde lane on foote, hard by the courte gate at saincte James's, with iiii or v anncyentes; his men marching in goode array. Cutbert Vaughn, and about ii anncyentes, turned downe towards Westminster. The erle of Pembroke's horsemen haveryd all this while without moving, untyll all was passed by, saving the tayle, upon which they dyd sett and cut of. The other marched forwarde, and never stayed or retourned to the ayde of thier tayle. The greate ordenaunce shott of fresly on bothe sydes. Wyat's ordenance overshott the troope of horsemen. The quenes ordenance one pece struck iii of Wyat's companye in a ranck, apon ther hedes, and, sleying them, strake through the wall into the parke. More harme was not done by the great shott of neither partie. The quenes hole batayle of footemen standing stille, Wyat passed along by the wall towardes Charing crosse, wher the saide horsemen that wer ther sett upon parte of them, but were soone forced backe.

At Charinge crosse ther stood the lorde chamberlayne [Sir John Gage], with the garde and a nomber of other, almost a thousande persons, the whiche, upon Wyat's coming, shott at his company, and at last fledd to the court gates, which certayn pursued, and forced them with shott to shyt the court gates against them. In this repulse the said lord chamberlayn and others were so amased that men cryed Treason! treason! in the court, and had thought that the erle of Penbroke, who was assayling the tayle of his enemyes, had gon to Wyat, taking his part agaynst the quene. There should ye have seene runninge and cryenge of ladyes and gentyll women, shyting of dores, and such a scryking and noyse as yt was wonderfull to here.

The said Wyat, with his men, marched still forwarde, all along to Temple barre, also thoroghe Fleete street, along tyll he cam to Ludgate, his men going not in eny goode order or array. It is saide that in Fleet street certayn of the lorde treasueres band, to the nomber of CCC men, mett theym, and so going on the one syde passyd by theym coming on the other syde without eny whit staying to theym. Also this is more strandge: the said Wyat and his company passyd along by a greate company of harnessyd men, which stoode on bothe sydes without eny withstandinge them, and as he marched forwarde through Fleet street, moste with their swords drawne, some cryed "Queene Mary hath graunted our request, and hath geven us pardon." Others said, "The quene hathe pardoned us." Thus Wyat cam even to Ludgate, and knockyd calling to come in, saying, there was Wyat, whome the quene had graunted their requestes; but the lorde William Howard standing at the gate saide, "Avaunt, traytor, thou shalt not come in here." And then Wyat awill stayed, and, as some say, rested him apon a seate [at] the Bellsavage gate; at last, seing he coulde not come, and belike being deceaved of the ayde which he hoped for out of the cetye, retourned backe agayne in arraye towards Charing cross, and was never stopped tyll he cam to Temple barre, wher certayn horsemen which cam from the felde met them in the face. . . .'

Wyatt's rebellion is the most fully described sequence of events in the whole reign, and these extracts cover only a small proportion of the action. The rebellion in Kent was intended to be part of a multiple armed protest against the queen's marriage plans, which should have seen similar demonstrations in Leicestershire, Devon and the Welsh borders. The conspirators were forced to act prematurely, and only Wyatt succeeded in raising a power. The Tower chronicler reflects accurately the confusion and near panic which accompanied the first reports of the rising, reports which falsely placed both Lord Cobham and Sir Thomas Cheney among the rebels. The desertion of the Londoners at Rochester marked a major escalation of the danger, and the chronicler broadly hints at the large measure of support which the rebels enjoyed in the capital. Wyatt entered Southwark on 3 February, but found the bridge held against him. Three days later he crossed the Thames at Kingston, and approached the city along the north bank. The final confrontation took place on the 7th. This chronicler appears to have been an eyewitness of the confusion within the court during the last engagements, but not of the events in Fleet Street and Ludgate, which he reports as though observed by someone else. The circumstances of Wyatt's final frustration (he surrendered almost immediately after the end of the recorded events) remain almost as mysterious today as they were to the chronicler, whose sympathies seem to have been as ambivalent as his story.

By contrast, the other extract is from a piece of official propaganda, written by the schoolmaster of Tonbridge, who was close to events in Kent, but not in London. His account is notable for its fulsome praise of the queen, and also for its emphasis upon the religious motivation of the rebels. This was the government explanation for the rebellion, as there was an understandable reluctance to admit that the queen's choice of a husband was so unpopular. Significantly the Tower chronicler does not mention religion.

NINE

Elizabeth Imprisoned

Extracts from 'The myraculous preservation of Lady Elizabeth, nowe Queene', in Foxe, *Actes and Monuments* (London, 1583), pp. 2091–7.

'In conclusion, they willed her to prepare agaynst the morning at nine of the clocke to goe with them, declaring that they had brought with them the Queenes Lytter for her. After much talk, the messengers declaring how there was no prolonging of times & daies, so departed to theyr chamber, being entertained and cheared as appertained to their worships.

On the next morow at the time prescribed, they hadde her forth as shee was, very faynt and feeble, and in suche case, that she was ready to swound three or foure tymes betweene them, what shoulde I speake here that cannot well bee expressed, what an heavy house there was to behold the unreverend and doulefull dealyng of these men, but especially the carefull feare and captivitie of their innocent Lady and Mistresse.

Nowe to proceed in her iourney from Ashrydge, al sick in the Litter, she came to Redbourne, where she was garded all night: from thence to S. Albones, to Syr Rafe Rowlets house, where she taryed that night, both feble in body, and comfortles in minde. From that place they passed to Maister Doddes house at Mymmes, where also they remayned that night: and so from thence she came to Highgate: where she being very sicke, taryed that night and the next day. During which the time of her abode there, came many Purseuvantes and messengers from the court: but for what purpose I cannot tell.

From yt place she was conveied to the Court: where by the way came to meete her many Gentlemen, to acco[m]pany her highnesse, which were very sory to see her in that case. But especially a great multitude of people ther were standing by the way, who then flocking about her Litter, lame[n]ted and bewailed greatly her estate. Now when she came to the Court, her grace was there staight waies shut up, and kept as close prisonner a fortnight, which was till Palme sonday, seeing neither King nor Queene, [Philip did not arrive until July] nor lord, nor frend, all that time, but only then the Lord Chamberlaine, Syr John Gage, and the Vicechamberlain, which were attendant unto the dores. . . .

In conclusion, after long debating of matters, they [the Council] declared unto her that it was the Queenes will & pleasure that she should go unto the tower, while the matter were further tried and examined.

Whereat she beyng agaste, said that shee trusted the Queenes Maiestie would be more gracious Lady unto her, and that her highnesse would not otherwise conceyve of her, but that she was a true woman: and declaring furthermore to the Lordes that she was innocent in all those matters wherein they had burdened her, & desired them therefore to be a further meane to the Queen her sister, that she beyng a true woman in thought, word and deed towardes her Maiesty, might not be committed to so notorious and dolefull a place. . . .

After this, she tooke her Barge with the two foresayd Lordes, three of the Queenes Gentlewomen, and three of her owne, her gentleman Usher, and two of her Groomes, lying and hoveryng upon the water a certaine space, for that they could not shoote the bridge, the Barge men beyng very unwilling to shoote the same so soone as they did, because of the danger thereof: for the sterne of the boate, stroke upon the grounde, the fall was so big and the water was so shallowe, that the boate beyng under the bridge, there stayed agayne a while. At landing, she first stayed, and denied to land at those staires where all traitors and offenders customably used to land, neyther well could she, unlesse she should go over her shoe. The Lords were gone out of the boat before, and asked why she came not. One of the Lordes went backe againe to her, & broght word she would not come.

Then sayd one of the Lordes which shall be nameles, that she should not chuse: and because it did then raine, he offered to her his cloke, which she (puttyng it backe wyth her hand with a good dash) refused. So she comming out, having one foote uppon the staire, saide: Here landeth as true a subiect beyng prisoner, as ever la[n]ded at these stairs: And before thee O God I speake it, havyng none other friends but thee alone. . . .

. . . In conclusion, on Trinitie Sonday being the 19. day of Maye, she was remooved from the Tower, the Lorde Treasurer being then there for the lading of her Cartes and discharging the place of the same. Where Syr Henry Benifielde (being appoynted her Gailer) did receive her wyth a companie of rakehelles to Garde her, besides the Lorde of Darbies bande, wayting in the Countrey about for the mooneshine on the water. Unto whome at length came my Lorde of Tame, ioyned in Commission with the sayd Syr Henry, for the guiding of her to prisone: and they together conveied her grace to Woodstock, as hereafter followeth. . . .

The next day her grace took her iourney from thence to Woodstocke, where she was inclosed, as before in the Tower of London, the souldiers garding and wardyng both within and without the walles, every day to ye

number of threescore, and in the night without the wals xl during the tyme
of her imprisonment there.

At length shee had gardens appointed for her walke, which was very
comfortable to her grace. But alwayes when she did recreate herselfe
therein, the dores were fact locked up, in as straite maner as they were in
the Tower. . . .'

Elizabeth was a constant problem to Mary, both because she was the heir,
and because the queen did not trust her religious conformity. For similar
reasons, her name was on the tongue of every malcontent. Although the
government professed to believe that Wyatt's rebellion was really aimed
at restoring Jane Grey and the Edwardian Church, some at least were
convinced that Elizabeth and the Earl of Devon were also involved. The
imperial ambassador, Simon Renard, was particularly insistent that the
conspiracy should be used as an excuse to get rid of Mary's troublesome
sister. He prevailed so far as to obtain her arrest and bringing to court
soon after the rising.

In spite of Foxe's dramatic presentation, it is not certain that
Elizabeth's illness was genuine. Gardiner obtained her transfer to the
Tower by challenging his fellow councillors to accept responsibility for
her safeguard, and strenuous efforts were then made to obtain evidence
against her. Partly because of her own discretion, and partly because she
had powerful friends, none was forthcoming and Renard's quest for her
head was frustrated. Having decided not to put her on trial, the council
then removed her to Woodstock, where she remained under secure guard
for almost a year. Foxe's narrative contains many circumstantial
anecdotes of her imprisonment, intended to emphasise her constant
danger, and the boorish behaviour of Sir Henry Bedingfield. In fact he
seems to have been no more than conscientious, and Elizabeth herself
understood that.

After Philip's safe arrival, the princess petitioned for her release, but it
was not granted, the queen's suspicions not being allayed. In April 1555
she was brought back to court in anticipation of Mary's confinement,
and continued under restraint until all expectation of an heir had been
abandoned. She was then released, but kept under surveillance by having
royal servants assigned to her household. Foxe believed that Gardiner
organised two attempts on Elizabeth's life during her detention, but there
is no conclusive proof of that, and it is intrinsically improbable. This
account was, of course, published during Elizabeth's reign, but in spite of
its generally laudatory tone, it is not without implied criticism of her
Nicodemism, so it is unlikely that she saw it in advance of publication.

TEN

The Marriage of Philip and Mary

I

Extracts from *The copie of a letter sente into Scotlande, of the arrivall and landynge, and most noble marryage of the moste illustre prynce Philippe, prynce of Spaine . . .*, by John Elder (1554). This is taken from the copy printed by John Gough Nichols as app. X to the *Chronicle of Queen Jane* (1850), pp. 139–43, 145–9.

'Than the next munday, which was the xxiv of Juli, his highnes came to the citie of Winchester at vi of the clocke at nighte, the noble men of Englande and his nobles riding, one with another, before him, in good order, through the citie, every one placed according to his vocacion and office, he riding on a faire white horse, in a riche coate embroidered with gold, his doublet, hosen and hat suite-like, with a white fether in his hat very faire. And after he lighted he came the hie waye towardes the weast dore of the cathedrall churche, where he was most reverently received wyth procession by my lorde the bishop of Winchester, now lord chauncellor of England, and v other bishops, mitred, coped and staved. . . .

So the nexte tuesdaye, at three of the clocke, he went to the quene from the deanes house afote, where everybody might see him; the lorde stewarde [The Earl of Arundel] the erle of Derbey, the erle of Pembroke, with divers other lordes and noblemenne, as well Englishe as others, went before him, he going alone in a cloke of blacke cloth embrodered with silver, with a paire of white hose. And after that he had entered the courte, where all kinde of instrumentes played very melodiously, and came within the hal, where the quenes majesty was standing on a skafhold, hir highnes descended, and amiably receaving him, did kisse him in the presence of all the people. And then taking him by the right hande, they went together in the chaumber of presence, where after they had, in sighte of all the lordes and ladies, a quarter of an houres pleasantly talked and communed together, under the cloth of estate, and each of them merily smylyng on other, to the greate comforte and rejoising of the beholders, he toke his leave of her grace. . . .

Then wednisdaye, being Sanct James daie, the xxv of July, his highnes (at x of the clocke) and his nobles before him, went to the cathedral churche, and remayned there (the dores beyng very straightlie kepte) until the quenes highnes came: whose magestie, with al her counsel and nobilitie before her, came thyther at halfe houre to aleven. And entring at the west dore of the said cathedrall churche (where her grace was receaved the saterday before, in like manner as his highnes was the munday following), her majestie ascended the foresaid, and came towardes the quere dore; where a little without the same dore was made a round mount of bordes, ascendyng also five steps above the skafholde. On which mount, immediately after her magestie and the king were shreven, they were maried by my lord the bishop of Winchester lord chancellor of Inglande, her magestye standing on the right side of the said mount, and the king on the left side. And this the mariage being ended and solemnised, which with the biddinges and the banes ther of was declared and done by the said lord chauncelor both in Latin and English, his lordship declared also there: How that the emperours magestie resigned, under his emperial seale, the kingdomes of Naples and Hierusalem to his sonne Philip prince of Spain, wherby it might well appeare to all men that the quenes highnes was then maried, not only to a prince, but also unto a king. The quenes mariage ring was a plain hoope of gold without any stone in it: for that was as it is said her pleasure, because maydens were so maried in olde tymes. . . .

And to make an ende here of their progres, your lordship shall understande, that after they had remayned at Windsor certaine daies after the kinges installation [to the Order of the Garter], they came to Richemont. When being advertysed that all suche triumphes and pageantes as wer devised in London agaynst their cumming thyther, were finished and ended, they came from thens by water, on friday the xvii of August, and landed at S. Marie Overes staires on Sothwarke side; where every corner being so straight kept as no man could passe, come or go, but those which were appointed to attende their landing. . . .

Now to begyn and declare their cumming to London, and to make an ende. Your revered lordship shall understande that both their moste excellent majesties made thier most noble and triumphing entries into the noble citie of London furth of Southwarke place, the next satterdaye, which was the xviii of August, at ii of the clocke at after none. Where after all the lordes of their moste honorable privie counsel, and the ambassadours of all nacyons, with the nobilitie of Englande and Spayne, and divers other noble and jentle men as wel English as straunge, wer al on horsebacke, two and two, in a ranke, the lord maior of London, as the two princes came out at the gate, kneled and delivered a mace, whiche signified his power and authoritie within the citie of London, to the quenes grace. Whose magestie delivering the said mace to the lord maior again, the kinges highnes and she ascended their horses, and so marchyng towardes London bridge, the quene of the righte hande, and the king of the left, with two swerdes of honour before theym, and before the swerdes the lord maior of London bearing the mace, the Toure of London begynneth to shoote.

. . . Which being done, they proceded forwarde until they came to Gracious [Grace Church] strete, where in their waye the conduit therof was finely trimmed, whereon was painted verye ingeniouslye the nine Worthies, with many notable proverbes and adages written with fayre Roman letters on every side thereof.

And at the signe of the Splaied Eagle they made a seconde staie, where the first pagent was devysed and made by the marchaunt straungers of the Stilliarde. Where emongsth divers notable stories, there was in the top therof a picture of the king sitting on horssbacke, all armed very gorgeously, and richly set out to the quicke. Under which picture were written in field silver with fayre Romaine letters of sable, these wordes followinge after this maner:

> Divo Phi. Aug. Max.
> Hispaniarum principi exopatissimo

That is to say,

> In honour of worthy Philip the fortunate and most mighty
> Prince of Spaine, most earnestly wyshed for. . . .

Which picture, and al other notable stories and wrytinges in the said pagent, pleasing their magesties very wel, they marched forward. . . .'

II

Extract from Richard Grafton, *A Chronicle at Large* (1569, 1809 edn), p. 548.

'The xix day of Iuly next followyng, Phillipe Prince of Spaine, sonne and heire unto Charles the fift of that name Emperour of Rome, pasing out of Spayne arrived at Southhampton. And the fourth daye after he tooke his iourney to Winchester, and came thether in the evening, where goyng to the church he was honorablye receaved of the Bishoppe and a great number of the Nobles of the Realme. The next day he came to the sight of Queene Mary, with whome he had long and familiar talke, and the xxv of the sayde Moneth being the day of Saint Iames (whome the Spaniards call their patrone) the mariage betwene them was in the sayd Citie of Winchester in most honorable maner solempnised. At which time the Emperors Ambassadour beyng present, openly pronounced that in consideration of that mariage the Emperour had graunted and geven to the sayd Prince his sonne the kingdome of Naples &c. Hierusalem with divers other states and seigniories. The solempnitie of that mariage ended, the king of Heraults called Garter openly in the Church in the presence of the king, the Queene, the Lordes as well of Englande as Spaine, and all the people being present, solempnly proclaimed the tytle and style of these two princes as foloweth.

Philyp and Mary by the grace of God king and Queene of England Fraunce Naples Ierusalem and Ireland, defendours of the fayth, Princes of Spaine and Sicile, Archedukes of Austriche, Dukes of Milleyn, Burgundy and Brabant, Counties of Hapsburge, Flaudyrs and Tiroll.

The proclamation beyng ended, the Trumpets blew and the king and the Queene came foorth of the Church hand in hande, and two swordes borne before them, and so returned to their Palace. And assoone as the featyng and solempnitie of the said mariage was ended, the king and Queene departed from Winchester, and taking Hampton Court in their waye, came from thence by water into Southwarke, and so over Lo[n]don bridge through the Citie of London unto Westminster. At which time the Citie was bewtified with sumpteous pagiaunts and hanged with riche and coastly Silkes and cloth of gold and silver.'

There are many descriptions of the marriage of Philip and Mary, several written in Spanish and Italian for the benefit of other Habsburg subjects. John Elder's 'Letter', written ostensibly to Robert Stuart, Bishop of Caithness, was a semi-official publication, as may be suspected from the fulsomeness of its narrative. Grafton's much briefer account was not published until long after Mary was dead and Philip had returned to Spain. Elder translated a number of laudatory banners and mottos which were displayed at the entry to London, for the benefit of his readership, but at the time they appear to have been presented in Latin only. Philip, of course, could not read English, but then most Londoners could not read Latin. The mood in the capital was not as joyous as Elder suggests, and there had been some doubt as to whether an entry was appropriate at all. The scaffolds bearing the bodies of those executed after the Wyatt rebellion had been removed only a week or two earlier, and Henry Machyn, usually garrulous about ceremonies, does not mention the pageants at all.

ELEVEN

Anglo-Spanish Entanglements

I

Extracts from *Tres Cartas de lo sucedido in el viaje de Su Alteza a Inglaterra* (La Sociedad de Bibliophilos Espanoles, Madrid, 1877), trs. by the editor.

'. . . Dona Maria de Mendoza was right in saying that we were never going to be in attendance again, for we are all hanging about with nothing to do and might as well go and serve his Majesty in this war . . .

. . . we are all desiring to be off, with such longing that we think of Flanders as a paradise . . .

. . . they say publicly that England is realm enough for one king, and if he is not satisfied, he can go away . . .

. . . I really believe that if it were not for the continual prayers and processions being offered in Spain on our behalf, that we should all have been dead by now, for these English are a barbarous and heretical race, with no fear of God or his saints. . . .'

II

Extracts from Nichols, *Chronicle of Queen Jane* (1850), pp. 31–2.

'The quene removed the [. . .] day of August to Hampton Court.

At this tyme the French king retyred.

At this tyme ther was so many Spanyardes in London that a man should have mett in the stretes for one Inglisheman above iiii Spanyerdes, to the great discomfort of the Inglishe nation. The halles taken up for the Spanyerdes.

About this tyme ther was half a rysing at Ypswych in Suffolk.

In September the noblemen dyd axe licence to repayre every man into his contry, whether for avoiding their expenses or any other cause ys as yit unknown.

The king's wordes for the ryding of the garde at his coming aland.

His words towching the nobillyty.

The [. . .] of September Syr Anthony Brown dyscharged of the mastership of the horse for the king, and so made a lorde by the name of the lorde Mountacute.

Browghte into the Tower iiii out of Suffolk for an insurrecion ther, and certayn executed.

The vth of September a talk of xii thousand Spanyardes coming more into the realme, they said to fethe the crowne. . . .'

III

Extracts from *The Diary of Henry Machyn*, pp. 71–2.

'The xi day of October was the obsequy of a Spaneard at Westmynster; ther wase a praty herse after the fassyon of Spayn, with blake, and a goodly mass of requiem; and the chapell that he was bered in was hong with blake; and ys harmes [alms] mony with a baner of armes and cote of armes, alle in gold, and a target and elmett and mony skochyon, and a fere hers-clothe of blake ans a crosse of cremesum velvet, done to the ground – the ii yer of quen Mare.

The xv day of October was kylled with-owt Tempall bare almost at stren [the Strand] a servand of ser Gorge Gyfford, shamfully slayne by a Spaneard, a-bowt iiii of the [clock] at after-non. . . .

. . . The xxvi day of October was hanged at Charynge-crosse a Spaneard that kyld a servant of ser Gorge Gefford, the wyche was slayne with-owt Tempull bare.'

For some unknown reason, Philip brought with him, in addition to the noblemen and grandees who were to grace his wedding, a full Spanish household. When he arrived, he found a full English household awaiting him. The result was tension, conflict and recrimination, which exacerbated relations, which were always going to be difficult anyway. The king's solution was to assign public duties to his English servants, and private ones to his Spanish servants. Inevitably, neither was satisfied, and both were semi-unemployed. There was frequent violence, even within the court. The problem was eased when Philip gave most of his courtiers leave to join his father's army in the Low Countries, but it was never solved as long as he was in England. A joint judicial commission was established to adjudicate disputes between the nations, and it worked up to a point; but murders, unless committed within the court, were handled by the normal common law – quite expeditiously if Machyn's observation is anything to go by. The king's secretary, Ruy Gomez da Silva, observed with fine impartiality that there were many thieves in England, but the natives had the advantage because they stole by force, while the Spaniards used fraud.

TWELVE

Reconciliation with Rome

I

Extract from a report sent to Ferdinand, King of the Romans, 10 December 1554, from the *Calendar of State Papers, Spanish*, XIII, pp. 120–1. The original, in Spanish, is in the State Archive at Vienna.

'On Thursday, 29th November, Parliament met in the accustomed place, and lords, prelates, representatives of the towns and gentlemen all agreed to repeal the laws and statutes passed under King Henry and his son, Edward, against obedience to the Pope and imposing the accursed and destable heresy of Luther, the destruction of images and the suppression of the mass; though the queen had already put a stop to Lutheranism and returned to the usages of the true and ancient religion. It was agreed to send a deputation of 24 men to beg the King and Queen, on behalf of parliament, to grant their approval and request the Legate to absolve them, for they, in the kingdom's name, spontaneously confessed the error in which they had lived, and submitted themselves to the Pope's will, whom they held to be Head of the Church and true and universal Vicar of Christ. The King and Queen most willingly heard and admitted their petition, promising to do precisely as they had been requested, speak with the Cardinal next day, and strive to get him to absolve them. Joy was so great, tears of gladness were shed from so many old eyes that had been looking forward to this day, that this sudden change would have appeared incredible to any but those who saw it happen, as we did. The fact is that existing laws were so rigorous, providing that a man should lose life and property for so much as speaking of the Pope, and so forth and so on, that now the same are repealed and the example set by this most catholic royal couple has had its effect, there turn out to be far more Christians than had ever been supposed, and their numbers will daily increase. . . .'

II

Extract from Grafton, *A Chronicle at Large* (1569, 1809 edn), pp. 550–1.

'This supplication being first openly read, the same was by the Chauncelour delyvered to the king and Queene with peticion to them to exhibite the same to the Lorde Cardinall. And the king and Queene rysing out of their seates and doyng reverence to the Cardinall did delyver the same unto him. The Cardinall perceyving the effect thereof to aunswere to his expectation, did receive it most gladly at their maiesties handes. And then after that he had in a fewe wordes geven thankes unto God, & declared what great cause he had to reioyce above all others, that his comming from Rome into Englande had taken suche most happie successe, then he caused his commission to be read (whereby it might appere that he had aucthoritie of the Pope to absolve them) which commission was verie long and large. And that beyng done and all the parliament on their knees, this Cardinall by the Popes authoritie gave them absolution in manner following.

Our Lord Iesus Christ which with his most precious bloud hath redeemed and washed us from all our sinnes & iniquities that he might purchase unto himselfe a glorious spouse without spot or wrinkle, and whome the Father hath appointed head over all his Church. He by his mercy absolve you; And we by the Apostolique aucthoritie geven unto us by the most holy Lord Pope Julius the thirde (his Vicegerent in earth) doe absolve and delyver you and every of you with the whole realme and the dominions therof, from all heresie and Schisme, and from all and every iudgements, censures and paynes for that cause incurred. And also we doe restore you agayne to the unitie of our mother the holy Church, as in our letters of commission more plainely shall appere. In the name of the father, the sonne and holye ghost. Amen.

After this generall absolution receayvd, the king and the Queene and all the Lordes with the rest went into the kings Chapell, and there sang *Te Deum* with great ioy and gladnesse for this newe reconciliation.

The report of this with great speede flewe to Rome, as well by the French kinges letters, as also by the Cardinalles, whereupon the Pope caused solempne Processions to be made in Rome, namely one, wherein he himselfe with all his Cardinalles were present, passyng with as great solempnitie & pompe as might be, geving thankes to God with great ioy for the co[n]version of England to his Church. At what time also he not a little co[m]mended the diligence of Cardinall Poole, and the devocion of the King and Queene.'

III

Extracts from John Elder's Letter, printed as app. X to Nichols, *Chronicle of Queen Jane* (1850), pp. 152–9.

'Further, youre lordeshippe shall understande that the xviii daye of the sayed moneth [November 1554], the righte reverendee father in God, lorde cardinall Poole, accompanyed with my lorde Paget, my lord Clynton, and sir Anthony Browne knight, late created lorde Montague, and dyvers other noble menne, came from Gravesende to the White hall in one of the kynges barges. Where the kinges majestie, beinge advertysed that he hadde shot London brydge, his highnes, with the swerde of honoure borne before hym, came down and receaved him very amiably, as he landed at the common landynge brydge of the courte. And from thence they bothe passed up to the chambre of presence, where the quenes majestie was sittinge under the clothe of estate, whose highnes also receaved him very joyfully. . . .

. . . Within fewe daies after hys cumminge to Lambeth, a daye was prefixed by appoyntment of the king and quenes majesties, that the three estates of England being called unto the parliament shoulde be brought unto the presence of the cardinal for the better understandinge of his legation. This assemble was appointed in the greate chambre of the courte at Westminster, where as the king and quenes majesties sitting under the cloth of estate, and al the three estates placed in theyr degrees, the cardinall sytting in a chaire on the right hand, out of the cloth of estate, my lord chaunceller of England began in this maner. . . .

. . . When his lordship had thus made an ende, my lord cardinall taking the occasion offred, without any studye, as it semed, spake in effect as followeth: "My lordes all, and you that are the commons of this present parliament assembled, which in effecte is nothing els but the state and body of the whole realme, As the cause of my repaire hither hath been both wisely and gravely declared by my lord chauncellor, so before that I entre to the particularities of my commission, I have somewhat to say touching myselfe, and to geve most humble and harti thankes to the king and quenes magesties. . . . I signifie unto you all that my principall travayl is, for the restitucion of this noble realme to the auncient nobilitie, and to declare unto you, that the Sea Apostolike, from whens I come, hath a special respect to this realme above al other; and not without cause seing that God himselfe, as it were by providence, hath geven this realme prerogative of nobilitie above other, which to make more playne unto you, it is to be considered that this iland first of all ilandes received the light of Christes religion. For, as stories testifie, it was *prima provinciarum quae amplexa est fidem Christi*. . . .

. . . I wil not reherse the manifold benefites that this realme hath receaved from the Apostolike Sea, nor how ready the same hath been to relive us in all our necessities. Nor I wil not rehearse the manifolde miseries and calamities that this realme hath suffred by swarving from that unitie. And even as in thys realme, so in all other countries which, refusing the unitie of the catholike fayth, have followed fantastical doctryne, the like plages have happened. Let Asia, and the empire of Grece, be a spectacle unto the world, who by swarving from the unitie of the churche of Rome, are brought into captivitie and subjeccion of the Turks. All storyes be full of like examples.

And to cum unto latter latter tyme, loke upon our nie neighbours of Germany, who by swarving from this unitie, are miserablye afflicted with diversitie of sectes, and devided in factions. . . .

. . . And when all lyghte of true religion seamed utterly extincte, as the churches defaced and aulters overthrowen, the ministers corrupted; even lyke as in a lampe the lyght being covered, yet it is not quenched, even so in a few remained the confession of Christes fayth; namely in the brest of the quenes excellency, of whom to speake wythout adulacyon, the saing of the prophet may be verified. *Ecce quasi derelicta.* . . . And yet for all these practises and devises of ill men, here you see hir grace established in hir estate, being your lawful quene and governes, borne amonge you, whome God hathe appointed to reigne over you, for the restitucion of true religion, and exterpacion of all erroures and sectes. . . ." '

The emotion and triumphalism of these accounts conceal a hard and prolonged process of bargaining, which is not reflected in any chronicle. Parliament had on two previous occasions refused to petition for absolution, on the grounds that a restoration of papal authority would mean the loss of title to all former ecclesiastical lands, purchased since 1536. Pole's mission was accepted only after Philip had persuaded the pope to relinquish all claim to such land, which he had been most reluctant to do. Parliament's petition, and Pole's absolution, were based on the assumption that the land issue had been addressed. However, between these highly charged exchanges and the actual Statute of Repeal, there remained another round of bargaining, because Pole's absolution was based only on a papal dispensation, waiving all legal penalties. As no pope could bind his successors, this concession did not confer the legal title which was sought. This problem was eventually solved by including the text of the dispensation in the statute itself, thus giving it the force of law irrespective of future papal decisions. Both Pole and Mary opposed this additional concession, but Philip insisted, and parliament accepted the compromise. Pole continued to urge that the absolution covered only canonical penalties, and not the sins themselves, but his attempts to pressure the aristocracy into restoring the lands were unsuccessful.

THIRTEEN

The City of London

I

> Extracts from the first charter of privileges granted by the Emperor of Russia to the English merchants, 1555; taken from Richard Hakluyt, *The Principall Navigations, Voiages and Discoveries of the English Nation* (1589), II, pp. 297–303.

'John Vasilivitch, by the grace of God Emperor of Russia, great duke of Novgorode, Moscovia etc. To all people that shal see, reade heare or understande these presents, greeting. . . .

Upon these respects and other weighty and good considerations, us hereunto moving, and chiefly upon the contemplation of the gratious letters directed from the right high, right excellent and right mighty Queene Mary, by the grace of God Queene of England, France etc., in the favour of her subjectes, merchants, adventurers for the discovery of lands etc.

Know ye therefore that we of our grace speciall, meere motion and certaine knowledge, have given and graunted, and by these presents for us, our heires and successors, do give and grant as much as in us is and lieth, unto Sebastian Cabota Governour, Sir George Barnes knight etc. Consuls; Sir John Gresham etc. Assistants, and to the communalitie of the aforenamed fellowship, and to their successours for ever, and to the successours of everie of them, these articles, graunts, immunities, franchises, liberties and privileges, and every of them hereafter following, expressed and declared. . . .'

II

> Extract from a set of articles presented to the English council by Charles Quarrentyne, 'councellor of the Council of Brabant', 'by commandment of the kinges Maiestie', 17 October 1556; taken from BL Lansdowne MS 170, f. 129.

'His Majesty findeth this to be the trewe way wholy to deverte the said traphique from his said lowe countries and to transport it into some other place and to separate the subjects of both partes from all mutual traphique, communication and affection. A thing contrived by certyn privat persons of the said nacion [England] for their singular proffyt and convenyneince. And may be by some evel disposed persons myndyng some other evel purpose, chiefly by those that be fledd into the said Hambourg, Empden and other places, the which go about for to bring the said realme of England into disorder to marre and destroy it. . . .'

III

Extract from *The Diary of Henry Machyn*, pp. 72–3.

'The xxix day of October [1554] the nuw lord mayre of London, master Lyons groser, toke ys hoathe at Westmynster; and alle the craftes of London in ther barges, and with stremars; and ther was a grett penoys decked with ii topes and stremars and . . . gones and drumes and trumpetes, rohyng to Westmynster up and don; and when they cam hom they landyd at Powlles warff, and ther mett the mayr lx in rosett gownes and with targetts and gyffelyns [javelins] and blue hattes; and then a goodly pagant, a gryffen with a chyld lyung in harnes, and sant John Baptyst with a lyon, and ii vodys [wild men] and a dulle [devil] with squybes bornyng and trumpets blohyng, and drums[s] and flute[s], and then the bachelers with cremesum damaske hedes [hoods], and then trumpeters and the wettes [waits] of the cete; and so to yeld-hall to denar, for ther dynyd my lord chanseler and all the nobuls, and the Spaneardes, and the juges and lernyd men. . . .'

London was by far the greatest and wealthiest city in England, with a population in excess of 150,000 at this point. It controlled about 70 per cent of England's foreign trade, and its aldermen were as wealthy as most nobles (and more numerous). It was also a strong centre of Protestantism, although most of this retreated into Nicodemism during Mary's reign. Relations between the city and the government were correct, but never amicable. The Merchant Adventurers had spent decades trying to dislodge the Hanseatic League from its privileged position, and had succeeded in 1552. Mary immediately restored the Hanse privileges in the autumn of 1553, and the Adventurers never forgave her. There were conscientious displays of amity on ceremonial occasions, as Machyn witnesses (even including 'the Spaneardes'), but no love was lost. The establishment of the Muscovy Company (a major initiative of great significance) was a carry-over from the previous regime, and was permitted by Mary because it was one of the few initiatives which did not upset Philip (whose other subjects had no interest in Russia). The king deeply distrusted London, and tried to prevent the diversification of foreign trade, which was rendered necessary by the difficulties in the Antwerp market after 1550; hence the protest from the council of Brabant, with its slightly paranoid tone. Philip endeavoured to forbid English voyages to the Guinea coast, but the London merchants ignored him, to his great indignation. The City was in a very strong position, because no government could do without the financial services it provided.

FOURTEEN

Religious Persecution

I

Extract from the reminiscences of John Louthe, contained in a letter written to John Foxe, BL Harleian MS 425, ff. 134 et seq., printed in *Narratives of the Days of the Reformation*, ed. J.G. Nichols (Camden Society, 77, 1859), pp. 15–59.

'The examynatyone of a blyde boy called the blynde boy of Gloucester afore doctor Wylliams the judge. And of the myserable ende of the same judge.

Thys boy called blynde Tome was browght afore the sayd doctor Wyllyams the chawncelor, and John Barkere, alias Taylore the register, in the consistory by the south dore in the nether ende of the churche [Gloucester cathedral]. The offycers in whose custody the boy remeyned, by commandment of the chawncelor, presented the poore boy at the barre before the judge. The doctor Wyllyams examined him apon sondry articles magistrall and usuall emonge the tormentors at that tyme, as ye may fynd folio [. . .] in mr Foxe. And namely he urged the article of Transubstantiatyone.

Wyllyams. Doest yow not beleeve that after the wordes of consecratione of the preest that ther remaynyth the veery body of Chryste?

Tome. No, that I doo not.

Wyllyams. Then yow arte an heretyke, and shalte be burnte. Who tawght thee thys heresy?

Tome. Yow, mr. Chawncelor.

W. Where, I pray thee?

Tome. When in yonder place (poynting with his hande and lokyng as it were towerde the pulpytt, standynge apon the north syde of the churche).

W. When dyd I so teache thee?

Tome. When yow preched there (naming the day) a sermone to all men as well as to me, apon the sacrament. Yow sayd the sacrament was to be receaved spiritually by fayth, and not carnally and really as the papistes have heretofore tawght.

W. Then do as I have done, and yow shalt lyve as I do, and escape burnynge.

Tome. Thoghe yow can so easily dyspense with yowr selfe, and mocke with God, the world, and yowr conscyence, I wyll not so doo.

Wyllyams. Then God have mercy apon thee, for I wyll reade thy condemnatory sentense.

Tome. Godes wyll be fulfylled!

Here the register stoode up and sayd to the chawncelor, Fye for shame man! Wyll ye reade the sentense and condemne yowr selfe? Away, away! and substitute another to gyve sentense and judgement.

Wyllyams. Mr. registere, I wyll obbey the lawe and gyve sentense me selfe accordynge to myn offyce.

And so he redd the sentense with an unhappy tounge, and more unhappy conscience.

Ex testimonio John Taylore alias Barker, Registrarii Glouc' olim ex cenobio Oxon. quod vocatur Omnium Sanctorum.'

II

> Extract from the Queen's memorandum, undated but probably January 1555; taken from G. Burnet, *The History of the Reformation of the Church of England*, ed. N. Pocock (1865), V, pp. 440–1. There are two (slightly different) MSS copies in BL Harleian MS 444, f. 27; and Cotton, Titus, C.VII, f. 120.

'. . . touching good preaching, I wish that may supply and overcome the evil preaching in time past. And also to make a sure provision that none evil books shall either be printed bought or sold without just punishment therefore. I think it should be well done that the universities and churches of this realm should be visited by such persons as my Lord Cardinal with the rest of you may be well assured to be worthy and sufficient persons. . . . Touching punishment of heretics methinketh it ought to be done without rashness, not leaving in the meanwhile to do justice to such as by learning would seem to deceive the simple, and the rest to be so used that the people might well perceive them not to be condemned without just occasion, whereby they shall both understand the truth and beware to do the like. And especially within London I would wish none to be burnt without some of the Council's presence and both there and everywhere good sermons at the same. I verily believe that many benefices should not be in one man's hands but after such sort as every priest might look to his own charge and remain resident there, whereby they should have but one bond to discharge towards God whereas now they have many, which I take to be the cause that in most parts of the realm there is overmuch want of good preachers and such as should with their doctrine overcome the evil diligence of the abused preachers in the time of the schism; not only by their preaching but also by their good example without which in mine opinion their sermons shall not so much profit as I wish. And like as their good example on their behalf shall undoubtedly do much good, I account myself bound on my behalf to show some example in encouraging and maintaining those persons well doing their duty (not forgetting in the meanwhile to correct and punish them which do contrary) that it may be evident to all this Realm how I discharge my conscience therein and minister true justice in so doing.'

III

Extract from Foxe, *Actes and Monuments* (London, 1583), pp. 1680–1.

'The apprehension, examination, condemnation and burning of Diricke Carver and Iohn Launder, who suffered martyrdome for the testimonie of Christes Gospell.

July the 22 & 23 [1555] Diricke Carver and Ihon Launder, Martirs, Edward Gage, gentleman, persecutor.

The 22 day of this moneth of July, was burned at Lewes, within the Countie of Sussex, one Diricke Carver, late of the parish of Brighthamsted in the same Countie. And the next day (being the 23 day of the same moneth) was also burned at Stening an other named Iohn Lander, late of Godstone in the Countie of Surrey, whych 2. men were (w[i]th others) aboute the ende of the moneth of October, An. 1554 apprehended by Edward Gage, Gentleman, as they were at prayer within the dwelling house of the said Diricke: and by him were sent up unto the Queenes Counsaile. who, after examination, sent them as prisoners to Newgate, there to attende the leisure of Boner Bishop of London, From whence (upon the Bishops receipte of a letter from the Lorde Marques of Winchester, now Lord Treasurer) they were brought by the keeper of the prison, the 8 of June next after, into the bishops chamber at his house in Lo[n]don: and there (being examined upon divers poynts of religion) they made their several confessions, subscribing them and signing them with theyr owne hands, which being read, the Bishop obiected unto them certaine other Articles, causing them to sweare truely and directly to aunswere thereunto: which Articles they confessed to be true, referring them selves chiefly to theyr former confessions. . . .

Diricke Carver and Iohn Launder sent downe into the countrey to be burned. The cruell spoyle of Dirickes goodes. Diricke learned to reade in the prison. . . .

. . . Diricke burned at Lewes.

Moreover, at his comming into the towne of Lewes to be burned, the people called upon him, beseeching God to strengthen him in the faith of Jesus Christ. Hee thanked them, and prayed unto God, that of hys mercy hee woulde strengthen them in the lyke Faith. And when he came to the sign of the Starre, the people drew neare unto hym, where the Sheriffe sayde that he had founde him a faithfull man in all hys aunsweres. And as he came to the stake, hee kneeled downe and made hys prayers, and the Sheriffe made haste.

Dirickes book commaunded in the Quenes name to be throwen againe into the fier. The testimony of Diricke at the stake.

Then hys Booke was throwne into the barrell, and when he had stript him selfe (as a ioyfull member of God) he went into the barrell him selfe. And as soone as ever hee came in, he tooke up the booke and threw it among the people, and then the Sheriffe in the Kynge and Queenes name, in paine of death, to throw in the booke againe. And immediately that faithfull member spake with a ioyfull voyce, saying:

(The exhortation of Diricke to the people.) Deare brethren and sisterne, witnes you all, that I am come to seale with my bloude Christes Gospell, for because I know that it is true: it is not unknowen unto all you, but that it hath bene truely preached heere in Lewes, and in all places of Englande, and nowe it is not. And for because that I will not deny heere Gods Gospel, and be obedient to mans lawes, I am condemned to die. Dear brethren and sisterne, as many of you as doe belelve upon the Father, the Sonne and the holy Ghost, unto everlasting life, see you do the woorkes appertaining to the same. And as many of you as doe beleeve uppon the Pope of Rome, or any of his lawes, which he sets foorth in these daies, you do beleeve to your utter conde[m]nation, and except the great mercy of God, you shall burne in hell perpetually.

Where finde you that in the Creede, to beleeve on the Pope.

Immediately the Sheriffe spake unto hym, and sayde, if thou doest not beleve on the Pope thou art damned body and soule. And further the Sheriffe sayde unto hym: speake to thy God, that he maye deliver thee nowe, or else to strike me downe to the example of thys people: but this faythfull member sayde, the Lorde forgeve you youre sayinges.

Horrible provoking of Gods iudgement.

And then spake hee againe to all the people there present, wyth a loude voyce, saying deare brethren, and all you whom I have offended in woordes or in deede, I ask you for the Lordes sake to forgeve mee, and I hartely forgeve all you, which have offended me in thought, word or dede.

. . . These were the last wordes of that Faythfull member of Christe, before the fire was put to hym. And afterward that the fire came unto him, he cried: Oh Lorde have mercy upon me, and spronge up in the fire, calling uppon the name of Jesus, and so ended.'

IV

Extract from a report by Giovanni Michieli to the Doge and Senate of Venice, 1 June 1555; taken from the *Calendar of State Papers, Venetian*, V, pp. 93–4.

'. . . two days ago, to the displeasure as usual of the population here, two Londoners were burned alive, one of them having been public lecturer in Scripture, a person sixty years of age, who was held in great esteem. In a few days the like will be done to four or five more; and thus from time to time to many others who are in prison for this cause, and will not recant, although such sudden severity is odious to many people. . . .'

Although Mary had made her intentions clear up to a point, the severity of the persecution was a great shock. Protestant services had been discontinued from December 1553, and many bishops and other clergy deprived. The foreign congregations were expelled, and numerous preachers imprisoned, but it was not until Cardinal Pole began to exercise his legatine jurisdiction in January 1555 that the actual heresy trials commenced. Lord Chancellor Gardiner, who was the driving force behind these trials at first, appears to have believed that Protestantism was merely a cloak for political ambition, and that the threat of death would be sufficient to expose its leaders as frauds. Instead, in February 1555 a number of respected Protestant leaders were burned. This encouraged the rank and file also to refuse submission, and the large-scale execution of ordinary men and women commenced. Gardiner immediately realised that, as a policy, severity had failed, but he was unable to influence the queen's conscience. Mary believed it to be her duty to extirpate heresy, and refused to be deterred by those who pointed out that her actions were having the opposite of the intended effect. In three and a half years some 280 people were burned alive, and many others died in prison.

FIFTEEN

The Queen's Pregnancy

I

Extracts from the *Calendar of State Papers, Domestic, Mary*, ed. C.S. Knighton (1998). The originals are PRO SP11/5, nos 29 and 48.

'[No date, but early June 1555.] The king and queen to all [?mayors], sheriffs, bailiffs, constables, cust[odians], searchers and other ministers and subjects.

We send Sir Henry Sidney to the kings of the Romans and of Bohemia [Ferdinand and Maximilian] to signify the happy deliverance of a prince. Suffer him to pass with servants, horses, money, jewels and other baggage without any search, let or molestation; see him provided of post horses, and all other necessaries for reasonable money, and a convenient vessel for transport [signed with the sign manual].'

'July 20, 1555. The Court at Brussels. The Earl of Devon to [Antonio] Bonvisi.

Whereas partly by credit of [James] Bassett and partly by your own friendship you have offered me a loan of money, I am bold to require you to deliver 1,000 crowns to Thomas Gresham, the queen's agent at Antwerp, which shall be repaid at Christmas. I shall subscribe and seal such writings as you think convenient.

I received yesterday a letter from Sir William Petre, secretary, who wrote that the king and queen are in good health, the realm quiet, and the queen's good hour near at hand. The king is here looked for very shortly.'

II

Extract from Foxe, *Actes and Monuments* (London, 1583), pp. 1596–7.

'Concerning the childebed of Queene Mary, as it was rumoured among the people.

Long perswasion had bene in England with great expectation, for the space of halfe a yeare or more, that the Queene was conceived with childe.

This report was made by the Queenes Phisitions, & other nie about the Court: so that divers were punished for saying the contrary. And commaundement was geven, that in all churches supplication and prayers should be made for the Queenes good deliverie: the certificate whereof ye may read before in the letter of the Counsel sent to Boner, pag. 1405. And also the same moreover may appeare by provision made before in the Act of Parliament for the childe, pag.1410.

And now for somuch as in ye beginning of this month of June, about Whitsontide, the time was thought to be nie, that this young Maister should come into the world, and that midwives, rockers, nurses, with the cradle & all, were prepared and in a readines, sode[n]ly upon what cause or occasion it is uncertaine, a certaine vaine rumour was blowne in London of the prosperous deliverance of the Queene, and the birth of the childe: In so muche that the Bels were rong, Bonfiers and processions made, not only in the Citie of London, and in most other partes of the realme, but also in the towne of Antwarpe, gunnes were shot off uppon the river, by the English shippes, and the Mariners thereof rewarded wyth an hundred pistolettes or Italian crownes by the Ladie Regent, who was the Queene of Hungarie. Such great reioysing and triumph was for the Queenes deliverie, & that there was a Prince borne. Yea, divers Preachers, namely one the Parson of S. Anne within Aldergate, after Procession and Te Deum song, tooke upon him to describe the proportion of ye child, how faire, howe beautifull, and great a Prince it was, as the like had not bene scene. . . .

. . . [but] in ye ende al proved clean co[n]trary, & the ioy and expectations of me[n] were much deceived. For the people were certified, yt the Queene neither was as then delivered, nor was in hope to have any child. At thys time many talked diversly: some sayd thys rumour of the Queenes conception was spread for a policie: some other affirmed that she was deceived by a Tympanie or some other like disease, to thinke herself with child, and it was not; some thought she was with childe, and that it did by some chaunce miscarie, or els that she was bewitched: but what was the truth therof, the Lord knoweth, to whome nothing is secrete. One thing of mine owne hearing and seeing I can not passe over unwitnessed.

There came to me, whom I did both heare and see, one Isabell Malt, a woman dwellyng in Aldersgate streete in Home alley, not far from the house where this present booke was Printed, who before witnes made this declaration unto us, that she beyng delivered of a ma[n]child upo[n] whitsonday in the mornyng, whiche was the xi day of June an.1555 there came to her the Lorde North and another Lord to her unknowe[n], dwellyng then about old Fish streete, demau[n]dyng of her if she would part with her child, and would sweare that she never knew nor had no such child. Whiche if she would, her sonne (they sayd) should be well provided for, she should take no care for it, with many fayre offers if she would part with the child.

After that came other wome[n] also, of who[m] one she sayd should have bene the Rocker, but she in no wise would let go her sonne, who at ye writyng hereof, being alive & called Timothye Malt, was of the age of xiii yeares & upward.

Thus much (I say) I heard of the woman her selfe. What credite is to be geven to her relation, I deale not withall, but leave it to the libertie of the Reader, to beleve it if that they list: to them that list not, I have no further warrant to assure them.

Among many other great preparations made for the Queenes deliveraunce of childe, there was a cradle very sumptuously and gorgeously trimmed, uppon the whiche cradle for the child appointed, these Verses were written, both in Latin and in English.

Quam Mariae sobolem Deus optime summe dedisti,
Anglia incolumen redde, tuere, rege.

The Child which thou to Mary, O Lord of might hast send
To Englandes ioy in health preserve, keepe and defend.'

This was the non-event of the reign, and also its turning point. Mary's phantom pregnancy deceived everyone, including herself, and was both a personal and a political tragedy for her. As a woman, she passionately wanted a child; as a queen, she needed an heir. It is most likely that the cause was a cancer of the womb, which killed her just over three years later. Although she refused to abandon hope of an heir, even after this debacle, no one else expected her to bear a healthy child, and that included Philip. This deprived her regime of momentum and credibility; because unless Philip was prepared to ignore his marriage treaty, and claim the Crown himself in the event of her death (an action which would almost certainly have led to civil war), her heir was her half-sister Elizabeth. The two women disliked and distrusted each other intensely, and Mary struggled in vain for the rest of her life to neutralise the threat which she presented. Foxe's circumstantial stories cannot be verified, but his general picture of intense expectation, disappointment and confusion is authentic enough. Of course Mary's failure was eventually to be the Protestant opportunity, but Foxe confines himself to a slightly smug invocation of Divine providence. The pathos of the gorgeous but empty cradle would have been for him a salutary warning of the perils of provoking the wrath of God.

SIXTEEN

The Religious Exile

I

Extract from *A Brief Discourse of the Troubles begun at Frankfort in Germany, anno Domini 1554* (1575); taken from the edition by Edward Arber (London, 1908), pp. 23–4.

'After that it pleased the Lord GOD to take away, for our sins, that noble Prince of famous memory King EDWARD the Sixth, and had placed Queen MARY in his room; sundry godly men, as well strangers as of the English nation, fled, for the liberty of their consciences, over the seas; some into France, some into Flanders, and some into the high countries of the Empire: and in the year of our Lord 1554, and the 27th of June, came EDMUND SUTTON, WILLIAM WILLIAMS, WILLIAM WHITTINGHAM and THOMAS WOOD with their companies, to the city of Frankfort in Germany; the first Englishmen that there arrived to remain and abide.

The same night came one, Master VALERAND POULLAIN, Minister, unto their lodging; and declared how he had obtained a church there, in the name of all such as should come out of England for the Gospel; but especially from Glastonbury, which were all Frenchmen.

Answer was made him, That as GOD was to be praised, who had moved the Magistrates' hearts to shew the French such favour; even so, for so much as few of them understood the French tongue, it would be small commodity to them, or to such as should come afterward to join themselves to that church.

The next day they communed with Master MORELLIO, another Minister of the French church, and also with Master CASTALIO, a Senior of the same; both of them godly and learned men. By their advice and counsel, it was determined that a Supplication should be drawn out, and offered to the Magistrates, to know first, Whether they would be contented that, not only the parties before named, but also all other Englishmen that would repair thither for the like cause, might, through their favour, be suffred safely to remain within their City. This Supplication was subscribed, as well by the said SUTTON, WHITTINGHAM and the rest of the Englishmen, as also by MORELLIO, CASTALIO and one ADRIAN, a citizen there, with whom they lodged.

And within three days after the offering up of their Supplication; they obtained their requests. . . .

When the church was in this sort granted; they consulted among themselves, what Order of Service they should use: for they were not so strictly bound, as was told them, to the Ceremonies of the French, by the Magistrates; but that if the one allowed of the other, it was sufficient.

At length, the English Order [1552 Book of Common Prayer] was perused; and this, by general consent, was concluded:

That the answering aloud after the Minister should not be used: the Litany, Surplice, and many other things also omitted; for that, in those Reformed Churches, such things would seem more than strange. It was farther agreed upon, that the Minister, in place of the English Confession, should use another, both of more effect, and also framed according to the state and time. And the same ended; the people to sing a Psalm in metre in a plain tune; as it was and is accustomed in the French, Dutch, Italian, Spanish and Scottish churches. That done, the Minister to pray for the assistance of GODS HOLY SPIRIT; and so to proceed to the sermon. . . . And as touching the Ministration of the Sacraments; sundry things were also, by common consent, omitted as superstitious and superfluous.'

II

Extracts from *Original Letters Relative to the English Reformation*, ed. Hastings Robinson (Parker Society, 1847), pp. 751–5. The originals, written in Latin, are preserved in the City Archive at Zurich.

'Letter CCCLVI: Robert Horn and others to the magistrates at Zurich [1554].

Forasmuch as we are exiled, most honourable magistrates, from England, our beloved country, and for the sake of that light of divine truth by which she was lately distinguished, we humbly request of your worthiness, that we may be permitted to sojourn in this most famous city, relying upon and supported by your sanction, decree, and protection against the violence of those, should any such be found, who would oppose and molest us. The Lord knoweth, for whose sake we have left our all, that we seek for nothing besides himself. And for this reason chiefly we have unanimously and with ready minds come to this place, where he is most sincerely preached and most purely worshipped. This being the case, we entertain the hope that, as you are most zealous defenders of the true Christian religion, so you will protect us by your authority, who by reason of the same are exiled and homeless. May the Lord Jesus long preserve you and this your illustrious state in safety and prosperity! Your most humble petitioners:

ROBERT HORN	RICHARD CHAMBERS
MARGERY HIS WIFE	THOMAS SPENCER

JAMES PILKINGTON   HENRY COCKRAFT
THOMAS LEVER   MICHAEL RENIGER
JOHN MULLINS   LAURENCE HUMPHREY
THOMAS BENTHAM   WILLIAM COLE

Letter CCCVII: Richard Cox and others to John Calvin; Frankfort, 5th April 1555.

Greeting. After that our very dear brother Thomas Sampson had communicated to us sometime since the letter that you wrote to him touching our common controversy with certain brothers, we considered it a mark of our duty and regard to you to inform you, as early as possible, of all that has been done, and with what design. But though it may perhaps seem to you somewhat late to write to you, when the matter is altogether brought to a termination; yet we implore you by Jesus Christ not to suppose that the delay has arisen from any desire unduly to undervalue your authority. For it both is, and ought to be, most highly esteemed and regarded, not only by ourselves, but by the world at large. But since your reverence was many days' journey distant from us, and because there was great hope that all that controversy would be settled with less inconvenience between the brethren themselves, we were unwilling to disturb your most important meditations by our trifling and domestic concerns. But though we are very loth to suspect our brethren of anything that savours of insincerity, we are nevertheless somewhat afraid that the whole affair and case has not been set before you with sufficient explicitness. For neither are we so entirely wedded to our country, as not to be able to endure any customs differing from our own; nor is the authority of those fathers and martyrs of Christ so much regarded by us, as that we have any scruple in thinking or acting in opposition to it. And we have not only very frequently borne witness to this by our assertions, but have at length proved it by our actions. For when the magistrates lately gave us permission to adopt the rites of our native country, we freely relinquished all those ceremonies which were regarded by our brethren as offensive and inconvenient. For we gave up private baptisms, confirmation of children, saints days, kneeling at the holy communion, the linen surplices of the ministers, crosses and other things of the like character. And we gave them up, not as being impure and papistical, which certain of our brethren often charged them with being; but whereas they were in their own nature indifferent, and either ordained or allowed by godly fathers for the edification of our people, we notwithstanding chose rather to lay them aside than to offend the minds or alienate the affections of our brethren. We retain, however the remainder of the form of prayer and of the administration of the sacraments, which is prescribed in our book, and this with the consent of almost the whole church, the judgement of which in matters of this sort we did not think should be disregarded. With the consent likewise of the same church there was forthwith appointed one pastor, two preachers, four elders, two deacons; the greatest care being taken that every one should be at perfect liberty to vote as he pleased; except only that by the command of the magistrate, before the election took place, were set forth those articles lately published by authority of King Edward, which contained a summary of our doctrine, and which we were all of us required to subscribe [the Forty Two articles of 1553]. For what kind of an election, they said, must be expected, unless the voters shall previously have agreed as to doctrine? Certain parties, who had before manifested some objection, subscribed to these articles of their own accord. Some few declined doing so, of whose peaceableness nevertheless we entertain good hope.

We have thought fit to write thus fully to your kindness, that you might ascertain the whole course of our proceedings from ourselves. Our liturgy is translated into French, and the articles above mentioned have very lately been printed in Zurich. Did we not suppose that they would be easily met with among you, we should take care that copies should be forwarded you. But we pray your kindness not to imagine that we have aimed at anything else throughout this whole business, and this we testify before the Lord, than the purification of our church, and the avoiding of most grievous stumbling blocks which otherwise seem to be hanging over us. May the Lord Jesus very long preserve your piety to us and to his church! Farewell. Frankfort, April 5 [1555]. Your piety's most devoted

English exiles:

RICHARD COX	EDMUND GRINDAL
DAVID WHITEHEAD	JOHN BALE
RICHARD ALVEY	ROB. HORN
THOMAS BECON	THO. LEVER
EDWIN SANDYS	THO. SAMSON.'

Somewhere between 700 and 800 English men, women and children went abroad to avoid coercion by the Marian Church. They started going before the persecution proper began, as soon as it was clear in which direction the queen was moving. They were mostly 'of the better sort' – clergy, students, merchants, yeomen and gentlemen. A few were nobles and ex-bishops. They settled in a variety of places, mostly in Switzerland and the Rhineland: Aarau, Basle, Emden, Frankfort, Geneva, Strasbourg and Zurich. Lutheran cities did not welcome them, but where the magistrates adhered to some form of the Swiss reformation, they were able to settle and establish their own congregations. Partly because of their own inclinations, and partly because the future of the Church in England looked so bleak, many of these exiles began to adopt a form of worship closer to that used in one of the 'model' churches, Geneva or Zurich, than that used in England under Edward.

Although they all continued to use the English language, there was much dispute over the need to preserve the 'face' of an English Church. The magistrates of the host cities normally required an acceptable statement of doctrine from each congregation before giving permission for them to worship collectively. Frankfort was happy to accept the Forty Two Articles, but the dispute within the congregation there later became notorious. Whittingham and his friends virtually abandoned the Prayer Book as 'superstitious', a decision which sounded alarm in the other congregations. Cox and his group therefore moved to Frankfort in order to bring the Church there back into some kind of uniformity. In that they succeeded, to Calvin's annoyance. Most of the dissidents eventually removed to Geneva. The Elizabethan establishment was drawn mostly from the Frankfort and Zurich congregations, while Puritan dissent had its roots in Geneva.

SEVENTEEN

The Court of Philip and Mary

I

Extracts from *Documents relating to the Revels at Court in the time of King Edward VI and Queen Mary*, ed. A. Feuillerat (Louvain, 1914). The original accounts are among the More Molineux MSS at Loseley.

'p. 149: 26 September 1553; to the Master of the Revels ". . . to make and delyver owt of our Revels unto the gentillmen of our Chapel for a play to be played before us at the feates of our coronacione, as in time past hath bene accustomed. . . .

p. 150: . . . The charges of apparelling . . . the said play [64*s* 2*d*].

[22–8 September] when as the same by reason of a new determinacion of appointment the play to serve at Christmas next following . . . surceased and were left unfinished. . . .

p. 152: The charges of finishing thaforesaid and putting in a redines . . . such thinges as were likely to be called upon at Christmas, w[i]th thattendaunce of the officers all the xii dayes at court, as hath bene accustomed . . . [£7 4*s* 8*d*]."

p. 159: 17–21 October 1554: New making (etc.) properties for "divers and sundry maskes both for men and women as plays set forth by Udall and other pastimes prepared furnished at set foorth out of the Revels this yeere to be shewed and done in the Kyng and Quenes Maiesties presence from time to tyme as the same was commaunded and called for. . . .

[13 December 1554] . . . whereas our welbeloved Nicholas Udall hath at sundry seasons convenyent hertofore showed and minded to show his diligence in settyng forthe of dyalogues and Interludes before us for oure roiall sport and recreation, to thintent that he may be in a better redines at all tymes when it shall be oure plesure to call [he to have all such things as he may require by virtue of this warrant].

p. 163: [23–30 November 1554] A maske of the vi Arclues [Hercules] or men of warre with vi Maryners for their torchbearers. . . .

. . . viii headpeces of past & symen moulded work like morican helmets the fronts like gryphons heds with ceneturs in the form of a greyhound with three heds standing on the rest very faire.

xvi hors faces of moulded work of paste & cyment tremed with hair for the breastes & backes of the said maskers.

. . . and for new making of certain other like faces broken . . . [£6 0s 4d].

p. 166: . . . At Christmas Annis primo & secundo Regis & Regine . . .

A maske of viii patrons of gallies like Venetian senators, with vi galley slaves for their torchbearers. A maske of vi Venuses or amorous ladies with vi cupids & vi torchbearers to them. And certain plays made by Nicholas Udall & their incidents. . . . "

p. 215: [To Sir Thomas Cawarden, Master of the Revels] "You shal understande sir that I hav made a commedie concerning the way to life, meet as yt is supposed to be plaied before the Quene, and there be of the Innes of Court that desire to have the settyng forth therof, but because y[ou]r Mastership now three yeares past offered in a sort to sett forthe some of my rude devices, I thought it good to knowe yor mynde herein before I gyve aunswere to eny other. The settyng forthe will be chargeable because the matter ys stately, comprehendyng a discorse of the hole world. There be in yt of sundry personages lxii and the play is iii howres long. It ys nowe in lerning and will be reddie within these x dayes. The matter is this, I bringe in a younge man whom I name Lemuel, who hath a servant called Lob, those two will attempt the worlde to seek theyre fortune, they mete with Lust, Luck and Love; Lust promiseth theym Lechery, Luck lordship; Love, life. They follow Lust and through Lechery be lost, then through Luck they recover. Luck bringeth them to lordship, which through largess and learninge they come to Love. Then through Love they go to Lyght and thereby attaine Lyfe. All the players names begin with L. . . . This is the proportion, wherein I praie you as shortly as you can to let me knowe yor mind. I pray God to kepe you and yours."

At London this tewdsay Christmas eve [1556]

Yours to do you plesure, William Baldwin.'

II

Extract from a letter of Don Pedro de Cordova to the King of the Romans, 10 December 1554; taken from the *Calendar of State Papers, Spanish*, XIII, p. 119. The original MS is in the Vienna State Archive.

'On Sunday it rained, but the king wished to have some distraction, and there was cane play. There were six gentlemen in each band, all dressed in silk and gold, and thus they entered the place where a great number of people were gathered together, with ladies in gold and silver cloth and great wealth of crimson and purple velvet, of which the king had ordered each one of them to be supplied with as much as they asked for. There must have been over thirty of them, married and unmarried, for the Queen's ladies here may be married or single. The Queen came out adorned with her brocades and jewels, the ladies all had head-dresses enriched with gold, and many of them jewels and silk fringes. Don Juan de Benevides and his band, ten in all, wcrc in white and gold; Luis Vanegas's in green and silver; Don Diego de Cordova's, in which the king rode, purple and silver; and all these were dressed at the king's expense. On the other side were Ruy Gomez in gold and blue, the Duke [of Alba] with his band of eleven in yellow and silver, and Don Diego de Acevedo in black and silver. They made a brave display when they appeared, and the play passed off without accidents, to the sound of trumpets and drums. The same evening the king supped in public with the Queen, and at another table sat the grandees of Spain, and the nobles of England, with their ladies. Afterwards there was dancing, and Don Fadrique de Toledo, *Commendador Major*, issued a challenge for a tournament on foot. . . .'

III

Extract from the 'order of the quenes privie chamber'. BL Add. MS 71009, f. 60.

'Now what every manes office is to doe. ferste the gentleman ussher or oon of them to be in the privie chambre betwene vi and vii oclocke or earlier if nede required and to see the gromes doe their dewte that is to saie; to take away the plates yf ani be and to make fiers and swepe the chambre to sette the chaers and koschins in their places and all their thinges nedfall to be done. that is for the plate and cobberd clothes the [. . .] stofe and pantrie stofe all these to be deliverid by a grome to the said officers afore named and likewise al silver vessell to be delivered safe as the other stofe al chandrie stofe grome porteres stofe and al thinges that is occupied in the privie chambre of ani office to be sente home to the offis for the officers feschest. & at viii a cloke when the gentlemen ussher shall see time to send a grome to the yoeman ussher w[i]thowte to goe for brekfaste and he to bringe yt to the doer and their the gromes to take it in a gentleman ussher standing by to geve the sees and when brekfaste is done then the gromes to feate owte the plate againe; so that in all thinges nedfull for the service of the quene the gromes to at commandemente to do it. The gentleman ussher always to be in the chambre and oon of the gentlemen yf yt sholde happen the quene to call for oon of them other to be their or else to leve worde w[i]th the gentleman ussher where he shall have him. The quene that ded is [Mary] had her borde of astate in hir privie chamber and their hir meate was sette and oon of the ordinari servantes w[i]th owte did go for yt when he was comanded by a gentleman usher and browte it to the dore and their the ladies and gentlemen did fesche yt in a gentleman ussher standing by w[i]th seeth in a plate seyng the seeth taken at the doer the karvar standyng

Jane Dudley (née Grey). 'The nine days Queen'.

Mary I – a medal by Jacopo
da Trezzo.

Edward Courtenay, Earl of Devon, who hoped to marry Mary.

William Lord Paget, Lord Privy Seal, who supported the marriage to Philip.

Jane Dormer, Countess, and later Duchess, of Feria. She provided a refuge for English Catholics.

Philip, King of England; and Philip II of Spain.

Simon Renard,
Charles V's
ambassador
with Mary.

Sir Thomas Wyatt the
younger, who led the
rebellion in Kent.

at the borde to reseave yt beynge a ladi or gentlewoman apowntid for it
and so the [. . .] ded sende into the quene suche meate as yt plesed her to
have. . . . [Her] her grace had dined then the wayters goethe to diner and
for the cobberde when the seller hathe browte in wyne ale and beer upp yf
the quene be not their they maye bringe it to the cobberd & they gentleman
ussher to geve the sees and so to charge a lady or gentlewoman w[i]th it to
sarve the coberar so often as she comes w[i]th the cope, and for thewer and
pantre the quene beynge not their came in and coverid the borde and the
panter the breade and salte theis mani did waite the carvar copberar and
the gentlewoman that kepeth the cobberde the gentleman ussher and
ii gromes theis to dyne w[i]th the wayters and the sewer. all others where
w[i]th mistris clarensius [Mary's Chief Gentlewoman of the Privy Chamber]
in her chambre she having ii messe of meate for them and the gromes oon
messe of meate for them that did not waite and thei to have a chambre for
them all to dine in and [they] be commanded to li in no other place and for
all nighte the gentleman knowethe all readi what is for to be done.
   this I have made you abresse what order was used in this tyme.'

The kindest thing to say about Mary's court was that it was
unremarkable. All the structures were in place, and she did nothing to
change them, but her own circumstances forced some innovations. For
the first time a monarch's Privy Chamber was predominantly female, and
this imposed its own rules and limitations on how it operated. This can
be glimpsed in the 'order of the quenes privie chamber', a handbook
probably compiled by John Norris, Mary's Chief Gentleman, for the
guidance of his successor.

   Mary herself was far more interested in ecclesiastical ceremonial than
in secular entertainments. She was the only Tudor not to hold a
coronation tournament, and as the accounts show, even the plays that
were prepared for her coronation were not performed, although it is not
known why. It was decided to postpone them until Christmas, but the
level of expenditure suggests that they were not staged then, either.

   The revels expenditure for Mary's first year was less than 10 per cent
of that of 1552–3. It was clearly Philip who injected life into the court.
From the autumn of 1554 the accounts show increased expenditure, and
some particulars of the masques and other entertainments provided.
However, the 'cane play' which was staged in December 1554 seems to
have been an all-Spanish occasion, and such English comments as survive
about this form of entertainment are not complimentary. Philip did better
with Anglo-Spanish tournaments in the early part of 1555, when he was
making a serious attempt to gain support among the English aristocracy.

   After the king's departure in August 1555 Mary clearly made an effort
to keep up a good show at court, and a modest level of activity and

expenditure is recorded for the rest of the reign, although it never approached the levels recorded under her father and brother. Philip had his own Privy Chamber, chapel and stables, but shared other service departments with the queen, a situation made easier by the fact that they were hardly ever apart. The Nicholas Udall whose name appears in the revels accounts was a gentleman of the Chapel Royal who was famous for his musical and theatrical entertainments. William Baldwin was not a member of the court, and it seems that his offer of a play was not taken up (hardly surprising, given his summary of it!). The text does not appear to have survived. A William Baldwin appears in London during Elizabeth's reign as a strong Protestant, but it is not certain that they were the same man.

The court was divided into the Chamber (including the Privy Chamber) which was ruled by the Lord Chamberlain, and the Household, or service departments, which were ruled by the Lord Steward. The latter was divided into some thirty departments, and had a permanent staff of over 200. The Chamber and Privy Chamber had a full-time staff of less than 100, but many part-time gentry servants. The orchestra, players and physicians were part of the Chamber staff, along with the various wardrobes, but the Chapel Royal, which provided the majority of the entertainers, was a separate department. The dean was directly responsible to the monarch, and answered neither to the chamberlain nor the steward. At this time the Revels Office, which dealt mainly with props and costumes, was also independent.

EIGHTEEN

Queen Mary's Navy

Extract from *The Acts of the Privy Council*, eds J.R. Dasent et al. (London, 1890), VI, pp. 39–41. The original is PRO PC2/6, pp. 487–8.

'Minute of 8 January 1557

Whereas heretofore the Queen's Majesty hath been sundry times troubled with the often signing of warrants for money to be defrayed about the necessary charges of her Highness's navy, and being desirous to have some other order taken for the easier conducting of this matter hereafter, did this day, upon consultation had with certain of my Lords of the Council for this purpose, desire the Lord Treasurer [William Paulet, Marquis of Winchester], with the advice of the Lord Admiral [Lord William Howard] to take this matter upon him, who, agreeing thereunto, was content to take the charge thereof with these conditions following:

First he required to have the sum of £14,000 by year to be advanced half yearly to Benjamin Gonson, Treasurer of the admiralty, to be by him defrayed in such sort as shall be prescribed by him, the said Lord Treasurer, with the advice of the Lord Admiral etc.

For the which the said Lord Treasurer took upon him to do these things ensuing:

First, to cause such of her Majesty's ships as may be made serviceable with caulking and new trimming to be sufficiently renewed and repaired.

Item to cause such of her Highness's said ships as must of neccessity to be made of new, to be gone in hand withal and new made with convenient speed, and he to have timber of the Queen's Majesty in such of her parks, forests, chases and manors as lie meetest for that purpose, by her Majesty's warrant.

Item, he is to see also all her Highness's said ships furnished with sails, anchors, cables, and other tackle and apparel sufficiently.

Item, he [is] to cause the charge and victualling of the shipkeepers and workmen in harbour to be paid and discharged.

Item he [is] to cause a mass of victuals to be always in a readiness, able to serve for one thousand men for one month, to be set to the seas upon any sudden [emergency].

Item, he [is] to cause the said ships from time to time to be repaired and renewed as occasion shall serve.

Item when the said ships that are to be renewed shall be nigh made and sufficiently repaired, and the whole navy furnished of such sails, anchors, cables and other tackle, then is the said Lord Treasurer content to continue this service in form aforesaid for the sum of ten thousand pounds yearly, to be advanced as is aforesaid.

Item the said Benjamin Gonson and Edward Baeshe, Surveyor of the Victuals for the ships, shall make their several accounts of the defrayment of the said money and of their whole doings herein once in the year at the least, and as often besides as shall be thought convenient by my Lords of the Council.

Finally, if upon the accounts made by the said Gonson and Baeshe there shall be found at the end of the year any of the said sums of money, or any grain or other victuals to remain in their hands undefrayed by the order aforesaid, then the same money and victuals to remain to be answered to the Queen's Majesty's use towards the charges of the next year following, or otherwise as it shall please her Highness to appoint.'

Mary inherited from her brother a navy of some fifty ships, and an Admiralty department called the Council for Marine Causes. The Lord Admiral was responsible for all operations, but it was the business of the council, chaired by the Vice-Admiral, to make sure that all the queen's ships were maintained, repaired, manned, victualled, and replaced as necessary. There was, however, no naval budget or 'ordinary'. Money was made available to the Treasurer by general warrant as it was needed (or could be found).

Mary was not much interested in her ships, but they were in good order at her accession, and the council was working efficiently. However, as the danger of war with France began to increase in 1556, the council decided to overhaul the naval administration. It seems that there was some suspicion of financial malpractice, although the surviving accounts do not reveal what that might have been. The result of an investigation is contained in the above minute. The Treasurer and the Surveyor of the Victuals are instructed to account separately, but more important, the Lord Treasurer is given overall control. This was not an infringement of the Lord Admiral's prerogative, but it does reveal distrust of the Council for Marine Causes. Winchester set himself an initial 'ordinary' of £14,000, which would reduce in time to £10,000. This suggests that he saw a backlog of repair work, although that is not visible in any other source.

In fact these regulations were overtaken by events, because the outbreak of war in the summer of 1557 saw a huge increase in naval expenditure, and it was not until 1559 (under Elizabeth) that the 'ordinary' was applied. Elizabeth did not like the system, and eventually reverted to earlier practice. The navy functioned competently during the war of 1557–9, but did not distinguish itself, much to Philip's disappointment. He recognised the English navy to be the country's main military asset, but he does not seem to have interfered at all in the running of it. If he was in any way responsible for the reforms of 1556–7, there is no evidence to substantiate it.

NINETEEN

The Problem of Elizabeth

I

Letter from Elizabeth to her sister, 2 August 1556. Printed in *Elizabeth I: Collected Works*, eds L.S. Marcus, J. Mueller and M.B. Rose (Chicago, 2000), p. 43; from BL Lansdowne MS 1236, f. 37.

'When I revolve in mind (most noble queen), the old love of paynims to their prince, and the reverent fear of Romans to their Senate, I can but muse for my part, and blush for theirs, to see the rebellious hearts and devilish intents of Christians in names, but Jews in deed, towards their oincted king. Which, methinks if they had feared God though they could not have loved the state, they should for dread of their own plague have refrained that wickedness which their bounden duty to your Majesty hath not restrained. But when I call to remembrance that the Devil *tanquam leo rugiens circumit querens quam devorare potest* [goes about as a roaring lion, seeking whom he may devour; 1 Peter, 5:8], I do the less marvel though he have gotten such novices into his professed house, as vessels (without God's grace) more apt to serve his palace than meet to inhabit English land. I am the bolder to call them his imps for that St. Paul sayeth, *Seditiosi filii sunt diaboli* [the seditious are children of the devil], and since I have so good a buckler I fear the less to enter into their judgement. Of this I assure your Majesty, though it be my part above the rest to bewail such things though my name had not been in them, yet it vexeth me too much tha[t] the devil owe[s] me such a hate as to put me in any part of his mischievous instigations. Whom, as I profess him my foe that is all Christians' enemy, so wish I he had some other way invented to spite me. But since it hath pleased God to bewray their malice afore they finish their purpose, I most humbly thank Him both that He hath ever thus preserved your Majesty through His aid (much like a lamb from the horns of these Bashan bulls), and also stirs up the hearts of your loving subjects to resist them and deliver you, to His honour and their shame.

The intelligence of which, proceeding from your Majesty, deserveth more humble thanks than with my pen I can render, which, as infinite, I will leave to number. And among earthly things I chiefly wish this one: that there were as good surgeons for making anatomies of hearts that might show my thoughts to your Majesty as there are expert physicians of the bodies, able to express the inward griefs of their maladies to their patients. For then I doubt not but know well that whatsoever other should suggest by malice, yet your majesty should be sure by knowledge, so that the more such misty clouds obfuscates the clear light of my truth, the more my tried thoughts should glister to the dimming of their hidden malice. But since wishes are vain and desires oft fails, I must crave that my deeds may supply that my thoughts cannot declare, and that they be not misdeemed there as the facts have been so well tried. And like as I have been your faithful subject from the beginning of your reign, so shall no wicked person cause me to change to the end of my life. And thus I commit your Majesty to God's tuition, whom I beseech long time to preserve, ending with the new remembrance of my old suit, more for that it should not be forgotten than for that I think it not remembered. From Hatfield this present Sunday, the second day of August.

Your Majesty's obedient subject and humble sister,

Elizabeth.'

II

> Simon Renard reports to Philip from France, 12 January 1557; taken from the *Calendar of State Papers, Spanish*, XIII, p. 285.

'The King of France has heard with great regret that negotiations are going on for a match between the Duke of Savoy and the Lady Elizabeth. The King wishes to prevent this if he possibly can. He has shown how he feels about it to the Venetian ambassador. Indeed the French fear this match more than any other calamity that might occur. They say that the queen has given her consent. They [the French] are devising means for upsetting the order of succession in England through the Queen of Scotland, whom they consider to come next. They intend to move the pope to declare that the Lady Elizabeth is a bastard, hoping thus to upset your Majesty's plans. . . .'

III

> Extract from a memorandum attributed to Don Bernardino de Mendoza, May 1557; taken from the *Calendar of State Papers, Spanish*, XIII, p. 293.

'The Lady Elizabeth has been declared by parliament heiress to the crown of England. The Queen is childless, and agrees that the Lady Elizabeth should marry the Duke of Savoy. If this marriage takes place and is consummated, and the Duke has a son or daughter by Elizabeth, he is to be obliged to hand over to the King [of France] the castles of Nice and Villefranche as security that, in case the Duke of Savoy or one of his children succeeds to the throne of England, the county of Nice and the port and town of Villefranche, with their dependencies, shall belong to the King, without his giving anything in Exchange. Pending the Duke's gaining possession of the Kingdom of England as heir to the said Elizabeth, or one of his children succeeding there, the Duke and his children are to enjoy the income of the county of Nice and Villefranche, but the castles are to remain in the hands of the King, who may put in them whatever troops he pleases. . . .'

IV

> Notes in the hand of Simon Renard, for a letter to Philip on the question of the English succession; taken from the *Calendar of State Papers, Spanish*, XIII, pp. 372–3, where it is dated March 1558. However, the references to Thomas Stafford seem to show that it was written before his execution on 28 May 1557. The true date is probably early May 1557. The original (in Latin) is in the Civic Archive at Besançon.

'The succession to the throne of England is a matter of such importance that your Majesty will certainly wish to examine the question in all its bearings, especially in view of the uncertainty and danger attending all developments in that country, on the assumption (which God forbid!) that the Queen will die without issue, in which case Elizabeth will be called to the throne in virtue of the will of Henry VIII, confirmed by parliament in spite of the taint of illegitimacy. Now Elizabeth was brought up in the doctrines of the new religion, she was formerly of the French faction, she hates the Queen and has many supporters who are suspect from the point of view of religion. If she succeeds and marries an Englishman, religion will be undermined, everything sacred profaned, Catholics ill treated, churchmen driven out, those monasteries which have been restored will again suffer, churches will be destroyed, affairs which had taken a favourable turn will once more be compromised. The heretics have no other intentions. Moreover the ancient amity, good neighbourliness and understanding that have so far been maintained, albeit with difficulty, between England and your Majesty's realms, will not only be impaired but disappear altogether. The French faction will prevail, and your majesty's interests will suffer so much, unless timely measures are taken, that no lasting good can be hoped for from this holy marriage [i.e. Philip and Mary], divine rather than human.

It must not be forgotten that all the plots and disorders that have troubled England during the past four years have aimed at placing its government in Elizabeth's hands sooner than the course of nature would permit, as witness the actions of Peter Carew, the Duke of Suffolk, Courtenay, Dudley, the Frenchman Bertheville, Stafford and others, in which affairs the French and Elizabeth were involved, not to mention Wyatt's rebellion. In spite of all this, Elizabeth is now honoured and recognised (as heiress to the Crown). Frequent communications reach and leave her, secretly, in regard to the succession. And I omit many other grave factors. What ought to be done in the circumstances is not easy to say, nor is it easy to debar her from the succession. If it were attempted to induce parliament to repeal the act by which Henry's will was confirmed, those who have espoused her cause would not consent. The religious factions would fight, Catholics against Protestants, with all the virulence customary among people of the same blood, to the prejudice of your Majesty's authority. If parliament were to repeal the act, it could as easily vote it over again, once the Queen had died, as happened when she mounted the throne, displaying the inconstancy natural to these islanders, among whom nothing is ever securely established. Besides repeal would altogether estrange Elizabeth's supporters from your Majesty, and prove a fresh source of conspiracy, and of alliance among your adversaries. The Queen is hardly safe as it is; and unless my information and judgement are at fault, the leading men of the realm are leagued together to prevent repeal. They know that some months ago the Queen thought of having Elizabeth declared a bastard by parliament and debarred from the succession. If that had been done the next of kin would have been the Queen of Scotland, and if she were ruled out as a foreigner, the wife of the Earl of Lennox or her children would come next, and then the daughters of the Duke of Suffolk. In none of these cases do I see the succession being firmly established. The realm would fall a prey to civil strife. And it is doubtful whether any of these persons would be more deserving of confidence than Elizabeth herself.

Both conscience and opportunity forbid the idea of throwing her into prison on suspicion, unless a further examination of Stafford supplies a reason for doing so.

Between these extremes, a middle course might be chosen, your majesty finding a husband for her abroad. Were she to marry an Englishman, all the evils above enumerated would result, both in religion and in politics; besides which it would be difficult to discover in the realm a man suitable for such preferment. One man only would appear to answer all requirements; and I doubt whether he desires this match. I leave the question to your Majesty's judgement. The Duke of Savoy is true to God and your Majesty. It seems possible that he might be attracted by the hope of the succession. Here it must be remembered that this hope would vanish if the Queen were to have issue, although all seem to be of the opinion that she will not, and that if Elizabeth were to wed a foreigner there might be a new conspiracy to induce parliament to repeal the act instituting her as heiress. Moreover, I hear that she and the leading men of the realm would refuse a foreign match. Latterly, it is true, the Queen and many nobles have not shared this view, as your Majesty knows.

In order to draw a conclusion from the foregoing, it would be desirable to know the Queen's own wishes, what she has discerned, whether she has spoken with the Privy Councillors about the question, and to marshal all the advantages and drawbacks. If a decision is reached on what should be done, it will remain to decide when to do it, making sure of the will of the kingdom and the Council, and that Elizabeth can be approached on the subject of matrimony with the Queen's assent, and if so how. . . .'

As far as can be discovered, Elizabeth made no move of any kind against her sister after her release from confinement in 1555. However, her name was constantly being invoked by malcontents, most notably those involved in the exile plot for a French-backed invasion, known as the Dudley conspiracy. Mary herself had notified her sister of this while the conspirators were being examined in the spring and early summer of 1556, which provoked the unctuous letter reproduced above. It is doubtful if the queen was much reassured. Simon Renard's extremely shrewd assessment of the situation errs only in supposing that Elizabeth had ever been particularly pro-French. She knew, as well as the imperialists, that the French candidate for the English succession was Mary Stuart.

Several potential marriages for Elizabeth were discussed, all aimed at neutralising her in the event of her succeeding. Mary had by this time discovered that no attempt to bar her via parliament would have been likely to prosper, and as failure would have been acutely damaging, she did not try. Reports that parliament had either barred her, or confirmed her right, were equally mistaken; there was no need to do the latter, as Renard realised. Elizabeth herself refused all offers of marriage, understanding perfectly well the motives behind them. The Duke of Savoy was Philip's preferred candidate, but reports that Mary had consented to this appear to have been mistaken. At this stage the queen seems to have disagreed with her husband, and opposed the match as being too honourable for a mere bastard. She continued to hope that her sister could be barred by some means (perhaps a papal pronouncement) until a few weeks before her death. By that time Philip recognised that Elizabeth could not be pressured, and had accepted the fact that she would succeed without any commitments. This he concealed from his wife during her last illness.

TWENTY

Plots and Conspiracies

I

Deposition by Henry Peckham, in the Tower, 18 March and 7 May 1556; taken from the *Calendar of State Papers, Domestic, Mary*, no. 423. Original, PRO SP11/18, no. 51.

'Deposition of Henry Peckham, of a conspiracy against the queen, and talk between him and Christopher Ashton, in Peckham's father's [Sir Edmund Peckham] house [at Blackfriars].

It was ordered that I, Henry, should have but £6 for 400 marks' lands. Being asked of Ashton why I was sad, I answered, for loss of my land. He bade me be of good cheer; if I would be sworn to him he would tell me news that would bring my land again ere long. I promised to keep his counsel, and he told me how Sir Anthony Kingston and a great many western gentlemen were in a confederacy to send the queen over to the king and make the Lady Elizabeth queen, and marry the Earl of Devon, and that the laws of the realm will bear it: Kingston has required me to hark to Henry VIII's will, for there is sufficient matter for our purpose. If you can, help me to it. I told him it was to be had in the rolls, in no case would he have it fetched out of there, but if I could get it by other means I should. [Said Ashton] Good, I will show you a token, and he took out of his purse a halfpenny, telling me the other half remains with Sir Anthony: Whenever I send this to Sir Anthony he will be ready with 10,000 men within three days; they shall cut off Lord Pembroke's power if he makes any resistance, and be in twenty days at the furthest in London. Then I trust to see good Sir Henry restored to your land and have 1,000 marks a year given you, and see your father made a duke, which he has well deserved, however ill he is now handled. Elizabeth is a goodly liberal dame, nothing so unthankful as her sister, and takes this liberality of her mother, who was one of the bountifullest women in all her time or since. Then shall men of good service and gentlemen be esteemed. He asked why I mused; I trust you will not betray him who has put his life into your hands. I told him, no. He said you have as little cause to mislike this as any, for you have served the unfaithfullest mistress on earth; she has given you 100 marks a year and taken from you 400. If you had done this service to her father or brother, or to our sweet Lady Elizabeth, you should have kept this land whoever had lost, and had twice as much more given you. I gave him my hand and bade him not mistrust. Said Ashton: I will tell you more. There will take our part the Earl of Westmorland, who will not come alone, and Lord Williams. I told him I thought that was not true, for he had served the queen well before, and by her was made lord. [Said Ashton]: Williams is a good fellow, and as unthankfully dealt with as you; he is fain to break up his house and lie at Beaconsfield, and must pay a great deal to the queen, which grieves him. He is sure on our side. Henry Dudley has spoken to all the gentlemen that are soldiers about this town [London] and they are all sure ours. We have left the queen never a man of war that is worth a button. Dudley came hither one night, purposing to win you. He was also determined, as the wife that keeps this house can tell, to ride to your house in the country. One of the special charges Dudley committed to me was to win you. Then Ashton told me how Dudley was gone into France, and Bedell with him, and he looked every day for Bedell's return, commending Bedell to be trusty, very secret, and with a wit able to beguile the best of them. Then Ashton took a rose penny and broke it, kept one half and gave me the other, and told me whenever he sent me that, that I should trust the bearer, who should bring me word how the world went. He told me I might trust Bedell without this token. Said Ashton, cousin Peckham, farewell. Deliver the will (if you can get it) to Bedell; then will he tell you news of Dudley. I trust it shall not be long ere you hear from me. If you cannot get the will make no ado, for I am sure Sir Anthony has got it.'

II

Extract from BL Harleian MS 537, printed in *The History and Antiquities of Hengrave*, by John Gage Rokewood (1822), p. 159.

'One Cleber, w[hi]ch sometyme kept a scoole at Dis in Norfolk, conspired w[i]th iii bretherne, whose names were Lyncolne. They pretended an insurrection, and woulde have gathered the people together, by pretence of a marriage, and eyther of the brethren promised to bring 100 horse, w[i]th men, to ye marriage pretended upon a Sondaye, in the forenoon, in somer time, in anno 1556. The sayd Cleber had a proclamation in redynes, and gave charge to a servant of his to give hys attendance, and to watch in a lane, nigh to the church, where they shoulde mete, and so soon as he dyd met any man on horseback riding in the same lane, to give thereof warnynge to his sayde m[aste]r, wyth all speede. Now yt chaunsed (by the wyll of God), yt certain men, rydinge through the lane, to some other place, about thyr busynes, came, about such hour as Cleber had appoynted, w[i]th his mates; upon sight of w[hi]ch men, hys sayde servant dyd returne to hys m[aste]r, w[i]th all speede, and told hym yt his frendes were come, and immediately, ye said Cleber stode up, in ye parishe church at Yaxsly, and did proclaim ye Ladye Elizabeth Quene, and her beloved bedfellow Lord Edward Courtenaye, Kinge, the w[hi]ch Lorde Courtenaye was, at that tyme, beyonde the sea, by the licence of her Majestie Lady Marye, the Quene of Englande. The said proclamation being ended by ye said trayter, he thought yt his mates woulde have bene w[i]th him in the churche to have defended his quarrel, but he, seeing yt his parte was so weake, seeing they were not come, beganne to flee, and a faithful subject, whose name was Scherman, pursued hym and toke hym at a towne called Eye, and was kept in prison untyl the next session at St. Edmundsbury, and his 3 mates were brought to him, and there they were altogether drawn, hanged and quartered.'

III

Extract from the proclamation of 30 April 1557, declaring the treason of Thomas Stafford and others; taken from Hughes and Larkin, *Tudor Royal Proclamations* (New Haven/London, 1969), II, no. 433.

'Whereas Thomas Stafford and others, malicious and evil disposed subjects his adherents, having conspired to perpetrate divers heinous treasons against the most royal persons of their majesties, and thereupon fearing to receive just punishment for his and their deserts, fled into the parts of beyond the seas and there remaining for a time, have, persisting in their said malice, devised and attempted divers times to stir seditions and rebellions within this realm to the great disturbance of the quietness, peace and tranquility thereof, by sending hither into the realm divers books, letters, and writings, both printed and written, farced and filled full of untruths and seditious and most false surmises of things said to be done and devised by the king our sovereign lord and his servants, which were never imagined nor thought; and to show their utter malice with more effect, the same Stafford did lately (with certain of his accomplices, unnatural Englishmen and some strangers) enter into this realm and by stealth took their majesties' castle of Scarborough in the county of York, and set out a shameful proclamation wherein he traiterously calleth nameth and affirmeth our said sovereign lady, the Queen's highness, to be unrightful and most unworthy queen, and that the king's majesty, our said sovereign lord, hath induced and brought into this realm the number of 12,000 strangers and Spaniards, and that into the said Spaniards' hands 12 [of] the strongest holds of this realm be delivered; in which proclamation also the said traitor Stafford did name and take himself to be protector and governor of this realm, by these most false and unnatural means minding to allure the good subjects of their majesties to withdraw their duty of allegiance from their said majesties and to adhere to him the said Stafford, to their confusion.

Albeit the said Stafford and other traitors his accomplices be (by the help of God and diligence of the Earl of Westmorland, and other noblemen and gentlemen, good subjects of those parts) repressed, apprehended and forthcoming to receive just punishment according to their deserts; and that it may be well thought that no wise nor honest man thinketh, or can justly gather any cause to think, that the king's majesty mindeth any other thing unto the queen's majesty and the realm but only to be careful and studious of all things tending to the benefit, surety, honour and defence of the same, and in this part most lovingly and daily bestoweth the great travail of his royal person, besides the large expenses of his goods and treasure. . . .'

There were a number of alarms in the last two years of Mary's reign, although none of them developed into a serious challenge. The most dangerous was that associated with Henry Dudley, a cousin of Lord Robert Dudley, later Earl of Leicester. His plan was for an invasion of southern England by a force of English exiles with French backing. That alone would not have posed much threat, but there was a related conspiracy involving a number of prominent West Country gentlemen, led by Sir Anthony Kingston of Gloucestershire, and it was in that part of the plot that Henry Peckham became involved. Peckham's father and brother were both members of Mary's council, and there was serious concern that many in high places were involved. That was probably not the case, but the full ramifications were never uncovered. French support was eventually withheld, and the conspirators formed another plot to remove £50,000 from the Exchequer, which came within an ace of success. The arrest, interrogation and trial of the conspirators occupied an immense amount of time between March and May 1556, and created an atmosphere of near panic at court. Eight conspirators were eventually executed (including Peckham); a few died (including Kingston) but most made good their escape abroad (including both Dudley and Ashton). By comparison, the adventure of Cleobury is trivial to the point of farce, but it also contributed both to the atmosphere of nervousness and to the suspicion with which Elizabeth was regarded. There is no evidence that she knew anything about either conspiracy, but both invoked her name.

Stafford, on the other hand, did not. Thomas Stafford was a younger son of Edward, Duke of Buckingham, who had been executed in 1521, and hence (to the latter's great embarrassment) a nephew of Cardinal Pole. His sense of grievance against the Tudors was not particularly focused on Mary, but the conspiratorial atmosphere of 1556–7 gave him an opportunity. He had been favourably received at the French court, but

Henry had withdrawn his support in January 1557, not wishing to incite hostilities. Stafford nevertheless managed to put together a small expedition which seized Scarborough castle in April 1557. The English council was warned in advance, and it seems likely that Stafford was used by a party in England who wanted to provoke war. His small force was quickly overpowered, and he and about two dozen of his followers were executed. War with France followed soon after.

TWENTY-ONE

War with France

I

Proclamation declaring war on France, 7 June 1557; taken from Hughes and Larkin, *Tudor Royal Proclamations* (New Haven/London, 1969), II, no. 434. Another version, in Spanish, remains in the archive at Simancas, and is recorded in the *Calendar of State Papers, Spanish*, XIII, pp. 293–4.

'Although we the Queen at our first coming to the crown were given to understand that the notable and heinous treason enterprised by the late Duke of Northumberland was supported and furthered by Henry the French king and his ministers by him put in trust, and that shortly after in the conspiracy moved against God and us by Wyatt and his traitorous band the said king's ministers did secretly practice and give their favourable comfort thereunto, contrary to the treaty of peace between both the realms, and all good amity and honour, yet the great love we bear to the peace of Christendom and to the quiet of our loving subjects moved us rather to impute to his ministers whom he used in service than unto himself, thinking ever by that our patience to have induced him to bear us true amity, and to use good neighbourhood towards us and our subjects; for the which respect we were not only contented to bear such injuries as to ourself had been by him done, but also travailed to be a mean of pacification between the Emperor and the said King, sending our ambassadors to Calais for that purpose to our great charge, as the world knoweth; which our travail and good zeal was not so well employed and taken of him as of us meant.

For not long after that time, when the devil had put in the heads of Dudley, Ashton and others their complices to enter into a new conspiracy against us, the said king's ambassador was not only privy thereof, but also received them into his house . . .

The like mind towards us he declared in receiving sundry famous and notorious pirates, enemies of Christendom and spoilers of our subjects, whom he maintained with men, money and ships, to exercise their piracy, and to declare that no patience or good demeanour of our part can move him to bear us good amity.

Of late he sent Stafford with other rebels whom he had entertained in that realm, furnished with armour, money, munition, and ships, to surprise our castle of Scarborough, not contented this long time to have borne with pirates and such as have robbed our merchants and other subjects by seas, and to have used dishonourable practices for the surprising of Calais, and our pieces on that side; the ministers whereof hath been openly known and the espials taken.

For the better maintaining of which ungodly doings and greater annoyance of our realm he hath continually suffered in his countries forgers of false moneys and counterfeiters of our coin; for the which causes, and also for that he hath with all hostility invaded the Low Countries to the defence and preservation whereof we are bound by special treaty; and considering that neither by demanding redress hereof we can obtain any, neither by good means which we have hitherto used enjoy any amity or good neighbourhood at his hand, neither by promise be assured of the same.

We have thought better to have him known and taken for an open enemy of whom we may beware than, under the pretence of amity, a secret worker against us and a privy enemy such as we have hitherto found him, to the great danger of our person, and loss and damage of our subjects. And therefore we give warning to all our loving subjects from henceforth to forbear all traffic and contracting with any of that realm, and to repute the said French King and his subjects as open enemies, annoying them by all such means as men may and are wont to do their enemies. . . .'

II

Letter from Thomas Martyn, secretary to the commissioners dealing with the Scots, to the queen, dated Carlisle, 11 June 1557; taken from the *Calendar of State Papers Relating to Scotland*, II, pp. 198–9.

'Please your highness to hear some private matters not contained in our general letters. After we and the Scottish commissioners had communed a good space at Sark water, and agreed of days of meeting &c, we talked apart with another of them. Seeing they were 'apalled' with this our new breech with France, we gave occasion of talk thus – my Lord of Westmorland said to the Earl of Cassillis, "my lord I thinke hit but foly for us to treate now togyther, we having broken with France, and ye beinge Frenche for youre lyves." "By the masse" quoth the Earl of Cassillis, "I am no more Frenche then ye are a Spanyard". "Mary", quoth my lord of Westmorland, "as long as God shall preserve my master and mystrys togyther, I am and shallbe a Spanyard to the uttermost of my powre." "By God", quoth the Earl of Cassillis, "so shall not I be Frenche, and I told ye ons yn my lord your fathers howse, yn Kynge Henry the viii his tyme, that we would dye every mothers sonne of us reither than be subiectes untill England. Even the lyke shall ye fynd us to kepe with Fraunce: and I may tell yowe there ar viiC Gascons arryved at Dunbryton mere than we wyll be knoen to yow of, wyche were sent to serve yn the borders heare, but we would not lette them passe the ryver, and they being alowyd but iiid a daye, have so scatered abrode, that iiiC of them be lycked up by the waye. Syk is the favour that owre men berythe unto the Frenche men heare!"

My lord of Durham [Cuthbert Tunstall] tells me the bishop of Orkney spoke to like effect, wishing in any wise, equal restitution on both parts to preserve amity, notwithstanding the French. Mr. Makehil told Mr. Henmar there was no cause to break with us on account of the French. "For", quoth he, "thEmperors warres with the French empeacheth not owre league and amytie with thEmperor."

Likewise Mr. Carnegy, hearing me avow with an express oath, your grace's sincere meaning for continuance of the league with Scotland, gave me his faith of a Christian, and honour of a Scottish knight, that his mistress meant the like. Mary to save his oath, he added, "As farre as we yet ken". And the Earl of Cassillis lastly said "Doe yowe my lordes, what yowre commissions directe ye to, and so wyll we." Now I find in their commission these words *Dedimus potestatem nostris commissariis audiendi, tractandi, concordandi, concludendi et finaliter dissidendi* [We give power to our commissioners to hear, negotiate, argue, conclude and finally dissolve]. Now if this is their meaning, and not the fault of the clerk penning, they may fall out with us notwithstanding the premises, by virtue of their commission, which is not *finaliter decidere*, but *finaliter dissidere*.

On the Earl of Cassillis pressing us to go to Dumfries, my lord of Westmorland told him plainly, they could not assure us, for they had 300 Frenchmen there. They promised to remove them before our coming. "If hit laye yn yowr powre", quoth my lord of Westmorland, "and how can ye assure us, seeing ye cannot assure yowr selfes of yowre owtlawes?" Even then we might see the Scottish outlaws bragg nigh the Scots with their "baufles" on their spears, and "Mathew Plumpe an owtlawe, took Cragyparill a Scote, yn all our sighte, and woonded another very sore, and kylled a Frenchman.""

III

Extracts from a report of events at St Quentin, sent to Philip, 11 August 1557, from the camp; taken from the *Calendar of State Papers, Spanish*, XIII, pp. 313–14. The original (in Spanish) is at Simancas.

'On Wednesday evening, the 4th August, the Duke of Savoy sent Count Mansfeld with his 1,000 horse, camp-master Navarrete with ten standards of Spanish infantry numbering as much as 800 men, and four standards of Germans from George Van Hol's regiment, to take up positions along the road leading from Ham to St. Quentin, in order to prevent any relief being thrown into St. Quentin. . . .

Two other regiments of Germans, with Count Schwarzenberg's thousand horse, were posted on the other side of the town in a very good position, so that the castle was masked, and the Duke was able to take the rest of his camp round to the other side so as to prevent the enemy from relieving the town, which they were trying to do with all their might.

The English were still delaying, and in order not to lose time his majesty ordered Alfonso de Caceres *tercio* to advance without waiting for him. . . .

In spite of all attempts to make them hurry, the English will not be here until tomorrow, Tuesday, 10th August, with the result that it has not been possible to put their battery in position. If this had been done, St. Quentin would have been hard pressed by now. The loss of six days is a serious matter.'

IV

Extract from a letter of Juan de Pinedo to Francisco de Vargas, 27 August 1557; taken from the *Calendar of State Papers, Spanish*, XIII, p. 317. The original (in Spanish) is at Simancas.

'The news are that between three and four this afternoon our troops fought their way into St. Quentin. Both sides fought most choicely, and the English best of all. I will give you further details by the earliest opportunity. For the moment there is no more to say, because blows are still being exchanged inside the town, although they say that the Admiral of France [Gaspar de Coligny] has already been taken prisoner. Our Lord will give Philip the victory, because he had behaved like a true Christian throughout.'

V

Extract from Grafton, *A Chronicle at Large* (1569, 1809 edn), pp. 557–8, describing the loss of Calais in January 1558.

'The Duke of Guise being Generall of the French Army proceeded in this enterprice with merveylous polecy. For approching the English frontier under colour to vittalyle Bulleyne and Arde, he entred the same upon a sodaine, and tooke a little Bulwarke at Sandgate by assaulte, and then devided hys armye into two partes, sendyng one parte with certaine peeces of great artillery along the Dounes by the sea side, towardes Rise Banke: & the other parte furnished also with battery peeces, marched strayte forth to Newnam Bridge: meaning to batter these two Fortris both at one tyme, which thing he did wyth such celerytie, that coming thether very late in the evening: he was maister of both by the next Morning, whereat the first shot discharged at Newnam Bridge, the head of the master Gunner of ye peece, whose name was Horsely, was cleane striken of. The Capitaine co[n]sidering the great power of the French army, & having his Fort but slenderly manned to make sufficient resistance, fled to Calice: And by ye time he was come thether: the other part of ye Fre[n]ch army that went by ye sea side with their battery had woone Rice Banke, being abandoned to their ha[n]ds. The next day the Frenchemen with five double Canones & thre Culverins began a battery from ye sande Hilles next Rice Banke, against ye towne of Calice & co[n]tinued the same by the space of two or three dayes untill they made a litle breache of the wall, next unto the Water Gate, which nevertheless was not yet assaultable, for that which was broken in the daye was by them within the towne made up again in the night stronger than afore. But the batterie was not begonne there by the French, for that they entended to enter in that place, but rather to abuse the Englishe to have the lesse regarde to the defence of the Castell, which was the weakest part of the towne, and the place where they were asserteyned by their espyalles to win an easie entrye. So that whyle our people travayled fondely to defende that counterfeyte breach of the towne wall: the Duke had in the meane season planted xv double Cannons against the Castell, which Castell being considered by the rulers of the towne to be of no such force as might resist the battery of the Cannon (by reason it was olde and without any rampiers) it was devised to make a trayne with certayne Barrels of powder to this purpose, that when the frenchmen should enter (as they well knewe that there they would) to have fyred the sayde trayne and blowne up the keepe, and for that purpose left never a man within to defend it. But the Frenchemen at their entry espyed the trayne and so avoyded the same, so that devise came to no purpose, and without any resistaunce they entred the Castell, and thought to have entred the towne by that waye: But by the prowes and hardy courage of syr Anthony Ager knight and Marshall of the towne with his souldiors they were repulsed and driven backe agayne into the Castell, and so hard followed after, that our men forced them to close and shut the Castell gate for their suretie, least it should have been recovered against them as it was once attempted by Sir Anthony Ager, who there with his sonne and heyre, and a Pursuivant at Armes called Calice with divers other to the number of xv or xvi Englishmen lost their lives.

The same night after the recule of the Frenchmen, whose number so encreased in the Castell that the towne was not able to resist their force. The Lorde Wentworth Deputie of Calice, sent a Pursuivant called Guynes unto the Duke of Guise requiring composition, which after long debate was agreed upon this sort. First that the towne with all the great artillary, victualles, and munition, should be freely yelden to the Frenche king, the lives of the inhabitaunts onely saved, to whome safeconduyte should be graunted to passe where they lysted, saving the Lord Deputie with fiftie such other as the Duke should appoint to remaine prisoners, and be put to their ransome.'

Although there was no shortage of pretexts for Mary to declare war on the French in 1557, the real reason for the breach was pressure from Philip. Henry's hostility to the Habsburg–Tudor link was inevitable, and although his support for English pirates and rebels was a constant irritant, it had done very little damage because it had never been carried through. Henry's indignant denial of any involvement with Stafford was probably justified. The Scots were not at all anxious to become involved, and used the regular meetings which took place on the borders for the adjustment of mutual grievances, to convey that message. The regent, Mary of Guise, did wish to support her countrymen, but her authority was shaky and there were no hostilities on the Anglo-Scottish border. Scottish politics were frequently unstable, and a major revolt among the Scottish lords was brewing, hence the opportunity given to the outlaws.

An expeditionary force under the Earl of Pembroke was sent across to Picardy at Philip's request (and at his expense) in July 1557. The Duke of Savoy was besieging St Quentin in early August, and the French sent an army to relieve the town. In the resulting battle, which both the English contingent and Philip missed because of logistical delays, the French were totally defeated. The town was taken by assault soon after, an engagement in which the English did take part.

Thereafter, the force did very little, and returned home in October. Believing the campaigning season to be over, and having very little enthusiasm for the war, the English council then economised by failing to reinforce the garrisons of the Calais Pale. The fortifications themselves had been neglected since 1552, and a surprise attack by the Duke of Guise in January 1558 was swiftly and dramatically successful. Philip had warned the English some weeks before of Guise's intention, but they had done nothing. When the attack came, he endeavoured to send in reinforcements, but was defeated by the speed of the French victory. He was therefore particularly chagrined to find himself being used as a scapegoat.

The small fortress of Guisnes held out after Calais had fallen, but a combination of widespread sickness in England and winter storms frustrated a relief mobilisation which had been left far too late anyway, and the whole Pale was lost. The English council endeavoured to blame 'heretics' in Calais for betraying the town, and accused Wentworth of treason, but the real reason for the loss was its own supine attitude. The English navy continued to be active thereafter, with mixed success, but the war was generally unpopular in England from the beginning, and even more so after the loss of Calais.

TWENTY-TWO

The Death of Queen Mary

I

Extract from John Foxe, *The Ecclesiasticall History* (2nd edn of the *Actes and Monuments*, 1570), II, p. 2296.

'Now then after these so great afflictions falling upon this realm from the first beginning of Queen MARYS reign, wherein so many men, women and children were burned; many imprisoned, and in prisons starved, divers exiled, some spoiled of their goods and possessions, a great number driven from house and home, so many weeping eyes, so many sobbing hearts, so many children made fatherless, so many fathers bereft of the wives and children, so many vexed in conscience, and divers against conscience constrained to recant, and, in conclusion, never a good man in all the realm but suffered something during all the time of this bloody persecution. After all this, I say, now we are come at length, the LORD be praised! to the 17th day of November, which day, as it brought to the persecuted members of CHRIST rest from their careful mourning, so it easeth me somewhat likewise of my laborious writing; by the death, I mean, of Queen MARY. Who, being long sick before, upon the said 17th day of November, 1558, about three or four a clock in the morning, yielded her life to nature, and her kingdom to Queen ELIZABETH, her sister.

As touching the manner of whose death, some say that she died of a tympany [dropsy, i.e. cancer]; some, by her much sighing before her death, supposed she died of thought and sorrow. Whereupon her council, seeing her sighing, and desirous to know the cause, to the end that they might minister the more ready consolation unto her, feared, as they said, that "She took that thought for the Kings Majesty her husband, which was gone from her".

To whom she answering again, "Indeed", said she, "that may be one cause; but that is not the greatest wound that pierceth my oppressed mind!" but what that was she would not express to them. Albeit, afterwards, she opened the matter more plainly to Master RYSE and Mistress CLARENCIUS (if it be true that they told me, which had it of Master RYSE himself); who (then being most familiar with her, and most bold about her) told her that "They feared she took thought for King PHILIPS departing from her".

"Not that only", said she, "but when I am dead and opened; you shall find Calais lying at my heart", &c.

And here an end of Queen MARY and her persecution. Of which Queen, this truly may be affirmed, and left in story for a perpetual Memorial or Epitaph for all Kings and Queens that shall succeed her, to be noted, that before her never was read in any story of any King or Queen in England, since the time of King LUCIUS, under whom, in time of peace, by hanging, heading, burning and prisoning, so much Christian blood, so many Englishmens lives were spilled within this realm, as under the said Queen MARY, for the space of four years, was to be seen; and I beseech the LORD may never be seen hereafter.'

II

Extracts from Mary's will, printed as app. 3 to David Loades, *Mary Tudor: a Life* (Oxford, 1989), from a transcript in BL Harleian MS 6949. The original does not survive.

'[30 March 1558] In the name of God, Amen. I Marye by the Grace of God Quene of Englond, Spayne, France, both Sicelles, Jerusalem and Ireland, Defender of the Faythe, Archduchesse of Austriche, Duchesse of Burgundy, Millayne and Brabant, Countesse of Habsburg, Flanders and Tyroll, and lawful wife to the most noble and virtuous Prince Phillippe, by the same Grace of God Kynge of the said Realms and Domynions of England, &c. Thinking myself to be with child in lawful marriage between my said dearly beloved husband and Lord, altho' I be at this present (thankes be unto Almighty God) otherwise in good helthe, yet forseeing the great danger which by Godd's ordynance remaine to all whomen in ther travel of children, have thought good, both for the discharge of my conscience and continewance of good order within my Realmes and domynions to declare my last will and testament. . . .

Fyrste I do commend my Soulle to the mercye of Almighty God the maker and Redeemer thereof, and to the good prayers and helpe of the most puer and blessed Virgin our Lady St. Mary, and of all the Holy Companye of Heven. . . . And further I will that the body of the vertuous Lady and my most dere and well-beloved mother of happy memory, Quene Kateryn, whych lyeth now buried at Peterborowh, shall within as short tyme as conveniently yt may be after my burial, be removed brought and layde nye the place of my sepulture. . . .

And as towchyng the dispocyon of this my Imperiall Crowne of englande and Ireland, and my title to france, and all the dependances of the same, wherof by the mere provydence of Almighty God I am the Inheritor and Quene: my will, mynde and entent ys, that the s[ai]d Imperiall Crowne of england and Ireland, and my Title to France, and all the dependances, and all other my Honours, Castells, fortresses, mannours, londs tenements, prerogatyves and heriditaments whatsover, shall wholly and entirely descend remayne & be unto the heyres, issewe, and frewte of my bodye, according to the lawes of this Realme. Nevertheless, the order Government and Rewle of my said issewe, and of my said Imperiall Crowne, and the dependances thereof, during the Minoryte of my said heyre and Issewe, I specyally recommend unto my said most Dere and well-beloved Husband, accordynge to the laws of this my said Realme for the same provided. . . .

And I do humbly beseeche my saide most deerest lorde and husbande to accepte of my bequeste, and to kepe for a memory of me one jewell, being a table dyamond which themperours Majesty, his and my most honourable Father, sent unto me by the Cont degment [Count of Egmont], at the insurance of my sayde lorde and husbande, and also one other table dyamonde whiche his Majesty sent unto me by the marques de les Naves, and the Coler of golde set with nyne dyamonds, the whiche his Majestye gave me the Epiphanie after our Maryage, also the rubie now sett in a Golde ryng which his Highnesse sent me by the Cont of Feria, all which things I require his Majestye to dispose at his pleasure, and if his Highnesse thynke mete, to the Issue betwene us. . . .

[Codicil of 28 October 1558] . . . Forasmuch as God hath hitherto sent me no frewte nor heire of my bodie, yt ys only in his most devyne providence whether I shall have onny or noo, Therefore both for the discharge of my conscyence and dewtie towards God and this Realme, and for the better satisfaction of all good people, and to thentent my said last will and Testament (the which I trust is agreeable to God's law and to the laws of this Realme) may be dewly performed, and my dettes (pryncipally those I owe to many of my good subjects, and the which they most lovyngly lent unto me) trewly and justly answered payed, I have thought it good, fealynge myself presently sicke and week in bodye (and yet of hole and perfytt remembrance, our Lord be thanked) to adde this unto my said testament and last will, viz. Yf yt shall please Almighty God to call me to his mercye owte of this transytory lyfe without issewe and heire of my bodye lawfully begotten, Then I most instantly desire et per viscera misericordiae Dei, requyre my next heire & Successour, by the Lawes and Statutes of this Realme . . . to permytt and suffer thexecutors of my said Testament and last will and the Survivours of them to perform the same. . . .'

Mary's death was poignant in many ways. Even John Foxe (whose rejoicing was more widely shared later than it was at the time) was aware of her sadness and isolation. Philip's absence was not mere callousness or indifference. He had no desire to become involved in a power struggle in England, and was quite happy to accept Elizabeth's succession without wishing to be on the spot to endorse it. He had never returned Mary's affection, and her death relieved him of the serious embarrassment of a barren wife. Saddest of all is the queen's refusal to accept her own childlessness. There was not the slightest chance that she could have been pregnant in March 1558, but nobody had the courage (or perhaps the heart) to tell her so. The codicil reflected ultimate defeat. Elizabeth is not mentioned by name, and Mary's successor returned the slight, not only by reversing most of her sister's policies, but by ignoring her last will and testament, the provisions of which were never fulfilled.

Mary died with her fortunes at a low ebb in other ways. The war was petering out, but the disastrous harvests of 1555 and 1556 had left a legacy of malnutrition, which in turn had brought on the influenza epidemic of 1557–8 – the most serious demographic setback of the century. Mary herself may have been a victim, and Cardinal Pole (who died the same day) certainly was. John Foxe's declaration that England was under Divine judgement for murdering the saints of God, thereby acquired a resonance it might otherwise have lacked.

PART II

Queen Elizabeth

TWENTY-THREE

The Accession of a New Queen

I

Extracts from the Count of Feria's despatch to Philip II, 14 November 1558; eds M-J. Rodriguez Salgado and Simon Adams, in the *Camden Miscellany*, 28 (1984), pp. 328–37. The original (in Spanish) is in the archive at Simancas.

'I arrived here on Wednesday, the ninth of this month, at lunchtime and found the queen our lady's health to be just as Dr. Nunez describes in his letter to your Majesty. There is, therefore, no hope of her life. . . .
. . . These councillors are extremely frightened of what Madame Elizabeth will do with them. They have received me well, but somewhat as they would receive a man who came with bulls from a dead pope. The day after I arrived, I went to a house belonging to a gentleman some twenty three miles from here, where Madame Elizabeth is staying. I arrived there some time before she might wish to dine, and she received me well, although not as joyfully as she did the last time. She asked me to dine with her and the wife of Admiral Clinton who was there when I arrived was also invited. During the meal we laughed and enjoyed ourselves a great deal. . . .
I made it very clear to her that your majesty was determined not to conclude peace with the French unless they also composed their differences with this kingdom and that I had informed the English commissioners to negotiate as best they could, because your majesty would defer the conclusion of peace until they had come to an agreement. She was very pleased to hear this and in turn made it very clear that she would have them beheaded if they made peace without Calais.
She told me that your Majesty had tried very hard to persuade the queen to arrange a marriage for her with the duke of Savoy, and she smiled at the thought of it. I told her that all your Majesty had tried to do was to persuade the queen to accept her as her sister and successor, and as far as marriage was concerned, your Majesty had never dreamt of concluding anything without her consent. Following this she commented that the queen had lost the affection of the people of the realm because she had married a foreigner. I replied in rather a luke warm fashion that on the contrary your Majesty had been well loved. However, I did not wish to continue discusing this particular issue. . . .

. . . I have been told (although not directly by her, as was the case with those whom I have already mentioned) of certain others with whom she is on very good terms. They are: the earl of Bedford, Lord Robert [Dudley], [Sir Nicholas] Throgmorton (one who went everywhere with the aforesaid earl during the last war), Peter Carew, and [John] Harrington (the man behind King Edward's uncle – the Admiral who was later beheaded – he is reputed to be able and devilish). I have been told for certain that Cecil, who was King Edward's Secretary, will also be secretary to Madame Elizabeth. He is said to be an able and virtuous man, but a heretic. . . .

Until now they [the council] knew that they had to negotiate with your majesty, now they realise that your majesty must negotiate with them. As far as I can judge from what I have seen, the situation could not be worse for your majesty. Four years ago your majesty could have disposed of Madame Elizabeth by marrying her off to someone of your own choosing. Now she will marry whomsoever she desires and your majesty has no power to influence her decision without initiating a new set of negotiations and once more buying the co-operation of all these councillors; because they will sell themselves to the highest bidder. Besides Madame Elizabeth already sees herself as the next queen and having come to the conclusion that she would have succeeded even if your majesty and the queen had opposed it, she does not feel indebted to your majesty in this matter. It is impossible to persuade her otherwise than that the kingdom will not consent to anything else and would take up arms on her behalf. . . .'

II

Proclamation announcing the accession, 17 November 1558; taken from Hughes and Larkin, *Tudor Royal Proclamations* (New Haven/London, 1969), II, no. 448.

'Elizabeth by the grace of God Queen of England, France, and Ireland, defender of the faith, etc. Because it hath pleased Almighty God by calling to his mercy out of this mortal life, to our great grief, our dearest sister of noble memory, Mary, late Queen of England, France and Ireland (whose soul God have), to dispose and bestow upon us as the only right heir by blood and lawful succession the crown of the aforesaid kingdoms of England, France and Ireland, with all manner titles and rights thereunto in anywise appertaining.

We do publish and give knowledge by this our proclamation to all manner people being natural subjects of every the said kingdoms, that from the beginning of the 17th day of this month of November, at which time our said dearest sister departed from this mortal life, they be discharged of all bonds and duties of subjection towards our said sister, and be from the same time in nature and law bound only to us as to their only sovereign lady and Queen: wherewith we do by this our proclamation straightly charge and ally them to us, promising on our part no less love and care towards their preservation than hath been in any of our progenitors, and not doubting on their part but they will observe the duty which belongeth to natural, good, and true loving subjects.

And further we straightly charge and command all manner our said subjects of every degree, to keep themselves in our peace, and not to attempt upon any pretense the breach, alteration, or change of any order or usage presently established within this our realm; upon pain of our indignation and the perils and punishment which thereto in anywise may belong.'

III

Queen Elizabeth's first recorded speech, at Hatfield, 20 November 1558; taken from Marcus et al. *Elizabeth I: Collected Works* (Chicago, 2000), pp. 51–2. The original is PRO SP12/1/7.

'Queen Elizabeth's speech to her secretary and other her lords before her coronation.

Words spoken by her majesty to Mr. Cecil:

I give you this charge, that you shall be of my Privy Council and content yourself to take pains for me and my realm. This judgement I have of you: that you will not be corrupted with any manner of gift, and that you will be faithful to the state, and that without respect of my private will, you will give me that counsel that you think best, and if you shall know anything necessary to be declared to me of secrecy, you shall show it to myself only. And assure yourself I will not fail to keep taciturnity therein, and therefore herewith I charge you.

Words spoken by the queen to the lords:

My lords, the law of nature moveth me to sorrow for my sister; the burden that is fallen upon me maketh me amazed; and yet considering I am God's creature, ordained to obey His appointment, I will thereunto yield, desiring from the bottom of my heart that I may have assistance of His grace to be the minister of His heavenly will in this office now committed to me. And as I am but one body naturally considered, though by His permission a body politic to govern, so I shall desire you all, my lords (chiefly you of the nobility, everyone in his degree and power), to be assistant to me, that I with my ruling and you with your service, may make a good account to Almighty God, and leave some comfort to our posterity in earth. I mean to direct all my actions by good advice and counsel. And therefore, considering that divers of you be of the ancient nobility, having your beginnings and estates of my progenitors, kings of this realm, and thereby ought in honour to have the more natural care for the maintaining of my estate and this commonwealth; some others have been of long experience in governance, and enabled by my father of noble memory, my brother, and my late sister to bear office; the rest of you being upon special trust lately called to her service only and trust, for your service considered and rewarded; my meaning is to require of you all nothing more but faithful hearts in such service as from time to time shall be in your powers towards the preservation of me and this commonwealth. And for counsel and advice I shall accept you of my nobility, and such others of you the rest as in consultation I shall think meet and shortly appoint, to the which also, with their advice, I will join to their aid, and for ease of their burden, others meet for my service. And they which I shall not appoint, let them not think the same for any disability in them, but for that I do consider a multitude doth make rather discord and confusion than good counsel. And of my goodwill you shall not doubt, using yourselves as appertaineth to good and loving subjects.'

IV

Extracts from Richard Mulcaster, *The Passage of our Most Dread Sovereign Lady, Queen Elizabeth, Through the City of London to Westminster, the Day before her Coronation* (1559); taken from A.F. Pollard, *Tudor Tracts, 1532–1588* (London, 1903), pp. 367–400.

'Upon Saturday, which was the 14th day of january in the year of our Lord God 1558 [1559], about two of the clock in the afternoon, the most noble and Christian Princess, our most dread Sovereign Lady, Elizabeth, by the grace of GOD, Queen of England France and Ireland, defender of the faith, &c., marched from the Tower to pass through the City of London, towards Westminster: richly furnished and most honourably accompanied, as well with Gentlemen, Barons and other of the Nobility of this realm, as also with a noble train of goodly and beautiful Ladies, richly appointed.

And entering the City, was of the people received marvellous entirely, as appeared by the assembly's prayers, wishes, welcomings, cries, tender words, and all other signs: which argue a wonderful earnest love towards their sovereign. And on the other side, Her Grace, by holding up her hands, and merry countenance to such as stood afar off, and most tender and gentle language to those that stood nigh to her Grace, did declare herself no less thankfully to receive her people's goodwill, than they lovingly offered it to her.

To all that wished her Grace well she gave "Hearty thanks!", and to such as bade "GOD save Her Grace!" she said again "GOD save them all!" and thanked with all her heart. So that on either side there was nothing but gladness! nothing but prayer! nothing but comfort!

. . . Near unto Fanchurch, was erected a scaffold richly furnished; whereon stood a noise of instruments; and a child, in costly apparel, which was appointed to welcome the Queen's Majesty, in the whole City's behalf.

Against which place, when her Grace came, of her own will she commanded the chariot to be stayed; and that the noise might be appeased until the child had uttered his welcoming oration, which he spake in English metre, as here followeth:

> O peerless Sovereign Queen! Behold what this thy town
> Hath thee presented with, at thy first entrance here . . .
> Welcome to joyous tongues, and hearts that will not shrink!
> "GOD thee preserve!" we pray; and wish thee ever well!

At which words of the last line, the people gave a great shout; wishing, with one assent, as the child had said. And the Queen's Majesty thanked them most heartily, both the City for this her gentle receiving at the first, and also the people for confirming the same. . . .

This pageant, standing at the nether end of Cornhill, was extended from one side of the street to another. . . . And in a comely wreath, artificially and well devised, with perfect sight and understanding to the people, in the front of the said pageant, was written the name and title thereof which is

THE SEAT OF WORTHY GOVERNANCE

Which seat was made in such artificial manner, as to the appearance of the lookers on, the forepart seemed to have no stay; and therefore of force, was stayed by lively personages. Which personages were in number four, standing and staying the forefront of the same Seat royal, each having his face to the Queen and the people; whereof every one had a table to express their effects. Which were Virtues, namely PURE RELIGION, LOVE OF SUBJECTS, WISDOM and JUSTICE. Which did tread their contrary vices under their feet: that is to wit PURE RELIGION did tread upon IGNORANCE and SUPERSTITION, LOVE OF SUBJECTS did tread upon REBELLION and INSOLENCY, WISDOM did tread upon FOLLY and VAINGLORY, JUSTICE did tread upon ADULATION and BRIBERY. . . .

Soon after that her Grace passed the Cross [in Cheapside], she had espied the pageant erected at the Little Conduit in Cheap; and incontinent required to know what it might signify. And it was told her Grace that there was placed TIME.

"TIME", quoth she, "and time hath brought me hither!" And so forth the whole matter was opened to her Grace as hereafter shall be declared in the description of the pageant. But when in the opening, her Grace understood that the BIBLE in English should be delivered to her by TRUTH (which was herein represented by a child) she thanked the City for that gift, and said that she would oftentimes read over that book. . . .

. . . And in the aforesaid Seat or Chair was a seemly and meet personage, richly apparelled in parliament robes, with a sceptre in her hand, as a queen; crowned with an open crown, whose name and title were in a table fixed over her head in this sort; *DEBORAH, the Judge and Restorer of Israel*. Judic. 4. And the other degrees on either side were furnished with six personages; two representing the Nobility, two the Clergy, and two the Comminalty. And before these personages was written in a table

DEBORAH, WITH HER ESTATES, CONSULTING FOR THE GOOD GOVERNMENT OF ISRAEL

At the feet of these, and the lowest part of the pageant, was ordained a convenient room for a child to open the meaning of the pageant. When the Queens Majesty drew near unto this pageant; and perceived, as in the others, the child ready to speak; Her Grace required silence, and commanded her chariot to be removed nigher that she might plainly hear the child speak; which said as hereafter followeth:

> Jabin, of Canaan king, had long by force of arms,
> Oppressed the Israelites; which for GOD'S People went;
> But GOD minding at last for to redress their harms;
> The worthy DEBORAH as Judge among them sent. . . .

In Cheapside, Her Grace smiled; and being thereof demanded the cause, answered "For that she heard one say 'Remember old king Henry VIII!'" A natural child! which at the very remembrance of her father's name took so great a joy; that all men may well think that as she rejoiced at his name whom the realm doth hold of such worthy memory, so, in her doings, she will resemble the same.'

Elizabeth's accession was unchallenged, largely because at the last moment her sister had reluctantly recognised her right. Philip had realised the strength of her position some time before, and nothing in Feria's despatch of 9 November would have come as any surprise to him. Elizabeth knew perfectly well that his friendship was self-interested, because he understood the threat posed by Mary of Scotland, and was not disposed to feign a gratitude which she did not feel. In fact, while Feria was writing, Elizabeth's affinity was secretly mobilising, not because she feared any challenge from Philip, but in case Mary should change her mind. That she professed to trust in 'the people' was perfectly genuine – but then Mary could have said the same thing five years before.

What is clear from all these early accounts is that Elizabeth was acting a part from the very beginning. Her calculated remarks to Feria about the way in which Mary had lost her subjects' affection; her studied responses to the pageants provided for her entry into London, particularly her reaction to the mention of Henry VIII; and the gift of an English bible, were all parts of an image which was being carefully constructed. All those pageants would have been approved in advance by the Revels Office, and the queen's responses were much less spontaneous than they were made to appear. Moreover the accounts themselves were officially sponsored, and Mulcaster was virtually an official propagandist. There is no reason to suppose that the pageants were not genuine expressions of London expectations; Mary's relations with the city had been bad for a number of reasons. However, their unanimity is suspicious, as are the broad hints which they offer of the desire to return to a Protestant Church.

Her speeches were similarly motivated. If they were ever actually made, and not fabricated later by her 'spin doctors', they were clearly intended for public consumption. Most particularly, her alleged words to Cecil appear so prophetic, and are now so much a part of her myth, that they arouse instinctive suspicion. Elizabeth managed every move and gesture of her first few weeks in power, to present the image of a queen who was 'mere English', at one with her people and dedicated to restoring her country's pride and independence. The reality, that many of her subjects were wondering if the realm could stand another female ruler, or where they could look for support in the dangerous world of 1558, was never publicly admitted; and her eventual success has meant that the official view of this early period is now almost unchallenged.

TWENTY-FOUR

The Settlement of Religion

I

Extract from Raphael Holinshed, *Chronicle* (1807 edn), IV, p. 179.

'Manie that for feare of persecution in Queen Maries daies were fled the realm and lived in voluntarie exile, now that all persecution ceased by the gratious clemency of this noble princesse queene Elizabeth, they returned with all convenient speed home to their native countrie, giving to Almightie God most humble thanks for that his mercifull deliverance, in sending them a governor, that not onlie permitted libertie of conscience, but also was readie to advance religion, and free exercise of common praier, preaching and administration of the sacraments, according to the right institution of the primitive churches. Fridaie the seaventeenth of Februarie, one of maister Hunnings servants (that was also one of the takers of fresh fish for the provision of the queenes house) was set on the pillorie in Cheapside, in the fish market over against the Kings head, having a bawdricke of smelts hanging about his necke, with a paper on his forehead written: For beieng smelts for twelve pence the hundred [weight] and selling them again for ten pence the quarter. He stood so likewise on the eighteenth and twentieth daie of the same moneth, everie one of those three daies from nine of the clocke until twelve. The last daie he should have had one of his eares slit, if by great sute made to the councell by the Lord Maior of London, he had not been pardoned and released out of prison. This penance was assigned to him by the queenes owne appointment, when to hir grace his trespasse was revealed. Whereby she gave a tast to the people of a zealous mind to have justice dulie ministered, and faultes accordinglie punished, namelie of those which under pretence of hir graces authoritie should go about to wrong and oppresse her loving subiectes.

This yeere in the Easter holidaies on the mondaie preached at the Spittle doctor Bill, on the tuesdaie doctor Cox and on the wednedaie doctor Horne: the first was hir majesties chaplaine, the other two had remained at Geneva, and in other places beyond the seas all Queene Maries time. On low sundaie maister Samson made the rehersal sermon: but when the Lord maior and aldermen came to their places in Pauls churchyard the pulpitt doore was locked, and the keie could not be heard of. Whereupon the lord maior sent for a smith to open the locke, which was doone, and when the preacher should enter the place, it was found very filthie and uncleanlie. Moreover the verger that had the custodie of the keie, which opened the doore of the place where the prelats and others use to stand at the sermon time, would not open the doore; but the gentlemen with a form broke it open, and so came in to heare the sermon. This disorder chanced by reason that since Christmas last past there was not a sermon preached at Paules Crosse by meanes of an inhibition sent down from the councell to the bishop of London, that he should admit no preacher, because of the controversie betwixt the bishops and other of the clergie that were nowe returned into the realm from the partes of beyond the sea.'

II

Extracts from Archbishop Heath's speech in the House of Lords on the Act of Supremacy, 18 March 1559; taken from *Proceedings in the Parliaments of Elizabeth I*, ed. T.E. Hartley (London, 1983), pp. 12–17. The original is in Corpus Christi College, Cambridge, MS 121, pp. 137B–Cv.

'My lordes all, with humble submission of my whole talke unto your wisdomes I propose to speake to the bodye of this acte as touchinge the supremacie; and that the doinges of this honorable assemble maye therin be always founde honorable, two thinges are right necessarie of your wisdomes to be considered. First, when by the vertue of this acte of supremacye we muste forsake and flee from the sea of Rome, it wold be considered of your wisdomes what matter lyeth therin, as what matter of weight, or force, what matter of daunger or inconvenience, or els whether there be none at all. Second, when th'intent of this act is to geve unto the Queene's Highnes a supremacie it wold be considered of your wisdoms what this supremacie is, and whether it dothe consiste in spirituall government or temporall; if in temporall, what further authoritye can this House geve unto her Highnes than she hathe alredy by right and inheritance – and not by our gifte but by thappoyntment of God – she being our sovereigne Lord and Ladye, our King and Queen, our Emperor and Empresse, other kinges and princes of duetie ought to paye tribute unto her, she being free from them all. If yow will say this supremacie doth consiste in spirituall government, then it wold be considered what this spirituall government is, and in what poyntes it dothe chiefly remayne; which being first agree upon, it wold further be considered of your wisdomes whether this House may graunt them unto her Highnes or not. And by the thoroughe examynacion of all these partes your honours shall proceede in this matter groundlye upon throughe knowledge, and not be deceyved by ignorance. . . .

As whether in spirituall government or in temporal; yf in spirituall, like as these wordes of th'acte do importe, *scilicet*, "suprem head of the

Churche of Inglond nexte and immediately under God", then it wold be considered of your wisdoms in what poyntes this spirituall government dothe consiste; and the poyntes being well knowne it wold be considered whether this House have authority to graunt them, and hcr Highnes abilytie to receave the same. And as touching the poyntes wherin spirituall government dothe consiste, I have in reading the gospell observed these iiii emonge manye, wherof the firste is to lose and bynd, when our Saviuor Christe in ordeyninge Peter to be the chief governor of his Churche sayde unto him, "*Tibi dabo claves regni celorum, quodcunque ligaveris super terram, erit ligatum et in celis, et quodcunque solveris, erit solutum et in celis.*" ["I give to you the keys of the kingdom of hcaven, and whatsoever you shall bind on earth shall be bound in heaven; and whatsoever you shall loose, shall be loosed in heaven."] Now it wolde be considered of your wisdomes whether ye have sufficient authoritye to graunt unto her Highnes this first poynt of spirituall government and to say to her, "*Tibi dabimus claves regni coelorum.*" If you do saye "Yea", then we do require the sight of the warrant and commission by the vertue of Gods worde; and if you say "No", then you maye be well assured and persuade yourselfes ye have insufficient authority to make her Highnes suprem head of the Churche heare in this realme. . . .

Thus muche have I heare said, right honoorable and my verie good lordes, agaynst this acte of supremacie for the discharge of my conscience, and for the love, dread and feare that I chieflie owe unto God, and my sovereigne ladie the Queen's Highnes, and unto your lordships all; when otherwise and without mature consideracion of all these premisses your honors shalbe never able to shewe your faces before your enemyes in this matter, beinge so raishe an example and spectacle in Christe's Churche as in this realme onelie to be found, and in none other. Thus humblie beseechinge your good honors to take in good parte this rude and playne speache that I have heare used of muche good zeale and will I shall nowe leave to trouble your honors anye longer.'

III

Extracts from Holinshed's description of the Westminster debate of March 1559; *Chronicle* (1807 edn), p. 180.

'The last of March, the parlement yet continuing, was a conference begun at Westminster concerning certeine articles of religion betwixt the bishops and other of the clergie of the one part, and certeine learned preachers of whom some had been in dignitie in the Church of England before that time of the other part. . . . The queenes most excellent maiestie, having heard of diversitie of opinions in certeine matters of religion amongst sundrie of her loving subiectes, and being verie desirous to have the same reduced to some Godlie and Christian concord thought it best by the advice of the Lords, and other of her privie councill, as well for the satisfaction of persons doubtfull as also for the knowledge of the verie truth in certeine matters of difference, to have a convenient chosen number of the best learned of either part, and to confer together their opinions and reasons, and thereby to come to some good and charitable agreement.

And hereupon by hir maiesties commandement certeine of her privie councell declared this purpose to the archbishop of Yorke (being also one of the same privie councell) [Nicholas Heath] and required him that he would impart the same to some of the bishops and to make choise of eight, nine or ten of them; and that there shoulde a like number be named of the other part. . . .

It was hereupon fullie resolved by the queenes maiestie, with the advice aforesaid, that according to their desire, it should be in writing on both parts, for avoiding of much altercation in words; and that the said bishops should, bicause they were in authoritie and degree superiors, first declare their minds and opinions in the matter. . . . And so each of them should deliver their writings to the other. . . . And this was fullie agreed upon with the archbishop of Yorke and also signified to both parties. And immediatlie hereupon devers of the nobilitie and states of the realme, understanding that such a meeting and conference should be, and that in certeine matters, whereupon (the court of parlement consequentlie following) some lawes might be grounded; they made earnest meanes to hir maiestie, that the parties of this conference might put and read their assertions in the English tongue, and that in the presence of them of the nobilitie, and others of the parlement house, for the better satisfaction and enabling of their owne iudgementes, to treat and conclude of such lawes as might depend hereupon.

. . . And nothwithstanding the former order appointed, and consented unto by both partes, yet the bishop of Winchester and his colleagues, alleging that they had mistaken that their assertions and reasons should be written, and so onlie recited out of the booke, said their booke was not readie then written; but they were provided to argue and dispute, and therefore would for that time repeat in speech that which they had to saie unto the first proposition. This variation from the order, and specialie from that which themselves had by the said archbishop in writing before required, adding thereunto the reason of the apostle, that to contend with words is profitable to nothing, but to the subversion of the hearer, seemed unto the queenes maiesties councell somewhat strange; and yet it was permitted without any great reprehension. . . .

And the same being ended with some liklihood, as it seemed, that the same was much allowable to the audience; certeine of the bishops began to saie contrarie to their former answer, that they had now much more to saie to this matter. Wherein although they might have bene well reprehended for such maner of cavillation, yet for avoiding of all mistaking of orders in this colloquie or conference, and for that they should utter all that they had to saie, it was both ordered, and thus openlie agreed upon both partes in the full audience, that upon the mondaie following, the bishops should bring their minds and reasons in writing to the second assertion, and the last also if they could, and first read the same, and that done the other part should bring theirs likewise to the same. And being read each of them should deliver to other the same writings. . . . Thus both partes assented thereto, and the assemble quietlie dismissed. And therefore upon mondaie the like assemblie began againe at the place and houre appointed; and there (upon what sinister or disordered meaning is not yet fullie known, though in some part it be understanded) the bishop of Winchester and his colleagues, and especiallie Lincolne [Thomas Watson], refused to exhibit or read, according to the former notorious order on fridaie, that which they had prepared for the second assertion. And thereupon by the Lord Keeper of the Great Seal [Sir Nicholas Bacon] they first being gentlie and favourablie required to keep the order appointed; and that taking no place, being secondlie as it behooved, pressed with more earnest request; they neither regarding the authoritie of that place, nor their own reputation, nor the credit of the cause, utterlie refused that to doo. And finallie being againe particularlie everie of them apart, distinctlie by name required to understand their opinions therein, they all saving one (which was the abbot of Westminster [John Feckenham] having more consideration of order and his dutie of obedience than the others) utterlie and plainlie denied to have their booke read, some of them more earnestlie than others, and some other more undiscreetlie and unreventlie then others.

. . . And afterwards for the contempt so notoriouslie made, the bishops of Winchester and Lincolne, having most obstinatlie both disobeid common authoritie, and varied manifestlie from their own order, and speciallie Lincolne (who shewed more follie then the other) were condignlie committed to the tower of London. . . .

The names of such as had conference in the propositions aforesaid.

The Bp. of Winchester [John White]
The bishop of Lincolne
The bishop of Chester [Cuthbert Scott]
The bishop of Carliell [Owen Oglethorpe]
The bishop of Lichfield [Ralph Baynes]
Doctor [Henry] Cole
Doctor [Nicholas] Harpesfield
Doctor [Alban] Langdall
Doctor [John] Chedsie

Dr. [John] Scorie B. of Chiche[ster]

Doctor [Richard] Cox
Maister [David] Whitehead
Maister [Edmund] Grindall
Maister [Robert] Horne
Maister doctor [Edwin] Sands
Maister [William] Gest
Maister [John] Elmer
Maister [John] Iewell.'

IV

Extracts from the acts of Supremacy and Uniformity (1 Elizabeth, c. 1 and 1 Elizabeth, c. 2); *Statutes of the Realm*, IV, pp. 350–5, 355–8.

'[Supremacy] Most humbly beseeches your most excellent Majesty your faithful and obedient subjects the Lords spiritual and temporal and the Commons in this your present Parliament assembled: that where in the time of the reign of your most dear father of worthy memory, King Henry the Eighth, divers good laws and statutes were made and established, as well for the utter extinguishment and putting away of all usurped and foreign powers and authorities out of this your realm and other your Highness' dominions and countries, as also for the restoring and uniting to the imperial crown of this realm the ancient jurisdictions, authorities, superiorities and preeminences to the same of right belonging and appertaining; by reason whereof we your most humble and obedient subjects, from the five and twentieth year of the reign of your said dear father, were continually kept in good order and were disburdened of divers great and intolerable charges and exactions before that time unlawfully taken and exacted by such foreign power and authority as before that was usurped, until such time as all the said good laws and statutes by one act of Parliament made in the first and second years of the reigns of the late King Philip and Queen Mary, your Highness' sister [1 & 2 Philip and Mary, c. 8], were all clearly repealed and made void, as by the same act of repeal more at large doth and may appear. By reason of which act of repeal your said humble subjects were eftsoons brought under an usurped foreign power and authority and yet do remain in that bondage, to the intolerable charges of your loving subjects if some redress by the authority of this your High Court of Parliament with the assent of your Highness be not had and provided. May it therefore please your Highness, for the repressing of the said usurped foreign power and the restoring of the rights, jurisdictions and preeminences appertaining to the imperial crown of this your realm, that it may be enacted by the authority of this present Parliament, That the said act . . . and all and every branch, clauses and articles therein contained (other than such branches, clauses and sentences as hereafter shall be excepted) may from the last day of this session of Parliament, by authority of this present Parliament, be repealed, and shall from henceforth be utterly void and of no effect. . . .'

Acts restored: 23 Henry VIII, c. 9 (foreign citations); 24 Henry VIII, c. 12 (appeals to Rome); 23 Henry VIII, c. 20 (payment of annates); 25 Henry VIII, c. 19 (submission of the clergy); 25 Henry VIII, c. 20 (consecration of bishops); 25 Henry VIII, c. 21 (exactions from Rome); 26 Henry VIII, c. 14 (suffragans); 26 Henry VIII, c. 16 (dispensations); 1 Edward VI, c. 1 (communion in both kinds); also repeals the heresy laws revived by Mary.

'[Uniformity] Where at the death of our late sovereign lord King Edward the Sixth there remained one uniform order of common service and prayer and the administration of sacraments, rites and ceremonies in the Church of England, which was set forth in one book entitled The Book of Common Prayer and Administration of Sacraments and other Rites and Ceremonies in the Church of England, authorised by act of Parliament holden in the fifth and sixth years of our late sovereign lord King Edward the Sixth, entitled An Act for the Uniformity of Common Prayer and Administration of the Sacraments [5 & 6 Edward VI, c. 1], the which was repealed and taken away by act of Parliament in the first year of the reign of our late sovereign lady Queen Mary [1 Mary, st. 2, c. 2], to the great decay of the due honour of God and discomfort to the professors of the truth of Christ's religion: Be it therefore enacted by the authority of this present Parliament that the said statute of repeal and everything therein contained only concerning the said book and the service, administration of sacraments, rites and ceremonies contained or appointed in or by the said book shall be void and of none effect from and after the feast of the Nativity of St. John Baptist next coming [24 June]; and that the said book with the order of service and of the administration of sacraments, rites and ceremonies, with the alteration and additions therein added and appointed by this statute shall stand and be from and after the said feast . . . in full force and effect according to the tenor and effect of this statute; anything in the aforesaid statute of repeal to the contrary notwithstanding.'

V

Extract from the royal injunctions of Elizabeth, early July 1559; taken from W.H. Frere, *Visitation Articles and Injunctions of the Period of the Reformation* (Alcuin Club, 1910), III, pp. 8–9.

'Injunctions given by the Queen's Majesty as well to the Clergy as to the laity of this realm.

The Queen's most royal majesty, by the advice of her most honourable council, intending the advancement of the true honour of Almighty God, the suppression of superstition through all her Highness's realms and dominions, and to plant true religion, to the extirpation of all hypocrisy, enormities and abuses (as to her duty appertaineth) doth minister unto her loving subjects these godly injunctions hereafter following. All which injunctions her Highness willeth and commandeth her loving subjects obediently to receive, and truly to observe and keep, every man in their offices, degrees and states, as they will avoid her Highness's displeasure, and pains of the same hereafter expressed.

[Usurped and foreign authority]

1. The first is that all deans, archdeacons, parsons, vicars and all other ecclesiasticall persons shall faithfully keep and observe, and as far as in them may lie shall cause to be observed and kept of other, all and singular laws and statutes made for the restoring to the Crown the ancient jurisdiction over the state ecclesiastical, and abolishing of all foreign power repugnant to the same. And furthermore, all ecclesiastical persons having cure of souls shall to the uttermost of their wit, knowledge and learning, purely and sincerely, and without any colour or dissimulation, declare, manifest and open four times every year at the least, in their sermons and other collations, that all usurped and foreign power having no establishment nor ground by the law of God is for most just causes taken away and abolished; and that therefore no manner of obedience or subjection within her Highness's realms and dominions is due to any such foreign power. And that the Queen's power within her realms and dominions is the highest power under God, to whom all men, within the same realms and dominions, by God's law owe most loyalty and obedience, afore and above all other powers and potentates in earth.

... The form of bidding the prayers to be used generally in this uniform sort.

Ye shall pray for Christ's Holy Catholic Church, that is, for the whole congregation of Christian people dispersed throughout the whole world, and especially for the Church of England and Ireland. And herein I require you most specially to pray for the Queen's most excellent majesty, our Sovereign Lady Elizabeth, Queen of England, France and Ireland, defender of the faith, and supreme governor of this realm, as well in causes ecclesiastical as temporal.

You shall also pray for the ministers of God's holy Word and Sacraments, as well archbishops and bishops, as other pastors and curates.

You shall also pray for the Queen's most honourable Council, and for all the nobility of this realm, that all and every of these in their calling, may serve truly and painfully to the glory of God and edifying of His people, remembering the account that they must make.

Also you shall pray for the whole commons of this realm, that they may live in true faith and fear of God, in humble obedience and brotherly charity one to another.

Finally, let us praise God for all those that are departed out of this life in the faith of Christ, and pray unto God that we may have the grace so to direct our lives after their good example, that after this life we may with them be made partakers of the glorious resurrection, in the life everlasting.'

VI

Extract from William Camden, *Annales rerum anglicarum et hibernicarum*, trs. H. Norton (London, 1635), p. 61.

'The pope Pius the fourth of that name, his letter sent unto Queene Elizabeth by his nuncio Vincent Parpalia.

To oure most deare daughter in Christ, Elizabeth, Quene of England.

Most deare Daughter in Christ, Salvation and Apostollical Benediction. God the searcher of all hearts, knoweth, and you may perceive, by the advice that we have given you, to behave yourselfe towards this our eldest son, Vincent Parpali, whom you know well, how much we tender and desire, according to our Office of Pastorship, to provide for your salvation and honour, together with the establishment of your Raigne, thereby exhorting and admonishing your greatness (most deare daughter) that in rejecting these lewd councellors, who love themselves better than you, and aime but at their private ends; you implore the feare of God to your Councell, and remembering the time of your visitation, you observe our fatherly admonitions & wholesome counsels, and we promise you of our part, all th'assistance you can desire, not only for the comfort of your soule, but for th'establishment and confirmation of your royall dignities, according to the authority, place and charge comitted to us from God: And if (as we most fervently desire and hope) you return unto the bosom of the Churche, we will receive you with the like affectionate love as the Father (of whom it is spoken in the Gospell) received his sonne when he returned to him: and our joy shall be farre greater that the joy of a father for his sonne onely. But you, in drawing after you the whole people of England, shall heape with joyes, not only your own particular salvation, but to your whole Nation; Us and the universitie of our brethren, whom you shall shortly (God willing) heare to be assembled in an Ecumenique and general councell for th'extirpation of Heresies: and the whole church together. You shall also cause the Heavens to reioyce, and by such a memorable act, purchase renewed glory to your name, and a far more glorious crowne than that werewith you are already crowned; but of that the said Vincent shall more amplie certifie you; whome we desire your Highness to receive courteously and graciously, hearing him attentively and give such credit to what he shall declare unto you as you would to our selfe. Given at Rome, at St. Peters Palace, the fifth day of May 1560, and of our papacy the first.

I have not found what propositions were made by Parpalia, for I cannot think he was put in writing, neither does it please me to suppos, as ordinarily Historians doe. As all the world knows Queene Elizabeth lived like herselfe and "Alwaies the same" and that the business succeeded not to the Popes expectation.'

Elizabeth had (more or less) conformed to her sister's Church. In her position it was almost impossible to do otherwise, but both Mary and the Protestant underground understood her submission to be reluctant and formal, not representing any real conversion. As Brice's *Register of Martyrs* (1559) put it 'we wish'd for our Elizabeth'. However, she was more concerned to be queen than to be godly, and what she actually did would depend upon the circumstances as she found them. The persecution stopped as soon as the news of Mary's death became known and without, as far as we know, any specific instructions from the new queen. Some Protestant exiles returned immediately, and celebrations began, long before there was anything particular to celebrate. Meanwhile, Archbishop Heath had been the first to hail Elizabeth in the House of Lords. These events conveyed their own message. Protestant expectations were high, and although many Catholics may have looked to the future with apprehension, there was no will to resist her accession on religious grounds.

Unlike Mary, Elizabeth did not encourage any immediate changes to the status quo, and inhibited all preaching to damp down speculation ahead of the policy decisions which would have to be quickly made. Although this caution persuaded some of the exiles to stay where they were for the time being, Londoners never seem to have had any doubt, either about what they wanted, or about what the queen would do. Her council appointments had excluded nearly all Mary's familiars, but reflected a careful balance between Protestants and Henrician conservatives. On the other hand her Privy Chamber appointments had swept away not only all the Marians, but almost all the conservatives as well, filling their places with women (and a few men) of the 'new learning'. All this had happened, even before she tested the water with studied gestures, not only at her coronation entry, but also during the ceremony itself.

What she learned seems to have convinced her that it would be possible to restore her brother's Church settlement. This was almost certainly what she wanted to do, and the early responses of the established senior clergy, particularly the bishops, convinced her that there was no future in attempting an Henrician compromise. She therefore introduced both a Supremacy bill and a Uniformity bill into parliament early in 1559, and began to turn up the heat on the bishops. Protestant preachers began to be heard by royal licence, and a traditional disputation was set up at Westminster. Such disputations had been used elsewhere (although not in England) and were usually a pretext for the secular authority to announce a programme of Protestant reform. The bishops had little option but to take part, and Nicholas Heath, who was the ranking cleric while Canterbury was vacant, was fully cooperative, whatever misgiving he may have felt.

What happened is something of a puzzle. The surviving Protestant accounts, such as that of Holinshed, make it appear that some of the Catholic team behaved with perverse pig-headedness, but the outcome inevitably arouses the suspicion that they were tricked into a false position. Perhaps the terms of debate were not as clearly laid down as Holinshed suggests, or not actually agreed. For whatever reason, the disputation was a non-event, and the bishops of Winchester and Lincoln ended up in the Tower for contumacy. While they were there, the acts of Supremacy and Uniformity passed into law. Their incarceration made little difference to the former; it passed the Commons without trouble, and the bishops who opposed it in the House of Lords were too few, and attracted insufficient lay support to come close to defeating it.

The Uniformity act, however, was a different matter. It, too, passed the Commons easily, but it was fought in the Lords, not only by the bishops but by a substantial body of lay peers, including some councillors. The queen considered giving up on it when parliament adjourned for Easter, but the imprisonment of White and Watson just tipped the balance. The act came back after the recess, and passed by a single vote. The fact that no fewer than eight out of the twenty-six sees were vacant early in 1559, plus the two imprisonments, weakened the Catholic party just sufficiently to ensure its defeat in this crucial division. It is not surprising that Catholics claimed that the imprisonment of White and Watson was contrived.

Once the Edwardian settlement was restored by these measures, the queen's emphasis in enforcement was at first very much on the supremacy rather than upon Protestant uniformity. This angered many of her new bishops, but she judged it to be necessary to promote a measure of conciliation on the basis of the most acceptable premise, and the outcome suggests that she was right. The new pope, Pius IV, may also have been deceived, since he thought it worthwhile to send an envoy, Vincenzo Parpaglia, bearing an invitation to Elizabeth to send representatives to the Council of Trent, which was just about to reconvene. Camden clearly knew very little about this mission, which was aborted by a combination of the queen's reluctance and Philip's hostility, without ever crossing the Channel.

TWENTY-FIVE

Intervention in Scotland

I

Extracts from an anonymous letter of advice addressed to the queen in January 1560; taken from *The Egerton Papers*, ed. J. Payne Collier (Camden Society, 1840), pp. 30–2.

'It may please your most Excellent Ma[jes]tie to understand, that yesterday Mr. Treasurer [the Marquis of Winchester] and Mr. Secretary [Sir William Cecil] were in hand with me againe on your Ma[ies]ties behalf for the voyage into Scotland by land. Whereupon the more I thinke, the more I do mislike it. . . . I am sure your Ma[jes]tie hath wise Counsailors, or els (I speake upon hope of your Ma[jes]ties pardon) the fawte is youres. If your Counsaill hath geven you advise in this matter, or in any other, good gracious Lady, folowe yt, and do that you are advised by them to do in tyme. . . . If your Ma[jes]tie be advised nedes to entre, entre so, as if there be falshod in felowship, you may trust to your self, and be able to come out againe with honour, or at the lest without daunger; but yet I can not see how you can well entre by land, specyally this tyme of the yeare. The Duke of Norfolkes granfather was sent by the King your father, to invade Scotland, well accompanied both with good headdes, and with a good nombre: an army also by sea went into the Frithe, well furnished with victualles to releive the army by lande at theire comyng to Edenborow, which the army by land was not able to do for lacke, and yet as much was done for the furtherance of the jorney as might be. In the Duke of Somersettes tyme, the victory was not folowed in Scotland for lacke. I doubt not but your Counsaillors for this warre, at this tyme, do considre what an enemy besides the French men, yea, and peradventure the Scotts, first the weather will be to your people and to there horses.
Item – how they shalbe furnished of victualls both going and comyng.
Item – what store of gunners you may have.
Item – what passage for their ordinaunce and the carriages.
Item – what store of carriages for their munition and victualles.
Item – what maner of encamping is at this tyme of the yeare by the waye.
Item – what forage is to be founde both for the horse of service and also for the horse of drawght.
Item – what maner of men be sent in to this invasion, and if they should

fortune to perishe for lacke of one thing or of another, how much the losse of them will importe to your Ma[jes]tie, and to this realme. It were good, if it may pleas your Ma[jes]tie, if you be not already enformed of these poyntes, and that you must nedes entre to understand particularly first how these thinges be forseen and provided. . . .'

II

Articles agreed upon at Berwick, 27 February 1560; taken from the *Calendar of State Papers Relating to Scotland, 1559–60* (1965), pp. 413–15. The original MS is BL Cotton Caligula B.ix, 34 and 38.

'At Berwick, 27 Feb. 1559 it was agreed between Thomas, Duke of Norfolk, Lieutenant in the North, on the one part, and the Lords James Stewart, Patrick, Lord Ruthven, Sir John Maxwell of Terricles, William Maitland of Lethington, younger, John Wyschart of Pyttarrow, and Master Hendry Balnevis of Hallhill, in the name of James, Duke of Chatellerault, second person of the realm of Scotland and the others joined with him for the defence of the ancient rights and liberty of their country, on the other part, in form following:

2. The Queen, understanding that the French intend to conquer the realm of Scotland, suppress the liberty thereof and unite it to France, and being required thereto by the nobility in the name of the whole realm, shall accept the said realm, the heir apparent to the crown, the nobility and subjects thereof, for the protection of their old freedoms and liberties from conquest or oppression.

3. For that purpose with all speed she shall send into Scotland sufficient aid of men to join with the Scots as well by sea as by land, not only to expel the present power of French, but also to stop all greater forces to enter therein, and shall continue the same until they are [utterly] expelled therefrom.

4. In case any forts within the realm be won out of the hands of the French by the Queen, the same shall be immediately demolished, or delivered to the said Duke and his party; nor shall the English fortify within Scotland but by advice of the nobility and estates of the realm.

5. The Scottish nobility shall aid the Queen's army against the French.

6. They shall be enemies to all such Scotch and French as shall be enemies against England.

7. They shall never assent that the realm of Scotland shall be knit to the crown of France otherwise than as it is already, only by marriage of the Queen to the French King.

8. If the French at any time hereafter invade England, they shall furnish at least 2,000 horsemen and 1,000 footmen to pass upon her charges to any part of England. And if the invasion be north of York they shall convene their whole forces at their own charges, and continue so long in the field as they are wont to do for the defence of Scotland.

9. The Earl of Argyll shall employ his force to reduce the north parts of Ireland to the perfect obedience of England, according to an agreement between the Deputy of Ireland and the said Earl.

10. For the performance and sure keeping hereof, they shall enter to the Duke of Norfolk certain pledges before the entry of the Queen's forces in Scottish ground, the time of the continuance of the hostages to be only during the marriage of the Queen of Scotland with the French King, and one whole year after. [Signed] James Stewart, Patrick, Lord Ruthven, John Maxwell, W. Maitland, John Wischart, Henricus Balnaves.

11. For the performance of the same on the part of England the Queen shall confirm the same by her letters patents, to be delivered to the nobility of Scotland at the entry of their pledges.'

III

Extracts from translations and paraphrases in relation to the settlement between England, Scotland and France; June/July 1560; taken from the *Calendar of State Papers Relating to Scotland, 1560–61*, pp. 150, 172–4.

'[Cecil's instructions to Norfolk, 26 June 1560]

2. The Scots shall choose twenty four noblemen, out of whom the queen of Scots shall choose seven, and the Lords five, and this Council (or the more part) shall rule Scotland. No Frenchman shall have any office in Scotland; no man shall lose any office, room or promotion by this business; no men of war shall remain, but fifty at Dunbar and fifty at Inchkeith, who shall be monthly mustered by the Lords of Scotland; they shall not bring any victual or munition into these places but by oversight of the Scots, and that from six to six months. All the new fortifications in Dunbar shall be demolished; and the men of war in them shall be answerable to the justice of Scotland. The Scots shall remain in their religion, as a thing the French dare not meddle with. All the men in Leith shall be embarked at the English appointment, and the fortifications demolished by their oversight. They shall either pay, or the French King be bound to the Scots, for all things taken from them since the beginning of this matter. The Duke of Chatellerault and all others shall be restored to their estates in France. The Scots shall not acknowledge any fault, but only require all the abovesaid

things; and for more assurance the French King and Queen shall convent with Elizabeth to ratify all these things to the Scots. The only thing they yield is for 100 men in two places; which it is also accorded shall be treated of in the next parliament; and if it be found unnecessary for the realm they shall be withdrawn.

[Articles proposed to the French commissioners on the part of the Scots, 6 July 1560]

1. All the French shall be removed save 120 to be stationed in Dunbar and Inchkeith, who are to be amenable to the laws of Scotland; they shall be mustered and paid monthly, and inspected by two Lords of Scotland to see that their numbers are not increased.

2. The fortifications of Leith and Dunbar shall be dismantled, and not rebuilt, and no artillery and munition imported without the consent of the estates.

3. Debts contracted by the French troops shall be paid.

4. Parliament shall assemble on the 10th July, and its acts shall be valid.

5. No war shall be commenced save with the consent of the estates.

6. A council of twelve shall be appointed to manage affairs.

7. No strangers shall be employed in offices of law, or as Treasurer, Comptroller, or the like.

8. Amnesty for all things done since 6th March 1558.

9. Any armed assembly exceeding twelve without the order of the council shall be deemed rebellious.

10. Neither the party of the Congregation nor their adversaries shall reproach one another with anything done since 6th March 1558.

11. The King and Queen shall not take vengeance for anything done since 6th March 1558.

12. It shall not be lawful for any nobleman to assemble in arms nor to invite foreign soldiers.

13. Wrongs done to the clergy are to be considered in parliament, nor is it lawful for any person to hinder their enjoyment of their goods.

14. Anyone breaking the treaty to be regarded as a public enemy.

15. The Duke of Chatellerault and other noblemen to be restored to their estates in France.

16. No other artillery shall be transported out of Scotland than what was sent thither since the death of King Francis [I].

17. Some persons of quality shall be chosen to repair to the King and Queen and remonstrate to them concerning religion and other matters in which the Lords Deputies cannot meddle.

[The treaty of Edinburgh, 6 July 1560]

1. The present treaty is intended to put an end to all disputes between the Queen of England and the King and Queen of France and Scotland. The Articles are as follows:

2. The treaty of Cateau Cambresis shall remain in full force.

3. The concord between the Dauphin and Dauphiness and the Queen of England executed at Cambrai shall remain in force.

4. All French land and sea forces shall leave Scotland, except the garrisons of Dunbar and Inchkeith, and all warlike preparations shall cease on both sides.

5. Eyemouth shall be dismantled according to the provisions of the treaty of Cambrai, within four days after the commencement of the demolition of Leith.

6. The French King and Queen shall abstain from using the arms and style of the Queen of England, and shall prohibit their subjects from doing the same.

7. A convention shall be held in London to consider the question of compensation for the injuries sustained by the Queen of England in having her arms usurped; and in case no agreement being arrived at, Philip, King of Spain, shall be appointed arbiter.

8. The convention concluded between the French King and Queen and their subjects [of Scotland] shall be observed by both parties.

9. Philip of Spain shall be included in this treaty.

10. This treaty shall be confirmed within sixty days.

11. All the Princes shall swear to keep these articles inviolate.'

Appended are: 1. The commission of Francis and Mary, appointing the Bishops of Valence and Amiens, and MM De La Brosse, D'Oysel, and Randan their commissioners to treat for peace; 2 May 1560. 2. The commission of Elizabeth appointing Cecil, Wotton, Sadler, Percy and Carew as her commissioners, 25 May 1560. The treaty is signed by the Bishop of Valence, Randan, Cecil and Wotton.

The final withdrawal of English forces from Scotland in 1550 had alerted many Scots to their increasing subservience to France. By 1559 the Francophile government of the Queen Mother, Mary of Guise, was becoming bitterly resented. At the same time Scottish Protestants, temporarily freed from any association with England, were beginning to represent themselves as a 'patriot' party. Elizabeth would have had no direct interest in this, had it not been for the fact that Mary, Queen of Scots had a more than respectable claim to the English throne. Henry II, having exerted himself to escape from war at Cateau Cambresis in April 1559, was not likely to do anything about pressing his daughter-in-law's claim, but he died in July, and his fifteen-year-old son and successor, Francis II, was dominated by the Guises. The Duke and the Cardinal of Guise were aggressive, anti-English, and only too anxious to aid their beleaguered sister, the Queen Regent of Scotland.

By the summer of 1559 Scotland was in turmoil as the Protestant Lords of the Congregation emerged as open rebels against the regency government. They were, however, too disorganised, and lacked the military power to overcome Mary's French troops unaided. In the autumn of 1559 they appealed to Elizabeth for assistance. The queen was extremely reluctant, partly because of the instinctive caution of her nature, and partly because she objected on principle to aiding rebels against governments which she considered to be legitimate. Cecil, who was very well informed about events both in Scotland and France, believed that intervention was necessary to frustrate Guise ambitions in Scotland, and possible because of the deteriorating stability of France itself. The Privy Council, and the queen's military advisers, were divided, as the letter cited here demonstrates.

By November 1559, when William Maitland of Lethington came on a mission from the Scottish lords the rebellion was in difficulties, and Elizabeth was sufficiently convinced to provide surreptitious financial and naval assistance. Cecil, however, continued to press for a more serious commitment, and by Christmas the queen had decided not only to send a fleet to the Firth of Forth to cut communications between Scotland and France, but also to send an army north under the command of the Duke of Norfolk. Consequently there was already a working partnership between Norfolk and the Scottish lords, well before it was embodied in a written agreement in February 1560. From an English point of view the risks were great, because intervention arguably constituted a breach of the treaty of Cateau Cambresis, but the risks of doing nothing and seeing the Protestant uprising suppressed, were greater still.

Francis II and Mary were at one with their Guise kindred in wishing to support the regent, but not only was Sir William Winter with a powerful

English fleet in the way, they also needed their forces at home to maintain control of an increasingly volatile religious conflict. Consequently, the war in the north developed without any direct intervention from France. For the time being the French forces already in Scotland were sufficient, and an Anglo-Scottish attack on Leith was beaten off with fatalities in early May. However, by then Francis had already decided to cut his losses, and had appointed commissioners to negotiate. It seems likely that the regent did not know that, because she continued to be intransigent until her death in June. This, together with the fact that no reinforcements were coming from France, forced the French commanders in Scotland onto the back foot.

Negotiations began before the end of June. Delays were caused by Elizabeth's ill-advised attempts to secure either the return of Calais or a substantial indemnity, but when Cecil effectively refused to press for these concessions, agreement was reached on 6 July. The French forces surrendered, and Winter shipped them back to France. Francis and Mary never ratified the treaty, but Francis died in December 1560 without taking any further action, and the French ceased to have the capacity to intervene. Although the situation in Scotland continued to be turbulent, Elizabeth's refusal to overexploit the treaty of Edinburgh ensured that Anglo-Scottish relations were henceforth on a new footing.

TWENTY-SIX

Marriage and the Succession

I

Extracts from an anonymous letter of advice written to the queen on 10 February 1563; taken from *The Egerton Papers* (1840), pp. 34–40.

'Most excellent Princesse, my most gracious Souveraigne and good Ladye. I crave of your Ma[jes]tie, prostrate before your feete, pardon for my boldnes in wryting unto youe at this tyme. . . . I understand that there hathe ben a sewte moved unto your Ma[jes]tie for the mariage of your most noble person (whome I beseeche God longe to preserve unto us), and for thentaille of the succession of youre crowne, if youe leave us without heires of youre bodye; which sewte [is] made unto your Ma[jes]tie in generallytie without lymitation for youre mariage or for the succession. . . . Itt is the greatest matter that ever I or anie man alive at this daie can remember hathe bin brought in deliberation in our daies, and therfore everie parte therof, aswell your Ma[jes]ties answer to the motion, did require good consideration (which I have heard youe did most prudentlie use) as the further progress by youre Ma[jes]tie in that parte of the matter which tocheth succession, must of necessytie have a tyme to be determined, bicause yt is subjecte to diverse affections and humours founded upon private respectes, some desyringe (after youre Ma[jes]tie and the heires of youre bodye) that a man should succeede, without anie regard to the tytle of a woman, whatsoever yt be, forgetting (as I have heard that most noble prince of worthy memorie, the King youre father, saie) that the greatest ancherhold of this crowne, after Kinge henrye the first, took roote from the heire generall Maud, daughter and heire to the said Henrye, who was maried first to themp'ror, and after his deceasse to Jeffrey Plantagenett, Ducke of Anjou, &c. Of which two came Kinge Henrye the seconde (none alien, though he were borne out off the realme), but rightfull Kinge by course of nature, and by discent of bloode; of whome your Ma[jes]tie ys rightfullie discended, and unto whome, by course of nature, discent of bloode and by lawes of this realme your Ma[jes]tie is right and lawfull heire and successor of this crowne. . . .

This discourse, wherin I note a disinherison of some right heires, and off callamities that fell thereuppon, ys to put your Ma[jes]tie in remembraunce to use great and deep deliberation, and to understand thorowghly wher the right resteth by the law of this land, which is the rule wherby all your subjectes must be ordred, and wherby they hold all that they have, and whereunto the Princes of this realme do promise solempnelie at ther coronation to have a speciall regarde. . . .

But if yt will please your Ma[jes]tie to be (after a sorte) a Christ unto us, a Redeemer, a Saviour off us by mortifying your own affection for us, and for our sakes, by mariage, take the paine to bring furth princely children, then shuld youe not nede to feare thentaill; then shuld your Ma[jes]tie be quiet; then shuld we be happie, and then your Ma[jes]tie with a better securytie and with longer deliberation (by understanding of everie body his pretens and by what everychone off them could saie for themselffes) establish the matter rightfully. But in this pointe I speake the less toching mariage, bicause I have heretofore, by your Ma[jes]ties goodnes, presumed not onelie to write unto you at large, but allso presentlie to move your Ma[jes]tie efstones by word of mouth therin. I praie God directe your harte in these two pointes speciallie, and in all other your doinges, according to his will and pleasure.'

II

Extracts from the report of the Count of Feria to Philip II, 18 April 1559; taken from the *Calendar of State Papers, Spanish, 1558–1567* (1892), pp. 56–8. The original MS is at Simancas.

'I note that your Majesty writes respecting the marriage of the Archduke Ferdinand with the Queen, and the same day that the courier arrived with the letter, I was about to despatch news to your Majesty of what was being done here in the matter, and about Lord Robert, which is as follows. When the Emperor's ambassador arrived here I understood that he had no instructions to treat of the matter, but as so many loose and flighty fancies are about, some of those people who went to and from with him to the palace must have broached the subject to him. One in particular I know of was [Sir Thomas] Challoner, who went to visit the Emperor on the Queen's behalf when she succeeded to the throne. He is a great talker, but a person of no authority. At the same time the matter must have been brought before Count [George] Helfenstein by the Queen's asking him whether he had instructions to speak to her on any other subject, which I believe she did two or three times. He must therupon have advised his master, and about a week ago the said Count sent hither a German who acts as his secretary, and who I am told is a lawyer, directed to Challoner with a letter from the Emperor to the Queen and a portrait of the Archduke Ferdinand. The secretary delivered the letter in person, and in it his Majesty says that he desires to send hither a person to treat with her [the Queen] of matters of closer friendship than those respecting which Count Holfenstein visited her. The Queen accepted the offer to send the person, and the German returned with her letter and message the day before yesterday. As I was assured that the matter was under discussion, and that the secretary was here for the purpose, I thought I ought so to approach the Queen and him that they might both understand that the negotiations had your Majesty's accord and goodwill without binding myself to them in a way that could cause inconvenience from my having acted without your Majesty's orders. I therefore only told the Queen, on the day the Portuguese went to take leave of her, that since she had not married your Majesty, I wished she would take the person nearest to you in kin and kindness, and so gave her to understand that I was informed of what was being discussed. . . .

The same day I sent to beg an audience of the Queen and spoke to her of this business, persuading her to it as your Majesty commands. She told me the Emperor had written to her, and that up to the present she did not know what he wanted to negotiate with her. All this in fair words, and I do not think that she faces this business badly, nor indeed do any of them, although to say the truth I could not tell your Majesty what this woman means to do with herself, and those who know her best know no more than I do.

During the last few days Lord Robert has come so much into favour that he does whatever he likes with affairs and it is even said that her Majesty visits him in his chamber day and night. People talk of this so freely that they go so far as to say that his wife has a malady in one of her breasts, and the Queen is only waiting for her to die to marry Lord Robert. I can assure your Majesty that matters have reached such a pass that I have been brought to consider whether it would not be well to approach Lord Robert on your Majesty's behalf, promising him your help and favour and coming to terms with him.'

III

Extracts from letters sent by Alvarez de Quadra, Bishop of Aquila, Spanish ambassador in England, to Philip II; taken from the *Calendar of State Papers, Spanish, 1558–1567*, pp. 225, 263.

'[31 January 1562]

My last letters were written on the 10th & the 17th instant, and since then Lord Robert has intimated to me, and has caused others to tell me that he is desirous that your Majesty should write to the Queen in his favour, and persuading her to marry him. He would like this boon to be obtained for him without writing himself to your Majesty, as he fears the answer might make conditions with regard to religion which were out of his power. He has let out in the course of the negotiations that the French are making him great offers, although he desired that I should not be told so. He recently sent word that if I would write to your Majesty he would send the letter by a special messenger as it was important for him to have the answer before Easter. I have replied, professing great desire for his advancement, and offering to speak to the Queen for him if he liked, assuring her that your Majesty would be glad of this marriage, as you wished to see her wedded, and had a good opinion of him. . . .

[25 October 1562]

The Queen was at Hampton Court on the 10th instant, and feeling unwell, thought she would like a bath. The illness turned out to be smallpox, and the cold caught by leaving her bath for the air resulted in so violent a fever that on the seventh day she was given up, but during the night the eruption came, and she is now better.

There was great excitement that day in the palace, and if her improvement had not come so soon, some hidden thoughts would have become manifest. The Council discussed the succession twice, and I am told there were three different opinions. Some wished King Henry's will to be followed and Lady Catherine declared heiress. Others who found flaws in the will were in favour of the Earl of Huntingdon. Lord Robert, the Earl of Bedford, the Earl of Pembroke and the Duke of Norfolk with others of the lower rank were in favour of this. The most moderate and sensible tried to dissuade the others from being in such a furious hurry, and said that they would divide and ruin the country unless they summoned jurists of the greatest standing in the country to examine the rights of the claimants, and in accordance with this decision the Council should then unanimously take such steps as might be best in the interests of justice and the good of the country. The Marquis Treasurer was of this opinion with others, although only a few, as the rest understood that this was a move in favour of the Catholic religion, nearly all the jurists who would be called upon being of that faith, and this delay would give time for your Majesty to take steps in the matter, which is the thing these heretics fear most, for upon your Majesty's absence they found all their hopes.

During this discussion the Queen improved, and on recovering from the crisis which had kept her unconscious and speechless for two hours the first thing she said was to beg her Council to make Lord Robert protector of the kingdom with a title and an income of £20,000. Everthing she asked for was promised, but will not be fulfilled. . . .

. . . The Queen protested at that time that although she loved, and always had loved Lord Robert dearly, as God was her witness, nothing improper had ever passed between them.'

At the beginning of her reign it was assumed by everyone (except Elizabeth herself) that one of her first priorities would be to marry in order to secure the succession. She was the last of Henry VIII's children, and beyond her life the future was deeply uncertain. By the normal rules of inheritance the heir (if not the lawful claimant) was Mary Stuart, Queen of Scotland in her own right, and in 1560 Queen of France by marriage. By the terms of Henry's will the heir should have been the eldest survivor of the 'Suffolk line', that is Catherine Grey, the younger sister of Jane.

However, among those who could not bear the thought of another woman on the throne, there was also some support for Francis Hastings, Earl of Huntingdon. Hastings' mother, Anne, had been the daughter of the 2nd Duke of Buckingham, and sister of Edward Stafford, the 3rd Duke, whose proximity to the throne had brought him to the block in 1521. The Stafford claim was fairly remote, going back to Thomas of Woodstock, one of the numerous sons of Edward III. Francis died in 1560, and his claim passed to his son, Henry. Henry was a strong Protestant and a loyal subject of Elizabeth, who never showed the slightest interest in his claim, so the only real contenders in the disputes of the early 1560s were Mary and Catherine.

Mary was both Catholic and Francophile (even after she ceased to be Queen of France in December 1560), and that meant that she was unacceptable, both to Protestants and to the Habsburg interest. Unfortunately, Catherine fell foul of Elizabeth by marrying the young Earl of Hertford without licence, and spent much of this period in the Tower. However, none of this would matter if the queen could be persuaded to marry, and she was bombarded with that advice from all sides. Elizabeth understood the reason for this pressure, but evaded it. Unlike her sister, the new queen did not believe that government was unsuitable work for a woman, and had no yearnings for domesticity. The phrase attributed to her, 'I will have one mistress – and no master', is probably authentic. There were, therefore, only two reasons for marriage, and not three: to secure the succession, and to secure a firm foreign alliance.

Philip's reception in England had demonstrated the hazards of the latter, and although he would have been the most powerful protector against the French threat represented by Mary, the price of renewing that connection would have been too high in several respects. Consequently, although he dutifully proposed within weeks of her accession, Elizabeth had no hesitation in rejecting him. The courts of Europe buzzed with alternative possibilities, but only three were serious: Eric, who threw his hat into the ring in 1559, and succeeded as Eric XIV of Sweden in 1560; Charles, the Archduke of Austria, younger son of the Emperor

Ferdinand; and Lord Robert Dudley, a younger son of Edward VI's mentor, the Duke of Northumberland.

Charles, who was reputed to be 'flexible' over religion, had strong support, not only from Habsburg representatives and English Catholics, but also within the council. However, he eventually turned out to be less flexible than he was reputed, and the negotiations broke down, much to the relief of the stronger English Protestants. They were Eric's chief backers, but Sweden was no great catch in international terms, and there were valid reasons for not marrying a man who already had his own country to run. It is not known that Elizabeth ever had any strong personal interest in either Charles or Eric.

The man she did have an interest in was Robert Dudley, her Master of the Horse and long-term friend. Dudley was married, but his wife Amy died in somewhat mysterious circumstances in September 1560. De Quadra was almost certainly right in attributing her death to the 'malady in her breast', which would now be recognised as breast cancer; however, at the time there was a great scandal, and although Dudley was officially (and probably rightly) exonerated, the course of true love became a distinctly rocky road. Most of the council were strongly opposed to his advancement, believing him to be politically and socially unsuitable, even if his wife had died in the most blameless circumstances. For about two years he exercised a powerful but unquantifiable influence over the queen, and several people (including de Quadra) were so convinced that he would succeed that they threw in their lot with him. Elizabeth, however, at great personal cost, eventually became convinced that such a marriage would be political suicide, and would involve losing the confidence of such trusted advisers as Cecil, and equally important, the affection of her subjects.

The scare over the queen's illness in October 1562, and her semi-conscious attempt to have Dudley made protector, in effect marked the end of that affair. He continued to entertain hopes for about another two years, until Elizabeth finally drew a line under his bid by making him Earl of Leicester in September 1564, and a privy councillor. Although they continued an emotional friendship until his death, after 1564 Dudley was a normal part of the political scene, instead of the unpredictable maverick he had been as Lord Robert Dudley. The question of the succession remained unresolved, but the issue did not go away.

TWENTY-SEVEN

Intervention in France

I

Extract from Holinshed, *Chronicle* (1807 edn), p. 205.

'She [Elizabeth] therefore lamenting that the King and queene mother [Charles IX and Catherine de Medici] should be thus in the hands of them that procured all these troubles [the Guises], and led up and downe at ther pleasures, and driven to behold the spoil and sacking of diverse his cities, and miserable slaughter of his subiectes; and againe hir grace thinking it expedient to prevent that such as were knowne to beare no good will, either to hir or to hir relame, should not get into their possessions such townes and havens as laie againste the sea coastes of hir said realme, whereby they stuffing the same with garrisons and numbers of men of warre, might easilie upon occasions seeke to make invasions into this hir said realme, to the great annoiance of hir and hir loving subiectes; at the request of the French themselves, thought it expedient to put in armor a certeine number of hir subiectes, to passe over into Normandie, unto such havens as neere approched unto this hir relame of England, as well for the safeguard of the same, as also for the reliefe and preservation of the inhabitants there; and other that professed the gospell, living in continuall danger to be murthered and oppressed, and therefore craving hir aid to save and deliver them out of the bloudie handes of their cruell adversaries, that sought their hastie destruction.

For the conduction therefore of such forces as she meant to send over that present she ordeined the Lord Ambrose Dudlie, Earle of Warwike to be hir principall lieutenant, captaine generall, chiefe leader and gouvenor of hir said subiectes, that should in such wise passe over into Normandie. Hereupon, the saide Earle the seventeenth of October in the fourth yeare of hir maiesties reigne, tooke shipping at Portsmouth . . . and directing his course forwards, on thursdaie morning about eight of the clocke, his lordship landed at Newhaven, where he was most ioyfullie received with a great peale of artillerie.

. . . The sixteenth of Maie [1563] was proclamation made, that all Frenchmen, being within the towne of Newhaven, otherwise called Havre de Grace, as well men, women, as children, should depart the towne betwixt the present time and six of the clocke at night on the next daie being mondaie, except surgians, apothecaries, bakers, butchers, smiths, masons, locksmiths, carpenters and other such artificers, upon paine to be attached as good and lawfull prisoners, and their goods to be confiscated.

. . . There died so manie dailie through the vehemencie of the infection, that the streets laie even full of dead corpses, not able to be removed or buried, by reason of the multitude that perished. Herewith theie were greevouslie annoied for want of fresh vittels; but chiefly of fresh waters, which the enemie by longe siege had cut off. And now the shot of the canon, being within six and twentie paces of the towne, was so terrible, as the like had not lightlie beene heard of: and sundrie breaches therwith were alreadie made; namelie two verie great and easie for the enemies to enter. All these daungers and miseries notwithstanding, the worthie earle of Warwicke and his captains and soldiers in courageous order stood at those severall breaches readie to defend the same, if the enemie had presumed to give the assault. . . .'

II

Extract from a letter of Bishop de Quadra to Margaret, Duchess of Parma, regent of the Low Countries, 10 October 1562; taken from the *Calendar of State Papers, Spanish, 1558–1567*, p. 261.

'. . . I have sent to ask for an audience, and will give advice at once as to the result of the interview.

The 3,000 men they have embarked in the ports of Portsmouth and Rye on the 26th ultimo were driven by contrary winds to shelter in the Isle of Wight, whence the captains wrote to the queen to know whether it was her wish that they should continue their voyage. They were told to proceed with the first favourable wind, as they did, leaving the island on the 3rd instant. As soon as the queen received news of their arrival and the good reception in Havre de Grace and Dieppe she gave orders to the earl of Warwick to leave with the other 3,000 men, as he will do within two or three days, the troops being already at the shipping place awaiting him. All the more speed will be displayed in the voyage because it is said that the King of France is nearer the coast, and they fear that as the troops that have gone over are few and fresh, they might be surprised and beaten.

The Duke of Norfolk arrived today at Hampton Court, where the Queen is, and people still say that if more troops are sent into France the Duke will take command of the whole force. Many persons offer their services to me every day in the belief that a rupture is imminent between his Majesty and the Queen. I think the best thing I can do in such cases is to pass them lightly over, thanking those who offer themselves, but not closing with them without orders [London].'

III

Extract from Sir John Hayward, *Annals of the First Four Years of Queen Elizabeth* (Camden Society, 1840), p. 104.

'Nowe, the French of the other faction, when they saw the English (their old unwellcome guests) thus to build their nest in France, beganne to look one upon another, as finding an error but unprovided of present remedie. Their witts were wavering, their courage irresolute, their feares generall, their hopes doubtfull, in their wills no agreement. . . .

The Queen Mother preferring to her remembrance how much it would savour of indiscretion, to consider indignities so farre – so farre to have small rule over her self, as not to preferre the safetie of her estate before the satisfieing of her will, dealt under hand with Monsieur Beauvois, and promised him 50,000 crowns with a coller of the order, and a companie of men-at-armes entertained, in case he would yield up the towne of Newhaven; but whether he had no minde to repose assurance in her word (as nothing more naturallie breedith suspicion than matters of state) or whether he had no power to effect that which she affected, she prevailled as little by this faire sollicitation as the Rhinegrave did before by presenting himself to the towne in armes. When this would not succeed, she attempted to induce the Queen of England to withdrawe her forces out of France; but she had given her word, and did think herself greater in being subject to that, then in the greatness of her estste.

In the mean time, between the French of Newhaven and the English soldiers (as litle time as they had byn together) much contention did arise; manie grievances did growe; whereof complaint was made from both sides to the Earl of Warwick. Hereupon a proclamation was made to appease this disagreement; and to remedie the grievances from whence it was occasioned. . . .'

In spite of ostensibly good relations with Spain in the early 1560s, Elizabeth's council was continually bombarded with rumours of Catholic plots to form a political league for the extirpation of Protestantism. There was little substance behind these rumours, but the final sessions of Trent, and the undoubted militancy of some Catholic extremists, spread paranoia through the Protestant world. Elizabeth found herself in a very difficult position, because outside England there were very few Protestant governments, and most of them were either weak, or in the wrong place, or both. At the same time she never accepted any religious criteria for legitimacy, and encouraging rebellion against lawful government was both dangerous and distasteful. This caution was wasted on de Quadra, who informed his master that 'This woman desires to make use of religion in order to excite rebellion in the whole world. . . .' The fact that her aim was purely defensive cut no ice with the bishop, even if he understood it.

The first crisis came in France, where the Duke of Guise seized control of the government in February 1562, and the Huguenot leaders took to arms, ostensibly in defence of the Crown, at the same time appealing for both English and German help. At first Elizabeth temporised, offering mediation, but as Sir Nicholas Throgmorton, her ambassador in Paris, pointed out to Cecil, the French appeal might give her the opportunity for a spectacular policy success in the recovery of Calais. This was a temptation which the queen could not resist, but at first the Huguenots were unwilling to purchase her support at such a price. However, by September 1562 the Protestant military position had deteriorated, and a compromise deal was struck. Calais could not be surrendered because it was not in Protestant hands, but Le Havre was offered as security. By the secret treaty of Richmond it was agreed that Elizabeth would garrison Le Havre (Newhaven to the English) with 3,000 men, place another 3,000 men at the service of the Prince of Conde, and loan the prince 140,000 crowns.

Philip wished to intervene to frustrate the English intention, but his forces in the Low Countries were so tied down by trouble there that they were unable to cross the frontier. The Duke of Guise, however, hardly needed Spanish help. In December 1562 he defeated the Huguenots at the battle of Dreux, and took the Prince of Conde prisoner. There were also several notable casualties, including Guise himself, struck down by an assassin in February 1563. By this time, both Conde and the queen mother were anxious for a deal, and the former had a guilty conscience about his treaty with Elizabeth. In March 1563 he signed the peace of Amboise, gaining some limited political and religious concessions, and ignoring (but not repudiating) his English treaty.

The French then turned their united forces against Le Havre. The town was supplied by sea, and adequately garrisoned, at first with about 5,000 men. However, by June plague was reducing the English force faster than it could be reinforced, and all local French help had long since disappeared. By 26 July the Earl of Warwick's position was untenable, and he surrendered on honourable terms. For several months Elizabeth refused to accept the logic of this disaster, blustering about cutting trade links (which was just about the only leverage she had), but in April 1564 she finally accepted the inevitable, and signed the treaty of Troyes, to all intents and purposes annulling that part of the treaty of Cateau Cambresis which related to Calais, and abandoning all future pretensions to the town.

TWENTY-EIGHT

The State of the Nation

I

Paraphrase extracts from Sir Thomas Gresham's letter to Sir William Cecil, of 12 May 1560; taken from the *Calendar of State Papers, Foreign, 1560–61*, p. 48.

'Since writing on the 7th, he has received the Queen's letter of the 2nd, and Cecil's of the 3rd, on the 9th by Richard Clough. The £25,000 that the Queen will presently pay has greatly advanced her credit. Gresham's friend that the Queen gave the chain of gold unto of 500 crowns has performed his promise, for on the 10th the payment of the mart was prolonged until August, with the interest of 50 shillings upon the £100, which is but 10% for the year, wherewith no man can say against. In respect of this worthy piece of service the Queen can do no less than write him a letter of thanks with at least 500 crowns. The same person has likewise given Gresham to understand that the assembling of the Estates [General] is only to come by money for the despatch of the 4,400 Spaniards for Spain and the payment of Lazarus von Swendlen's band and other soldiers, so that the money that the Regent gathered is spent already, for which Count Egmont is departed into Flanders, and the Prince of Orange remains in Holland. . . .

. . . Hans Kecke yet remains behind in England; it were good Cecil despatched him thence for the money matter if it takes place, whom he will handle well enough; his price to him was five per cent interest and five for obligation of service. It were well for the Queen to set her laws at liberty that her subjects and all other nations might let the money out upon interest not exceeding £5 per cent, as in King Henry's time, with a penalty that no man use any after manner of chevaunce with wars or otherwise; and this doing he doubts not that she will find store of money upon interest within her own dominions. For since the exchange being risen in King Edward's time there has been brought all the fine gold and silver from all places thither, which will continue while the exchange is 23 shillings [Flemish, to the pound sterling] at London and 22s 6d from hence [Antwerp]. Wishes Cecil never to consent to the banishing of the exchange, as it would bring it down again and cause all the fine gold and silver to be transported out of the realm. The money merchants are not to be suffered to lower the exchange by their greediness. Mr. Hussey, the civilian [lawyer] has no understanding in these matters. Banishing the exchange will decrease the Queen's customs, for when men find more profit in carrying hence gold than delivering by exchange, they will employ it on English commodities, so that the present exchange augments the customs, to the great estimation of all English commodities, and hindrance of foreign.'

II

> Proclamation of 19 February 1561, reforming the coinage; taken from Hughes and Larkin, *Tudor Royal Proclamations* (New Haven/London, 1969), II, no. 478.

'The Queen's Majesty, continuing her most gracious purpose to the reformation of the base moneys of this realm, and having already caused to be coined in fine sterling moneys such quantity as, being added to other fine moneys coined in the times of her late dear brother and sister, King Edward and Queen Mary, doth far exceed the quantity of moneys used of ancient time in this realm, hath, by advice and good deliberation had with her council, thought necessary to proceed to the diminution of certain base moneys yet remaining current within her realm. And because her Majesty desireth nothing more than to discharge her subjects, and specially her poor commonalty, of all manner of burden to be sustained herein, her Majesty, by advice of her said council, hath thus ordered as followeth:

First, her Majesty giveth all her subjects to understand that all pieces of base moneys, lately valued and now current at 4½d., shall not be taken nor allowed as current money after the 9th of April next following (which is 15 days after Our Lady Day in Lent, and is by her Majesty so specially appointed because the tenants and meaner sort of her subjects that live as tenants and farmers may have a convenient time to pay their rents at our said Lady Day without trouble if they shall chance to have prepared any part of the same in the said sorts of money); and from the said 9th day of April, the said pieces of 4½d. to be accounted not current but bullion.

And because neither the poorer nor the richer sort of her Majesty's subjects should take any loss by the converting of the same at that time into bullion, her Majesty is pleased that whomsoever will bring any of the same moneys betwixt this and the 25th of April to her mint in the Tower shall have for the same both the value, according to the rate of 4½d. the piece and 3d for the pound, in new sterling moneys within the space of 20 days or less; and that after, until the 20th day of May, to have for the same the like rate, saving and excepting the 3d. upon the pound; and from thence forward her Majesty meaneth to receive no more of the same into her mint.

Mary I as princess. 'She is a perfect saint, and dresses badly'.

Pope Julius III, from the reconciliation medal.

Greenwich Palace, drawn in the later years of Henry VIII. It was a favourite royal residence.

John Foxe's 'Bloody Bonner', a rough diamond who left himself open to misrepresentation.

John Foxe and 'popish cruelty' – the burning of Rose Allin's hand.

GVLIELM' CAMDEN'
CLARENTI'

PRÆLECTVRÆ HISTORICÆ
FVNDATOR MVNIFIC?

PONDERE, NON NVMERO.

Hic oculos similes vultusq. hic ora tueri
Poteris, nec vltra hæc artifex quiuit manus.
ANNALES ipsum, celebrisq BRITANNIA monstrant
Perenniora Saxo et ære μνήματα.
Quisquis et Historiæ Cathedram hanc conscenderit, esto
Benignitatis vsq monumentum Loquax.

DEGOREVS WHEAR PRIM'
HIST. PR·P·F·POSVIT

Marius Gheeraerts pinxit.

William Camden,
author of the *Annales*.

AN' DNI
1587

ÆTATIS SV
7

John Foxe, the influential
martyrologist.

Furthermore, her Majesty thinketh meet to admonish her subjects that, although in the beginning of this refining and coinage such difficulties happened as the expedition of exchange could not be so speedily made as was meant, yet for that it is manifest that use and experience hath taken away all those difficulties, and that now the ministers of her mints be able to make speedy return of fine moneys for the base: her Majesty would that her subjects should not forbear to come to her said mints, without doubt there to be satisfied, for small sums at sight or within two or three days, and for greater within eight or ten, and at the furthest not to continue above 20; for so her Majesty understandeth the ability of her officers now to do it, and so hath directed them to execute the same.

Finally, her Majesty chargeth all manner her subjects to endeavour themselves to bring unto her mints not only the said base moneys of 4½d. but also, as they may conveniently, the other pieces of 1½d and ¾d., which her Majesty doth permit to remain current for the ease of her people, for lack of small moneys; of which sort is meant to have a coinage as shortly as may be in good and fine sterling moneys. And because it may be that divers of her Majesty's own proper tenants, farmers, bailiffs, or receivers, may after the said 9th of April have in their hands parcel of her Majesty's revenues, her pleasure and contentation that her officers in the receipt of her echequer shall receive the same as current money until the 25th of May next.'

III

Preamble to the Statute of Artificers, 5 Elizabeth, c. 4 (1563); taken from *Tudor Economic Documents* (1924), eds R.H. Tawney and Eileen Power, l, p 338.

'An Acte towching dyvers Orders for Artificers Laborers Servantes of Husbandrye and Apprentises.

Althoughe there remayne and stande in force presentlie a greate nombre of actes and Statutes concernyng the reteynynge departinge wages and orders of Appre[n]tices Servantes and Laborers, aswell in husbandrye as in divers other Artes Misteries and occupacions, yet partlye for thimperfeccion and contraritie that is founde and doo appere in sondrie of the saide Lawes, and for the varietie and nombre of them, and chieflie for that the wages and allouances lymytted and rated in many of the said statutes are in dyverse places to small and not answerable to this tyme, respecting thadvauncement of pryses of all thinges belonginge to the said servantes and laborers, the said lawes cannot convenyentlie withoute the great greyfe and burden of the poore laborer and hired man, be put in good and due execution: and as the said severall Actes and Statutes were at the tyme of the makinge of them thought to be very good and beneficiall for the common welthe of this Realme, as dyvers of them yet are, So yf the substaunce of the manny of the saide lawes are as mete to be contynued shalbe digested and reduced into one sole lawe and statute. And in the same an unyforme ordre prescribed and lymytted concernynge the wages and other ordres for apprentices servauntes and laborers, their is good hope that it will come to passe that the same lawe, beinge duelie executed, shoulde bannyshe idlenes, avaunce husbandrie, and yelde unto the hyred persone bothe in the tyme of scarcitie and in the tyme of plentie a convenyent proporcion of Wages.'

Elizabeth inherited from her sister a debt of about £300,000, occasioned very largely by the war, which was then coming to an end. Thanks to her continuation of the Marquis of Winchester as Lord Treasurer, and her appointment of Thomas Gresham as agent in Flanders, Mary's financial management had been competent, and it was an achievement that the debt was no larger. However, it was mostly in Antwerp, and although Gresham managed to secure the cooperation of the City of London in servicing the debt, it was a somewhat grudging cooperation, as London was deeply unhappy about several aspects of government policy, notably the restoration of the Hanseatic privileges and Philip's determination to keep English merchants out of the American and west African trades. Gresham had actually rescued the exchange rate (which had at one point been as low as thirteen shillings sterling to the pound Flemish) before the end of Edward VI's reign, and had proved extremely adroit at manipulating credits and securing deferment of repayment dates. He and Winchester served throughout Mary's reign, and Elizabeth reappointed them both, the best (and almost the only) example of continuity between the two reigns.

At first, Elizabeth continued to borrow heavily in Antwerp, exploiting the fact that her credit was good. Unlike both Philip and Henry II, Mary and Elizabeth never defaulted. However, Elizabeth's slightly longer-term policy was to run down the Antwerp debt, transferring most of her credit transactions to London. This was partly because her relations with the City were very much better than her sister's had been, and partly because the political stability of the Low Countries was becoming increasingly problematic. By 1565, when the troubles in the Netherlands began in earnest, the transfer had largely been achieved.

The queen's good relations with London, mediated by Gresham, and her willingness to support the aspirations of the London merchants, is one of the main keys to the understanding of her policy in the 1560s. One consequence of this was the recoinage of 1561. From 1545 until 1551 the silver coinage had become increasingly debased, because first

Henry VIII and then Protector Somerset needed quick profits to pay for wars. At one point the minting touched 30 per cent fine, and the effect upon inflation was disastrous. The Duke of Northumberland checked this downward spiral (eventually) and began minting fine coin, a practice continued by Mary. However, until the base coin was recalled, all that happened was that the fine coin went to pay overseas debts, and the circulating medium continued to be poor. Two attempts to 'cry down' the face value of coins alleviated the problem, but did not cure it.

Until 1558 the council continued to believe that it could not afford the cost of a complete replacement, but urgent (and better informed) advice from the London financiers changed this perception, and in 1561 all the base coin was called in and replaced. Because the baseness of different issues varied, and redemption had to be at a fixed rate, the government ended by making a small profit on this transaction, as well as restoring stability to the currency. Inflation was checked, but only temporarily, as it was driven by a variety of other economic forces.

Elizabeth had nothing particularly original to offer by way of social policy. It had been received wisdom since at least the middle years of Henry VIII that it was the government's responsibility to protect domestic trades and manufactures, and to promote fair practice in employment, apprenticeship, and wage payment. The corpus of legislation developed for this purpose had, however, often responded to initiatives from the trades concerned. It was incoherent, and individual laws became unenforceable with changing circumstances. The great Statute of Artificers of 1563 was thus an attempt to codify employment law rather than to develop any new initiative. It was very long, extremely detailed, and decidedly overambitious. The way in which it was created, and the attempts thereafter to enforce it, form one of the major themes in the social history of Elizabethan England, exposing the limitations both of early modern economic thinking, and also of the resources of government.

TWENTY-NINE

New Departures

I

Memorandum by Sir William Cecil on the export trade in cloth and wool, *c.* 1564; taken from *Tudor Economic Documents* (1924), eds R.H. Tawney and Eileen Power, II, p. 45. The original MS is in the Domestic State Papers, PRO SP12/35, no. 33.

'Reasons to move a forbearyng of the restitution of the entercourse to Antwerpe.

It is to be confessed of all m[en] that it were better for this realme for manny considerations, that the commodities of the same wer issued owt rather to sondry places, than to one, and specially to such one as the lord therof is of so great power, as he may therewith annoye this realme by waye of [embargoes].

Secondly, it is probable that by the carryeng over into Antwerpe of such a quantity of commodities owt of the realme, as of late yeres is used, the shortnes of the retorn multeplyeth manny marchantes, and so consequently also this realme is overburdened with unnecessary forrayn wares, and if the trade therof shuld contynew but a whyle, a great part of the treasor of the monny of the realme wold be carryed thyther to answer for such unnecessary triffles, consideryng it is to be seene that very lately the commoditees carried out of the realm beyond the seas hath scantly answered the vallor of the merchandise brought in. And if the lawes for apparrell and taverns for excessyve abundance of wynes shall not be better observed, it is to be feared that the quantitie of our english commodities will be to small a great deale to answer the forrayn commodities.

Thirdly, it is to be thought that the deminution of clothyng in this realme wer proffitable to the same for manny causees; first, for that therby the tilladg of the realme is notoriosly decayed, which is yerly manifest in that, contrary to former tymes, the realme is dryven to be furnished with forrayn corne, and specially the Citee of London. Secondly, for that the people that depend uppon makyng of cloth ar of worss condition to be quyetly governed than the husband men. Thyrdly, that by convertyng of so manny people to clothyng, the realme lacketh not only artificers, which wer wont to inhabitt all corporat townes, but also laborers for all comen workes.

Whereuppon it followeth probably that it wer proffitable for the realme to have some alteration of the great trade of carrying of clothes out of the realme to Antwerp.

A second question.

But now the Question may be wyther the tyme as it is be mete to attempt such an alteration or no; wherin are to be considered these thynges following:

1. The unabilitie of the merchantes adventurors at Embden to endure any longer from bryngyng ther clothes to Antwerp to be ther dressed and dyed, without which help there qualitie of clothes is not vendable.

2. The staye of clothyng within the realme, what inconvenience it may bryng.

3. The forbearyng of the revennew which ought to grow to the Queens Maiesty of hir customs, both uppon clothes and uppon forrayn commodities to be brought inward.

Answer.

Consyderyng the matter of it self [it] wer to be wished to have the trade to Antwerp deminished, and that all redye a great part of the greefe is passed that tooched both the Queens Maiesty for hir customs, and the merchantes for there trade, it wer better to proceede, and to devise how these incommoditees both to the Queens Maiesty, the realme, and the merchantes might be eased, as the causes may beare, than to make a reverse, without any fruict to be had or gathered of these troobles now passed.

And in this behalf is to be considered:

First, for the Queens Maiestys customs, although the trade of drapyng and carryeng out of clothe shuld decaye, yet therby the quantitie of woll to be sent out of the realme shuld evidently incress, and though it shuld come but to the half of that quantitie that was wont to be carryed by the staplors, yet, as the custom therof is at this daye, the revennew to hir Maiesty will farr excede the custom that is of the clothe, or that hath bene sence the increase of the customs. And where exception is taken by the subiectes of the twoo kynges of france and spayne, that the customs of cloth ar increased contrary to the treaty, by convertyng the trade of cloth into woll, they could not have any cause to fynd fault with the increase of the custom of wolls, for that the same is a trade of ancient tyme appertayning to the staplors of England, establyshed before the tymes of the treatyes.

Secondly, for the merchantes adventurors, consideryng they have alreddy borne so much as they have, and that therby it will fall out that the unhable and unsufficient merchantes not mete to be favored shall break of and discontynew, it is no evill pollycy to suspend ther trade from the low contrye, wherby the trade may rest in the handes both of a fewer nombre of merchantes, of those that be rycher and that will deale and trade lyke merchants with ther stockes, and not with the exchange, as all the yong merchantes doo.

Thirdly, for the stay of the cloathyng in the realme, wherof is to be douted some inconvenience in the realme: first in that part is to be considered that this stey from antwerp will brede no stay of clothyng to such as make any collered clothes, or to them which make carseys, or to them of the north that mak course clothes, for that the vent of them remayneth as good as before, both into spayne, france, and into the est contreys. And the carseys that wer wont to be sent into Italy by experience may pass thyther from Embden. Wherfor the care that is to be taken is onely of such townes and contreys as make fyne whyte clothes. For order wherin, if the statutes that ar provyded for makyng of trew clothes, for prohibiting of men to be clothyars that have not bene brought upp in the faculty, and for such lyke [were enforced], it wold brede to make a smaller nombre of clothyars of that sort; and for the order of the multitud that now presently is therin occupyed, it wer to be hoped that if men of discretion and creditt wer appoynted to see therto ther might be devisees how to kepe that multitud occupyed, partly by procuryng the makers of those whyt clothes to dye and coller them, partly by employeng some of those people about handy craftes or other labors. And rather than therof shuld grow by Idlenes any inconvenience, it wer better to collect the sturdyer and stronger sort of the men, and to send them into Ireland to helpe the peoplyng of the contrees ther.'

II

Extracts from Hakluyt, *Principall Navigations*; taken from the facsimile edition by D.B. Quinn and R.A. Skelton (Hakluyt Society, Extra Series, 39, 1965), p. 553.

'The 3. unfortunate voyage made with the Jesus, the Minion and foure other shippes, to the partes of Guinea, and the West Indies, in the yeeres 1567 and 1568 by M.Iohn Hawkins.

The shippes departed from Plymouth, the second day of October Anno 1567 and had reasonable weather until the seventh day, at which time fortie leagues north from Cape Finister, there arose an extreame storme, which continued foure daies in such sorte that the fleete was dispersed . . . but the eleventh day of the same moneth, the wind changed, with faire weather, whereby we were animated to followe our enterprise, and so did. . . .

. . . From thence we past the time upon the coast of Guinea, searching with all diligence, the Rivers from Rio grande unto Sierra Leona, till the twelfth of Ianuarie, in which time we had not gotten together a hundred and fiftie negroes; yet notwithstanding the sickness of our men and the late time of the yeere commanded us away; and thus having nothing wherewith to seeke the coast of the West Indies, I was with the rest of our companie in consultation to goe to the coast of the Myne [El Mina], hoping there to have obtained some golde for our wares, and thinking to have defraied our charge. But even in that present instant, there came to us a Negroe, sent from a king, oppressed by other kings his neighbours, desiring oure aide, with promise that as many Negroes as by these wares might be obtained, as well of his part as of oures, should be at oure pleasure: whereupon we concluded to give aide, and sent 120 of our men, which the fifteenth of Ianuarie, assaulted a towne of the Negroes of our Allies adversaries, which had in it 8,000 Inhabitantes, and very strongly impaled and fenced, after their manner, but it was so well defended, that our men prevailed not, but lost six men and 40 hurt; so that our men sent forthwith to me for more helpe, whereupon considering that the good success of this enterprise might highly further the commoditie of our voyage, I wente myselfe, and with the helpe of the kinge of our side, assaulted the towne both by land and sea, and very hardly with fire (their houses being covered with dry Palme leaves) obtained the towne and put the Inhabitants to flight, where we took 250 persons, men, women and children, and by our friend the king of our side was taken 600 prisoners, whereof we hoped to have had our choice; but the Negroe (in which nation is seldom or never found truth) meant nothing lesse; for that night he removed his campe, and prisoners, so that we were faine to content us with those fewe which we had gotten ourselves. . . .

[They then cross the Atlantic] . . . thus leaving the towne [Rio de la Hacha], with some circumstance, as partly by the Spanyardes desire of Negroes & partly by friendship of the Treasorer, we obtained a seconde trade; whereupon the Spanyards resorted to us by night & bought of us to the number of 200 Negroes; in all other places where we traded the Spanyardes inhabitantes were glad of us and traded willingly. . . .

. . . & taken with a new storme which continued other 3 daies, we were inforced to take for our succour ye Port which serveth the Citie of Mexico called Saint John de Ulua, which standeth in xix degrees . . . the sixteenth day of september at nyght, being the very day of our arrivall, in the next morning which was the sixteenth [*sic*] day of the same moneth, we saw open of the Haven xiii great shippes, and understanding them to be the fleete of Spaine, I sent immediately to advertise the General of the Fleet of my being there, doing him to understand that before I would suffer them to enter ye Port, there should some order of condicions passe between us for our safe being there. . . .

. . . then we laboured ii daies, placing the English ships by them selves & the Spanish ships by them selves, and the captains of each part and inferioure men of their partes promising a great amity of all sides, which even as w[i]th all fidelity was ment of our part, so the Spanyardes ment nothing lesse for theire partes. . . . The vice Roy . . . forthwith blew the trumpet and of all sides set upon us; our men that were warded ashore, being striken with sudden feare, gave place, fled, and sought to recover the succour of the shippes . . . a few of them escaped aboard the Jesus. The great shippe which had by estimacion 300 men placed in her secretly, immediately fell aboard the Minion which by Gods appointment in the time of the suspition, which was onely one half houre, the Minion was made ready to avoide, and so leesing hir hedfastes, and hayling away by the stearne fastes, Shee was gotten out . . . the Mynions men which had alwaies theire sayles in a redinesse, thought to make sure worke, and so without eyther consent of the Captayne or Master cutte their sayle, so that very hardly I was received into the Minion.

The most part of the men that were left alyve in the Jesus, made shift and followed the Minion in a small boat, the rest which the little boate was not able to receave, were enforced to abide the mercy of the Spanyardes (which I doubt was very little); so with the Minion onely and the Judith (a small barke of fiftye tunne) wee escaped, which barke the same nyght forsook us in our great myserie. . . .'

III

Further extracts from Hakluyt, *Principall Navigations*, p. 594.

'The first voyage attempted and set foorth by the expert and valiant Captaine M. Francis Drake himselfe, with a ship called the Dragon, and another ship, and a Pinnesse, to Nombre de Dios and Dariene, about the year 1572. Written and recorded by one Lopez a Spaniard, in this manner followinge, which Spaniard, with the discourse about him, was taken at the River of Plate by the Ships set forth by the Right Honorable the Earle of Cumberland, in the year 1586.

There was a certeine English man named Francis Drake, who having intelligence howe the Towne of Nombre de Dios in Nova Hispania, had but small store of people remaining there, came on a night & entered the Porte with foure Pinnesses, and landed about 150 men, and leaving 70 men with a trumpet, in a Forte which was there, with the other 80 he entered the Towne, without doing any harme, till he came to the market place, and there discharged his calivers, and sounded his trumpet very loud, and the other which he had left in the Forte answered him after the same maner, with the discharging their calivers and sounding their trumpets; the people hereupon, not thinking of any such matter, were put in great feare, and waking out of their sleepe fled all into the mountaines, inquiring one of another what the matter should be, remaynyng as men amazed not knowing what the uprore was which happened so suddenly in the Towne. But fourteene or fifteene of them ioyning together with their harquebuses, went to the market place to knowe what they were that were in the Towne, and in a corner of the market place they did discover the English men, and seeing them to be but fewe, discharged their calivers at those English men: their fortune was such that they killed the Trumpeter, and shot one of the principall men thorow the leg, who seeing himselfe hurt, retyred to the Forte, where the rest of ther company was left; they which were in the Forte sounded their Trumpet, and seeing that they in the Towne did not answer them, and hearing the calivers, thought that all they in the Towne had been slaine, and thereupon fled to their Pinnesses; The English Captaine coming to the Forte, and not finding his men which he lefte there, hee and his were in so great feare, that leaving their furniture behinde them, and putting off their hose, swamme and waded all to their Pinnesses, and so went with their shippes again out of the Porte.

Thus the English Captaine called Francis Drake departed from Nombre de Dios, and slewe only one man in the Towne which was looking out of a window to see what the matter was, and of his men had only his Trumpeter slaine.

But he being discontented with the repulse which he had received there, came to the sound of Dariene, & having conference with certeine Negroes which were fled from their masters of Panama and Nombre de Dios, the Negroes did tell him that certaine mules came laden with golde and silver from Panama to Nombre de Dios, who in company with these Negroes went thereupon on land, and stayed in the way where the treasure should come with 100 shot, and so tooke two companies of mules, which came onely with their drivers, mistrusting nothing, and he caried away the gold only, for they were not able to carie the silver through the mountaines. And two dayes after he came to the house of the Crosses, where he killed six or seven merchantes, and found no golde nor silver, but much merchandise; so he fired the house, where was burnt above 200,000 Duckets in merchandise, and so went to his shippe againe; and within half an houre after he was a shipborde, there came downe to the sandes 300 shot of the Spaniards in the sight of his shippes, of purpose to seeke him, but hee cared little for them being out of their reache, and so departed with his treasure.'

At the end of Henry VIII's reign, England's overseas trade had been heavily dependent upon the export of unfinished woollen cloth from London to Antwerp. In the early 1550s that trade had got into difficulties for purely commercial reasons, and a period of economic instability was then followed by increasing political instability in the Netherlands after 1565. There were a number of possible solutions to this problem: one was to cut back on the manufacture of unfinished cloth, thereby reviving the trade in raw wool, which had been in decline for over a century; another was to build up the trade in finished cloth, which went mainly to other markets; and a third was to diversify the existing trade, not only beyond the Low Countries, but beyond Europe.

Cecil was quite clear that the temporary closure of Antwerp was a good thing, and he was not keen to see it reopened. His rather conservative brand of mercantilism would have preferred to see a reduction in the existing trade, which would, in his view, have had the beneficial effects of reducing the fringe of merchant interlopers (thereby strengthening the big companies), and improving the balance of trade. The Merchants Adventurers, however, were not very responsive. The trade in wool had gone too far to be revived, and the social effects of cutting back the well-established clothmaking industry would have been both damaging and dangerous. Their main remedy, and the policy actually pursued, was to seek new markets. It was this drive which sent explorers out in search of routes to China and Persia, as well as to Guinea and the New World.

In the course of these voyages, the adventurers also began to explore other possibilities, one of which was the Atlantic slave trade. The original idea had been to buy slaves for cloth, and supply them to the labour-starved Spanish colonies. Hawkins, however, had other ideas about how to acquire slaves, and his trading cannot have done much for the cloth industry. Such trading was strictly forbidden by the authorities in New Spain, but the profits were worth the risks.

Elizabeth was more adventurous than Cecil in this respect, and had become a shareholder in Hawkins's voyages as early as 1564. This was a new departure for the English Crown, and was of momentous significance. Hawkins was using royal ships, and holding the queen's commission when he was caught at San Juan d'Ulloa in 1568, and this gave his discomfiture diplomatic significance. Philip regarded such voyages as openly provocative, but neither Elizabeth nor the adventurers were deterred. The commander of the *Judith* (which so basely deserted Hawkins, according to his reminiscence written over twenty years later) had been Francis Drake. Drake emerged from that experience with a burning hatred of Spain, which he was to work out in many voyages, some private and some in the queen's service. Most were more successful than the one described here (from a Spanish source), and El Draque became a figure of terror as well as the spearhead of a new breed of English seamen. As explorers, merchants and pirates, they were driven by royal encouragement, by the financial interests of the City, and by their own ambition and greed.

THIRTY

Tragedy in Scotland

I

Extract from Camden, *Annals*, trs. A. Darcie (1625), p. 116.

'[1565] Darley [Henry, Lord Darnley] in the meane time, by the intercession of his mother [Margaret, Countess of Lennox], with prayers and diligence to Queene Elizabeth obtained (though with much difficulty) leave to goe into Scotland, and to stay there three moneths, under pretext to be partaker of his fathers establishment; and came to Edenborrough in the Moneth of Februarie, in the great winter, when the Thames was so frozen, that people passed dry over on foot. Hee was a youth of a most worthy Carriage, fit to beare rule, of an excellent composition of members, of a milde spirit, and of a most sweet behaviour. As soon as the Queene of Scotland had seen him, she fell in love with him; and to the end to keep her love secret, in discoursing with Randolph the English Ambassador in Scotland, she often times intermixt her discourse with the marriage of Leicester, and at the same time seeks a dispensation from Rome for Darley, shee being so neere in bloud, that accoring to the Popes Ordinance, they stoode in need of one. This being come to every bodies knowledge, she sent Lidington to Queene Elizabeth, to have her consent to contract with Darley, and not to be any longer detained with a vaine hope of marriage.

Quene Elizabeth propounds the matter to her most intimate Counsaillers; who, by the secret suggestions of the earle of Murray, easily beleeved that the Quene of Scotland had no other designe, but to strengthen herself by such a marriage, to carry the right which she pretended for the Kingdom of England, and at length to establish it, and likewise the Romish religion. . . . That to prevent these accidents, it was chiefly requisite, first, to pray the Quene to marry speedily, to the end that the affairs and hopes of England should not depend else-where, but of the certainty of Succession, which should come by her and of her lineage: (for they feared that if the Queene of Scotland did marry, and should have issue first, many would incline towards her for the certainty and assuredness of succession). Secondly, to ruine (as much as may be) the Romish religion in England, and to advance and carefully establish the reformed; the one by using more moderately in things indifferent, such protestants as are carried with a fervent zeale; the other in setting guards again upon the deposed papisticall bishops, who were dispersed through the Country. . . .

And that to hinder the marriage of Darley, it was fit to levy soldiers upon the Frontiers of Scotland, to the end to raise a terror. . . .

From hence, [Sir Nicholas] Throgmorton is sent to the Quene of Scotland, to advise her that it behooved her to deliberate long of a thing that can be but once determined on, and that a precipitate marriage was followed with repentance; to recommend Leicester to her again and again; and that it was altogether contrary to the Canon Law to contract with the son of her Aunt by the Father-side, for Queen Elizabeth desired above all that some of the English race should by her means succeed to both the kingdoms albeit there fayled not who for matter of Religion, and for the two Kingdoms, made account to succeed, if shee died without issue.

She answers that it is now past revoking, and that Queen Elizabeth had no cause to be angry, seeing that by her Counsell she had made choyce of a husband which was no stranger but an Englishman borne of the royall blood of both kingdoms, and the most noble of Great Brittain. . . .

The Queen of England, to interpose some hindrance to this so hastened marriage, calls back Lennox and his sonne Darley as being her subiectes, according to the form of leave which she had granted them. The father excuses himself modestly by letters, the Sonne prays her not to hinder his advancement, representing unto hir that he might be usefull to England his dearest contry . . . five months after his coming into Scotland she marries him with the consent of many peers, and declares him King.'

II

Extract from Holinshed, *Chronicle* (1807 edn; 9 Elizabeth), p. 231.

'Charles Iames, the sixt of that name, son to Henrie Stuart lord of Darnleie and Marie King and Queene of Scots was borne in Edenburgh castell, the nineteenth of Iune last past; and the eighteenth of December this year solemnlie christened at Stirling, whose godfathers at the christening were Charles K. of France and Philibert duke of Savoie, and the queenes maiestie of England was the godmother, who gave a font of gold curiously wrought and inameled, waieing three hundred and three and thirtie ounces, amounting in value to the summe of 1,043 pounds, nineteen shillings.

The tenth of Februarie in the morning, Henrie Stuart lord of Darnlie before named K. of Scots, by Scots in Scotland was shamefullie murthered, the revenge whereof remaineth in the mightie hand of God. The two and twentieth of Februarie, the lady Margaret Dowglas, countesse of Lineux, mother to the said king of Scots, was discharged out of the tower of London. . . .'

III

Extract from Camden, *Annals* (1635), p. 148.

'He [the Earl of Murray] was scarcely arrived in France, but they, who absolved Bothwell of that crime, and gave consent to this marriage, took up armes, as if they would have seyzed on his person. But in effect, under hand, they privily admonished him speedily to withdrawe himselfe, for feare lest, being taken, he might have revealed the whole Complot, and that from his flight, they might draw argument and subiect whereof to accuse the Queene, for the murder of a king, they seyzed on her person, and intreated her so ignominiously and disgracefully, that although she had nothing on, but a very homely night-Gowne, yet they so clapt her up in prison at Lake Levin, under the custody of the earl of Murray's mother, who was James the 5 his Concubine, who further persecuted her with most shamlesse malice, during her restraint, boasting how she was lawfull wife to james the 5. and her sonne lawfully descended from him.

So soone as Queene Elizabeth had certaine notice of all these proceedings, detesting in her heart this unbridled insolency of subiectes towards a Princesse who was her Sister and Neighbour, terming them perfidious, rebellious, ingratfull and cruel: She sent into Scotland Nicho. Throgmorton, to complaine hereof unto the Confederates, and to consult some meanes how to restore the Quene to her former liberty and authority, for the punishment of the kings murderers, and that the young prince might be sent into England, rather than France, for his more secure preservation and safety. . . .

. . . Finally, through feare of death, and without ever hearing her answers, they forced her to seal three Patents: the first of which contained that she assigned the government over to her sonne, who was scarcely thirteen months old; the second comprehending how she constituted Earle Murray to be Vice-Roy during her sonnes minority; and the third implyed, that in case Murray refused this charge, she ordeined for Rectors and Protectors of her sonne, the Duke of Chastelrault, and the earls of Lenox, Arguile, Athol, Morton, Glencome and Mar. . . . Five days after this Resignation or Grant, Iames, Sonne to the Queene was consecrated and Crowned king. . . .

. . . About the same time, the second day of May [1568] the prisoner Queen at Lake-Levin, made an escape out of prison, and retired to Hamilton Castle, by means of George Dowglasse, to whose Brother she was committed in guard; where, upon the testimonies of R. Melvin and others, and with the unanimous [consent] of all the Nobles who flocked thither in great numbers, Sentence definitive was uttered, That the Grant or Resignation, extorted by meere feare from the Prisoner Queene, was void from the beginning: and the Queene herself being present, tooke a solemne oath that it was extorted and forced from her. By meanes whereof, in two days such multitudes of men repayred to her out of all partes, as she raised an Army of six thousand brave soldiours, who notwithstanding, when they came to ioyne battell with Murray & fighting rather hare brainedly, then with wit or discretion, they were soon discomfited. This timorous Lady, being daunted with that hard success, betooke herself to flight, and rode the same day threescore miles; when, coming by night to Maxwells house, Baron of Herie, she had rather expose herselfe to the mercy of the Sea, and rely upon Quene Elizabeths protection, than upon the fidelitie of her subiectes. . . .

. . . What pitty and commiseration soever Queen Elizabeth had of her, the Councell of England deliberated gravely and advisedly, what in this case was to be done. They feared that if she remained any longer in England, having a persuasive and a moving tongue, she might drawe manie to her party who favoured the Title which she pretended to the Crowne of England. . . . Besides they considered that the fidelitie of her Guard might be doubtful, and that if she chanced to dye in England, though it were through some infirmitie or sicknesse, many slanders might be raised and so the Queene should be dayly encumbered with new cares. If she were sent into France, the Guizes her cousins would againe set on foot the Title whereby she laid claime to the crown of England. . . . That the Amity betwene England and scotland, so behoofefull and beneficiall, would be broken, and the ancient alliance between Scotland and France renewed. . . . Wherefore the greater part ioyned in opinion, that shee was to be retained in England, as beeing taken by the law of Armes, and not to be releast, till she had given over her present claime to the Crowne of England, which she tooke upon her, and answered for the death of the Lord Darley her husband, who was a naturall subject of England.'

Elizabeth's piqued comment, that Mary's marriage in haste would be repented at leisure, turned out to be tragically prophetic. The queen's decision offended many Scottish nobles, including the Earl of Murray, but the momentum of her actions succeeded in brushing their objections aside, and Murray's attempt to persuade Elizabeth to intervene was unsuccessful. Mary ordered the confiscation of the estates of those who had opposed her, and broke off diplomatic relations with England. Darnley, however, for whose sake she was pursuing this perilous course, proved to be an extremely unsatisfactory husband, let alone king. About two months before the birth of James he became involved in what was effectively a Protestant plot against the increasingly autocratic queen. He appears to have believed that Mary could be frightened into adopting a lower profile, and was under the impression that this would enhance his own role and importance.

The means chosen was the murder in the queen's presence of David Rizzio, her harmless Italian secretary. The plot failed in its intended purpose, but after the birth of James (which was Mary's moment of triumph), the couple became increasingly estranged. Mary found out about Darnley's involvement in the murder of Rizzio, and Darnley's behaviour became even more jealous and irresponsible. The christening of James (with full Catholic ritual) in December 1566 brought a brief period of apparent reconciliation. Suffering from a mild attack of smallpox, Darnley withdrew to the old provost's house in Kirk o' Fields, just outside Edinburgh. There, on 10 February 1567, he was murdered. The crime was brutal, and the responsibility never firmly established. Mary's position could have been strengthened; instead it was destroyed by her own reactions.

The man generally blamed was the Earl of Bothwell. Bothwell may have been the victim of a deliberate campaign of vilification, but the charge was plausible, as was the suspicion that the queen herself had been implicated. James Hepburn was a loyalist who had supported Mary of Guise against the Lords of the Congregation, and had many enemies in consequence; he also had many claims on Mary's gratitude. So the queen ignored the urgent advice of her more sober supporters (and Elizabeth), that the first priority was to clear her own name. Instead, she had Bothwell exonerated by a process which may have been authentic, but did not look it, and created him Duke of Orkney. Shortly after she allowed (and possibly encouraged) him to abduct her to his fortress near Dunbar, and on 15 May 1567 married him with Protestant rites. The transparency of this charade is demonstrated by the fact that he had divorced his previous wife just twelve days earlier.

Mary had now contrived to offend everyone, not least her loyal Catholic followers, and just a month later she and Bothwell were defeated by the outraged Lords of the Council at Carberry Hill. He managed to escape to Denmark, but she was captured and imprisoned in Loch Leven castle. Elizabeth had her own views about how to resolve this situation: that Mary should renounce Bothwell, and that the lords should restore her, on conditions. However, emotions in Scotland were running high, and her intervention was rejected by both sides. Relations between England and Scotland deteriorated, temporarily but dangerously. In July 1567 Mary was forced to abdicate in favour of her year-old son, and the Earl of Murray assumed the regency.

At first Elizabeth refused to recognise the new government, and endeavoured to put pressure on Murray. In May 1568 the ex-queen escaped, and made a determined attempt to recover her position, but was swiftly defeated by the regent at Langside. Faced with a return to prison, and possible execution as a rebel, Mary fled into England, supposing

Elizabeth to be her strongest source of support. The latter, however, now found herself caught in a web of her own weaving. The Scots had overwhelmingly rejected Mary, and to seek to restore her would mean war; similarly, to send her back without an army would have been to sign her death warrant. In spite of the obvious risks involved, Elizabeth decided to retain her unwelcome guest, using as a pretext the charges of murder and adultery which the Scottish lords were quick to present. Thereafter, Mary's role in Scotland was over, and she became a fiercely controversial player in English domestic politics.

THIRTY-ONE

Dangerous Courses, 1568–72

I

Extract from Camden, *Annals* (1635), p. 195.

'. . . it happened that certaine Marchants of Genoa and other parts of Italy, sent out of Spain and Flanders a quantity of coine, to have it put out to use, in a great ship of Biscay, and foure lesse, which the Spaniards term Zabras, which being chased by Chasteler a Frenchman, and defended by Winter an Englishman, had much ado to save themselves in the ports of Plimouth, Fawmouth and Southampton in England. So soon as the Quene was advertised of it, she commanded all the Magistrates of those parts to use the Spaniards very kindly, and to defend their Shipping against the French. . . . And therefore it was thought expedient to land it, for better security, which was done out of hand. But, notwithstanding it was not all brought on shore: for d'Espes, supposing the Queenes intention to be other then it was, gave the D. of Alva to understand, how she had seized upon it. While he was in consultation with him, Odet de Chastillon, Cardinal, who was retired into those parts by reason of the troubles in France, certefied the Queene that this money belonged to certaine Marchantes of Genoa, and not to the Spaniard, and that hee would seize upon it against their wills, to employ it to the ruine of the Protestantes. And this was the reason why the Councell made a question whether they should deliver it or no; and the greatest of them that sat in Councell were of opinion that it should be sent into the Low-Countries, for feare of provoking the Spaniard, who was a great Prince, and stood already but hardly affected to England. But Queen Elizabeth, being assured by two of them to whom it belonged, that the Marchants were only interested in it, the Kinge of Spaine nothing at all, she resolved to take it up of the Marchantes by way of loane, and give them [credit] for it, as princes many times use to do with such goods as they find in their ports, and the Spaniard not long before had done the like. And when the Spanish ambassador shewed her the Letter the Duke writ unto her, for the transportation of this money, she told him that she had taken it by loane, and religiously protested to restore it againe so soone as she should truely understand that it belonged to the King of Spain. The very same day, which was the twenty ninth of December [1568], the Duke in hot rage and furie, seized on the Englishmens goods, all the Low Countries over, where he found any, and taking their persons prisoners, comitted them to the gard of his soldiers. . . .'

II

Extracts from a statement made by the English ambassador resident in France to Don Frances de Alava, January 1569; taken from the *Calendar of State Papers, Spanish, 1568–1579*, p. 114.

'At the end of November last her Majesty the Queen received reports from her governors and officials in the West of England, namely in certain ports of Cornwall and Devon, that some ships had arrived there on their voyage to Flanders, and that there were certain armed French ships at sea, for fear of which neither they nor the English merchants dared put to sea, particularly such as desired to go to Bordeaux for wine, and the said ships on their way to Flanders . . . the master, one Lope de la Sierra . . . seeing the danger in which his ship was, begged the Governor in writing to help him place the treasure on shore, which was done three or four days before Christmas, and was put into a safe place under the seal of Lope de Sierra himself, so that no portion of it could be touched without his consent. On Lope de Sierra requesting that one of the boxes should be opened that he might take a sum out for his own expenses, this was done, and in this box as in other parts of the ship, documents were found proving that the money belonged to certain merchants, and was not the property of the King of Spain. . . . This was confirmed by the statement of some of the Spaniards who came with the treasure, to the effect that it belonged to certain merchants . . . and that as they [the merchants] were sure they would be paid a fair interest, they were willing that the Queen should have the use of it for a year, or longer, if she desired. . . . While her Majesty was awaiting the reply, the Spanish ambassador came to court on the 29th of December, asking that all the treasures should be removed from the places where it was; affirming that it was all the property of the King of Spain. . . . She, however, was now informed, she said, that the money belonged to Merchants, and, as in four or five days she would have further particulars, she assured him on her word that nothing should be done that could displease her brother the King. . . . The ambassador took his leave without any sign of being dissatisfied with this reply. On the 3rd January, which was the fifth day after the ambassador saw her, he having in the interim not seen the Queen or requested a reply, she learnt that Count Lodron had called together all the numerous English merchants residing in Antwerp on the 28th December, and told them that the Duke of Alva had given orders for the arrest of all their persons and property. This was the day before the ambassador had his answer. . . .'

III

Extracts from Camden, *Annals* (1635), p. 212.

'And finally the earl of Leicester being at Tichfield, found himself ill (or else counterfeited the sicke), and being visited and graciously comforted by the Queene, he was seized with such feare, that her Maiestie could easily descerne it, beholding the blood and vital senses to shrinke in himselfe: which was the cause, that after he had asked pardon, and implored forgiveness with sighs and teares of the Queene, he declared unto her all the busines from the beginning.

In that very same time, the Queene tooke the Duke [of Norfolk] aside into a Gallery, where she rebuked him sharply for having sought the Quene of Scotland in marriage without her leave and permission, commanding him to free himself of it for the fidelity and loyalty which he ought to beare unto his Sovereigne. The Duke most willingly promised the same, as if he despised the match. . . . But . . . her anger rather augmented then diminished, also many Noble men withdrew themselves by little and little from his familiarity, saluting him but with much adoe, and breaking off in haste their discourses. At this the Duke took his journey to London, without leave, and upon his way took his lodging at the Earl of Pembrokes house, who counselled him to be cheerfull. . . . That very day, Queene Elizabeth, moved with anger, refused to set at liberty the prisoned Quene, to the Scottish ambassadors who implored it of her Maiestie, and commanded that she should behave herself peaceably, or else she should see shortly, those upon whom she most relyed, cut off and beheaded. . . .

In the meane time the Duke, affrighted with the false rumour of the rebellion in the North, and being certefied of Leicester that he should be committed to prison, went into Norfolk, till his friends at court (as they promised) had stilled the storm, and he pacified the offended mind of the Queene with submissive, supplicative Letters. When he found no comfort among his owne, and Heiden, Cornwallis and others of his traine perswaded him that if he were guilty, should flye to the Queenes mercy, he was almost distracted with sorrow . . . he most submissively intreateth pardon, and forthwith prepareth to goe to the court . . . after his confession of the greater part, and a bitter check given him for departing the Court without leave, and being further accused of Innovation, was sent to the Tower of London. . . . Two dayes after the Bishop of Ross was likewise examined, and Ridolphi that Florentine Councillor, of whom both he and others made familiar and common use, committed in keeping to Sir Francis Walsingham. . . .

. . . the rumour of that rebellion to be excited in the North Country was daily augmented. To relate the matter more originally, there ran a great fame and bruit of this rebellion, about the beginning of autumn [1569], which at the first being continued, it presently strengthened and encreased, by reason of the frequent meetings of the Earles of Northumberland, Westmorland and some others; so that the Earl of Sussex then Governour and Deputie of the North, cited them before him, and interrogated them precisely about these reports and rumours. They could not deny but they had heard of it, marry so, they were in no wise guilty or culpable, with many and deep protestations, offering to lose their lives in the Queenes service against any rebels whatsoever; and thus he sent them back to their owne houses, with authoritie to enquire and search out the authors of this report, which nevertheless daily so augmented, as her Maiestie conceiving that nothing was rashly to be credited of so great men, so commanded them by the Lord of Sussex, to repaire presentlie to London, for the removing of all suspition. Notwithstanding my Lord of Sussex, I know not for what drift or policy, enioyned them to come and meet him, as if he meant to consult with them about some occasions of that Province. At the firste they drew backe, but presently after expressly refused to repaire thither. This ministered occasion to the Queenes Maiestie to command them by preremptory letters, which shee writ, and caused to be conveyed with all expedition, that laying apart all delays and excuses, they should incontinently appear in her roiall presence; and this onlie to terrify and absolutely divert them from entering in to this rebellion, or at the least that they might precipitately undertake the same, before they had rallied their forces, or that the matter grew to any maturitie. For they relyed uppon some secret succours, which the Scots Leaguers and the Duke of Alva were to land at Herripoole, within the Bishopricke of Durham, as afterwards it was manifest. . . .

. . . For to amasse and drawe together an ignorant multitude, they commanded some to take up armes for the Queenes defence; others were made to believe that all the great men of England conspired with them, to re-erect the Romish religion; other some they told how they were forced to take up armes for prevention that the auncient Nobility of England might not be trampled under foot by up-starts, and their country yielded as a prey to strangers. This carried them violently into a manifest rebellion. . . .'

IV

Extract from Holinshed, *Chronicle* (1807 edn), p. 235.

'On thursdaie the ninth of November [1569], Thomas Persie earle of Northumberland received the queenes maiesties letters to repaire to the court. And the same night other conspiritors perceiving him to be wavering and unconstant of promise made to them, caused a servant of his called

Beckwith (after he was laid in his bed) to bustle in, and to knocke on his chamber doore willing him in haste to arise and shift for himselfe, for that his enemies (whom he termed to be Sir Oswald Ulstrop and maister Vaughn) were about the parke, and beset him with great numbers of men. Whereupon he arose, and conveied himselfe awaie to his keepers house. In the same instant they caused the bels of the towne to be roong backwards, and so raised as manie as they could to their purpose. The next night the earle departed thense to Branspith, where he met with Charles earle of Westmerland, and the other confederats. Then by sundrie proclamations, they abusing manie of the queenes subiectes, commanded them in hir highnesse name, to repaire them in warlike manner, for the defence and suretie of hir maiesties person, sometimes affirming their dooings to be with the advice and consent of the nobilitie of this realme, who in deed were wholie bent (as manifestlie appeared) to spend their lives in dutifull obedience, against them and all other traitors, sometimes pretending for conscience sake to seke to reforme religion; sometimes declaring that they were driven to take this matter in hand, least otherwise forren princes might take it upon them, to the great perill of this realme.

Upon mondaie the thirteenth of November, they went to Durham with their banners displayed. And to get the more credit among the favorers of the old Romish religion, they had a crosse with a baner of the five wounds borne before them, sometime by old Norton sometime by others. As soone as they entered Durham they went to the minster, where they tore the bible, communion books and such other as were there. The same night they went againe to Branspith. The fourteenth daie of the same moneth, they went to Darington, and there had the masse, which the earles and the rest heard with such lewd devotion as they had. Then they sent their horsemen, to gather togither such number of men as they could. The fifteenth daie the earles parted; he of Northumberland to Richmond, then to Northallerton, and so to Borowbridge; and he of Westmerland to Ripon and after to Borowbridge, where they bothe met againe. On the eighteenth daie they went to Wetherbie, and there taried three or foure daies, and upon Clifford moore, nigh unto Bramham moore, they mistrusted themselves, at which time they [numbered] about two thousand horssemen and five thousand footemen, which was the greatest number that ever they were. From the which they intended to have marched toward Yorke, but their minds being suddenlie altered, they returned. . . .

. . . Sir George Bowes having surrendered Bernards castell (as before ye have heard) met the earle of Sussex thus marching forward with his armie at Sisaie, from whence they kept forward to Northallerton; and resting two nights there, they marched on to Croftbridge, then to Akle, and so to Durham and after to Newcastell. And the twentieth day of December they came to Hexham, from whence the rebells were gone the night before to

Naworth, where they counselled with Edward Dacres concerning their owne weakness, and also how they were not onlie pursued by the earle of Sussex and others with him, having a power with him of seven thousand men, beinge almost at their heels, but also by the earle of Warwicke and the lord Clinton, high admirall of England with a far greater armie of twelve thousand men. . . .

. . . the same night advertisement came from the earle of Sussex . . . that the two earles of Northumberland and Westmerland were fled . . . into Scotlande, without bidding their companie farewell. . . .

The fourthe and fifth of Ianuarie did suffer at Durham to the number of threescore and six, conestables and others, amongst whom the alderman of the towne and a priest called Plumtree were the most notable. Then Sir George Bowes being made marshall, finding manie to be fautors in the foresaid rebellion, did see them executed in divers places of the countrie.'

V

Extracts from a memorandum of letters written by Antonio de Guaras, chargé d'affaires to the Duke of Alva, 11, 17 and 22 June 1570; taken from the *Calendar of State Papers, Spanish, 1568–79*, p. 249.

'The English demand . . . that the earls of Northumberland and Westmorland shall be expelled, with the rest of the English outlaws. . . . The queen of Scotland and her people will not agree to these terms, which would be to their ruin, as the object of the queen of England, it is suspected, is to at once kill the Prince [James] and place on the throne the eldest son of Catherine [Grey] sister of Jane who was beheaded, he being a heretic. She would at once do this if the Queen of Scotland were to die. They much fear an agreement in France, and Councils are held every day in order to provide funds for the Admiral [Coligny], whom they urge not to come to terms. . . .

The object of the queen of England in sending the fleet with merchandise to the value of a million [ducats?] to Hamburg is mainly to place funds there in order to raise troops whenever they may be wanted by her, or whenever she may decide to help [William of] Orange, under the conviction that in due time through him something may be attempted in the States. . . .

. . . two gentlemen named Norton have been drawn and quartered in consequence of their steadfastness in the catholic faith. This has greatly scandalised and alarmed the people. . . .

The proclamation made by the Queen of England is simply a trick with the object of satisfying her people and entertaining his Majesty and the Duke [of Alva], since under the flags of the Admiral, Vendome, and the prince of Orange, the whole channel, from Falmouth to the Downs is infested with ships to the number of forty, and twelve frigates, each one of which contains a dozen or fifteen Englishmen. They assail every ship that passes, of whatever nation, and after capturing them equip them for their own purposes, by this means continually increasing their fleet, with the intention on the part of the Queen, thus to make war on his Majesty, without its costing her anything, and under the specious pretence that she is not responsible since the pirates carry authority from Chatillon, Vendome and Orange. . . .

It is useless, therefore, to treat for a settlement with the English since, however just may be our demands, they will claim absurd terms. They demand that his Majesty should again assure them the following conditions, namely: That they may have freedom to trade in the Indies; that the English property confiscated for years past by the Holy Office should be restored; that the English pirate Hawkins should have returned to him the property taken from him by the Viceroy a year and a half since, and that which was captured from him in the Indies, valued at a great sum. . . . They demand that his Majesty should guarantee them all these absurdities, because they know very well that such terms will not even be listened to. . . .

The declaration of the Pope against the Queen has been posted on the bishop of London's gate, which has caused great sorrow to the bad people and much delight to the godly, who are convinced that, as a consequence of it, redress for their evils will follow by the arms of Christian princes, since this declaration can only have been made by the consent of such princes, and especially of his Majesty. The first result of the declaration has been the persecution and imprisonment of catholics . . . [the Queen's] heart is much corrupted, and she herself [has] answered the Pope's declaration in Latin verse, scoffing at the apostolic authority, saying that the boat of St. Peter should never enter a port of hers, and other heresies of a like nature.'

Two events of 1568 destroyed the relative domestic calm of the first decade of Elizabeth's reign. The first was the unwelcome arrival of Mary, Queen of Scots, and the second was the attack upon John Hawkins at San Juan d'Ulloa. Mary's sudden availability, and the fact that her marriage to Bothwell was generally considered to have been unlawful, prompted the thought among conservative nobles (and even councillors) that an ideal solution to the problem of the succession would be to marry her to a conformist English noble. At the very least the prospect of such a match would force Elizabeth's hand. It might also have the effect of diminishing the authority of the powerful Principal Secretary, Cecil, or even of removing him from office altogether.

Consequently, a scheme, or plot, was concocted, to marry Mary to the Duke of Norfolk. Whether the queen was supposed to be persuaded into giving her consent to this match, or to be faced with a fait accompli, is not entirely clear. A number of nobles and councillors opposed to Cecil, including the Earl of Leicester, were implicated in the plot. Elizabeth, however, became suspicious, and Leicester, sensitive to her mood and anxious above all to retain his own position, revealed the whole matter. Her anger was immediately apparent, and Norfolk fled from court without licence, taking refuge on his extensive estates in East Anglia. There were immediately rumours that he was 'raising a power', which drew fears of widespread rebellion; but in fact Norfolk's affinity refused to back him, and he seems to have done hardly more than consult their opinions. He had little stomach for a fight, and when it became clear that he could expect no support, he returned to court in an attempt to make his peace.

Hawkins's discomfiture had no connection with Mary, or Norfolk, but it exacerbated tensions in a different way. In November 1568 a number of Genoese ships carrying coin were driven into Plymouth and Falmouth by a combination of bad weather and French privateers. Elizabeth had already issued instructions to her own fleet to protect Spanish vessels against the French, but no sooner had these ships sought refuge than word arrived of what had happened at San Juan d'Ulloa. It is not certain how this news was transmitted, because Hawkins did not return until January, but demands were immediately made that the Spanish treasure should be seized in reprisal. Exactly what happened is not clear, but it seems that neither the English nor the Spanish versions given here are strictly accurate.

The money was plainly intended to pay Alva's troops in the Netherlands, but Elizabeth discovered that it had not been handed over, and therefore was still technically the property of the Genoese bankers. Acting on Cecil's advice, and probably against the advice of more cautious councillors, the queen moved swiftly to impound the coin, and borrow it herself. She had already done this when she fobbed off the Spanish ambassador with a delaying answer on 29 December, so her response to him was less than honest. On the other hand, it seems that this was already known to Alva when he ordered the impounding of English goods on the 28th, so Spanish indignation about the outcome was also disingenuous.

Elizabeth was left, in a sense, with the moral high ground as well as the money, because she could (and did) claim that her action was provoked by Alva's precipitancy, rather than the other way round. Cecil was denounced by his opponents as a danger to the state, because he had provoked so serious a rupture with the Low Countries. Elizabeth, however, took the full responsibility herself, and this so strengthened the Principal Secretary's position that it became apparent that any attempt to unseat him would be doomed to defeat. It was at that point that Leicester decided to salvage his own position by revealing the Norfolk marriage plot which was an essential part of the anti-Cecil conspiracy.

Norfolk was sent to the Tower, and that left all the others who had been in the plot (except Leicester) dangerously exposed. The Earls of Northumberland and Westmorland were in that position. Both had grievances against the regime, and were hoping to mobilise conservative opinion to remove Cecil and persuade Elizabeth to recognise Mary as her heir. They were probably also hoping to modify the religious settlement in a conservative direction, having misinterpreted the queen's cautious approach to enforcing that settlement. Unfortunately for them, they were being used as stalking horses by a more radical Catholic group in the north-east, led by the Nortons, whose aim was to depose the queen with Spanish help, and install Mary on the throne. The Earl of Sussex gave them every opportunity to dissociate themselves from the rumours of impending rebellion, but they failed to do so, and the queen forced the issue by summoning them to court.

In the ensuing confusion, it is unclear who was deceiving who. Northumberland, at least, seems to have been bounced into action by one of his servants who was in league with the radicals, and thus the latter were apparently controlling the agenda. Norton was well aware that support for an open attack upon the queen would have been small, but loyalty to the Percy and Neville families, together with widespread discontent over the religious settlement, enabled him to dissemble his real intentions and to raise a force by what were virtually false pretences. However reluctantly the earls may have acted, once they had done so there was no going back.

The symbolic march on Durham, and the capture of Barnard Castle from Sir George Bowes were the rebels' two main achievements. The intention seems to have been to emulate the Pilgrimage of Grace of 1536, but as they moved south it became clear that they had nothing like the appeal of the earlier movement. Once they were outside the Percy and Neville estates, which were mostly in Northumberland, Durham and the North Riding of Yorkshire, hardly anyone joined them. The pilgrims had mustered 30,000 men by the time they advanced on Doncaster, but the earls never had more than a quarter of that number. Moreover, the force which the Earl of Sussex had mustered against them at least matched their own strength, and was better armed. At Bramham Moor they halted, and then turned back. The Spanish aid which the Nortons had hoped for did not materialise, and was never going to do so, because the Duke of Alva had no opinion of their chances, and had no men to waste on a wild-goose chase.

The dwindling rebel force retreated north, first to Newcastle, then to Hexham, and finally to Naworth, where the decision was taken to disband. The earls themselves took refuge temporarily in Scotland, and their followers were for the most part left to face the consequences of their actions. The majority of the gentlemen of the north-east were now desperate to prove their loyalty to the queen, and a large number of trials and executions followed. The government was not only anxious to deter any further such action, but also was keen to grasp the opportunity to restructure the politics of the northern borders. The Percy and Neville estates were seized and redistributed, and the leadership of the area passed permanently into the hands of loyal gentry such as Sir John Forster, or courtiers such as Lord Hunsdon and the Earl of Huntingdon. As a result of this rebellion, the power of the border magnates was broken for the last time.

The other main consequence was a rapid sharpening of the religious focus. For ten years Elizabeth had been as ambivalent as possible within the parameters her own settlement had laid down. There had been no religious persecution, and only mild coercion. The rebellion changed all that because the rebels had appealed to Pope Pius V to legitimate their action in the name of the Catholic Church, arguing that they would have enjoyed overwhelming support if the pope had given a lead. Pius duly obliged by issuing the bull *Regnans in Excelsis*, declaring Elizabeth to be deposed, and the allegiance of all her subjects annulled. Not only did this come far too late to do the rebels any good, it also constituted a declaration of war to which the queen was forced to respond.

The Nortons would probably have been executed as traitors anyway, but from this point on all Catholics were (at least potentially) tarred with the same brush. In spite of Guaras's blinkered view, this caused no rejoicing among the English Catholics, who were now faced with a cruel dilemma which they would have much preferred to avoid. Nor was Pius's action welcomed by Catholic princes, such as Philip II, who had no intention of launching a crusade which did not coincide with their own political interests. The logic of this situation drove loyal religious conservatives (the great majority) away from the Catholic Church into reluctant conformity. Those who now perceived their primary allegiance to belong to the Church became recusants, an identifiable and increasingly alienated minority.

THIRTY-TWO

French Connections

I

Extract from Holinshed, *Chronicle* (1807 edn), p. 252.

'Whilst this iornie was made (as ye have haerd) into Scotland, the five and twentieth daie of Maie [1570] in the morning was found hanging on the bishop of London's palace gate in Paul's churchyard, a bull which latelie had beene sent from Rome, conteininge diverse horrible treasons against the queenes Maiestie; for the which one John Felton was shortly after apprehended, and committed to the Tower of London. And because the saide bull may appeare and shew itself in nature and kind, it is behoofull here to interlace some roringes of the same, as I have gathered them out of one that I am sure had a conscience to tell the truth; which I am therefore the willinger to insert, that the world may iudge the heinousness of Felton's fact, in fixing so pestillent a libell upon a prelates gate in a place of common concourse and against the Queenes excellent maiestie.

[Latin text]

A Sentence Denounced against Elizabeth etc.

Pius bishop, servant of God's servants etc. Shee [Queen Elizabeth] hath clene put awaie the sacrifice of the masse, praiers, fastings, choise of difference of meats and single life. She invaded the kingdom and by usurping monstrouslie the place of the Supreme head of the Church in all England, and the chiefe aucthoritie and iurisdiction of the same, hath againe brought the saide realme into miserable destruction. Shee hath removed the noble men of England from the Kings councill. Shee hath made her councell of poore, darke, beggerlie fellowes, and hath placed them over the people. These councillors are not only poore and beggerlie, but also heretikes. Unto her all such as are the woorst of the people resort, and are by hir received into safe protection etc. We make it knowen, that Elizabeth aforesaid, and as many as stand on hir side in the matters abovenamed, have cum into the danger of our cursse. We make it also known that we have deprived hir from that right shee pretended to have in the kingdome aforesaid, and also from all and everie hir authoritie, dignitie and privilege. We charge and forbid all and everie the nobles, and subiectes and people, and others aforesaid, that they be not so hardie as to obeie hir or her will and commandments, or lawes, upon paine of the like acursse upon them. We pronounce that all whosoever by anie occasion have taken their oth unto hir, are for ever discharged of any such oath, and also from all fealtie and service which was due to hir by reason of hir government etc.

Heere hath everie true subiect to see whether Felton was not a friend to Pius Quintus, in so easilie being induced and drawne to prefer his proceeding against the lords annointed; for whose sake if he had a thousand lives, true loyaltie would have invited him to the losse of them all if occasion had so required; considering that her maiestie hath alwaies deserved well of her people. . . .

. . . .The first of June [1571] Iohn Storie, a doctor of the canon law, who before had been condemned of high treason, was drawen from the tower of London to Tiburne, and there hanged, bowelled and quartered, his head was set on London bridge, and his quarters on the gates of the citie. Of this monster disguised in the likeness of a man, it is very material to record what master Fox hath noted in his historie. . . .

. . . The 22nd of August [1572] Thomas Persie earle of Northumberland late of Topcliffe, who had beene before attainted by parliament of high treason, as one of the principall conspiritors in the late rebellion, and was brought out of Scotland, whither he had fled, was beheaded at Yorke about two of the clocke in the afternoone, on a new scaffolde set up for that purpose in the market place. . . .'

II

Extracts from the despatch of Sir Thomas Smith and Sir Henry Killigrew in France, 8 January 1572; taken from the *Calendar of State Papers, Foreign, 1572–1579*, pp. 8–10.

'[They] had audience with the Queen Mother in her chamber on the 6th instant, the king her son and all the rest being most busy with their dancing; when in answer to Smith's earnest demand the Queen Mother declared that the only stay of the marriage between the Queen of England and the duke of Anjou was religion, wherein he was so earnest that he thought he would be damned if he yielded in anything. Smith asked whether if they yielded to him in religion, would all then be done. The Queen answered that there were other things which he would require towards his honour and dignity, but that this was the chief. Smith replied that the matter of religion would be the most honourable to break off with, both for his mistress and the Duke. The Queen Mother declared that they meant no breaking off, and never desired anything more in their lives than this, but that he was so "assotied" that they could not tell how to rule him, his conscience being so troubled if he might not have the exercise of the religion Catholic. Hereupon both Killigrew and Smith declared that the Queen meant at this time effectually to marry, and although of herself she had no mind thereto, yet the continual crying unto her of her Privy Council, the necessity of the time, and the love of her subjects, had turned her mind; and Smith further rehearsed what her Majesty had said to him at Walden, when she sent him to search out the Duke of Norfolk's doings, and at other times touching her inclination for the weal of her realm to marry. After further declarations of their mutual desires for the completion of the match, Smith desired to know what was required touching religion, saying that liberty of conscience and the private exercise of his religion had already been granted, and that there was nothing excepted but such part of the mass as cannot agree with God's word. The Queen Mother said that he had always been brought up in the Roman Catholic religion, and without he had his mass he thought he would be damned. Smith asked whether if he were suffered for a time to have his mass private, in some little oratory or chapel, so that there should be no scandal to any of the Queen's subjects whether that would suffice. The Queen Mother replied that he must have the exercise of his religion open, lest he should seem to be ashamed of it, and that he was now of late so devout that he heard his two or three masses every day, and fasted the Lent and vigils so precisely "that he began to be lean and evil coloured", so that she was angry with him and told him that she "had rather he were an Huguenot than be so foolishly precise to hurt his health"; and therefore he will not be content to have his mass in a corner, but will have a high mass and all the ceremonies thereof according to the time, and in song, and after all solemn fashion of the Roman Church, and a church or chapel appointed where he may openly have his priests and singers, and use all their ceremonies. "Why Madame" (quoth Smith), "then he may require also the four orders of friars, monks, canons, pilgrimages, pardons, oil and cream, relics and all such trumperies", that in nowise can be agreed. "Well, this was given to M. de Foix to demand" (quoth she). On Smith's pointing out the danger that would arise from suffering two religions in England, the Queen Mother said that the king her son suffered two in his realm, and that all was quiet and that the people agreed well enough. . . . Smith said that in Queen Mary's days many hundreds and thousands had been put to death, some by hunger, some burned and some hanged, and yet when the Queen's Majesty came one day turned all, and that by the whole consent of the three estates and of all England the religion was established again. . . .

. . . On the following day M. de Foix and M. de Limoges had conference with them, and told them that the Queen Mother had talked with the King and Monsieur [the Duke of Anjou], and that the latter would nothing relent, but caused his answer to be put in writing, which they delivered to them. Smith said that he would rather die than move the Queen to agree to it. M. de Limoges said that they were so earnest with Monsieur that he never saw the king in greater chafe, and the Queen Mother wept hot tears. If this alliance might not be, which was not likely, yet the King and Queen Mother said that if the Duke of Alençon [Francois, the Duke of Anjou's younger brother] might be thought meet, or if there were any other league or amity that the Queen might require, they would be ready to do it.'

III

Extract from Camden, *Annals* (1635), p. 311.

'. . . At that very time a pleasing serenity seemed to shine upon the Protestantes in France, and Charles the Ninth pretending only a war in Flanders, which he affirmed to be [for] the preservation of France, and covering himselfe with this maske, he feigned as though he meant to contract alliance and amitie with the Queene of England, and the Princes of Germany, to give some testimonie herein of his love to the Protestantes, whose absolute ruine nothwithstanding he covertly intended. And as if he leaned to them of the one side, and the Spaniard on the other, he substituted to this end the Duke de Mont-Morency, Biray de Amboise, the Bishop of Limoges, and of Foix. The Queene of England, who secretly apprehended the secret plots and strategems of the Duke of Alva, deputed Sir Thomas Smith and Sir Francis Walsingham. And Articles were drawn between them, whereof you shall see an abridgement in the same expresse wordes and termes: "This alliance shall not tye Princes allyed, to leave other Treaties past betweene them, so they be not opposite and contrary thereunto. There shall be a consideration, League and Union betweene them, to defend themselves mutually against all, who, under some pretext, or any other occasion whatsoever, shall invade or attempt to invade their persons or Territories, whereof they are now possesst. It shall remaine firme betweene them, not onely while they live, but also betweene their successors, so the Heire of the first deceased give notice to the survivant within the space of a yeare, by Ambassadors and letters, that hee accepts the same conditions. Otherwise the survivant shall be reputed discharged of the observance of the same. It shall be validious against all, yea even against those that are ioined in affinitie to the one or other Prince, and against all other Alliances contracted or to contract. If the Queene of England be required to send succours, by Letters sealed and subscribed with the King of France his owne hand, shee shall be bound to passe over into France within two moneths after, a thousand foot armed, or five hundred horse at her choyc, whom the king must pay, from the first day of their arrivall in France. Shee was to find for the warre of Flanders eight Ships of equall greatnesse, wherein twelve hundred souldiers must be imployed, with all things necessary, and there must be no Marreners nor Souldiers but English, but yet they must be commanded by the Admirall of France, payed and victualled by the king, from the first day they enter into service. Shee was also to victuall her ships for two moneths, which the king was also to pay within two moneths. And if the Queene be moved to any warre, the King having received Letters subscribed with her own hand, was to send over into England, or Ireland, within two moneths, sixe thousand foote, or at her choyce, five hundred Conductors, armed at all poynts, who should bring fifteene hundred horse, and about three thousand foot, with good Horse and armes, after the French manner, whom shee must pay, from the time they set foote in her countries. And for the Warre by sea, he was to furnish eight shippes, with twelve hundred souldiers, in manner and forme above mentioned. Order agreed upon for succours and pay, to be digest in writing, running on this form, that the one shall be bound to sell unto the other Armes and all necessary things, to the Prince assayled. They shall innovate nothing in Scotland, but defend it against strangers, and [not to?] permit them to enter and nourish Scottish particularities. But the Queene of England was permitted to pursue with armes those amongst them who maintained or fostered the English rebels, who were at that present in Scotland. That this alliance shall be so taken and understood, as the onelie proprietie and meaning of the wordes imported. Each of the two Princes shall confirme every one of these Articles by Patents, and faithfully and really to deliver them into the hands of Ambassadours, for the one and the other within three moneths".

. . . While Mont-Morency remayned in England [for ratifying the treaty] he moved certain propositions in the King of France his name, that the Queene of Scots might find favour, so farre as it might be performed without danger. That there might be a cessation of Armes in Scotland, and that a Concord might be established by Act of Parliament. And if a Parliament could not commodiously be summoned, that there might be elected of the one and of the other part, among the Scots, to repayre to London, to settle affairs with the deputies of the King of France and the Queene of England.

But answere was made him, that more favour had been showed to the Queene of Scots then shee deserved, and yet for the King of France, more should be shewed her, though the Estates of the Kingdom assembled had iudged, how the Queene of England could not live in security, except some rigour were used to her. That the Queene had carefully employed her whole power to establish Concord, and procure a cessation of Armes, having for this end lately sent into Scotland Sir William Drewry, Governour of Berwick, with la Croce, the French ambassador. But they could by no means induce

Grange to peace, nor the garrison of the Castle of Edenborrough, out of the hope they conceived to be succoured from France and Flanders; though Huntly and Hamilton Arbroath for the Duke their father had obliged themselves in writing to Queene Elizabeth, to enter it, and other of the Queens partakers had plighted their faith and promise thereto.

After these motives, he also propounded many other, touching the marriage of the Duke of Anjou, but in that they could not agree about some circumstances concerning religion, the matter grew hopeless, and he returned to France. . . .'

In the years 1570–2 the various threads of Elizabeth's policy were closely interwoven. She was afraid of Alva's threatening posture in the Netherlands, and of the danger of Catholic rebellion or conspiracy in the wake of the papal bull. She also wanted to be rid of Mary Stuart, preferably by a negotiated and conditional restoration to the throne of Scotland. All this pointed to a rapprochement with France, and her diplomatic efforts began to be directed to that end. As early as 1568 some motions had been made in France for a marriage between her and the king's younger brother, Henri, Duke of Anjou, but with civil war raging in that country, the time was not ripe.

However, in 1570 the peace of St Germain promised (wrongly, as it turned out) a more stable future for France, and the king's party in Scotland absolutely refused to have anything to do with the return of Mary, except as a private citizen. Encouraged by Elizabeth's attitude, and believing that the French were bound to aid them, the queen's party returned to arms, and this increased rather than diminished the need for a deal with France. After the peace of St Germain the Huguenot leaders had returned to court, and Charles IX had fallen increasingly under the influence of the admiral Gaspard de Coligny. Coligny's objective was to consolidate Huguenot political influence by persuading the king that Alva constituted a threat to France which must be countered. This brought an alliance with England, and the Anjou marriage to the top of the agenda.

Meanwhile, the Catholic conspiracy which Elizabeth feared had taken shape, through the complex machinations of the Italian financier Roberto Ridolfi. Ridolfi had papal support, and believed that he had enough backing in England to engineer a Catholic coup in favour of Mary. He also thought that he had the support of Alva. How serious a danger Ridolfi really represented is still controversial. As early as February 1571 he secured Mary Stuart's backing, and the much more reluctant cooperation of the Duke of Norfolk, still smarting under his earlier humiliation. However, Alva refused to be drawn into what he regarded as a hare-brained scheme, and by September 1571

Walsingham's agents had the whole plot in their hands. The Duke of Norfolk was convicted of treason in January 1572, although it was to be six months before he was executed, and there could no longer be any question of supporting Mary's claim to return to Scotland. Instead, there was mounting pressure in England for her to be tried and executed, a pressure which Elizabeth resisted at great cost to herself, for another fifteen years.

Simultaneously with these developments, and obviously influenced by them, negotiations for the Anjou marriage began in earnest. There is no reason to suppose that Elizabeth felt any affection for the duke (whom she had never seen), but she may well have been honest in admitting that the constant pressure from her own subjects was wearing her down. She was now thirty-eight, and time was running out. However, the most compelling motive was the need to seal (with some security) an agreement with France. The present alignment of political forces in that country not only offered the promise of a lasting solution to the Scottish problem, but also of a defensive alliance against the increasingly likely threat of Spanish aggression.

It soon transpired that marriage was not the most convenient way to achieve such an agreement. The Duke of Anjou (who was not a particularly stable character at the best of times) was apparently going through a *devot* phase, and regarded anything akin to heresy with pious horror. Charles and Catherine de Medici (the Queen Mother) may well have been as put out as they claimed by this behaviour, because such a marriage offered enormous potential advantages to France. They also wanted the alliance, for completely different reasons, and that eventually gave Elizabeth what she wanted, without having to pay the price that she feared. On 21 April the treaty of Blois was signed. The Anjou marriage had foundered on the rock of religious conflict, but that did not prevent the signature of a treaty of mutual defence, which also gave the English a virtual free hand in Scotland, and spelt the end for the queen's party there. The Earl of Northumberland was duly handed over by James's regency council, and executed at York.

Catherine's optimistic remarks about the peaceful religious situation in France were mere whistling in the dark. Within a few months the St Bartholomew's day massacre, a Guise coup which implicated both Charles and Catherine, had blown away the semblance of religious peace, and rendered the treaty of Blois a dead letter. It was never abrogated – because Catherine clung to it as a slender means of resisting Guise control, and Elizabeth clung to it as her relations with Philip went from bad to worse – but neither side invoked it either, or believed that it would be possible to do so. It was still there when the Duke of Alençon returned to the frame as a candidate for the queen's hand.

THIRTY-THREE

The Problem of the Netherlands

I

Extract from 'Memoires des sources et causes des troubles des Pay d'Enbas . . .' by Cardinal Granvelle (August 1559); taken from the translation by H.H. Rowen in *The Low Countries in Early Modern Times* (London, 1972), pp. 27–9.

'The first and principal [cause] is the will of God, and his infallible and irrefutable decision to punish the sin of insolence. This country was already too prosperous, so that the people were not able to resist luxury and gave in to every vice, exceeding the proper limits of their stations. They sank into debt as a result and were no longer able to support themselves in the style to which they had grown accustomed; they found their resources eaten up by the interest which they owed to the merchants. They could see no better way out of their situation than to change the government and avoid the authority of the courts of law, which would not be able to compel them to pay their debts. . . . This is why, when the Estates General met at such an unfortunate time, the nobles and merchants reached agreement and took away the management of taxation from the financial officials and put it into the hands of the merchants. The merchants then lent money to the nobles and supplied pay for their soldiers, while making their own profit from the use of the tax monies. Finally, when the soldiers became dissatisfied, this became a pretext for alienating the affection which the soldiers owed to His Majesty, their prince and natural lord, and for bringing them into their own service; they made a show of compassion for them and took care of their complaints, offering aid and placing responsibility upon the king and his ministers in order to get them hated.

Great harm, especially in the matter of religion, also resulted from intercourse with foreigners, which could not be avoided because of the needs of commerce. Various Germans, Italians, Burgundians and others among the nobles made use of the Netherlanders, turned them into dangerous men, preaching freedom to them and blinding them with a belief in their own greatness and that they did not have to accept being governed but should seek to govern themselves. . . .'

II

Proclamation banishing pirates from English ports, 1 March 1572; taken from Hughes and Larkin, *Tudor Royal Proclamations* (New Haven/London, 1969), II, no. 585.

'The Queen's Majesty doth straightly charge and command all the searovers, commonly called freebooters, of what nation or country soever they be, to depart and avoid all her highness' ports, roads and towns with all speed, and hereafter not to return to any of the same again, upon pain of forfeiture of their ships and goods, and imprisonment of their bodies at her Majesty's pleasure.

And that no subject of her majesty nor any other inhabitant of this realm do send or convey any victuals, munitions or other necessaries to them or any of them, or by any ways or means directly or indirectly do traffic with them, or buy any wares, merchandise, or other things of them, upon pain of death. . . .'

III

Extract from Camden, *Annals* (1635), p. 322.

'[1573] The proceedinge of Spaine in the Low Coutries, being wonderfully lost by the taking of Flushing, the revolt of the Townes of Holland, and the losse and discomfiture of the Spanish fleet by the Hollanders, with which the Duke of Medina Ceoli had a commission with Captain Vitelli to succour the papists in England. The Duke of Alva was constrained in despight of himself, to show himself more favourable to the English; and so it happened in the month of Ianuarie, the commerce of the English with the Flemmings, which in the same month of the year 1568 was interdicted, at last came to be open for two years, and the articles were agreed upon at Bristol, confirmed by the Spaniard in the month of Iune, amongst which this clause was inserted:

"That though this mutual correspondencie and amitie hath been obscured, yet it was in nowise to be reputed dissolved and broken; and it was accorded that if the Deputies within a certain prescript time, could not arbitrate the business, that then the said entercourse should be expired, when the two yeares came to an end."

But when the troubles renewed in Flaunders, it grew dead by little and little; nay and before the two yeares were fully accomplished, and a new one was commenst, between the united States. And as for Queene Elizabeth, she recommpensed all the dammages of the English merchants, with such

Flemish goods as she retained in her hands, restored the rest to the Duke of Alva, and amply contented the Genoa merchants for the mony of theirs she seized upon and took up at loan, which was the first cause of the warre, although the Duke of Alva restored not one shilling to the Flemmings of the Englishmens goods, which did accrue to the wonderful honour of Queene Elizabeth. And yet she preferred a far more glorious action than this, and more pleasing to her Subiectes, by discharging England of those debts which her Father and Brother had taken upon credit of strangers, which were greatly augmented by reason of the long interests due; and to the inexplicable [*sic*] ioy of the inhabitauntes of the Citie of London, calling in all the Citie obligations, which had been so often renewed. . . .'

IV

Extract from a letter of intelligence sent anonymously from London to the Duke of Alva, 16 September 1572; taken from the *Calendar of State Papers, Spanish, 1568–1579*, pp. 413–15.

'I wrote to your Excellency on the 8th by Antonio de Tassis, and the news now is that, the court learns that the prince of Orange has entered the States in force and that the towns have received him, and nearly all Holland is for him. A gentleman of this city, named Thomas Gresham, a very rich and important man, has therefore been sent secretly to Holland by sea. He has lived in the States for many years as factor of the kings and queens of England, speaks Flemish well, and has been a great friend of the prince of Orange. He is taking a large sum of money, and bills for the purpose of supporting the Prince if he prospers in his enterprise, which God forbid, but one of the causes of his going is to claim the countess of Northumberland, wife of the earl whom they recently beheaded, who resides at Malines, the Earl of Westmorland, Lord Morley and others who live at Louvain, if they should have been found in any of the towns which have welcomed Orange. He is ready to pay a large sum of money to get these people into his hands and send them hither, and much importance is attached to this, so that if the poor people have not fled before the towns surrender, they will be bought by these English. If the Prince of Orange prospers, they have ready here some 7,000 men who have been collected secretly to aid him; 3,000 in London, 2,000 in the ports on the East coast, and 2,000 in the West country. The seven Queen's ships, of which I recently wrote, are ready to carry over the 5,000 here and on the East coast, as well as seven other ships of from 100 to 250 tons, which were sailing to the coast of Spain to plunder, but have now been ordered to stay for this purpose if necessary. John Hawkins is in the port of Plymouth preparing 17 of his ships to take over the men from the West country. . . .'

V

Extract from a letter by Antonio de Guaras in London to Gabriel Zayas, secretary to Philip II, 17 September 1575; taken from the *Calendar of State Papers, Spanish, 1568–1579*, pp. 503–4.

'In accordance with his Excellency's orders, as soon as news arrives of the appearance of our fleet on the coast, I will at once go to the Queen and deliver the letter personally. I will also endeavour to get a letter from her to all the justices of the ports, so that our men may be supplied, by purchase with such victuals as they require, and be welcomed as friends. This order I will take or send to wherever the fleet may be, and will serve the commander personally to the best of my ability. In the meantime, not a word shall be whispered on the subject. I wrote on the 10th that the Queen and Council knew of the coming of the fleet, and had consequently raised eight hundred soldiers to send to the Isle of Wight, prompted by their unnecessary suspicion, the king being as affectionate to this queen as ever, and as desirous of maintaining old friendship. When certain news comes of the arrival of the fleet, I will write advising his Excellency thereof, as well as taking the necessary steps at Court. News from Holland and Zeeland make us hope that our army will prevail at Dordrecht, and that that bad town will soon be confounded. All the news received at Court and by the rebels here is that Orange and his friends are so routed that they cannot resist much longer. . . .
    On the 10th I wrote that the English Colonel Chester had been sent back to Orange from the Court with a curt reply, but they sent after him and he returned. I do not know whether it was for the promotion of the enterprise I have mentioned, or whether it was to provide help for Orange. I have been told that they have collected two sums, one of sixty thousand crowns in cash which has been sent abroad, and the other of forty thousand which they have sent to Antwerp through Thomas Smith. A person who knows tells me that the cash is going to the Englishmen in Conde's army, and the other money to be remitted to Orange, which is to be repaid from the sums collected from the rebels here. . . .'

VI

Letter from de Guaras to Zayas, 30 December 1576; taken from the *Calendar of State Papers, Spanish, 1568–1579*, pp. 536–7.

'I enclose copies of the last letters, dated 3rd instant, whic I wrote to Don John of Austria, and I have now to report that Dr. Wilson has sent hither several of his servants, one after the other, with despatches, and lately sent two men, named Rogers and Herll, cautious and zealous heretics, all to persuade the queen, that if she will help the States secretly, at present, with troops and stores, and afterward send aid openly, they will deliver to her all the coast of Flanders. They tell her that she will be acting in the common interest to resist his majesty's forces, and expel the Spaniards from the States, in which she will be supported by all. To confirm this the traitor Zweveghem arrived here today and they have sent to France a similar man, such as D'Aubigny. The Council has been considering the matter all this week, and Rogers has been despatched to Dr. Wilson with letters instructing him to hold out hopes to the States that the Queen will consent. The principal people of London have been summoned by the Queen and Council, in order that this determination may be communicated to them, and the matter is already so public that it is spoken of openly by the councillors themselves, in order that the public may be favourably impressed with it. The earl of Sussex, Lord Steward, publicly declared that if the Queen would give him leave he would go over with such a force as to turn the Spaniards out of the States, and they are talking of sending the Governor of the Isle of Wight, one [Edward] Horsey, to the Count Palatine, to induce him to continue the alliance which his late father had with the Queen. . . .'

The situation in the Low Countries was already becoming tense before Philip returned to Spain in 1559. Nobles who had served his father loyally disliked his strongly Hispanic style, and the merchants upon whom the prosperity of the provinces depended soon realised that he did not share, or even understand, their priorities. It was the vulnerability of the Antwerp markets to political disruption which caused English merchants to look elsewhere in the 1560s, and hence begin to undermine the supremacy of that once dominant centre. At the same time the opening of the border with France after 1559 brought French-speaking Calvinist preachers into the populous cities of Flanders and Brabant. The combination of declining prosperity, rising unemployment and radical preaching had produced a volatile situation by 1566, when iconoclastic riots began. By that time it was also clear that the Council of State which Philip had left behind was largely a facade, and that the king had no intention of allowing the local nobility any real say in government. He also had plans to rationalise the ecclesiastical government of the provinces in ways of which they disapproved.

Philip's scheme, which would have established two new archbishoprics coextensive with the political region, was sensible enough, but it looked like (and was) a move towards centralised control, which would have replaced the traditional chaos of jurisdictions and immunities with something much more like a modern state. Given the king's distrustful attitude towards them, this was a serious threat to the power and wealth of the nobility, and they objected strongly. They also wanted to defuse the religious tension by forcing the king to make some concessions on that front as well.

They succeeded in forcing Philip to withdraw the unpopular Granvelle, but that was as far as they could get. The regent, Margaret of Parma, made some concessions, both religious and political, but the king repudiated them, and replaced her with the Duke of Alva. Alva arrived with a large army and instructions to suppress all dissent by force. In this he was successful, but his opponents scattered, into France, Germany and England, and Elizabeth was forced to confront the threat which Spanish control of the Netherlands coast represented. Her risky riposte of taking up the Genoese money intended for Alva's troops resulted, as has been seen, in another trade embargo, but by this time London could cope with such interruptions better than Antwerp. The Duke was not in a position to make any more aggressive response, and although in the short term his position remained unchallenged, in the longer term it contributed to his eventual failure.

Elizabeth, meanwhile, equivocated. At first she was prepared to turn a blind eye to the activities of the so-called 'sea beggars', who were minor Protestant nobles driven out by Alva. Her subjects welcomed them, and some cooperated with them in their plundering expeditions, or in disposing of the loot. The danger of the northern rebellion and the Ridolfi plot had made most of the political nation of England more self-consciously and aggressively Protestant, and there was widespread sympathy with the Dutch.

For the time being, however, Elizabeth refused to intervene. This was partly because Alva's refusal to respond to appeals from the northern rebels had indicated that he had no aggressive intentions against England (at least not yet), and partly because she hoped that the French would do the job for her. During the period of Huguenot ascendancy at court in early 1572, this seemed likely enough, and Alva himself expected no less. This enabled the queen to draw back. On 1 March she issued a proclamation, ostensibly aimed at ridding her coasts of all foreign freebooters, but in fact aimed mainly at the sea beggars. On 21 February she had told Count Lamarque, who had authorisation from the Prince of Orange, that he was no longer welcome. Over the next few months, the position in the Low Countries was stood on its head. Deprived of their English base, the sea beggars headed for Brill, which they took almost unopposed. Over the next few weeks they gained many adherents, and began to spread their revolt; some towns they took, against more or less determined opposition, some declared for them. Alva, whose armies were along the French border, awaiting a Huguenot-inspired invasion, was powerless over events so far away. By the time the massacre of St Bartholomew's day had removed the French threat, and paralysed the treaty of Blois, the revolt in the northern Netherlands was out of control.

This led to rethinking on both sides. Alva was withdrawn, and replaced with the less-aggressive Luis de Requescens, probably in the search for a political solution. At the same time, as long as the rebels looked as if they were able to look after themselves, Elizabeth was not keen to provoke Philip further by getting involved. William of Orange did not see things in the same light. With no prospect now of support from France, he was keener than ever to secure English backing, and not slow to point out the interests which they had in common. The negotiations were continuous, complex and inconclusive. Quite a lot of English support did in fact cross the North Sea. Some of it was genuinely voluntary, either from Dutch exiles in England or from their English sympathisers, but some of it (as the Spanish ambassador well realised) was coming indirectly from Elizabeth. Both sides dissembled, and this atmosphere of mutual suspicion is well reflected in Guaras's despatches. He regarded the English as covert enemies, and was well aware that they saw him from a similar viewpoint.

Meanwhile, in the Low Countries themselves, the situation continued to develop. Between 1572 and 1575 large numbers of Calvinists from Flanders and Brabant, which were still under Spanish control, fled to the rebel-held lands of Holland and Zeeland, so that the religious profile of the population changed significantly. Spanish claims that the rebels faced imminent defeat were largely wishful thinking. At the end of 1575 it had looked briefly as though Requescens might make a major breakthrough in Zeeland, but he lacked adequate resources and as he failed to exploit his gains Elizabeth's enthusiasm for intervention, which had briefly waxed, waned again.

In March the Spanish governor died, and in the interval before his replacement could arrive, the unpaid Spanish army mutinied and sacked Antwerp. For a few weeks the whole of the Netherlands was outraged by these atrocities, and the Catholic and Protestant provinces united in the pacification of Ghent (8 November). When the king's bastard brother Don John arrived as governor later that month, he had no option but to accept the pacification, and the position of the rebels was far stronger than can be gauged from Guaras's guarded reports.

This, of course, gave Elizabeth the opportunity to retreat further and renew her professions of friendship for Philip. There had been a significant quarrel between the queen and Orange during the summer, when privateers from Zeeland were unwise enough to seize an English ship and refuse restitution. The queen then pointed out to the prince in no uncertain terms that her safety in no way depended upon his success, and that he should not presume upon her friendship. None of this altered the fact that it would be a disaster for England if Spain recovered full control of the deep-water ports of the Netherlands, and both sides understood that perfectly well.

THIRTY-FOUR

Elizabeth's Court

I

Extract from *The Book of the Courtier* by Baldesar Castiglione, translated into English by Sir Thomas Hoby in 1561; taken from the translation and edition by George Bull (London, 1967), pp. 262–3.

'. . . And to a lady of this character I should not know how to add anything, save that she should be loved by a man as excellent as the courtier fashioned by these gentlemen, and that she should love him in turn, so that both may attain absolute perfection.

Having spoken in this way, the Magnifico then fell silent; and signor Gaspare remarked with smile:

Now you cannot complain that the signor Magnifico has not formed a truly excellent Court lady; and from now on, if any such lady be discovered, I declare that she deserves to be regarded as the equal of the courtier.

Signora Emilia retorted: I will guarantee to discover her, if you will find the courtier.

Roberto added: Certainly, no one can deny that the lady fashioned by signor Magnifico is most perfect. Nevertheless, with regard to those last qualities pertaining to love, I still think he has made her a little too hard, especially in wanting her, in her words, gestures and behaviour, to rob her lover of all hope, and do all she can to plunge him into despair. For as everyone knows, no men desire what is hopeless. Admittedly there have been some women, proud perhaps of their worth and beauty, who have immediately told their suitors that they need not imagine they would ever get from them what they wanted, and yet subsequently they have been a little more gracious in their reception and the way they look, and thus their kindly behaviour has tended to modify their haughty words. But if this lady drives away all hope by her acts and looks and behaviour, then I think that if he is wise our courtier will never love her, and so she will lack the perfection of having someone who does.'

II

Extract from 'The joyfull Receyving of the Queenes most Excellent Majestie into her Highnesse Citie of Norwich, the thinges done in the

time of her abode ther and the Dolor of the citie at her Departure. . . .';
taken from *The Progresses . . . of Queen Elizabeth*, ed. J. Nichols
(Society of Antiquaries, 1788), vol. 2.

'On Saterday, being the xvith of August, 1578, and in the twentieth yeere of
the raigne of our most gratious Souvereign Lady Elizabeth, by the Grace of
God, Queene of England, France and Ireland, Defender of the Faith etc.
The same our most dread and sovereign lady (continuing her progresse in
Norfolk) immediately after dinner set forward from Brakenashe, where she
had dyned with the Lady Style, beeinge fyve miles distant from Norwich,
towardes the same her moste dutifull citie. Sir Robert Wood, then Esquier
and now knight, maior of the same citie, at one of the cloke of the same
happy day, sette forward to meet with her Maiestie, in this order; First
there roade before him, wel and seemely mounted, threescore of the most
comelie yong men of the citie, as bachelers, apparreled all in black satten
doublets, blacke hose, blacke taffeta hattes and yellow bandes, and their
universall liverie was a mandylion of purple taffeta, layde about with silver
lace; and so apparreled, marched forward, two and two in a rank. The one
which represented king GURGANT, sometyme king of England, which
buylded the castle of Norwich called Blanche Flowre and laid the
foundations of the citie. He was mounted on a brave courser, and was thus
furnished, his body armed, his bases of greene and white silke, on his head
a blacke velvet hatte, with a plume of white feathers. . . .

Thus everything in due and comely order, they all (except GURGANT,
which stayed her Maiesties comyng within a flight shotte or two of the cittie,
where the castle of Blanche Flowre was in most beutifull prospect), marched
forward to a bridge called Hartford bridge, the uttermost lymit that way,
distant from the citie about two miles or thereaboutes, to meete wyth her
Maiestie, who, within one houre or a little more after their attendaunce,
came in such gratious and princely wise, as ravished the heartes of all hir
loving subiectes, and might have terrified the stoutest heart of any enemy to
beholde. Whether the maiestie of the Prince, which is incomperable, or ioy
of her subiectes, which exceeded measure, were the greater, I think would
have appalled the iudgement of Apollo to define. The acclamations and cries
of the people to the Almighty God for the preservation of her Maiestie ratled
so loud, as hardly for a great tyme coulde anything he heard; but at last, as
everything hathe an ende, the noiyse appeased; and the maior saluted hir
Highnesse with the oration following; and yelded to hir Maiestie therewith
the Sword of the Citie, and a fayre standing cup of silver, and guilt, with a
cover, and in the cup one hundreth poundes in golde. . . .

Whiche oration ended, her Maiestie accepting in good part everything
delivered by the maier, did thankfully answer him in these words, or verie
lyke in effecte; "We heartily thank you, master maier, and all the rest, for

these tokens of good will; neverthelesse princes have no neede of money; God hath endowed us abundantly, we come not therefore but for that whiche in righte is owre owne, the heartes and true allegeance of our subiectes, whiche are the greatest riches of a Kingdom; whereof as we assure ourselves in you; so do you assure yourselves in us of a lovynge and gratious Sovereign", wherewith was delivered to the maier, a mace or sceptre, which he carried before hir to hir lodging, which was in the bishop of Norwich his pallaice, two miles distant from that place. . . .'

III

Extract from Ben Jonson's *Oberon*, lines 252–88; taken from Roy Strong and Stephen Orgel, *Inigo Jones, the Theatre of the Stuart Court* (London, 1973), I, pp. 208–9.

> '*Sylvan* This is a night of greatness and of state,
> Not to be mixed with light and skipping sport:
> A night of homage to the British court,
> And ceremony due to Arthur's chair,
> From our bright master, Oberon the fair,
> Who with these knights, attendants, here preserved
> In fairyland, for good they have deserved
> Of yond' high throne, are come of right to pay
> Their annual vows; and all their glories lay
> At feet, and tender to this only great
> True majesty, restored in this seat;
> To whose sole power and magic they do give
> The honour of their being, that they live
> Sustained in form, fame and felicity
> From rage of fortune and the fear to die.
> *Silenus* And may they well. For this indeed is he,
> My boys, whom you must quake at when you see.
> He is above your reach, and neither doth
> Nor can he think within a satyr's tooth.
> Before his presence you must fall or fly.
> He is the matter of virtue, and placed high.
> His meditations to his height are even,
> And all their issue is akin to heaven.
> He is a god o'er kings, yet stoops he then
> Nearest a man when he doth govern men,
> To teach them by the sweetness of his sway,
> And not by force. He's such a king as they
> Who're tyrant's subjects, or ne'er tasted peace,

Would in their wishes form for their release.
'Tis he that stays the time from turning old,
And keeps the age up in a head of gold;
That in his own true circle doth still run,
And holds his course as certain as the sun.
He makes it ever day and ever spring
Where he doth shine, and quickens everything
Like a new nature; so that true to call
Him by his title is to say, he's all. . . .'

IV

Extract from *King Henry VIII*, by Shakespeare and Fletcher; act 5, scene 4, lines 17–38.

'This royal infant – heaven still move about her! –
Though in her cradle yet now promises
Upon this land a thousand thousand blessings,
Which time shall bring to ripeness: she shall be –
But few now living can behold that goodness –
A pattern to all princes living with her,
And all that shall succeed: Saba was never
More covetous of wisdom and fair virtue
Than this pure soul shall be: all princely graces
That mould up such a mighty piece as this is,
With all the virtues that attend the good,
Shall still be doubled on her: truth shall nurse her:
Holy and heavenly thoughts still counsel her:
She shall be lov'd and fear'd: her own shall bless her:
Her foes shake like a field of barley corn,
And hang their heads with sorrow: good grows with her:
In her days every man shall eat in safety,
Under his own vine, what he plants; and sing
The merry songs of peace to all his neighbours;
God shall be truely known; and those about her
From her shall read the perfect ways of honour,
And by those claim their greatness, not by blood. . . .'

V

Extract from 'The Booke of Household of Queen Elizabeth, as it was ordered in the 43rd yeare of her Reign . . .' (1601); taken from *The Household Ordinances* (Society of Antiquaries, 1790), p. 281.

'The Counting House

Lord Steward. He hath for his entertainment [. . .] a yeare and two messes of meat furnished at his pleasure; for he is the sovereign and chiefe officer of the household. He hath the charge and government of the whole household; the commandment, discreation and appointment of all matters therein; and the placing and displacing of all her Maiesties servants. He is to be counselled and assisted by the Treasurer, Comptroller and the rest of the officers of the board, but is full and absolute of himself for appointment of anythinge.

Mr. Treasurer. He hath for his entertainment £130 16s 8d a yeare, and 10 dishes of meate to his firste messe, and six to his second, every meal. He and Mr. Comtrouler (there being no Lord Steward) have the government of the whole household, and placing of all her Maiesties servantes. They are likewise to be counselled and assisted by the officers of the boarde; but they two together are absolute of themselves.

Mr. Comptroller. He hath for his entertainment £107 17s 4d a yeare, and the like dyett and authority that Mr. Treasurer hath.

Mr. Cofferer. He hath £100 a yeare, and seven dishes of meate every meale, for his diett; and when he is absent he hath 8s the day for boardwages, and 3 dishes of meate a meal to his chamber for his men. He hath also £20 a yeare for his expenses, for being at sundry places of store twice a yeare to take the remains. This officer hathe the receiving and disbursing of all her Maiesties moneys for household affairs, and is the chief purveyor for provisions, so that all purveyours are to be directed by him.

Clerkes of the Greencloth. Master of the Household and Clerke of the Greencloth, he hath £64 6s 8d a yeare. These two, both of them, have seven dishes of meate apeece every meale, for their dietts when they waite, and when they are absent they have 5s a day boardwages apeece, and 3 dishes of meate a meal to their chamber for their men; they have also £4 a yeare apeece for their expenses in taking of remaynes twice a yeare, at sundry places of store. They are the auditors of the household, for they cast up and perfect all the parcelles, roules and brevements, and finish up all the accompts throughout the yeare.

Clerkes Comptrollers. They have £44 6s 8d a yeare apeece, and the like dietts and boardwages that the clerkes of the greenecloth have, and £4 a yeare apeece likewise for expences at remaynes taking. These two (under the White Staves) bee controllers of all household affaires; that is to say, of all her Maiesties servants, if they doo not the dutyes in their severall places. They have authoritie to check all prises for meales or necessaries belonging to houysehold expences. They prise all billes for allowances, all brevements and rolles of expenses, and turn backe and refuse all meates and drinkes unsavoury or not convenient to be spent.

Yeoman of the Counting House. He hath 100s a yeare and three dishes of meate every meale for him and his fellow the Groom; he and his saide fellow kepe the Counting House, and the bookes and records there, and doe daylye wayte to supply every want, and execute every commandment imposed upon them by the officers of the boarde.

Groom of the Counting House. He hath 4 markes a yeare, and his meate with his fellow the yeoman; and is to waite in the absence of his fellow, and with his fellow, as need shall require.

Messenger of the Counting House. He hath 100s a yeare, and is to go upon all messages, wherein the white staves or officers of the boorde shall employ him, and his charge allowed according to the discretion of the officers of the boarde; but if he be sent to fetch up any man, or gather up the wants and compositions not duely answered, then his charges are to be payde alwayes by the defaulters and not by the Queene.'

VI

Extract from *The Countess of Pembroke's Arcadia* (1593), ed. M. Evans (Harmondsworth, 1977), pp. 353–5.

'. . . the manner was that the forenoon they should run at tilt, one after the other, the afternoon in a broad field in the manner of a battle, till either the strangers or the country knights won the field.

The first that ran was a brave knight, whose device was to come in all chained, with a nymph leading him. Against him came forth an Iberian, whose manner of entering was with bagpipes instead of trumpets; a shepherd's boy before him for a page, and by him a dozen apparelled like shepherds for the fashion, though rich in stuff, who carried his lances, which though strong to give a lancely indeed, yet so were they coloured with hooks near the morne that they prettily resembled sheephooks. His own furniture was dressed over with wool, so enriched with jewels artifically placed that one would have thought it a marriage beween the lowest and the highest. His impresa was a sheep marked with pitch, with this word "Spotted to be known". And because I may tell you out his conceit (though that were not done, till the running for that time was ended) before the ladies departed from the windows – amongst whom there was one, they say, that was the Star whereby his course only was directed – the shepherds attending upon Philisides went among them and sang an eclogue; one of them answering another, while the other shepherds, pulling out recorders, which possessed the place of pipes, accorded their music to the others' voice. The eclogue had great praise. I only remember six verses, while having questioned one with the other of their fellow-shepherd's sudden growing a man of arms and the cause of his so doing, they thus said:

> Me thought some staves he miss'd: if so, not much amiss;
> For where he most would hit, he ever yet did miss.
> One said he brake across; full well it so might be;
> For never was there man more crossly crossed than he.
> But most cried, "O well broke"; O fool full gaily blest;
> Where failing is a shame, and breaking is his best.'

The court of Elizabeth was the political and cultural heart of the kingdom. It was not the centre of government, which remained at Westminster, but the queen was the chief executive. When the court was close to Westminster, at Hampton Court or Greenwich, for example, the Privy Council met at court, although by custom the monarch no longer attended except on special occasions. When the court was at a more distant residence, or on progress, it was customary for some councillors to travel with the monarch and some to remain at Westminster. By the reign of Elizabeth, the court was divided into three parts: the Privy Chamber, which consisted of the monarch's personal attendants; the Chamber, which was the formal and ceremonial part; and the Household, which contained the service departments.

Elizabeth's Privy Chamber was predominantly female, and was connected to the rest of the court (and the government) by marriage and kinship. The Chamber, headed by the Lord Chamberlain, included such groups as the Gentlemen Pensioners, the Yeomen of the Guard, and the queen's music (the court orchestra); it was also the main location for the numerous gentlemen servants, mostly part-time, who kept the court in touch with the gentry of the shires. The Chamber was the public setting for the monarch, and was structurally ill-defined.

The Household, by contrast, which was the domain of the Lord Steward, was tightly organised into departments (about twenty-five in number), and was predominantly professional and plebeian. It contained such departments as the kitchen, the buttery, the porters, the woodyard, and so on. The Household was managed by the Counting House, or Board of Greencloth; and there, as this extract makes clear, there was a sharp distinction between the gentleman officers (White Staves) and the rest. Unusually in the Household, the Counting House was predominantly aristocratic. Although this schedule ostensibly dates from 1601, it appears to have been drawn up during the vacancy in the office of Lord Steward, which ran from 1593 to 1597.

The court was also the theatre of monarchy, and it is to that aspect that most of these extracts relate. Castiglione's work, which had originally appeared in the 1520s, was widely admired and applied in all the courts of western Europe. It is included here mainly because it makes the function of the court lady almost entirely romantic – the inspirer of good and great deeds – but also because the court that Castiglione described was actually dominated by a woman, Emilia Pia. Emilia was clearly prepared to use the (largely fictitious) devotion of her male courtiers for her own purposes, and this was a cue which Elizabeth picked up. The jousts and other entertainments of the court became focused upon the cult of courtly love, wherein the lady is always superior, aloof, unattainable and hard to please.

The last extract, although published in 1593, is thought to describe the Accession Day tilts of 1581, which concentrated on the cult of Gloriana in the latter part of the reign. Although theoretically feats of athletic and military prowess, these tilts were in fact theatrical events in honour of the queen, when her courtiers competed as much in flattery as in jousting. Competitions in which strong men fought for no more than a smile or a dropped handkerchief suited the queen's thrifty style admirably. It was also a style which translated easily into genuine loyalty and devotion, and embraced ordinary subjects no less than courtiers.

Observers commented from the very beginning of Elizabeth's reign on how much she cultivated popularity; the cheers of her devoted subjects were music to her ears. The various descriptions of her progresses, one of which is quoted here, are not necessarily misrepresentations, but they were published to emphasise precisely that point. Such popularity (which was genuine enough) gave Elizabeth a little room to manoeuvre when she was forced to embrace policies which were rather less popular, and that was probably why she followed such a course, although ordinary vanity was probably a factor as well.

It was, of course, a hard act to follow, as the passage from *Henry VIII* makes clear. This was written after the queen's death, when 'Good Queen Bess's Glorious Days' were already passing into legend. It pretended to be a prophecy uttered over her cradle, but was in fact a piece of nostalgia for a world which had passed – insofar as it had ever existed at all. Jonson was more positive. He was also writing in James's reign, and for the king's benefit, pointing out (correctly enough) that all the imagery of traditional monarchic power had been male. It was not, perhaps, wise to remind James that it had also been military, but he was able to leave that sort of wish-fulfilment to his son Henry, until the latter's early death in 1612.

Elizabeth used her court with consummate skill to present a unique image of female mystery and power – alternatively Astrea, Belphoebe,

Gloriana or Deborah, according to circumstances – and making what capital she could out of the fact that she could only preserve her integrity, and that of her realm, by foregoing a secure succession. Sir John Davies wittily compared the politics of her reign to a courtly dance, in the course of which no one (except, presumably, Elizabeth herself) ever knew quite when the movements were in earnest, and when for form.

THIRTY-FIVE

Protestant Nonconformity

I

Letter from Dr (Lawrence) Humfrey to the Lord Treasurer Burghley, 'Certifying his Conformity in Apparel' (1576); taken from J. Strype, *Annals of the Reformation* (London, 1725), I, p. 68.

'I received your honourable letter, and withal perceive your care for bettering of my state. I would be loth her Majestie, or any other honourable, should think that I am so forgetful of my Dutie, or so far from Obedience, but that I would submit myself to those Orders in that Place, where my Being and Living is. And therefore I have yielded, that no further surmise of any wilfulness should be gathered: and would have done the like heretofore, but that having a Toleration, I was glad to enjoy it, and I hoped still for some points of Redresse; wherein I was no open Intermeddler, but onlie a private Solicitor, and humble suiter to her Majestie and your Lordships. My hope is, that as I have offended some by this my Obedience, so I shall have such Favour and Countenance at her Majesties hande, that I shall now more frelie and fruitfullie proceed in my Vocation. It was a remorse, to seme by singular Apparel to sundrie myself from those Bretherne, whose Doctrine and Life I always loved and liked. And I protest to your Lordship before God, that my standing before, and conforming now, cometh of one Cause, *viz.* the Direction of a clear Conscience; and tendeth to one end, which is Edification. And if in the Proclamation, which I heare shall be set forth for Apparel, one clause may be added for Ministers and Students in the Universitie, and a plain Signification given, that it is enjoined, not so much for an ecclesiastical ceremonie, as for a Civil policy and Ordinance, it would, I think, satisfie many in conscience. But I refer these Cases to your Wisdome, myself and my Cause to your Goodness. And so, with my humble thanks, I recommend your Lordship, and yours, to th'Almightie.

Yours Lordships to command,
Lau. Humfrey.'

II

Petition by the House of Commons for the reform of Church discipline, with the queen's reply, 2 and 9 March 1576; taken from T.E. Hartley,

Proceedings in the Parliaments of Elizabeth I (Leicester, 1981), vol. I, 1558–81, pp. 445–7. The original MS is BL Add. MS 33271.

'To the Queen's most excellent Majestie, our most sovereigne Ladye.

In most humble wise beseechinge your Highnes, your Majesties most lovinge, faithfull and obedient subjectes the commons in this present parliament assembled, that whereas by lack of the true discipline of the Churche amongest other abuses a greate number of men are admitted to occupie the place of ministers in the Churche of England, who are not only alto[ge]ther unfurnished of such guiftes as are by the word of God necessarelie and inseperablie required to be incident to their callinge, but also are infamous in their lives and conversat[i]ons. And also many of the ministry whome God hath endewed with habilitie to teache are by meane of non residences, pluralities, and such like dispensacions so withdrawen from theire flockes that their guiftes are almost altogeither become unprofitable, whereby an infinite number of your Majesties subjectes for want of the prechinge of the word – the onlie ordinary meane of salvation of soules and th'only good meanes to teach your Majesties subjectes to know their true obedience to your Majestie, and to the magistrates under you, and withjout which the Lord God hath pronounced that the people must needes perishe – have already runne headlonge into destrucion, and many thowsand of the residewe yet remaine in great perill (if speedy remedie be not provided) daylie to fall into the diche, and to dye in their sinnes, to the great danger and charge of those to whom the Lord hath committed the care of provisions for them in this behalf. And by meanes whereof the common blaspheaminge of the Lordes name, the most licenciousness of life, the abuse of excommunication, the greate number of atheists, schismatiques and heretiques daylie springing upp. And to conclude, the hindrance and increase of obstinate papistes, which ever since your Majesties sworne enemy the Pope did by his bulles pronounce definitive sentence against your Highness person and proseedinges, have given evident testimonie of their corrupt affection to him, and of their wilfull disobedience to your Majestie, in that they forebear to participate with your Majesties faithful subiectes in prayer and administracion of sacramentes, wherein they moste manifestlie declare that they carry very unsound and undutifull heartes unto your Majestie.

In consideration therefore of the premises . . . we are most humblie to beseech your Highnesse, seeing the same is of so greate importance, yf the parliament at this present may not be so longe continued, as that by good and Godly lawes established in the same, provision may be made for supplie and reformation of these great wantes and grevous abuses, that yet by such other good meanes as to your Majesties moste Godly wisdom shall seeme best, a perfecte redresse may be had of the same; which doinge you shall doo such acceptable service to the Lord God which cannot but procure at his handes the sure establishment of your seate and sceptre, and the number of your Majesties most faithfull subjectes (the bonde of conscience beinge of all other most streightest) by mean of preachinge and discipline be so multiplied and the great swarmes of malefactors, schismatiques, atheists, anabaptistes and papistes, your most daungerous enemies, so weakened and diminished, that by the helpe and assistance of allmightie God, yf all popishe treasons and trayterous pratizes should conspire together in one against your Majestie, they should not be able to shake the estate. . . .

An answeare to the petition of the common house exhibited to her Majestie, delivered by her commaundment by the Lord Treasurer and other lordes, and uttered in the house by Sir Walter Mildmay.

The Queenes majestie had of these thinges consideracion before, in such sorte as thoughe this motion had not beene, the reformation thereof should have followed. And yet she alloweth well that her subiectes, being agreved therewith, have in such sort and discreet manner both opened theire griefes and remitted them to be reformed by her Majestie. And considering that reformation hereof is to be principally sought in the cleargie, and namelie in the bishops and ordinaries, her Majestie did in the beginning of her Convocation conferr with some of the principalls of them and such as she thought were best dispoased to refom theis errors in the churche; from whom if she shall not find some directe dealinges for the reformation, then she will by her supreme authoritie with th'advise of her Councell directe them herself to amende; whereof her Majestie doubteth not but her people shall see that her majestie will use that aucthoritie which she hath to the encrease of th'onour of God and to the reformation of th'abuses in the Churche.'

III

Queen's letter to the Bishop of Lincoln (Thomas Cooper), to 'cause the Exercises, called Prophesyings, to cease in his Diocese' (1577); taken from Strype, *Annals of the Reformation* (London, 1725), II, p. 111.

'Right Reverend, etc., Although we doubt not, but that you do well and effectually remember our Speeches unto you, to continue and increase your Care and Vigilancy over your Charge in Gods Church, (a Matter of no small Weight) warning you also of the dangerous Presumptions of some in these Dayes, who by singular exercises in Public Places, after their own Fancies, have wrought no good in the Minds of the Multitude, easy to be carried with Novelties: Yet forasmuch as we have been sithence credibly enformed, that in sundry Places in your Dioces, namely in Hertfordshire, those exercises, or as they term them Prophesyinges, are yet or were very lately continued, to the great Offence of our orderly subjectes; and therefore, and for divers good reasons, we thinke requisite that they shall be forborne to be used: WEE let you to wit, that having in singular recommendation God's people under our government, whom we desire to have guided in an Uniformity as near as may be, wee charge and command you, as a Person, who by your function wee look should ease and satisfy us in this behalf, within your charge to have dutiful consideration hereof: and Furthermore to take express order through your dioces that none other Exercises be suffered to be publickly used, than Preaching in fit times and places, by persons learned, discreet, conformable and sound in religion, heard and allowed by you without Partiality; Reading of Homilies, as is set forth by publick authority, by the Injunctions appointed, and the Order of the Book of Common Prayer.

And further, that ye signify unto us, or to some of our Privy Council, attending about our Person, the names of all such Gentlemen, and others, as have been the Setters forth and maintainers of those Exercises; and in what places; and of such as shall impugn this Order. And also, what you shall have done herein from time to time. Hereof not to fail, as you tender our Plesure, and will avoid the contrary at your Peril.'

IV

'Wright, a Puritan, his answers to the matters urged against him, upon his own answers in the Consistory: By notes thereof taken by the Register' (1581); taken from Strype, *Annals of the Reformation* (London, 1725), III, app., p. 38.

'First, he most humbly desired, that it might be considered, Whether any man by our Lawes be bound to accuse himself upon his oath, for any Deed or Word; much less to declare his Thoughts. Item, Forasmuch as he was driven to answer at the first by word; and not suffered leisurely to peruse the Answers which the Register set down; and that these notes did much respect those Answers; he therefore with like duty desired, that both his Answers before might be poised with the weight of the former circumstances; and also that if his Memory failed him now in any Point, which then was answered, he might be charitably judged of, as he protested before almighty God, that he meant well to speak the Truth. Thirdly, he desired that it might be noted, that the collector of those notes dealt Partially.

[Then follow the contents of his answers.]

To speak in general of the Book of Common Prayer, he thought it good and godly.

His practice of resorting to churches where ceremonies have been used, did sufficiently clear him in that Point (where being before demanded what he thought of Ceremonies, he was silent).

About the form of Ordination, he answered, he remembered not that he had read and perused any such Form. He sent for it to the stationers, and could not get it; but he judgeth so reverently of those Rites, that he acknowledgeth, there is the Substance of the Ministry.

He did that private duty (of preaching and catechizing in my Lord Rich's Family) being thereto requested by the Householders, for their own and their Families profit; and other means of instruction failing them. For where they had means to be instructed, they were reverently used: as Mr. Berriman, minister of Rochford, must needs testify; that both the Prayers and Preaching were resorted unto. And Wright, conferring with him at first, meant no otherwise to deal in my Lord's house, being there, but with the minister's leave; and for his assistance in discharging the Duty.

He prayed as preachers use to do in all places, and altogether in Prescript words; but as the occasion fell out in some points. Yet he ever prayed for the Queen's Majesty, and for the Lords of the Council, and for all Ministers of Gods word. And so for Archbishops and Bishops, seeing they be Ministers. (This was in answer to that Article, that he used prayer of his own devising; and never used to pray as in the Book of Common Prayer; nor for Archbishops and Bishops). . . .

To the Article, That he said, that the election of ministers ought to be by the flock; he only said, that he supposed it not to be an error, that the Ministers should be chosen with the Consent of the Flock; so that their Flock were first well taught.

To the Article, That he was chosen in this sort (by the Family) in the house of the Lord Rich; he confesseth that the late Lord, calling his household together (in the absence of the said Wright, and not moving him thereto) to the end it seems that they might more willingly hearken to good Instruction, having one to teach them, whom themselves had before approved, Asked, whether any of them could shew any Reason, for Life or otherwise, why he might not be their Teacher. Whereupon, no man objecting anything, my Lord sent for him, and perhaps esteemed him as his Pastor. But that he took not himself to be any other than a private man to do them some good, till they might have a sufficient Pastor. For at Rochford, the Minister was distracted between his two Benefices. And at Leez his Provision was worse. . . .

To the Article, that he preached on a Holy Day, Jan. the 24th. Reginae, in the Hall at Rochford; and divers people thereabouts resorted to his preaching: He answered, he did then as at other times; neither drawing nor shutting out any man, nor omitting any public duties in the Churche.

Concerning his ordination at Antwerp, he said not that he went over for that End; but being at Antwerp, whither he went to see the churches from whence Idolatry had been lately driven; and English merchants desiring him to assist in the ministry; he was religiously ordained thereunto; and there did execute it. As also at Vilfort, where was a garison of 600 Scots, by the earnest suit of their Band, and a Colonel, one Mr. Bombridge, Governor of the Town; and with consent of the ministers of the three several Languages in Antwerp. The manner also of his admitting, he declared, so long as they would hear him. And he is ready to declare it at all times when it shall be demanded of him.

Touching that he said 'Every minister is a bishop'; it is true that he said he is *episcopus*, which we call bishop, according to the Word of God. But he said not, every one is a Lord Bishop. My Lord of London himself said as much in effect, when I was last before him in the Consistory. For rebuking Mr. White for smiting one of his parishoners, he alleged the scripture, 1 Tim.iii.3. "That a Bishop must be no striker", there had been no reason in the speech, if Mr. White, being only a minister, had not been a bishop.

To the last Article, that Mr. Greenwood served the Lord Rich, and did that which he did for him only: that he used the Book of Common Prayer, saving that for brevity sake, he read not all. He hath answered himself, that he continued not a Curate, for want of Audacity and Utterance; he being otherwise both Godly and well learned.'

In exercising her ecclesiastical authority, Elizabeth trod a delicate course. She was well aware that the majority of her subjects disliked the Prayer Book, which she had imposed upon them, and would have preferred the traditional rites. On the other hand, most such conservatives had little time for the papacy, and none at all for Spanish influence. They saw themselves, and wished to be seen, as loyal subjects. At the same time, because of the confessional polarisation which had occurred among the senior clergy, most of her new bench of bishops were more zealous in their Protestantism than was convenient. Having made a Protestant settlement, Elizabeth therefore had to restrain those who thought that settlement incomplete, in the interests of reconciling those who thought that it had gone too far.

The first push for further reform came in the convocations of 1563 and 1566 among those who objected to wearing the prescribed clerical apparel. This was an issue which had first surfaced over a decade earlier through the protests of John Hooper. Hooper had eventually given way, urged thereto by his models and mentors, particularly Heinrich Bullinger, in the interests of waging the common war against the Catholics. Bullinger now performed the same service again, pointing out that an imperfect reformation was greatly to be preferred to no reformation at all. Open defiance of the queen's injunctions was rare, but Laurence Humphrey, protected to some extent by his position in Oxford, held out longer than most. He eventually conformed, like others, when the Catholic threat became more explicit in 1569 and 1570. In the face of a fundamental challenge, it was easy to represent such matters as vestments as 'things indifferent', especially when the queen, upon whose life the Protestants depended, was under threat.

However, if vestments were largely symbolic, there were other issues which were more substantial. Poverty led to an undereducated clergy and to pluralism; a shortage of preachers; and a lack of professional training. Those who became known as Puritans, both clergy and laity, wanted to improve the economic status of the ministry; to recruit the better educated; and to encourage preaching, partly in the interests of creating a godly society, and partly in the life-and-death struggle against popery. Elizabeth saw this agitation as a threat to her own control, and even after 1570 gave a high priority to reconciling the conservative.

Her strategy continued to be to undermine the conservatives by insidious conformity, rather than to drive them into recusancy. Hence her conciliatory but unexplicit response to the petition of parliament, and her specific orders to suppress the so-called 'prophesying movement'. The latter was a system of educational self-help which Elizabeth distrusted because she had no control over it. Her bishops reluctantly accepted her orders in 1577, except Edmund Grindal, Archbishop of Canterbury, who refused on conscientious grounds and was suspended from office. The Puritans were not, with a few exceptions, separatists. They continued to accept the queen as a godly prince, and to endeavour to reform the Church from within. Mr Wright was not untypical. He clearly stretched conformity in a number of directions, but the real objection to his ministry was that he had been ordained abroad, and in uncertain circumstances. The questions addressed to him, however, reveal clearly what the authorities were looking for in their attempts to enforce uniformity. Wright enjoyed the support of Robert, the 2nd Lord Rich, but had no intention of making a martyr of himself.

THIRTY-SIX

Towards War

I

Memorandum of points submitted to Philip II by Sir John Smith, the English ambassador to Spain, December 1576; taken from the *Calendar of State Papers, Spanish, 1568–1579*, p. 535.

'A short statement of the memoranda which I have this day handed to your Majesty on behalf of my mistress, the Queen of England, begging your Majesty, as I do, to be pleased to order redress to be provided. . . .

1. Memorandum respecting the Inquisition of Seville, which has interfered with the title and royal style of my mistress, the queen of England, and in the other points contained in the memorandum.

2. Respecting the shameful and unworthy insult committed by the Prior of Cambre near Corunna against the person of my lady the Queen and her royal estate; with other things contained in this memorandum.

3. Respecting the liberation of eight Englishmen who are prisoners condemned to the galleys and perpetual imprisonment by the Holy Office in Seville.

4. Respecting the promises made by the duke of Alba in your Majesty's name to the ambassador, Sir Henry Cobham, respecting the decree of the general Inquisition in Spain as regards the subjects of my mistress the Queen.

5. That permission should be given to a certain subject of my Queen, to take his wife and son to England.

6. That the English ambassadors with their households should be allowed to live in this Court in conformity with the laws of their country, on condition that they do so privately, in their own house.

7. Respecting the injuries committed on the subjects of my mistress the Queen in the recent sacking of Antwerp.

8. Respecting the injuries and vexations to which English merchants trading on the coast of Biscay and elsewhere in this country are subjected.'

II

Extract from the queen's letter to Sir Amyas Paulet, her resident ambassador in France, May 1579; taken from Marcus et al., *Elizabeth I: Collected Works* (Chicago, 2000), pp. 233–5.

'Trusty etc., Finding de Simier [the Duke of Alençon's representative in England], at a certain late conference between him and some of our Council about the treaty of marriage between the Duke his master and us, to insist very peremptorily upon certain articles that have always heretofore been denied to such princes as in former time have sought us in way of marriage, as also to the king, the said Duke his brother (a thing falling out far contrary to our expectation considering that before his repair hither we caused one of our secretaries to advertise him upon view of certain letters of his directed to the king's ambassador here, by which he signified unto him that he was to repair hither about th'interview and the concluding of th'articles), that our meaning was not to enter into any treaty of articles, being resolved not to yield to any other than were before agreed on between us and other princes that have sought [the said marriage with us] in like case; and therefore advised him to forbear to rep[air thus to us], if he were sent to any such end. Only thus (b[eing resolved] that in case any of the said articles were doubtful or obscure, to explain and make them more clear), we have therefore thought meet, for that we know not what to judge of such a strainable kind of proceeding, even at that time when to our seeming we were growing to a conclusion touching the interview, to acquaint you therewith to the end that you may let both the king and Monsieur what we conceive thereof.

    And for that you may the more substantially and fully deal therein, you shall understand that the articles upon the which he did at the said conference with certain of our Council insist, were three. The first that the said Duke might jointly have authority with us to dispose of all things donative within this our realm and other our dominions. The second, that he might be after marriage crowned king, offering certain cautions that nothing should be done thereby to the prejudice of our realm. And lastly, that he might have threescore thousand pounds' pensions during his life. Touching the first, the inconveniences were laid before him by our said Council, who declared unto him that it was a matter that greatly toucheth our regality, in so much as Monsieur might have thereby *vocem negativum* [veto]. And also that in the marriage between the king of Spain and our late sister, the contents of that demand was by an especial article prohibited in the treaty between them, which afterward was ratified by parliament; yet was he not without great difficulty drawn to desist from urging us to yield our consent therein, notwithstanding he was plainly given to understand that our consenting thereto could not but breed dangerous alienation of our subjects' goodwill from us. And for the other two articles, it was showed unto him that the consideration of the said articles being committed to our whole Council, it was by them, after long deliberation had thereon, resolved that they were not presently to be granted or considered of, but by the Council of the whole realm in parliament, without whose consent they could nowise be accorded unto, and therefore thought meet to be held in suspense until the Duke's coming over. . . .'

III

Extracts from an account of Sir Francis Drake's circumnavigation, 1577–80; taken from Hakluyt, *Principall Naviations*, ed. D.B. Quinn (1965).

'The famous voyage of Sir Francis Drake into the South Sea, and there hence about the whole Globe of the Earth, begun in the yeere of our Lord, 1577.

The 15 day of November, in the yeere of our Lord, 1577, M. Francis Drake, with a fleete of five ships and barkes, and to the number of 164 men, Gentlemen and Sailers, departed Plimmouth, giving out his pretended voyage for Alexandria; but the wind falling contrary, he was forced the next morning to put in to Falmouth haven in Cornewall, where such and so terrible a tempest tooke us, as few men have seene the like, and was indeed so vehement, that all our ships were like to have gone to wracke, but it pleased God to preserve us from that extremitie, and to afflict us only for that present with these two particulars: The Maste of our Admiral, which was the Pelican, was cut over boord for the safegard of the ship, and the Marygold was driven ashore & somewhat bruised, for the repairing of which damages we returned againe to Plimmouth, and having recovered those harmes, and brought the ships againe to good state, we set forth the second time from Plimmouth, and set saile the 13 of December followinge.

The 25 day of the same moneth we fell in with Cape Cantine, upon the coast of Barbarie, and coasting along the 27 day we found an Island called Magador, lying one mile distant from the maine, betweene which Island and the maine, we found a very good and safe harbour for oure shipes to ride in, and void of any danger. . . .

The 17 day of Ianuarye we arrived at Cape Blanko, where we found a ship riding at anker within the Cape, and but two simple Mariners in her, which ship we tooke, and caried her further into the harbour where we remained 4 dayes, and in that space our Generall mustered, and trayned his men on land in warlike manner, to make them fit for all occasions.

In this place we tooke of the Fishermen suche necessaries as we wanted, and they could yeld us, and leaving here one of our little barkes called the Benedict, we tooke with us one of theirs which they called Canters, being of the burden of 40 tunnes or thereabouts.

All these thinges being finished, we departed this harbour the 22 of Ianuarie, carrying along with us one of the Portingall Carvels which was bound to the Islands of Cape de verde for salt, whereof good store is made in one of those Islands. . . .

Being returned to our ships, our Generall departed hence the 31 of this moneth, and sayled by the Island of S. Iago, but farre inough from the danger of the inhabitantes, who shot and discharged at us three pieces, but they all fell shorte of us and did us no harme. The Island is fayre and large, and as it seemeth rich and fruitfull, and inhabited by the Portigalls, but the mountains and high places of the island, are said to be possesed by the Moores, who having been slaves to the Portingals, to ease themselves, made escape to the desart places of the Island, where they abide with great strength. . . .

Being departed from these Islandes, we drew towardes the line, where we were becalmed the space of 3 weekes, but yet subiect to divers great stormes, terrible lightnings and much thunder: but with this miserie we had the commoditie of great store of fish, as Dolphin, Bonitas and flying fishes, whereof some fell into our shippes, where hence they could not rise againe for want of moisture, for when their wings are drie, they cannot flie. . . .

From Iava Maior we sailed for the Cape of Good Hope, which was the first land we fel withall: neither did we touch with it, or any other land, until we came to Sierre Leone, upon the coast of Guinea: notwithstanding we came hard aboord the Cape, finding the report of the Portingals to be most false, who affirme that it the most dangerous Cape of the world, never without intollerable stormes and present danger to travailors which come near the same.

This Cape is a most stately thing, and the fairest Cape we saw in the whole circumference of the earth, and we passed it the 18 of June.

From thence we continued our course to Sierra Leone, on the coast of Guinea, where we arrived the 22 of July, and found necessarie provisions, great store of Elephantes, Oisters upon trees of one kinde, spawning and increasing infinitely, the Oister suffering no budde to growe. We departed thence the 24 daye.

We arrived in England the third of November 1580, being the third yeare of oure departure.'

IV

The impact of Drake's voyage; taken from Camden, *Annals* (1635), p. 426.

'Queene Elizabeth received him graciously, with all clemency, caused his riches to be sequestered and in redinesse whensoever the Spaniard should reclaim them. Her Maiestie commanded likewise for a perpetual memory to have so happily circuited round about the whole earth, his ship should be drawen from the water and put aside neere Deptford upon Thames, where to this houre the body thereof is seene; and after the queene's feasting therein, she consecrated it with great ceremonie, pompe and magnificence, eternally to be remembered; and her Majestie forthwith honoured Drake with the dignitie of knighthood. As these things were performed, a slight bridge made with boordes, by which the people went up into the ship, was broken downe by the multitude, and about a hundred persons fell with it; they nevertheless received no harm at all; insomuch that the Ship seemed to have been built at a happy coniunction of the planets. That very day, against the great mast of the said ship, many verses, composed to the praise & honour of Sir Francis Drake, were fastened and fixed. . . .

Nothing angered worse Sir Francis Drake than to see the Nobles and the Chiefest of the Courte, refuse that Gold and Silver which he presented them withal, as if he had not lawfully come by it. The Commons nevertheless applauded him with all praise and admiration, esteeming he had purchased no less glory in advancing the limits of the English, their honour and reputation, than of their Empire.

Bernard Mendoza, then Ambassador for Spain in England, murmuring at it and was not well pleased, demands vehemently of the Queen the things taken. But he was answered:

"that the Spaniards had provoked unto themselves that evil through their iniustice towardes the English, in hindering against the right of Nations, their Negotiations; That Sir Francis Drake was always readie to answer the law, if by iust indictments and certain testimonies they could convict him, to have committed anything against equitie. That to no end but to give satisfaction to their king, the riches he brought in were sequestered, though her Maiestie had spent (against the rebels which Spain had moved and instigated in Ireland and England against her) more money than Drake was worth. Moreover that her Maiestie could find no reason why Spain should hinder her subiectes, and those of other Princes, from sayling to the Indies; that she could not be persuaded that they were his owne, although the Pope had ne'er so much given them unto him; that she acknowledged no such prerogative in the Pope, muche less the leaste authoritie as to oblige Princes, who owe him no obedience at all, under his power invest & put the Spaniard, as in fee and possession of that New World; also that she could not see how he could derive the least right, but by those descents and landinges here and there of his Subiectes, who built their small cootages to inhabit, and named the Promontorie; Thinges nevertheless that can purchase no Propriety. So that by vertue of such donation of other mens goods, which in equitie is nothinge worth, and of this propriety which is meerley imaginary, he cannot iustlie hinder other Princes to negotiate in those Regions: but they, without infringing any waies the Lawes of Nations, may lawfully bring in Colonies in those partes that are not yet inhabited by the king of Spaines subiectes; sith prescription without possession is of no validity; even as to sayle upon the mayne Ocean, that the use of the Sea, as of the Ayre, is common to all, and that publique necessitie permits not it should be possessed; that there is no people, nor particular, that can challenge or pretend any other rights therein."'

V

Extracts from a despatch by Bernardino de Mendoza to the King of Spain, 13 January 1580; taken from the *Calendar of State Papers, Spanish, Elizabeth, 1579–1590*, p. 1.

'The latter [the Duke of Alençon] told her that he was making ready for his departure, and would come as she pleased, either with or without a company, and either before or after the signing of the capitulations. He said that he was very sorry that they had cut off the hands of the men concerned with the book [John Stubbs, the author of *The Gaping Gulf*, attacking the queen's marriage plan, lost one hand], and he would indeed be glad if he could remedy it, even at the cost of two fingers of his own hand; but as that was now impossible, he entreated her to pardon the men, and award them some recompense, so that they might understand that they owed their lives and her favour to his intercession. . . . He entreated her not to bear illwill to Leicester and the other councillors who had opposed the match, as they no doubt did so, as they thought, in her interests. . . .

The French ambassador had high words with Leicester the other day about his trying to persuade him to confess to the Queen that he was married, as Simier and he, the ambassador, had assured her. [They had informed Elizabeth of Leicester's secret marriage to the Countess of Essex, in order to secure his loss of favour and removal as an obstacle to the Alençon marriage.] This is one of the grievances that Leicester has against him, and the ambassador in his desire to be reconciled with him, sent word by a confidant of his to say that he, Leicester, might see by what Alençon wrote, the good offices which he, the ambassador, had effected, and that the French were as friendly with him as ever. Leicester replied that he knew all about it, and that it was nothing but French chatter. When Alençon came to marry the Queen, he said, he would be obliged to treat him as his master. He said besides that, that he wanted to have no more to do with Frenchmen, and would never trust them again. . . .

Leicester has a ship ready to sail on a voyage for plunder on the route to the Indies. It will leave in ten days and they have collected the most experienced English sailors for the voyage. Although I understand the main object to be robbery if opportunity offers, the design also is to aid Drake, if they can come across him, and strengthen him with their vessel, as Leicester and his party are those who are behind Drake. With a similar object, three ships of 100, 80 and 70 tons are being fitted out at Plymouth in the name of John Hawkins, the pretence being that they are taking merchandise to the coast of Brazil. . . .'

VI

The Alençon negotiation; taken from Camden, *Annals* (1688), Book 3, p. 12.

'He [Alençon] arrived safe in England, and was magnificently entertained and received with all royall courtesies [that] could be expected, evident testimonies of honour and love, which her Maiestie showed apparently, insomuch that on a time on the day of the solemnisation of her coronation (he being entered into amourous discourse with her Maiestie) the great love which she bore him, drew a Ring from her finger, which she gave him upon certain conditions meant and agreed between them. The assistants took that for an argument and assurance that a marriage was by reciprocall promise contracted betwixt them. Amongst others Aldegondy Governor of the City of Antwerp despatched messengers suddenly over into the Low Countries, where for great ioy at the hearing thereof, both in Antwerp and all over Flanders were made great bonfires and their great Artillerie shot off. But this bred sundrie opinions among the Courtiers; for as some reioyced exceedingly, others were astonisht at it & some quite stricken down with sadness. The earl of Leicester who had laid a secret plot to prevent the marriage, the Vice-Chamberlain, Hatton and Walsingham were most of all malcontented, as if the Queene, Religion and Kingdome had been undone. Her women which were about her fell all in sorrow and sadnesse, and the terror they put her into, so troubled her mind that shee passed all that night without sleep amongst her household servants, who made a consort of weeping and sighing. The next morning, finding the Duke and taking him aside, had serious discourse with him. The Duke returning himself after he left her, into his Chamber, plucketh off the Ring, casteth it on the ground, taketh it up againe, rayleth on the lightness of women, and the Inconstancie of Islanders.

As shee was perplexed with these passions, she called to mind what once the Lord Burley and the earl of Sussex had told her, that there was no Alliance Offensive to be hoped for without marrying the Duke; nor being alone and without assistancy was able to withstand the greatness of the Spaniard. . . .'

The late 1570s were increasingly dominated by fear of Spain. This was manifested in intensified, if extremely complex, relations with the Dutch rebels, and by further maritime adventures. It was a period of maximum duplicity in Elizabeth's dealings with the outside world, which are reflected here in Drake's voyage of circumnavigation and in the queen's negotiations for a French marriage. The Earl of Leicester was Drake's most visible backer, but Elizabeth was also supportive, and although it was originally given out that the voyage was bound for Alexandria, no one was really deceived. The instructions (if there were any) were so secret that they have never come to light. It is clear that a plundering expedition of some kind was intended, but the eventual achievement may have happened more or less by accident. Drake was out of contact with England for a long time, and his whole voyage took three years, in the course of which complaints of his activities filtered back to Europe. He was so uncertain of his reception that he took the precaution of despatching a lavish gift to the queen immediately he landed. Elizabeth's reaction was typically ambiguous. She praised him to the skies, conferred the honour of knighthood, and ordered that his ship be converted into a national monument. She also accepted his gift. Conversely, she ordered his cargo to be sequestered, as though she intended to return it, and members of the 'peace party' at court carefully refused Drake's gifts, much to his annoyance. However, when Mendoza officially requested that the loot should be returned, he got what can only be described as a 'dusty' answer.

One of the reasons for Elizabeth's unexpected boldness at this point may have been the state of her negotiations with France. In spite of the massacre of St Bartholomew's day, the treaty of Blois had not been abrogated, and the possibility of a French marriage had never entirely gone away. Henri, Duke of Anjou, had earlier proved recalcitrant over religion, and that negotiation had collapsed; but even before that happened the likelihood of his younger brother, Francois, Duke of Alençon as an alternative had already been mooted. When Henri became King Henri III on the death of his brother, Charles IX, in 1574, François became (confusingly) Duke of Anjou. He is subsequently referred to sometimes as Anjou and sometimes as Alençon.

Elizabeth's motives for pursuing a marriage negotiation with Anjou still remain uncertain. By 1578 she was forty-five, and can have had no reasonable expectation of bearing children. So the logical grounds for the negotiation should have been the sealing of a firm alliance with France, to oppose Spanish ambitions without running the risk of war, or at least a war that would have to be sustained alone. It was for that reason that the 'peace party' at court, led by Burleigh and Sussex, supported the marriage, and the 'war party', led by the Earl of Leicester, opposed it.

The young Elizabeth, before her 'sober phase' in her sister's reign.

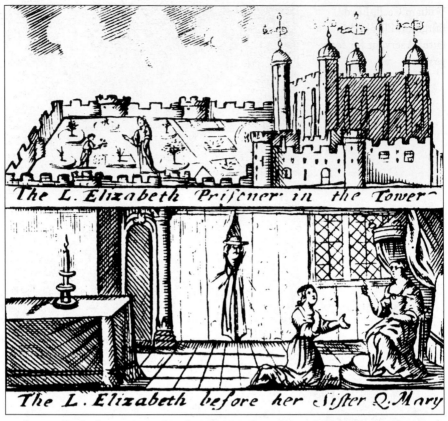

The L. Elizabeth Prisoner in the Tower

The L. Elizabeth before her Sister Q. Mary

Above: Elizabeth imprisoned in the Tower – the gaoler's child brings her flowers;
Below: Elizabeth before her sister Mary. The figure behind the arras is supposedly
Stephen Gardiner.

Nonsuch Palace, Henry VIII's homage to Francis I.

William Cecil, Lord Burghley, Elizabeth's faithful servant for forty years.

Robert Devereux, second Earl of Essex, a flamboyant and self-destructive talent.

Robert Dudley, Earl of Leicester, the Queen's favourite who became a statesman.

Sir Henry Lee, the inventor of the Accession Day tournaments.

The latter were by this time militantly Protestant, willing to risk war with Spain in defence of the faith, and strong advocates of an interventionist strategy in the Netherlands. They saw a French marriage as an undermining of England's confessional stance, whereas the peace party saw concessions on that front as a price well worth paying for security. Articulate popular opinion was vehemently opposed to the marriage, and was expressed by John Stubbs, who would probably have lost his life as well as his hand if he had not been supported by Leicester.

However, this fairly straightforward situation was confused by the queen's personal attitude. It used to be supposed that the whole negotiation was political, and that Elizabeth was play-acting when she expressed such warm affection for her 'little frog'. However, it now seems clear that it was the queen herself who reactivated a moribund negotiation, and pursued it with apparent avidity. Either she was suffering from the last pangs of youth, or she was an even better actress than has been recognised.

The reaction of the Flemings is also significant. Although opposed to Spanish rule, they were mostly Catholics and saw their best hope of survival in intervention from France, rather than England. For Elizabeth to make common cause with the Catholic but anti-Spanish Anjou would therefore be very good news for them. However, in May 1579 the Walloon provinces made their peace with Spain, and their attitude became irrelevant. Finally, with her council completely divided, and her people irreconcilably opposed to the marriage, Elizabeth herself began to blow hot and cold, to Anjou's intense frustration. Later in 1580, she gave up the negotiation although not, it would seem, without regrets. By the end of that year Don John had died, and the Netherlands were under the governorship of Alexander Farnese, Duke of Parma. At the same time Philip made good his claim to the Portuguese succession, thus greatly increasing his resources. Meanwhile, Henri III made his position clear: no Anjou marriage, no Anglo-French alliance. Also, with the Anjou marriage went the last lingering hope of an heir of the queen's body.

THIRTY-SEVEN

The Fate of Mary, Queen of Scots

I

Extract from Holinshed, *Chronicle* (1807 edn), p. 536.

'A True and perfect declaration of the treasons practised and attempted by Francis Throgmorton, late of London, against the Queenes Maiestie and Realme.

. . . You shall understand therefore, that the cause of his apprehension grew first upon secret intelligence given to the Queenes Maiestie that he was a privie conveier and receiver of letters to and from the Scottish Queen; upon which information nevertheless divers months were suffered to pass on before he was called to answer the matter to the end that there might some proof more apparent be had to charge him therewith directly; which shortlie after fell out, and thereupon there were sent unto his houses in London and at Levesham in Kent, to search and apprehend him, certeine gentlemen of no meane credit and reputation. . . . In that search were found the two papers containing the names of certeine catholike noblemen and gentlemen, expressing the havens for the landing of forren forces, with other particulars in the said papers mentioned, the one written in the secretarie hand (which he at the barre confessed to be his own handwriting) and the other in the Roman hand, which he denied to be his, and would not shew how the same came into his handes: howbeit in his examination he hath confessed them both to be his owne hand writing; and so they are in truth. There were also found among other of his papers, twelve petidegrees of the descent of the Crown of England, printed and published by the bishop of Rosse, in the defence of the pretended title of the Scotish Queene his mistresse; with certeine infamous libels against her maiestie printed and published beyond the seas. . . .
  . . . He hath further confessed that he used his fathers advice and opinion in setting downe the names of the catholike noblemen and gentlemen, and did acquaint him with the description of the havens for the landing of forces, which he conceived and put in writing onlie by view of the map and not by particular sight or survie of the said havens.
  Item he hath also confesed, that upon the intermision of writing of letters, and the accustomed intelligences passed between Sir Francis

Englefield and him, he was made acquainted by his brother Thomas Throgmorton, by letters and conferences, and by Thomas Morgan by letters (two of the principall confederates and workers of these treasons residing in France) with a resolute determination agreed upon by the Scottish Queen and her confederates in France and in other forren partes, and also in England, for the invading of the realme.

That the Duke of Guise should be the principall leader and executor of that invasion.

That the pretention (which should be publiclie notified) should be to deliver the Scottish Queene to libertie, and to procure even by force from the Queenes maiestie a toleration in religion for the pretended catholics. But the intention (the bottom whereof should not at the first be made known to all men) should be upon the Queenes maiesties resistance, to remove her maiestie from her Crowne and estate. That the Duke of Guise had prepared the forces, but there wanted two things, monie, and the assistance of a convenient party in England to join with the forren forces; and a third thing, how to set the Scottish Queen at libertie without peril of her person. . . .'

II

Extracts from 'An Act for provision to be made for the surety of the Queen's most royal person', 27 Elizabeth, c. 1; taken from *Statutes of the Realm*, IV, pp. 704–5.

'Forasmuch as the good felicity and comfort of the whole estate of this realm consisteth (only next under God) in the surety and preservation of the Queen's most excellent Majesty; and for that it hath manifestly appeared that sundry wicked plots and means have of late been devised and laid, as well in foreign parts beyond the seas as also within this realm, to the great endangering of her Highness's most royal person and to the utter ruin of the whole commonweal, if by God's merciful providence the same had not been revealed: therefore for the preventing of such great perils as might hereafter otherwise grow by the like detestable and devilish practices, at the humble suit and earnest petition and desire of the Lords spiritual and temporal, and of the Commons in this present Parliament assembled, and by authority of the same Parliament, be it enacted and ordained, if at any time after the end of this present session of Parliament any open invasion or rebellion shall be had or made into or within any of her Majesty's realms or dominions, or any act attempted tending to the hurt of her Majesty's most royal person, by or for any person that shall or may pretend any title to the crown of this realm after her Majesty's decease; or if anything shall be compassed or imagined tending to the hurt of her Majesty's royal person by any person or with the privity of any person that shall or may pretend title to the crown of this realm, that then by her Majesty's commission under her great seal, the lords and others of her Highness's Privy Council and such other lords of Parliament to be named by her Majesty as with the said Privy Council shall make up the number of 24 at the least, having with them for their assistance in that behalf such of the judges of the courts of record at Westminster as her Highness for that purpose shall assign and appoint, or the more part of the same Council, lords and judges, shall by virtue of this act have authority to examine all and every the offences aforesaid and all circumstances thereof, and thereupon to give sentence or judgement as upon good proof the matter shall appear unto them. And that after such sentence or judgement given and declaration thereof made and published by her majesty's proclamation under the great seal of England, all persons against whom such sentence or judgement shall be so given and published shall be excluded and disabled for ever to have or claim, or to pretend to have or claim, the crown of this realm or any of her Majesty's dominions; any former law or statute whatsoever to the contrary in any wise notwithstanding. . . .

And whereas of late many of her Majesty's good and faithful subjects have, in the name of God and with the testimony of good consciences, by one uniform manner of writing under their hands and seals and by their several oaths voluntarily taken, joined themselves together in one Bond and Association to withstand and revenge to the uttermost all such malicious actions and attempts against her Majesty's most royal person: now for the full explaining of all such ambiguities and questions as otherwise might happen to grow by reason of any sinister or wrong construction or interpretation to be made or inferred of or upon the words or meaning thereof, be it declared and enacted by authority of the present parliament that the same Association and every article and sentence therein contained, as well concerning the disallowing, excluding or disabling of any person that may or shall pretend any title to come to the crown of this realm, and also for the pursuing and taking revenge of any person for any such wicked act or attempt as is mentioned in the same Association, shall and ought to be in all things expounded and adjudged according to the true intent and meaning of this act, and not otherwise nor against any other person or persons.'

III

Dispatch from Giovanni Dolfin, Venetian ambassador in France, to the Doge and Senate, 12 September 1586; taken from the *Calendar of State Papers, Venetian*, VIII, p. 202.

'Letters from London, dated 30th August, reached here on the 6th. A conspiracy against the Queen's life has been brought to light. In order to discover the culprits, no one was allowed to leave the kingdom for eighteen days. As rumours here vary very much, I have learned from the English ambassador, and from some large merchants who have correspondence with London, how the facts really stand. They say that the plot was hatched in Paris, in the house of Don Bernardino de Mendoza, the Spanish ambassador, with the intervention and participation of one Charles Paget, an English exile, and brother of my Lord Paget who lately went to Spain, and also of a priest named Ballard, who is likewise an Englishman. This priest, although outlawed, volunteered to go to England, and to secure a rising of some of the principal catholic gentlemen who were, in a body, to slay the Queen as she was walking in a garden. The priest left, with letters, so all say, from Don Bernardino and from Paget. He won over six rich young men, between twenty and twenty five years old, of whom one named Babington took the lead. Babington induced many others to join the plot, and the execution of the murder was fixed for the 28th of August. But while the conspiritors were in treaty with others still, for the better securing of their intent, the priest Ballard was arrested and condemned to death as an outlaw. To save himself, he betrayed the plot, revealing the names, not only of the conspiritors in Paris, but also the names of those whom he himself had induced to join him in London. They were all instantly arrested, as were also two secretaries of the Queen of Scotland. All their papers were seized; and the English ambassador tells me that it was understood from the examination of the prisoners that the Queen of Scotland had given her consent to the attempt; to clear up the whole affair arrests are being made every day. The ambassador has orders from his mistress to communicate these occurrences to his Most Christian Majesty, and to point out to him that in virtue of the good relations between the two Crowns it would be right and proper for him to refuse asylum in his kingdom to men of such quality. . . .'

IV

Proclamation declaring sentence against the Scottish queen, 4 December 1586; taken from Hughes and Larkin, *Tudor Royal Proclamations* (New Haven/London, 1969), II, no. 685.

'Whereas we were given to understand very credibly (although to our great grief) that divers things were and of late time hath been compassed, imagined, and resolutely intended directly to the hurt and destruction of our royal person and to the subversion of the estate of our realm by foreign invasions and rebellions at home, as well by the Queen of Scots remaining in our realm under our protection as by many divers other wicked persons with her privity, who hath freely confessed the same and have thereupon received open trial, judgement and execution according to the laws for their deserts; and though in very truth we were greatly and deeply grieved in our mind to think or imagine that any such unnatural and monstrous fact should be either devised or willingly assented unto against us by her, being a princess born, and of our sex and blood, and one also whose life and honour we had many times before saved and preserved: yet were we so directly drawn to think all the same to be true by the sight and understanding of such proofs as were manifestly produced afore us upon matters that had as well proceeded from herself as from the conspiritors themselves, who voluntarily and freely without any coercion had confessed their conspirations both jointly with her and directed by her, against our person and our realm; and therefore also we saw great reason to think the same over dangerous to be suffered to pass onward to take their full effect.

Wherefore . . . we yielded, by good advice given to us, to proceed in the most honourable sort that could be devised within our realm to the examination hereof, according to a late Act of Parliament made the 23rd November in the 27th year of our reign [27 Elizabeth, c. 1 (1584)].

Whereupon by our commission under our Great Seal of England bearing date at our castle of Windsor in our county of Berkshire the 6th day of October now last past [1586] we did for that purpose (according to the said statute) assign, name, and appoint all the lords and others of our Privy Council, and so many other Earls and Barons, lords of the parliament of the greatest degree and most ancient of the nobility of this our realm as with the same lords and others of our Privy Council made up the number of 42; adding also thereto a further number, according to the tenor of the aforesaid act of parliament, of certain of the chiefest and other principal judges of the courts of record at Westminster, amounting in the whole to the number of 47, to examine all things compassed and imagined tending to the hurt of our royal person, as well by the said Queen of Scots by the name of Mary, the daughter and heir of James V, late King of Scots, commonly called the Queen of Scots and Dowager of France, as by any other of her privity, and all the circumstances thereof; and thereupon, according to the tenor of the said act of parliament, to give sentence or judgement as upon good proof of the matter unto them should appear; as by the same commission more fully appeareth.

And where afterwards the more part of the said councillors, lords and judges in our said commission names (that is to say the number of 36) did in the presence and hearing of the said Queen of Scots, where she remained in our castle of Fotheringhay, at divers days and times in public place very exactly, uprightly and with great deliberation, examine all the matters and offences whereof she was charged and accused, tending to the dangers afore rehearsed and mentioned in our said commission, and all the circumstances thereof: and heard also at large in all favourable manner what the same Queen did or could say for her excuse and defence in that behalf.

Whereupon afterwards, on the 25th day of October now last past, all the said council, lords and judges that had heard and examined the same cause in the said Queen's presence as afore is mentioned with one assent and consent after good deliberation did give their sentence and judgement in this sort following:

That, after the 1st day of June in the 27th year of our reign and before the date of our said commission, divers things were compassed and imagined within this realm of England by Anthony Babington and others with the privity of the said Mary, pretending title to the Crown of this realm of England, tending to the hurt, death and destruction of our royal person. . . .

And whereas also, sithen the same sentence and judgement so given and recorded, the lords and commons in this present parliament assembled have also at sundry times in open parliament heard and considered the principal evidences, proofs, and circumstances whereupon the same sentence and judgement was grounded, and have by their public assent in parliament, affirmed the same to be a just, lawful and true sentence, and so have allowed and approved the same in writing presented unto us, and have also notified to us how deeply they did foresee the great and many imminent dangers which otherwise might and would grow to our person and to the whole realm if this sentence were not fully executed; and consequently therefor they did (by their most humble and earnest petitions in that behalf, of one accord, having access unto us upon their sundry requests most instantly upon their knees) pray, beseech, and with many reasons of great force and importance, move and press us that the said sentence and judgement, so justly and duly given, and by them approved as is aforesaid, might (according to the express tenor of the said act of parliament) by our proclamation under our Great Seal be declared and published, and the same also finally executed. . . .

. . . Whereupon, being not only moved to our great grief but also overcome with the earnest requests, declarations and important reasons, of all our said subjects, the nobles and commons of our realm, whose judgement, knowledge, and natural care of us and the whole realm we know doth far surmount all others being not so interested therein and so justly to be esteemed; and perceiving also the said sentence to have been honourably, lawfully and justly given, agreeable to justice and to the laws of our realm, we did yield. . . .'

V

Extract from Camden, *Annals* (1688), Book 3, p. 202.

'The fatall day beginning to appeare, which was the 7 of February [1587], she attired herselfe in such garments as she usually wore upon Festivall dayes, and calling her servants about her caused her Will to be read, desiring them to take in good part the Legacies she had given them, seeing it was not in her power to make them better. Then wholly fixing her mind upon God, she betook herself into her Oratory or place of Prayer, where with sighs, grevous gronings and fervent prayers she called upon God; till such time as Thomas Audrey, Sheriefe of the Shire, signified to her that it was now time for her to come forth. Then forth she came, in gesture, carriage and demeanour right Princely and majestike; cheerefull in countenance, and in attire very modest and Matron like: she wore a linnen vaile upon her and before her face, which she discovered; at her girdle hung her rosarie or rowe of Beades, and in her hand she held a Crucifix of Ivory.

In the porch or passage of her lodging, met her the Earles and the rest of the Noblemen, where Melvine (one of her servants) falling on his knees, and pouring forth teares, lamented his unlucky fortune, that he was designed the man that should carey into Scotland the sad message of the tragicall death of his deerest Mistresse:

Oh weep not (quoth she) for you shall shortly see Mary Stuart at the end of all her sorrowes. You shall report that I dye true and constant in my religion, and firm in my love to scotland and to France. God forgive them that have thirsted after my blood, as the hart doth for the water-brooke. Thou (oh God) which art truth itself, and which soundest the deepest secrets of mine inward heart, even thou knowest how earnestlie I have desired the union of the two Kingdoms of England and Scotland. Reccommend me to my sonne, tell him for certaintie I never did nor attempted anything prejudiciall to the Kingdome of Scotland. Councell him to entertaine amitie with the Queene of England, and be you his true and trustie servant.

By this, the teares flowed from her eyes, she repeating againe and againe, Adieu, Adieu, Melvine; who wept all the while no less lamentably. Then turning her towards the earles, she intreated them that her servants might be gently used, that they might enjoy the things she had given them by her Will, that they might be permitted to be with her at her death, and lastly might be saflie conducted and sent home to their Countries. Her first two requestes they granted, but for the having of her servantes by at her death, the Earl of Kent seemed scrupulous, fearing there might be some superstition in that. To him she said:

Feere you not, Sir; the poore wretches desire nothing but to take their last leaves of me. And I know my sister, the Queene of England, would not that you should deny me so small a request: For the honour of my sex, my servants should be in presence. I am the nearest of her Parentage and Consanguinitie, grand childe to Henry the seventh, Dowager of France and annointed Queene of Scotlande.

Which when she had said, and turned her about, it was granted her to have such of her servants as she would nominate. Then she named Melvine,

Bourgon her Physician, her Apothecarie, her Chyrurgion, two of her maids, and some others, of which Melvine carried up her traine. Then the Noblemen, the two Earles and the Sherife of the Shire going before her, she came to the scaffold, which was built at the upper end of the Hall, upon which was a Chair, a cusion and a Block, all covered with black. So soon as she was set, and silence commanded, Beal read the Warrant or Mandate, to which she listened attentively, as if it had been some other thing. Then Doctor Fletcher (Deane of Peterborough) made a long discourse of the condition of her life past, present, and of the life to come. Twice she interrupted him, intreating him not to importune her; Protesting that she was settled and resolved in the ancient Roman Catholicke religion, and ready even now to shed her blood for the same. He vehemently exhorted her to be repentant and with an undoubted faith to put her whole trust and confidence in Christ: But shee answered him; That she had been borne and brought up in this Religion, and was ready to die in the same. Then the Earls saying they would pray for her; Shee replied, she would give them great thankes if they would pray together with her, but to communicate in Praier with them that are of a different religion were a great scandall, and a great sinne. Then they bade the Dean to pray; with whom, whilst the Assembly about him joined in prayer; Shee, falling on her knees, and holding the Crucifix betwixt her handes, prayed in Latin, with her owne people, out of the Office of our Blessed Lady.

After the Deane had ended his Praiers, shee prayed in English for the Church, for her Sonne, and Elizabeth, Queen of England, beseeching God to turn his heavy wrath from this Iland, and protesting (as she held up the Crucifix) that she reposed her hope of salvation in the Blood of Christ Jesus; she called upon the Holy Company of the Saints in heaven to make intercession for her unto Him. Shee forgave all her enemies; then kissing the crucifix and making the sign of the Crosse, she said: As thine armes (oh Lord Jesus Christ) were spread forth upon the Crosse, so receive me into the same armes of thy Mercy, and pardon my trespasses. Then the Executioner asked forgiveness, whom she forgave; and her servants (shee making haste) tooke off her upper garments, crying and lamenting aloud; yet neither by her kissing or crossing of them, did she ever change her cheerefull countenance, but bade them forbeare their womanish weeping, saying: That she was at the end of all her calamities. Likewise, turning herself towards her other servants, most pitiously weeping, she signed them with the sign of the crosse, and smilingly bade them all Adieu. Then having a linnen cloth before her face, and laid her head upon the blocke, she recited the psalm In thee (O Lord) have I put my trust, let me not be confounded for ever. Then stretching forth her body; and many times together ingeminating the word; Lord into thy handes I commend my spirit, her head at the second blow was cut off; the Deane crying aloud and saying

So perish all the enemies of Queen Elizabeth; to which the earl of Kent answered Amen, so likewise did the people weeping. Afterwards her body being imbalmed, and solemnly made ready, was with princely Funerals interred in the Cathedral Church of Peterborough. And in Paris were her obsequies in most magnificent maner, also celebrated by the Guises, who neither in her life omitted any office of love and kindred towards her, nor yet after her death, to their great laud and glory.'

Mary's position in England spelt trouble, both for Elizabeth and herself. As long as she was alive there would be conspiracies and plots in Scotland for her restoration, backed by the Guise party in France, if not by the French Crown. More seriously for Elizabeth, as her misdemeanours faded from memory, and the religious issue sharpened after 1570, Mary inevitably became the focus for plots, both in England and abroad, against the English queen. As a discredited exile, suspected of having had her husband murdered, and linked to the Protestant Earl of Bothwell by an alleged third marriage, she was not a plausible Catholic candidate.

However, even by 1572 that position had changed. Her French title was now no more than a memory; her complicity in Darnley's murder unproven; and Bothwell no more than an aberration, in which she could easily be represented as the victim. Her Catholic credentials were being rapidly restored; both Philip and the pope began to regard her with favour; and her imprisonment in England became a form of martyrdom. This was well-enough understood by the English parliament, and indeed by Elizabeth's council. Mary's complicity in the Ridolfi plot of 1571 was sufficiently established for parliament to pass an Act of Attainder against her, but the queen vetoed it, and ignored the mounting clamour for her death, particularly from the House of Commons. She considered sending her rival back to Scotland, where she would almost certainly have been executed for Darnley's murder, but apparently lacked confidence in the Earl of Mar, who was regent at that point, and thought that the responsibility for Mary's fate would still be laid at her door.

Elizabeth's attitude has never been satisfactorily explained. She was under no illusions about the danger, but clung obstinately to the belief that there could be a diplomatic settlement. Mary, for her part, was so convinced of the righteousness of her cause, both religious and political, that she would yield to no threat or pressure to surrender on either point. From 1569 to 1585 her custodian was the Earl of Shrewsbury, and her main place of confinement Sheffield castle. She lived in some state, but without any possibility of escape. Theoretically all her correspondence passed through Shrewsbury's hands, but in practice his system was full of leaks. This worked both ways; on the one hand it enabled her to keep in touch with the restless plotting which was occurring on her behalf all over western Europe; on the other hand, it subjected her to the much more rigorous and unsympathetic scrutiny of William Cecil, Francis Walsingham and their agents.

Mary's behaviour was indiscreet to the point of recklessness. She must have known after 1572 that it was only the personal protection afforded by Elizabeth that stood between her and death at the hands of an outraged parliament. And yet she would neither concede her right to the succession, nor desist from her restless plotting. More than once Elizabeth believed that she had found a formula, either with the French or the Scots, or both, which would enable her to get rid of her unwelcome captive safely, but as Mary would make no concessions whatsoever, they all came to nothing.

A further crisis was reached in 1584, when the assassination of William of Orange drew stark attention to the queen's peril. That year Mary had several irons in the fire for securing her release from Sheffield by force, by either foreign or domestic means. One of these was represented by Francis Throgmorton, who fell victim to Walsingham's intelligence system. Throgmorton's confession, and the evidence of intercepted letters, led to renewed efforts, both in parliament and on the council, to persuade Elizabeth to change her mind. In what was virtually despair at her obstinacy, a Bond of Association was formed by Protestant noblemen and gentlemen (many of them members of parliament), effectively giving notice that if Elizabeth should fall victim to the assassin's bullet, they would not only have no truck with Mary as her successor, but would immediately proceed to her execution. The Queen of Scots was not named, but the intention was obvious.

In the following year, in the wake of the Parry plot and as the hysteria mounted, parliament explicitly sanctioned the bond and its purpose, setting out a procedure to be followed in the event of its being invoked. This Elizabeth did not veto, and it became the statute of 27 Elizabeth, c. 1. In 1586, with the country already at war with Spain, another plot was exposed. Like the others, this involved Guise agents in France, Mary's own servants in Scotland, and disaffected English Catholics. It became known by the name of one of its English protagonists, Anthony Babington, but in fact he was not a prime mover. Again Mary's complicity appears to have been established by intercepted letters, and after Babington's execution the pressure upon Elizabeth became overwhelming. A judicial process was set up under the terms of the statute of 1584, because there was no 'normal' method of proceeding against an anointed queen, even a deposed one. Mary defended herself with theatrical flair and high moral righteousness, but having got so far, the commissioners were only going to reach one verdict. Reluctantly,

Elizabeth also complied with the provisions of the statute by proclaiming the verdict, but it took weeks of further pressure before she would sign the warrant for Mary's execution, and even then, if her servants had not acted with unprecedented despatch, she might have drawn back.

There has always been a suspicion that Mary was trapped into approving plots against Elizabeth by English agents, and that may have been so in the case of Babington (or at least of the mysterious Ballard). It may also have been that some of her own agents acted without her knowledge, or beyond their instructions. However, the evidence of her general attitude throughout this period is wide ranging and conclusive. She wanted Elizabeth dead, and wanted the English Crown herself. Buoyed up by false expectations, she seems to have believed that only a handful of Protestant fanatics stood in the way of a Catholic English consensus which would have accepted her. She went to her death in February 1587 in the grip of this invincible self-deception.

William Camden, writing in 1615 in the reign of Mary's son, presents her execution very much as she would have wished it to be seen; effectively as a martyrdom. Camden's account is delicately poised, and without any overt criticism either of Elizabeth or of the English council, but it clearly presents Mary as a tragic heroine on a grand scale. Its accuracy may be questioned, but its theatrical impact is undoubted. At the time, however, England had more urgent things to worry about than the exit of this passionate and deeply flawed diva.

THIRTY-EIGHT

The Presbyterian Challenge

I

Extracts from a petition 'For a learned ministry to preach the Gospel, and to be resident in every parish; and for further regulation of the Bishops, Officers and Governors of the Church' (1584); taken from Strype, *Annals of the Reformation* (London, 1725), III, app. 1, p. 68.

'. . . I. That there may be a view taken of all the Market Towns, and other Townes of most inhabitantes within the Realm of England; to see what hable preaching Pastor is now resident among them, and in every of them. And also to know, what Sufficiency of Living there is now provided in them, and in every of them, for the Maintenance of such a learned, Godly, Preaching, Pastor, to be resident among them. And what Want there is in every of them, as well of such a Pastor, as also of a sufficient sustentation, or living of a meet Pastor. Thus shall the truth of our former complaint appear concerning the Want of Teaching. Which we English subjects of this Land do not endure.

   . . . V. If this will not suffice for the Provision of all the resident Preaching Pastors, which shall be found to want a Sufficient Living, then let the Prebends of all the cathedral and Collegiate Churches, by the Bishops of the Dioces, or by him or them, in whom the gift of such Prebends are, be annexed to the said Offices of the Preaching Pastors, which do remain unprovided of Sufficient Livings. That by this Annexion, a further provision for a sufficient living may be made for the said Preaching Pastors. And in this behalf it would be provided, that those Prebendaries, which have not any benefices impropriate belonging to their prebends, either should be compelled to be resident upon the same benefice, to teach and guide the people in understanding thereby the Word of God, or severing the Benefice from the Corps of the Prebend, the same Parsonage Impropriate should be united with, and joined unto the Vicarage of the same Benefice. So that he, the said Vicar, having the whole charge of his Flock, may have also the whole living appointed to the teaching Pastor.

   . . . XIII. That no one Bishop do hereafter proceed in admitting, or depriving of any Pastor by his sole authority: nor in excommunicating any faulty person; nor in absolving any person that is excommunicated: nor in the deciding and determining of any cause Ecclesiastical, without the

Advice and Consent of the aforesaid seniors and associates joined with him. And that their consent may be testified by their own Names in Writing to every Act and Actes, which shall be determined and ordained by their common consent.

XIV. Moreover, that it be established, that it shall not be lawful for any man to appeal from the sentence and judgement of the bishop, given with the advice aforesaid, to any manner of Person or Persons, but only to ther next Provincial Synod, which shall be kept in this Church of England.

. . . XXIX. That there may be some godly, learned, zealous men appointed by the Queenes Highness, with the Advice of her Honourable Council; to Visit the present state of all Archbishops and Bishops of England and Ireland. And first to consider of such doinges and actions as have passed by the authority of the said Archbishops and Bishops, and through the hands of their officers, under the name of the said Archbishops and Bishops, sithence the beginning of her Blessed and Peaceful Government. That so the Queenes Highness may perfectly understand how the said Archbishops and Bishops have, sithence the beginning of Her Majesties most happy Reign, behaved themselves in their Offices. And whether they have in all Actions faithfully discharged their Duty, according to the Trust which was reposed in them, served the Church of God faithfully, or have don unfaithfully, and neglected their Duty to God, to his Church, to Her Highness, or not.

Again, that the said Commissioners or Visitors may have Authority, and that it be given in streight charge unto them, to look Godly into the very state itself of the said Bishops and Archbishops; as it is now: And to consider whether it be such as the State of those old true Bishops was, of whom God himself doth speak by St. Paul in His Holy Word, and of such other Pastors as were called Bishops in the first and sincere age of the Primitive Church. . . .'

II

Extract from 'Martin Marprelate', *Hay ye any work for Cooper?* (1588).

'. . . a briefe Pistle directed by waye of an hublication to the reverende Bisshopps . . . wherein worthy Martin quits himself like a man. . . . Printed in Europe/ not far from some of the Bounsing Priests. . . .

And I will have my pennyworths of all of you brethrene ere I have done with you/ for this pains which your T.C. hath taken with me. This is the puritans craft in prooving me to be confuted I know: Ile be even with them to. A craftie whoresons brethren Bp. did you think that because ye puritans T.C. did set John of Cant. [Whitgift] at a nonpluss, and gave him the overthrow that therefore your T.C. alias Thomas Cooper bishop of Winchester or Thomas Cooke his Chaplaine could set me at a nonplus. Simple fellows/ methinks he should not.

I guess your T.C. to be Thomas Cooper (but I do not preremptorily affirm it) because the modest old student of 52 yeares standing/ setteth Winchester after Lincoln & Rochester in the contents of his booke which Blasphemy would not have been tollerated by them that saw and allowed the same booke/ unless mistres Coopers husband had been the author of it.

Secondly because this T.C. the author of this booke is a bishop/ and therefore Thomas Cooper/ he is a bishop because he reckoneth [himself] charged amongst others/ with those crimes whereof non are accused but bishops alone/ pag. 101 lin. 26. Ha. olde Martin yet I see thou hast it in thee/ thou wilt enter into the bowels of the cause in hand I perceive. Nay, if thou wilt command me, I will give you more reasons yet. The stile and the phrase is very like her husbands, yt was sometimes woont to write unto doctor Day of Welles. You see I can doo it indeed. Again, non would be so grosehead as to gather/ because my reverence telleth Deane John/ that he shall have twenty fistes about his eares more than his owne (whereby I meane indeede that many would write against him by reason of his bamination learning, which otherwise never meant to take pen in hande) that I threaten him with blowes, and to deale by Scaffold lawe: whereas that was far from my meaning, and could by no meanes be gathered out of my woordes/ but only by him that pronounced Eulojin for Enlogeni in the pulpit; and by him whom a papist made to beleeve that the Greek word, that is to give thanks, signifieth to make a crosse on the forehead: py hy hy hy. I cannot but laugh. py hy hy hy. I cannot but laugh to thinke that an olde soaking student in this learnéd age is not ashamed to be so impudent as to presume to deale with a papist/ when he hath no gere in his pocked. But I promise you sir/ it is no shame to be a T. bishop if a man could/ though he be neere as unlearned as John [Bullingham] of Gloucester or William [Overton] of Liechfield. And I tell you true our brother Westchester [William Chaderton] had as live play twentie noble in a night/ at Priemeero on the cardes as trouble himselfe with any pulpit labour. . . .'

III

Extracts from the examinations relating to the press of Martin Marprelate, and the books printed, held at Lambeth, 15 February 1589; taken from Strype, *Annals of the Reformation* (London, 1725), III, app. 1, p. 261.

'Sir Rich. Knightly in his examination confessed, that at his house at Fausley, a Book called *The Epitomes*, was printed. The Printing Press brought to his House there by one Jeffs, a Tenant of his son. From whence the press was carried to his House at Norton about Christmas last [1588]. And touching the author of the book, he knoweth not, unless it were Penry. Who came and moved him that he might have a Room in his House to Print a like Book to that which he had made before, concerning the unlearned ministry of Wales. He likewise said that Waldegrave was the printer. And further confesseth, that Newman, the Cobbler, had his Livery and Conizance, and that Stephen, his servant, carried the Press and Letters from Norton to Coventry, to the house of John Hales Esq. . . .

. . . Henry Sharpe deposeth, That the press settled at Hale's House, Waldegrave there printed three Books, *viz. The Mineral Conclusions*, the *Supplication to the Parliament*, and *Have you any Work for the Cooper? Martin Junior* and *Martin Senior*

Appeareth by Roger Weekston Gentleman, his Confession, that his Wife moved him, that Hodgkins might do a piece of Work in his House; which he saw not, but heard afterwards that *Martin Junior* and *Martin Senior* were printed there in a Low Parlour of his House.
Udal, *Demonstration, Diotrephes*

Henry Sharpe deposed, that Penry (which appears to be a principal Dealer in all the Acts everywhere) told him, that Udall was the author of the *Demonstration of Discipline*.

Tomkyns [a Printer] also deposed, that he believed Udal was also the author of the Dialogues, called *Diotrephes*; because in a Catlogue of such Books, as is said, Udal had made, this Examinate saw as well the said Dialogue, as the *Demonstration* mentioned. And that Udal resorted sundry times to Mrs. Crane's House at Mowsely, while Penry and Waldegrave were there.

Stephen Chatfield, Vicar of Kingston, deposed, That before the coming forth of the first Martin, he saw in Udal's study certain written Papers, importing such matter as is contained in the Libel; and saith further, that about a fortnight before Michaelmas [1588] the said Udal, in conference with this examinate, said, It were best for the Bishops not to stop his Mouth. For if they did, he would then set himself to writing, and give such a Blow as they never had the like in their lives.

Udal himself confesseth, that some things contained in the first Martin proceded from his Report, but saith that he knoweth not how it came in writing. And yet being asked, Whether he made not a collection of some things that are contained in that Book; and whether he did show those his collections to Mr. Field [a Puritan minister] and Mr. Chatfield, or to either of them, saith that he did. He said further, that he told Mr. Chatfield, that if the Bishops and others restrained him from preaching, then he would give them occasion to employ themselves in writing the more against their Government. . . .'

Puritan dissatisfaction with the Church was widespread and varied. It was symbolised by the Vestiarian controversy of 1563 and 1566, but embraced pluralism, non-residence, the lack of preachers, and the poor education of many clergy, as well as the apparent toleration of surviving Catholic practices. For straightforward political reasons, Elizabeth was reluctant to use her ecclesiastical authority directly to suppress these dissidents, preferring to rely on the traditional visitational powers of the bishops. Archbishop Parker was consequently forced to issue a series of *Advertisements* in 1566, on his own authority, ordering conformity to the established order. These were bitterly resented, resisted and evaded, and Parker got little support from the queen. Instead the Puritans began to see the bishops themselves as the main cause of their grievances, which was deeply embarrassing to many of them who sympathised with the campaign for further reform.

In 1570 Thomas Cartwright, the Lady Margaret Professor of Divinity at Cambridge, began to articulate this newly focused anger, urging the dismantling of the whole episcopal structure of Church government, and its replacement with a Genevan, or Presbyterian, system. Cartwright lost his chair and was driven into exile, but his views were represented in two *Admonitions* to parliament in 1571 and 1572. These were well received in the House of Commons, and the queen was forced to come to the aid of her beleaguered bishops by suppressing discussion.

In the conflict which then developed, both sides were to some extent hamstrung by their own consciences. Most of the Puritans accepted the queen's ecclesiastical authority, and had no desire to withdraw from the Church; hence their somewhat artificial fury against the bishops. Most of the latter accepted the need for further reform, and had no desire to alienate those who were their most effective allies against the Catholics. On the other hand, the development of the Presbyterian attack forced them to defend themselves, and drove the episcopate and the Crown closer together.

Parker died in 1575, and two years later his successor, Edmund Grindal, was suspended for refusing to suppress the Prophesying movement, which he regarded as educational and necessary and the queen regarded as subversive. For about six years the bishops were without effective leadership, and it became abundantly clear that the real enemy of the demand for further reform was the queen herself.

Neither side made any real progress until Grindal was replaced by John Whitgift in 1583. Whitgift believed as strongly as any of the dissenters in the need to upgrade the Church's ministry, but he was as clear explicitly as Elizabeth was implicitly that this could only be achieved by the Crown and the episcopate working together without the distraction of self-appointed advisers. In 1583 he issued six articles which required unconditional submission. This inquisitorial style offended many of the Puritans' influential backers, including Lord Burghley and the Earl of Leicester; but Whitgift had what both Parker and Grindal had lacked – strong backing from the queen.

Then the Presbyterians shot themselves in the feet. The outbreak of war focused attention on the Catholic threat to a new degree, and the view that the English Church could not afford internecine strife gained ground. In 1587 a series of fierce, scurrilous and mocking attacks upon the episcopate began to appear under the pseudonym 'Martin Marprelate'. They were clearly the product of deep-seated frustration, but both their tone and their timing were unfortunate. One of the most irreverent, *Hay ye any work for Cooper?*, appeared during the euphoric period after the repulse of the Armada, when the prevailing feeling was that God was well pleased with England, and with its ways of conducting its business. Moreover, the mocking, colloquial tone of such works alarmed all those in positions of authority. If the bishops could be insulted with impunity, might not the Lords, or even the queen, be next?

Whitgift's countermeasures consequently attracted a degree of magisterial cooperation which neither Parker nor Grindal had ever enjoyed. The presses were found and broken up, and a number of suspects were arrested. One, John Penry, was eventually executed for high treason. The Marprelate controversy broke Presbyterianism as a political force, but it did not go away. Its more moderate advocates resumed a low-key campaign of 'in house' criticism, and the more extreme resorted to separatism. Time was to show that there was no future in the latter course, because the Presbyterian theory depended upon close cooperation with secular authority; it was an establishment, or nothing.

THIRTY-NINE

War, 1585–90

I

Extract from Camden, *Annals* (1688 edn); taken from the selection edited by Wallace MacCaffrey in 1970, p. 206.

'After the Queen had seriously and carefully for some time considered of things, and had thoroughly waighed the barbarous Cruelty of the Spaniards towards her neighbours the Netherlanders, and their Hatred against England and the Religion which she embraced (for the Spaniard was certainly persuaded that the Netherlands could never be reduced to his Obedience, unless England were first Conquered); lest the war should be brought home to her own Doors (Scotland yet wavering) and the Spaniards power should too far extend and increase in Countries so near adjoining unto her, and for Situation so convenient, both for translating the War into England, and for the Trade of Merchants as well by sea as up and down the River Rhyne, as also for prohibiting the carriag of all Provisions for Shipping to the Enemy; Countries provided of a strong fleet, and stout and able seamen, insomuch as if they were ioyned with the English, she might easily become Mistres of the Sea, and withall so rich and strong that they had for long time curbed their insulting enemies, without Foreign assistance; as also lest they should put themselves under the Protection of the French; she resolved, that it was both Christian Piety to relieve the afflicted Netherlanders, Embracers of the same Religion which she professed; and good wisdom also to provide for the safety of the people committed to her charge, by preventing the Pernicious Designs of her enemies; and that not out of any desire for Glory, but out of mere necessity for Preservation of her own and Peoples security. Hereupon she undertook the Protection of the Netherlands, whilst all the Princes of Christendom admired at such manly fortitude in a Woman, which durst, as it were, declare War against so puisant a Monarch; insomuch as the King of Sweden said "That Queen Elizabeth had now taken the Diadem from her head and adventured it upon the doubtful Chance of War".

Betwixt her and the Confederate Estates these Conditions were agreed upon:

The Queen shall send the Confederate Provinces an auxilliary force of 5,000 foot and 1,000 horse, under a Governor General, an Honourable

Person, and shall find them pay during the War, which the estates shall repay when a peace shall be Concluded; namely in the first year of the peace, the expenses disbursed in the first year of the War, and the rest in the Four Years next following. In the mean time Flushing and the Castle of Ramekins in Walcheran in the Isle of Briell, with the City and two Forts, shall be delivered into the Queens hands for Caution. The Governors of those places shall exercise no authority over the Inhabitants, but only over the Garrison-Soldiers, who shall pay Excise and Impositions as well as the Inhabitants. The said places, after the money is repaid, shall be restored again unto the Estates, and not delivered to the Spaniard or to any other enemy whatsoever. The Governor General, and two Englishmen whom the Queen shall name, shall be admitted into the Council of the Estates. The estates shall make no league with any without the Advice and Consent of the Queen; neither shall the Queen without the Advice of the Estates. Ships for the common defence shall be rigged and set forth in equal numbers by both Parties, and at the Common charges, to be commanded by the Admiral of England. The Havens and Ports shall be open and free to both sides.'

II

The English attack on Cartagena, 9 February 1586 (an eyewitness account); taken from *Papers Relating to the Spanish War, 1585–87*, ed. J.S. Corbett (Navy Records Society, 1898), pp. 18–20.

'. . . The eleventh day we came to an anchor at Cartagena, and ten days ere we came thither they had warning of us, and had carried away the most part of their goods having fortified and made such rampires that it was impossible by man's reason for us to win. But God fought for us, for our ships could not come near the town for lack of water to batter it, and where our pinnaces should go in was but the length of two ships, and it was chained over from the Castle with sixteen pieces pf ordnance in this narrow gutter; yet we did attempt it, [so] that we had the rudder of our pinnace struck away, and men's hats from their heads, and the top of our mainmast beaten in pieces, the oars stricken out of our men's hands as they rowed, and our captain like to have been slain. They had planted sixteen pieces against us in the Castle. Also they had planted two galleys and a galleass with ordnance, and another fort with six pieces, that we had not the length of a pike left us for passage to enter, and there were 400 horsemen and footmen in arms and still bent against us. The two galleys and galleass were well furnished with men and ordnance, and this was then their saying, as afterwards they did confess, that we shall all die but twenty of the best, and they should be made galley-slaves, they did so presume of their fort and strength.

Indeed it was not likely that any man of us should escape; but what God will have shall be done, who put it into our minds that we should enter upon them in the morn before day. Yet they were ready to resist us, and had set in the ground thousands of poisoned arrows, yet very few of our men received hurt thereby.

The Spanish horsemen met us without the fort very courageously, but our pikemen made them soon to retire, and we followed so fiecely upon them that we made them forsake their fort.

The two galleys and galleass, with the other fort, did so ply their ordnance against us that it was wonderful; their calivers, muskets and arquebuses did play their parts. But God is all in all, by whose good help we made them fly into the town like sheep, but they galled many of our men in the town.

We lost in this skirmish 28 men besides those that were hurt, yet constrained the Spaniards to fly like sheep into the mountains.

Thus we enjoyed the town, but found little store of victual therein, the most we found was wine and oil. They had hid many things in the ground, which we found notwithstanding. . . .'

III

Dispatch by Hieronimo Lippomano, Venetian ambassador in Spain, to the Doge and Senate, 6 September 1586; taken from the *Calendar of State Papers, Venetian*, IX, p. 201.

'Two days before the news of Drake's return to England arrived here, a spy in his Majesty's employ reached the Escurial with the information that the Queen of England had recalled Drake on account of the great mortality which existed in the fleet and threatened the safety of the whole squadron if it remained longer in those parts. Furthermore she was afraid that she might lose Drake himself at the very moment when she most needed him. The spy declares that the Queen is really anxious for peace, both because she is afraid that the King of Spain will take some resolution against her, for she knows that she has most seriously provoked him, and because the maintenance of troops in Holland and Zeeland is costing her very dear, while she is growing suspicious of the Earl of Leicester, whose popularity with the Dutch is on the increase. She is always anxious about the English, and above all, about the Irish catholics; and every precaution is employed to prevent anyone from entering the royal palace who has not taken the oath of allegiance. She has given Letters of Marque to a large number of English; and she, and private owners as well, are building vast numbers of ships. The ships of private owners are subsidised at the rate of one thousand crowns each [about £250] on condition that the Queen may call for them when she requires them. She has raised and paid for three months eight hundred infantry, and is going to send them to Holland. Finally, while negotiating for a peace she does not cease to prepare for the defence of her kingdom. And although Drake, they say, has not brought home as much as the Queen hoped for at first, yet he has most assuredly advanced his reputation. Here the preparations for war continue, but they hold that Drake's return to England will make it more easy to conclude a treaty, without loss of honour, on the subject of Holland and Zealand. The Prince of Parma writes that everything can be arranged except the religious clauses, and he implores his Majesty to find out some means of toning these down; but they consider that the King will not easily change upon this point.

The Spaniards are firmly convinced that the Republic [Venice] is little pleased at their successes in Flanders, and still less with the projected attack on England.'

IV

Extract from Philip's instructions to the Duke of Medina Sidonia, July 1588; taken from 'Spanish documents relating to the Armada', ed. C.C. Lloyd in *The Naval Miscellany*, IV (1952), p. 16.

'. . . If you do not encounter the enemy until you reach Margate, you should find there the Admiral of England with his fleet alone – or even if he should have united with Drake's fleet, yours will still be superior to both in quality, and also in the cause which you are defending, which is God's – you may give battle, trying to gain the wind, and all possible advantages from the enemy; and trusting to the Lord to give you victory.

As far as the battle formation and tactics to be adopted in the fight are concerned, I can give you little advice, since those questions must be decided at the time of the action by circumstances. I nevertheless urge you to lose no opportunity to improve your position, and gain all possible advantages; and to have the Armada so drawn up that every unit takes part in the fight, and is ready to give its support to the others, without any confusion nor disorder. You should take especial note, however, that the enemy's aim will be to fight from a distance, since he has the advantage of superior artillery, and of the large number of fireworks [explosive missiles] with which he will come provided; while ours must be to attack, and come to grips with the enemy at close quarters; and to succeed in doing this you will need to exert every effort. That you might be forewarned, you will receive a detailed report of the way in which the enemy arranges his artillery, so as to be able to aim his broadsides low in the hull and so sink his opponents' ships. The precautions which you feel to be necessary you must take against such action.'

V

Extract from a letter by Sir William Winter to Sir Francis Walsingham, 1 August 1588; taken from *The Defeat of the Spanish Armada*, ed. J.K. Laughton (Navy Records Society, 1896), vol. 2, pp. 8–10.

'Upon Sunday, being the 28th day [of July] my Lord put out his flag of Council early in the morning, the armies both riding still; and after the assembly of the council it was concluded that the practice for the firing of ships should be put in execution the night following, and Sir Henry Palmer was assigned to bear over presently in a pinnace for Dover, to bring away such vessels as were fit to be fired, and materials apt to take fire. Because it was seen, after his going, he could not return that night, and occasion would not be over slipped, it was thought meet that we should help ourselves with such shipping as we had there to serve that turn. So that about 12 of the clock that night six ships were brought and prepared with a saker shot, and going in a front, having the wind and tide with them, and their ordnance being charged, were fired; and the men that were executors, so soon as the fire was made they did abandon the ships, and entered into five boats that were appointed for the saving of them. This matter did put such terror among the Spanish army that they were fain to let slip their cables and anchors; and did work, as it did appear, great mischief among them by reason of the suddeness of it. We might perceive that there were two great fires more than ours, and far greater and huger than any of our vessels that were fired could make.

The 29th day, in the break of the day, my Lord Admiral did bear with them with all his fleet; and his Lordship perceived a galleass to go along the French shore, as near as she might possibly, striving to recover Calais, which could not use no more but her foresail and oars. The which vessel my Lord did cause to be followed with small vessels and boats, which did force her to run aground upon the bar of Calais haven, the tide being half spent. Great fight was made between our men and them; and one William Coxe, master of a bark of mine called the Delight, did first board her; who sithen that time is slain. And so others in boats and small pinnaces, did very valiantly behave themselves; which was better done by reason that my Lord Admiral did stay off and on, with some good ships with him, to give comfort and countenance to our men. But after his Lordship perceived that our men had quietly possessed her, as we might judge of it, then his Lordship, with such as were with him, did bear after the Spanish fleet, the wind being at the SSW, and the Spanish fleet bearing away NNE, making into the depth of the channel; and about 9 of the clock in the morning, we fet near unto them, being then athwart of Gravelines. They went into a preparation of a half moon. Their Admiral and vice-admiral, they went in the midst, and the greatest number of them; and there went on each side, in the wings, their galleasses, armados of Portugal, and other good ships, in the whole to the number of sixteen in a wing, which did seem to be of their principal shipping. My fortune was to make choice to charge their starboard wing without shooting of any ordnance, until we came within six score [paces] of them, and some of our ships did follow me. The said wing found themselves, as it did appear, to be so charged, as by making of haste to run into the body of their fleet, four of them did entangle themselves one aboard the other. One of them recovered himself, and so shrouded himself among the fleet; the rest, how they were beaten, I will leave to the report of some of the Spaniards that leapt into the seas and [were] taken up, and are now in the custody of some of our fleet.

The fight continued from 9 of the clock until six of the clock at night, in the which time the Spanish Army bear away NNE and N by E, as much as they could keeping company one with another, I assure your Honour in very good order. Great was the spoil and harm that was done unto them, no doubt. I deliver unto your Honour, on the credit of a poor gentleman, that out of my ship was shot 500 shot of demi-cannon, culverin and demi-culverin; and when I was furthest off in discharging any of the pieces, I was not out of the shot of their arquebuses, and most time within speech one of another. And surely every man did well; and as I have said, no doubt the slaughter and hurt they received was very great, as time will discover it; and when every man was weary with labour, and our cartridges spent, and munitions wasted – I think in some altogether – we ceased and followed the enemy, he bearing hence still in the course as I have said before.'

VI

Dispatch written by Anthony Ashley to Sir Francis Walsingham from Portugal, 2 June 1589; taken from *The Expedition of Sir John Norris and Sir Francis Drake to Spain and Portugal, 1589*, ed. R.B. Wernham (Navy Records Society, 1988), p. 181.

'May it please your honour, since the departure of the army from the Groyne, the Generals have landed the soldiers within 12 leagues of Lisbon at a place called Ataguia, lying to the eastward of the Burlings. Wherewith Sir John Norris marched through the country unto the city of Lisbon, having by the way repulsed and defeated the encounters of the enemy sundry times proferring [to assail] him. He entered and held the suburbs 3 days and then, having spent the powder and match brought in the army on land and not finding any succour or relief to be yielded to the King by the Portugals, as also wanting other munition and necessaries meet for assault, retired with the forces to Cascaes, four leagues from the city.

In the meantime Sir Francis Drake with the fleet, leaving in the bay aforesaid for the service of the garrison left in a castle there, which upon the Generals' landing was yielded to the King by the Portugals, a ship and two flyboats, departed to Cascaes, where at his arrival the town being yielded unto him by the Portugals there inhabiting, he besieged the castle with 1,000 soldiers and mariners which he landed. Wherewith he did so environ the same that for want of water and munition, which could not by that means be supplied by the enemy, he forced the Spaniard to yield the same upon composition for their lives, etc. within two days after the retreat thither of Sir John Norris.

This is the sum of all which hath been hitherto performed and may be hoped to be here done. The causes thereof being chiefly for lack of the timely supplies out of England, the King's not being able to make good his party in the country, not above 200 Portugals having repaired unto him since his arrival, besides the loss as well of soldiers as mariners in great numbers by an extreme sickness still remaining in the army. Besides that the landing at the Groyne is judged to have been the special hindrance of good success here, the enemy upon knowledge thereof having in the meanwhile assembled great strength for defence of the city and defeated Don Antonio by all possible means of any favour or aid in these parts, as is particularly declared in my letters to my Lords of the Council, whereunto for sundry other particularities, for lack of convenient time, I am bold to refer your Honour, whom I beseech God to continue in happiness long health – From Cascaes, the 2nd of June 1589.'

The assassination of William of Orange in 1584, and the desperate straits to which the Dutch were reduced by the Duke of Parma in the aftermath of that loss, forced Elizabeth to come to their aid. The Duke of Anjou proved to be a broken reed, both to the English and the Dutch, and having attempted, and failed, to seize power in Antwerp in the same year, left the Netherlands discredited, and died soon after. Camden's assessment of the queen's priorities is accurate, and is supported by other evidence; her response to the Dutch plight was in many ways pusillanimous, but the rebels were in no position to be critical. The Earl of Leicester was sent to command the English forces in the Netherlands, and was at first both well received and moderately successful. However, it was not long before he became embroiled in the domestic politics of that country, and Elizabeth feared that he was overcommitting her. She also suspected that he was overplaying his hand for his own purposes, and he was recalled in disfavour. He died in September 1588.

Philip regarded Elizabeth's intervention in the Netherlands as an act of war, but he had already decided upon action against England, and had seized large numbers of English trading ships in Spanish ports, before the news of the treaty of Nonsuch reached him. Drake was instructed to recover as many of these ships as possible before proceeding to the Caribbean, and partly fulfilled that aim in a raid on La Coruna. The attack on Cartagena was part of the same voyage, and the account quoted here gives a very good impression of the spirit in which many of the English were entering the war with Spain. Just as Philip considered an attack on England to be the service of God, Protestant Englishmen (the vast majority by 1588) considered war with Spain to be the same service. The Venetian report, later in 1586, is remarkably shrewd and well informed. Elizabeth never gave up hope of a negotiated settlement, but in pursuing that did not neglect the preparation of her defences. By this time Philip, following the advice of his veteran admiral, the Marquis of Santa Cruz, had decided to make a major effort to knock England out of the war. The Duke of Parma was less than enthusiastic, believing that if the king were prepared to be flexible over religion, both the English and the Dutch could be brought to terms. He may have been right, but Philip was not prepared to listen.

Philip intended to launch his Armada in 1587, but a combination of Santa Cruz's administrative incompetence and a damaging raid on Cadiz by Francis Drake, threw the preparations out of gear. The whole operation was becoming unsustainably expensive, and if Santa Cruz had not died in the winter of 1587/8, it might well have had to be abandoned. However, the Duke of Medina Sidonia was efficient, precisely where Santa Cruz had been inefficient, and the fleet was ready to sail by July 1588. Although fully manned and well victualled, it was in other respects ill prepared; in particular it was short of suitable guns, and the shot was ill matched to the weapons. At the other end Parma was still unenthusiastic, realising that he had no deep-water anchorage to receive such a fleet, and that his troop carriers could not get out to sea without encountering the Dutch inshore warships. Medina Sidonia was weak where Santa Cruz would have been strong, in the effective improvisation of tactics, and followed the king's orders to the letter. Unfortunately, these were firm on religious rhetoric and shaky on tactical understanding.

As a result, the Armada found itself stuck in an open anchorage at Calais, not knowing when Parma would be ready. The English tactics, reported by Winter, were simple and obvious: to disrupt the Spanish formation with fireships, and then attack with everything they had. Winter takes some pains to explain Lord Howard's assault on the galleass, which many considered to have been an unnecessary distraction, and his account makes clear that the Spanish formation was partly recovered in the course of the battle. However, as he rightly suspected, subsequent evidence confirmed that the Armada had taken a very heavy mauling off Gravelines, and many of the ships which were subsequently wrecked had been rendered unseaworthy in that encounter.

The odds were always stacked against the Spaniards, both for logistical and strategic reasons, and both sides were engaging in a kind of battle for which neither had relevant experience. The outcome did not cripple Spain, or free England from the fear of invasion, but the psychological effects on both sides were immense.

As soon as Elizabeth had taken breath, her first thought was to destroy that part of the Armada which had limped home. Consequently, the counter-attack she launched in 1589 had that as a prime objective. Unfortunately, it also attempted to place the Portuguese pretender, Dom Antonio, on the throne of that country, which had been occupied by Philip in 1580. Dom Antonio was full of lavish promises, and attracted major private investment in the expedition. Although this made the fleet much larger, it also led to conflicts of priority. As a result, the queen's first instruction was neglected completely. The remnants of the Armada were untouched, and after an ineffective raid on La Coruna (the Groyne), the expedition proceeded straight to Lisbon. There it quickly transpired that the promises of Dom Antonio were so much hot air. Hardly any Portuguese joined him, and after a few minor successes, the expedition was forced to withdraw with heavy losses. The queen was furious, and both the leaders were temporarily disgraced. Norris had recovered a measure of favour by 1592, but Drake's career was at an end. By 1590 the honours of war were fairly even, but in the circumstances that meant success for England.

FORTY

Catholic Recusancy

I

Extract from Robert Persons's 'Confession of Faith', written for the magistrates of London, 19 July 1580; taken from *Letters and Memorials of Robert Persons*, ed. Leo Hicks (Catholic Record Society, 1942).

'Most Noble Lords,

From the very day on which I was appointed to England by my superiors for this purpose which I am presently about to declare with the utmost candour, I did not fail to weigh in my mind all the things that were in store for one who undertakes an affair of this sort; as for instance that you may arrest me or that I may happen to fall into your hands; again that God may permit you to take every harsh and extreme action against me, and that I may have to undergo what in various parts of the world my comrades are suffering every day, or expecting to suffer, in this same cause from the enemies of Christ and of the aforesaid faith; moreover the fact that, before I came here I was informed (though to be sure the fact is not hidden, and now we are about to learn from actual experience whether it is true) that men who are Catholics have been arrested and brought before your Worships, and that magistrates of lower rank and sprung from the people are still less inclined than you to tolerate any man producing in his defence anything containing a vindication of his faith or an account of his conferences; nay, that, on the very threshold as it were, they are overwhelmed with questions that are clearly irrelevant and of their own home invention and usually by recourse to the statutes so that they may be brought within the scope of these and thereby the people may be made to believe that these men are punished, not for their religion and for conscience sake, as is plainly the case (two things which so far as words go, the Protestants proclaim should be free) but on the count of high treason and on the pretext of violation of the general laws of the realm; and for this they are quietly shut up in prison, either to be consumed and waste away there, as being implicated in these matters, or, if they should so decide, to be condemned to death under cover of some decree or other and done away with; lastly the fact that it was made known to me that once a man was arrested as a Catholic and shut up (especially if he bore some reputation for learning) there was no hope of his being allowed to speak, however humble and abject the prayers with which he strove for permission; nay, that anyone thus imprisoned was not only refused permission to speak again, but that even the words and arguments he had previously used were all suppressed or were reproduced in an entirely changed form, sayings of his being slyly quoted in a distorted sense, or certain monstrous crimes being falsely attributed to him, such as conspiracy, rebellion, or the crime of high treason or such like. This with the sole object that he may be involved in the meshes of this deceit and so be less in favour with the people. . . .'

II

    Letter of information sent to Lord Burghley, concerning the activities of Englishmen in Rome, 1583; taken from Strype, *Annals of the Reformation* (London, 1725), III, app. i, no. XXXV.

'A private letter of one Touker to the Lord Treasurer, Lord Burghley, informing him of English men in Rome; and of some matters relating to them.

Right Honourable, since my last being with your Honour I have been three times at the Marshalsai's. Where I find one Tither, who was acquainted with me in Rome. This Tither, at my request, profered Christopher Tater's wife to write unto the Rector of the English Seminary in Rome for the delivery of her husband out of the Gallies; who was condemned with Peter Backer. He said also with some Travail she might have the Queen of Scots letter to the Pope, or Fecknam's to the Cardinal. He profered me to convey my letters at any time, to Nicholas Fitz Harbord in Rome: I think the conveyer of these letters would be known with some diligence. Tither hath written two times since his imprisonment; but not answered. He warned me to beware of one Robert Woodward: who served sometime D. Wenden in Rome. They have great intelligence, and fear him much.

    In April last there came from Rome to Naples an Irish man, whom the Pope created bishop of Ross, in Ireland; and gave him authority to make priests. By which authority he gave orders to as many as came; and got much money: The Archbishop of Naples forbade him. But the Nuncio maintained his doings. This bishop stayed in Naples only for passage into Spain: and so directly for Ireland. He carried with him great store of pardons and Agnos Deis to the Pope's friends in Ireland. He hath to his servant one Thomas Galtrope, a merchant's son of Dewlin. This Galtrope pretendeth to leave the bishop's service and return to his father at their coming home.

    Also there died one John Davies in Rome: who served the Lord William Howard, as he said. This Davies said in Rome, that happy shall they be one day that have languages. For when God taketh our Prince from us there will be much trouble in England, and great revenging of old quarrels. But he said if the earl could get Norwich on his head, they did not care; with many like words.

Upon Sunday next I go towards Exeter, and return by the end of August. If it be your Honours pleasure, that I shall come to you before I depart, Mr. Cope may let me know of it.

Francis Touker.'

III

Letter from the Justices of the Peace in Suffolk to the Privy Council, 1586; taken from Strype, *Annals of the Reformation* (London, 1725), III, app. ii, no. XIII.

'Our humble duties to your Lordships remembered.

It may please you to be advertised, that according to the commandment exprest in your Lordships Letters, we have called before us all the Recusants; whose names in a schedule we received enclosed in your Lordships said Letters. To whom we imparted the contents therof. Advising them to consider of her Majesties gracious favour, extended towards them; and mesuring the Benefit which hereby they are to receive, to make Offer by Writing severally under their Hands what reasonable portion they can be contented yearly, of their own Disposition, to pay unto her Receipt, to be eased of the Common Danger of Law for their recusancy. Whose several offers under their own Hands, which herewith we send unto your Lordships, may particularly appear. Their several Rates and Valuations by your Lordships former Letters upon the disarming of them we before Certified unto your Lordships. So humbly we take our Leaves &c. From Ipswich, the 23 of April 1586.

Signed:

Rob. Wingfield	Nic. Bacon
Ph. Parker	Will. Singer
William Walgrave	Joh. Heigham

Mr. Fr. Mamock, Esq., mentioned in the schedule received from your Lordships, hath of long time, and doth, ordinarily and dutifully repair to his Parish Church; and there doth continue the time of the reading Divine Service, and preaching of the Word of God.

I Ro. Rokewood of Stanfield in ther county of Suffolk, am content yearly during my Recusancy, to contribute and pay to Her Majesties Receipt of her Highness Exchequer, the sum of £20. Thereby to receive and enjoy the

Benefit of Her Majesties gracious Favour, to be exempt from all Forfeitures, Vexations, Perils and Penalties, that may hereafter happen unto me, my Heirs or Executors, by reason of any Offence or Forfeiture, heretofore by me committed, or that hereafter by me shall be committed against the Law established touching Recusancy, for not resorting unto the Church, or other place assigned by the said Laws, in that case made and provided. March the 28 1586.

Rob. Rokewood

Will. Yaxley, offered £40 per ann. His estate he asserted was but £220 per ann. He writ, he had been levied for his lands, for recusancy, £280.

Wal. Norton £20 per ann.	Marg. Daniel £20
Henry Drury, £20	John Bedingfield, £20
H. Everard, £10	Rob. Jetter £6.13.4
Ri. Martin, £6	Joh. Daniel, £20
Edward Sulliard, £40	Mich. Hare, £50
Tho. Sulliard, 20 nobles	Edw. Rokewood of Euston, £30
Ambr. Germin, 20 marks	Roger Martin, 40 marks.'

IV

Extract from the statute 35 Elizabeth I, c. 2 (1593), an act against popish recusants; taken from the *Statutes of the Realm*, IV, pp. 843–6.

'For the better discovering and avoiding of all such traitorous and most dangerous conspiracies and attempts as are daily devised and practised against our most gracious sovereign lady the Queen's Majesty, and the happy estate of this common weal by sundry wicked and seditious persons, who terming themselves Catholics and being indeed spies and intelligencers, not only for her Majesty's foreign enemies but also for rebellious and traitorous subjects born within her Highness' realms and dominions, and hiding their most detestable and devilish purposes under a false pretext of religion and conscience do secretly wander and shift from place to place within this realm to corrupt and seduce her Majesty's subjects and to stir them to sedition and rebellion: Be it ordained and enacted by our sovereign lady the Queen's Majesty and the Lords spiritual and temporal and the Commons in this present Parliament assembled and by the authority of the same, that every person above the age of sixteen years, born within any of the Queen's Majesty's realms or dominions or made denizen, being a popish recusant and before the end of this session of Parliament convicted for not repairing to some church, chapel or usual place of common prayer to hear Divine service there, but forbearing the same contrary to the tenor of the laws and statutes heretofore made and provided in that behalf, and having any certain place of dwelling and abode within the realm, shall within forty days next after the end of this session of Parliament (if they be within this realm and not restrained or stayed, either by imprisonment, or by her Majesty's commandment, or by order and direction of some six or more of the Privy Council, or by such sickness or infirmity of body as they shall not be able to travel without imminent danger of life, and in such cases of absence out of the realm, restraint or stay, then within twenty days next after they shall return into the realm, or be enlarged of such imprisonment or restraint, and shall be able to travel) repair to their place of dwelling where they usually heretofore made their common abode, and shall not any time after pass or remove above five miles from thence. And also that every person being above the age of sixteen years born within any her Majesty's realms or dominions or made denizen, and having or which hereafter shall have any certain place of dwelling and abode within this realm, which being then a popish recusant shall at any time hereafter be lawfully convicted for not repairing to some church, chapel or usual place of common prayer to hear Divine Service there, but forbearing the same contrary to the said laws and statutes, and being within the realm at the time that they shall be convicted, shall within forty days next after the same conviction (if they be not restrained or stayed by imprisonment or otherwise as is aforesaid, and in such cases of restraint and stay then within twenty days next after they shall be enlarged of such imprisonment or restraint and shall be able to travel) repair to their place of usual dwelling and abode, and shall not at any time after pass or remove above five miles from thence: upon pain that every person and persons that shall offend against the tenor and intent of this act in anything before mentioned shall lose and forfeit all his and their goods and chattels, and shall also forfeit to the Queen's Majesty all the lands, tenements and hereditaments, and all other the rents and annuities of every such person so doing or offending, during the life of the same offender. . . .'

Before 1570, absence from church, or the clandestine hearing of mass, were misdemeanours. After the papal declaration of that year they became crimes, for the simple reason that they were the gestures of allegiance to a foreign power which had declared war on the queen. This created many dilemmas of conscience, because the great majority of those who adhered to the 'old religion' had no desire to be traitors, or in any way associated with treacherous activities. Robert Persons was a political activist, and his statement may be regarded as disingenuous, but many missionary priests honestly sought the salvation of souls, and had no political agenda. Conversely there were those, both within England and abroad, who after 1570 became fully committed to the overthrow of Elizabeth's government by whatever means might come to hand. Papal policy also was two-faced. On the one hand the Curia pursued a spiritual agenda, seeking the conversion of individuals through missionary activity; and on the other hand supported every conspiracy for the assassination of the queen, or the invasion of England by a Catholic power.

As Scotland ceased to be a promising point of entry, Catholic attention turned increasingly to Ireland. Both Burghley and Francis Walsingham countermined this conspiratorial activity through agents planted within the Catholic community, of whom Francis Touker appears to be a good example. Under the pressure of conflicting allegiance there were a number of defectors from 'political Catholicism', and the English intelligence system was surprisingly effective.

Although they got no credit for it among the Catholic exiles, or among the Catholic powers, both the council and parliament struggled to disentangle non-seditious recusants from the genuinely dangerous. They did this to some extent by crudely distinguishing priests from laymen. It became a capital offence to accept Roman ordination, or to function as a priest within England, but it was never a capital offence to be a Catholic. Theoretically, the penalties for ordinary recusancy were severe, but they were mainly financial, and were applied with a considerable amount of discretion, as is clear from the report of the Suffolk justices. Harbouring a priest was more dangerous, and could lead to imprisonment, or even in a few cases to a traitor's death, but a quiet refusal to attend church was regarded as no more than an inconvenience. Even at the height of the Spanish war, when anti-Catholic sentiment was running high in some parts of the country, fines and restriction orders were the main penalties imposed upon ordinary recusants.

Broadly speaking, this policy worked. There was no Catholic rebellion during the war (except in Ireland, which is a different matter), and under unremitting pressure many Catholic families became 'Church papists' in one generation, and conformists in the next. The missionary priests continued to report great success, but to some extent they were deceiving themselves, which is understandable given their extremely dangerous calling. There were many executions to give the tincture of martyrdom to their efforts, but they never came anywhere near to overthrowing the Protestant settlement of the English Church. In the 1560s religious conservatives held the middle ground. Thanks to *Regnans in Excelsis* and the strenuous measures of self-defence which Elizabeth was compelled to adopt, by the 1590s the middle ground was held by Protestant conformists. The 'survivalist' Catholicism of the early period had largely disappeared, and the recusant community which remained, although tough and resilient, was contained and had ceased to be a political threat.

FORTY-ONE

The Elizabethan Navy and the Privateers

I

Survey of the navy, and mobilisation plan, 1559; taken from *British Naval Documents, 1204–1960*, eds J.B. Hattendorf et al. (Navy Records Society, 1993), pp. 62–6. The MS is PRO SP12/3, ff. 131–4.

'A book for sea causes made by the Officers of the Queen's majesty's Navy, the 24th March [1559].

A declaration of an army which may be made as well of the queen's Majesty's own ships and barks as of her subjects' ships and barks, with an estimate of the charges that will grow upon the same.

As also certain remembrances appertaining thereunto hereafter followeth.

These ships are thought meet to be kept and preserved for the service of her Majesty.

The Queen's Majesty's own ships

The Great new ship [*Elizabeth Jonas*]	800 tons	550 men
The *Mary Rose* [second version]	600	350
The *Great Bark*	600	350
The *Philip and Mary*	500	300
The *Lyon*	450	300
The *Jennet*	300	220
The *Hart*	300	220
The *Antelope*	300	220
The *Swallow*	300	220
The *New Bark*	200	140
The *Mary Willoughby*	200	140
The *Greyhound*	160	120
The *Bull*	160	120
The *Falcon*	100	80
The *Phoenix*	70	60
The *Saker*	70	60
The *Bright Falcon*	60	50
The *Bark of Bulleyn*	60	50

The *Sun*	60	50
The *Hare*	60	50
The *Brigandine*	–	120
	1,510	3,880
	[*sic*, recte 5,350]	[*sic*, recte 3,770]

The ships underwritten are very much worn and of no continuance without great reparation to be done upon them. And besides that they might not be worth the new making, so that it is thought if there be a peace, the Queen's pleasure being declared for the putting of them to sale or otherwise for her Majesty's most profit, and to cease the charges to be bestowed in keeping of them afloat, of wages, victuals and tackle, which charges so saved will be a great help towards the making of the new ships of better service in their place. Nevertheless the present charges of the said ships are thought meet to be continued during the doubtful time of the peace.

The Queen's Majesty's own ships

The *Jesus*	600 tons	350 men
The *Salamander*	300	220
The *Anne Gallant*	300	220
The *Sacrette*	140	120
The *Gerfalcon*	140	120
The *Double Rose*	40	30
The *Fleur de Lys*	40	30
The *Red Galley*	–	300
The *Black Galley*	–	300
	1,600	1,720
	[*sic*, recte 1,560]	[*sic*, recte 1,690]

Merchant ships which may be put in fashion of war:

Item there is to be had 45 English merchant
ships which may be put in order of war
whose tonnage and number of men amounteth
by estimation as hereafter doth appear: 7,040   4,600

Victuallers for the army:

Item the said army will require to have 20 sail
of victuallers of 80 tons apiece or thereabout,

with 20 men in every of them to attend upon
the said army:　　　　　　　　　　　1,600　　　　　　400
　　　　　　　　　　　　　　　　　　　―――――　　　　―――――
　　　　　　　　　　　　　　　　　　　8,640　　　　　　5,000

Totals of:

The Queen's Majesty's ships and barks	32
The merchants ships and barks for war	45

　　　　　　　　　　　　　　　　　　　―――――　　　　―――――
　　　　　　　　　　　　　　　　　　　　　　　　　　77 for war

The victuallers ships	20
The tonnage of the Queen's ships	7,100
The tonnage of the merchants' ships	8,640

　　　　　　　　　　　　　　　　　　　―――――　　　　―――――
　　　　　　　　　　　　　　　　　　　　　　　　15,640 tons
　　　　　　　　　　　　　[*sic*, recte 15,760]

The men in the Queen's ships	5,610
The men in the merchants' ships and victuallers	5,000

　　　　　　　　　　　　　　　　　　　―――――　　　　―――――
　　　　　　　　　　　　　　　　　　　　　　　　10,600 men
　　　　　　　　　　　　　[*sic*, recte 10,610]'

II

Extracts from John Dee, *The Perfect Arte of Navigation* (London, 1577),
p. 3 (writing of himself in the third person).

'And Mr. Dee . . . who also I have heard often and most heartily wish that
all manner of persons passing or frequenting any our seas, appropriate and
many ways next environing England, Ireland and Scotland, might be in
convenient and honourable sort (at all times) at the commandment and
order (by beck or check) of a PETTY NAVY ROYAL of three score tall ships
(or more, but in no case fewer). And they to be very well appointed,
thoroughly manned and sufficiently victualled. . . .

To conclude herein. This Petty Navy Royal undoubtedly will stand the
realm in better stead than the enjoying of four such forts or towns as Calais
and Boulogne only could do. For this will be as great strength, and to as
good purpose, as any coast of England, Ireland or Scotland, between us and
the foreign foe, as ever Calais was for that only one place that it is situated
in. And will help to enjoy the royalty and Sovereignty of the Narrow Seas

throughout, and of our other seas also, more serviceably than Calais or Boulogne ever did, or could do. . . .

And how can any man reasonably doubt of the ability of so mighty a kingdom to set forth and maintain most easily only three or fourscore tall and warlike ships, where so many thousands of folks are contributors to the charges requisite? Seeing only forty or fifty worthy subjects, of their own private ability do very easily, and (in a manner) continually maintain in trade at sea so many (and more) such tall ships. And the same well appointed, well victualled, well manned, and they duly paid. . . .

And chiefly, seeing such a petty navy royal of threescore tall ships, and each of them between eightscore and 200 tons of burden, and twenty other smaller barks (between 20 and 50 tons) may be new made, very strong and warlike, and all well victualled for 6,660 men, and those men liberally waged, both ships and men, to all needful purposes sufficiently appointed, and so maintained continually and that very Royally FOR EVER for less than 200,000 pounds charges YEARLY sustained. . . .

One other chapter (yet more) hereunto annexed will make it most certain that treasure will not fail us for the royal and triumphant maintenance of this our Petty Navy Royal. And that is, if it would please the Queen her most gracious goodness to be so bountiful to the commons as to give, grant and assure FOR EVER to the treasury of the foresaid Petty Navy Royal all that her right, title and interest, to the TENTH of all foreign fishings within the royal limits and jurisdiction of her BRITISH SEAS of England and Ireland. Where now no man in her Highness' behalf, or to her use, receiveth of any foreign fisherman any one penny in token of their dutiful acknowledging her royalty within her due limits of the foresaid seas. . . .

Unto which peculiar great blessing of God our enjoying no certain readier and easier means can be devised than by the continued circuits of our PETTY NAVY ROYAL. . . .'

III

Extract from 'The Taking of the Madre de Dios' by Francis Seall (1592); taken from the edition by C.L. Kingsford in *The Naval Miscellany*, II (1912), pp. 106–9.

'The 9th of August some dozen or fourteen leagues from the Island westward, and in the morning very timely, the Dainty having descried a sail very far to windward of her, set sail and gave chase, the rest of the fleet likewise doing no less (for before our ships were all on hull): but the Dainty and the Dragon (not long after her) were the first that came up to her, and, finding her to be no less than a carrack, might not offer any meaner courtesy than to hail them with a cannon. But she, not unthankful, bestowed the like of them again, and by the miss she found no niggard; for she yielded bountifully both powder and shot, which very unluckily effected a fire endangering of the Dainty, for she struck the foremast by the board, and forced her to get her farther off (for she made small account of these ships). The next that came up with her was the Roebuck, who fought a great while with her, still holding her good tack, till the Foresight of her Majesty came to her. And then they did determine with them two ships to lay her aboard before the luff [the bow] and the Foresight to lay her aboard in the quarter. And so fitting everything ready, the Roebuck bear up with her, and how missing to lie at the head appointed I cannot tell, but he was aboard in the quarter. The Foresight attending as it was determined, came thinking to lay the carrack aboard; but in fine she laid the Roebuck aboard, to the great endangering of them both, but especially of the Roebuck, seeing she was next the enemy and thrust between two such great ships; where she received a shot but from whether of those two she was between I know not, and before she could get clear away from them, they found six or seven foot water in her hold; and so the company being in good haste to labour, at the same time had enough to do to pump the ship and stop her leak, and left the carrack as the Dainty had done (reinforced by their enemies), to a better bickering than they could give them; but his good will is to be accepted. The Foresight, having fitted herself, went aboard again, and continued a very dangerous fight, being close aboard and lashed fast to the carrack's side (who bore her away by their own men's report, all her sails standing, as lightly as if she had been made fast and jammed in her chain holes). The Assurance of my Lord of Cumberland's coming up unto her, laid her aboard, discharging even withal four or five cast pieces and a volley of small shot, and ranging up along the starboard quarter of the carrack, shot forward into the Foresight's stern, into which all her men, being eager of entering leapt (some of them) into her. And so both of them together maintained a strong fight, until the Tiger of my Lord of Cumberland's, who was furthest of all to leeward, came up unto them, and had passed by once before the Assurance was aboard; unto whom they of the Foresight called, desiring that they would with speed come rescue them, for they were in danger and could not get off from thence. They of the Tiger resolved that they would so do, and not only that, but also proceeding farther would take the carrack (for whom they had waited there all that year), or else, though with the hazard of their lives, burn or sink her. To effect which resolution, they cast about again, and with a great noise and shout (of at the least nine score men), who crying "God and St. George for England, a Cumberland, a Cumberland", advanced themselves on her shrouds and netting, fighting pellmell with sword and pike, still crying (with the Assurance's men that fought against us on the other side of the carrack, and were ready to enter at once upon the least recoil of the foe); God and it forcing the affrighted Portuguese from their fight, and to stow themselves, that shiveringly could yield forth nothing to ease their stomachs but "A quo deabala est a Cumberland". But we not to lose the least opportunity entered farther into the ship, where each ships company, of those three that were then aboard, might bid each other welcome aboard the carrack. And in short time after, or much about this time, the Dragon before spoken of, came likewise aboard of her. But the companies of valiant gentlemen and courageous soldiers with the rest of stout and skilful mariners, that had there most bravely fought, and found themselves near-hand possessed victors, stood not long to give salutations to their friends, but with eager force some tear and cut up the nettings, some break up scuttles, not ceasing to cry "a Cumberland" till the quaking Portuguese, that before would rehearse nought but a piteous "diabolos" and "viliacoes", now in a corner lamentably pronounceth "misery corde", humbly crying for mercy, yielding themselves over again, their ship and goods worthily won, and Englishmen then their victors best deserving thereof; in estimation to be worth (as I have heard some of the Portuguese confess upon examination) four millions of ducats, which amounteth to no more than one million pounds sterling. . . .'

IV

Extract from 'A project how to make war upon Spain' by Sir William Monson (1601); taken from *The Naval Tracts of Sir William Monson*, ed. M. Oppenheim, V (Navy Records Society, 1914), pp. 53–6.

'Our only security must be to cut off Spain's forces by sea, seeing their means of invasion and strength of defence depends upon their shipping. How this service may be effected, and the benefit that will arise by it, is here briefly handled.

First and principally, we must keep employed two main fleets upon the coast of Spain eight months in the year, that is from March to November. Every fleet to consist of 45 ships, to be divided into three squadrons; one to lie off the Rock [Cape Roca] to intercept all traders of Lisbon; the second at the South Cape, to stop all intercourse of San Lucar and Cadiz, to and from the Indies; the third to the [Canary] Islands, lest they should there stop, and put their goods ashore, having intelligence of our being upon the coast of Spain. Our fleet being thus divided, no army at sea can be prepared, or at least gathered to a head, but we shall intercept them. We shall not only debar the Spaniards and Portuguese their own trade but all nations to them. They will not be able to feed without our permission, nor no nation can be brought to greater extremity than they will be. Perhaps the number of these ships will exceed the proportion her Majesty is willing to employ. But if Holland will be drawn from the trade of Spain and join with us the number may be easily raised by them and our maritime towns in England, so that her Majesty needs employ but six ships of her own in each fleet, to serve for Admiral and Vice-Admiral of every squadron.

It is not the meanest mischief we shall do the King of Spain, if we war thus upon him, to force him to keep his shores still armed and guarded, to the infinite vexation, charge and discontent of his subjects. For no time or place can secure them so long as they see or know us to be upon their coast. The terror is so great they conceive of her Majesty's ships, that a few of them presenting themselves in view do commonly divert their actions, as may appear by these brief observations following. . . .

[Summary of actions between 1585 and 1600]

The sequel of all these actions being duly considered we may be confident that, whilst we busy the Spaniards at home, they dare not think of invading England or Ireland, for by their absence the fleet of the Indies may be endangered. And in their attempts they have as little hope of prevailing. . . .'

The navy Elizabeth inherited, and of which this stocktaking was made (inaccurately) at the beginning of the reign, was in good working order, and of manageable size. A policy document drawn up at the same time suggested an optimum size of thirty ships, but the actual number maintained was always a little greater than that. There was a regular programme of repair, maintenance and replacement. Most of the ships listed as 'worn' had been discarded by 1562, but the elderly *Jesus of Lubeck* survived to be used (and lost) on John Hawkins's voyage of 1568.

Although England was officially at peace until 1585, both the intervention in Scotland in 1560 and that in France in 1563 required the use of the navy. Elizabeth's strategy was different from that of her father, who kept most of his 'Great Ships' laid up for years at a time. With the exception of one or two of the largest, the queen used all her ships, either for high-profile patrols, for operations against pirates, or for participation in privately funded ventures, like those of Hawkins. This was partly because there was no genuine peace in the tense religious climate after 1560 – and so there was a constant need for vigilance – but also because the queen was beginning to respond to the idea of using sea power in a more far-reaching manner than her father had ever imagined. Her seamen were venturing further and further afield, in search of trade and plunder, and often taking her ships with them; so although there were no acknowledged acts of war outside European waters until 1586, the idea of a global strategy was under discussion.

One of the main protagonists of these expansionist ambitions was John Dee, who had been involved in London enterprises since the 1550s. Dee envisaged the creation of a 'British Empire', which would inevitably require a large expansion of the existing navy. Hence his plan for a Petty

Navy Royal, designed to secure command of the seas, thereby safeguarding trade (both existing and proposed) and deterring attack, which was a major consideration by 1577. The navy he proposed was about three times the size of the fleet the queen actually possessed, in terms of the number of ships, but only just over twice the size in terms of tonnage, because the ships he envisaged were relatively small.

During this period of uneasy peace, the real navy was costing between £25,000 and £35,000 a year, so £200,000 a year was a very generous estimate for Dee's proposal, and in fact would have been almost the whole of the Crown's ordinary revenue. His idea for raising so large a sum was ingenious – a tax on foreign fishing fleets, enforced by the navy it paid for – but quite unrealistic. So Dee's vision was not realised for nearly another hundred years; but his ambition to defend England by controlling the seas was taken seriously, and was even achieved, up to a point.

What actually happened when war broke out was that Elizabeth effectively more than doubled the size of her fleet by using privateers. These were despatched in large numbers, sometimes as many as 200 in a year, to intercept Spanish shipping and to raid the colonies in the New World. Many of them were small, and were sent out by individual gentlemen or merchant groups; but some were large private warships, usually owned by noblemen, or by major groups like the London livery companies. Almost two-thirds of the fleet which fought against the Armada was made up of such ships.

The problem with such auxiliaries was that (except for major crises like the Armada) they were very hard to control, and their use sometimes impeded military operations; as was the case with the Lisbon expedition of 1589. On the other hand, they could be spectacularly successful, and the greatest coup of the later years of the war was the capture of the *Madre de Dios*. This was effected by a small fleet, partly made up of royal warships and partly of privateers owned by the Earl of Cumberland. Several similar targets escaped, but one capture of such value more than paid for years of effort. The officially declared value was a good deal less than £1 million, but the queen was convinced that she had been cheated out of hundreds of thousands of pounds. She was probably right, but the undeclared balance was enough to keep the privateers at sea for several more years.

By 1601, what was later to be known as a 'blue water strategy' against Spain had been conceived: a year-round blockade to strangle the enemy's commerce, and cut off his supplies of bullion. Monson's plan was probably not capable of implementation at that time, and was never attempted, but it clearly reveals the ambitious thinking of English naval commanders by the end of the Spanish war. A similar strategy was to be successfully applied two-hundred years later.

FORTY-TWO

The Spanish War, 1590–1604

I

Extract from William Camden, *The History of the Most Renowned and Victorious Princess Elizabeth, Late Queen of England* (4th edn, 1688).

'For when the King [Henry IV] (who had happily weakened the Leaguers by his arms, and by his arts and policies disjoyned them, embracing the Romish religion the last year) was in the beginning of this year solemnly inaugurated, and had granted a truce, some of the noblemen being won by large promises, strove who should first return to his obedience; others submitted upon condition that he would permit them to hold the Governments which they had gotten. . . . Hereupon some of the rebellious cities surrendered themselves, others were suddenly surprised, yea, even Paris itself, inviting the King secretly into the city, was yielded up to him with Festal rejoycing of the citizens, and the Spaniards (having now their hope of getting the French sceptre and of the marriage of the Infanta with the Duke of Guise quite dashed, through the Emulation of the Duke of Mayn against his nephew) were dismissed from thence with bag and baggage, and not without taunts and scoffs from the French, who repented them of what they had lately done. But in regard to those Spaniards who were called into Bretaigne by the Duke of Mercoeur, stood out obstinately, and strengthened the maritime places with strong Garrisons to keep the possession they had gotten; [Sir John] Norris (who had been called home out of Bretaigne to inform the Queen in person of the state of the war there) was commanded again into Bretaigne, with charge to take in the Spaniards fort at Crodon near the haven of Brest, and arrived at Pimpol with fresh forces on the first of September [1594]. . . . The Quimpercoresstin being taken by the marshall and Sir Henry Norris, the French and English made their approach on the first of November to the fort of the Spaniards at Crodon, where Sir Martin Frobisher with ten English men of war rode at anchor expecting their coming. This fort is compassed on two sides with water; to landward there stand two large and high Forts between which there runneth a wall 37 feet wide, and within that a thick earthwork; the Forts were defended on each side with Rocks, whereupon pieces of Ordnance were planted. The English and French, having drawn several battering pieces out of the Ships, cast up Mounts and drew a trench on that side of the fort that looked to landward. The Spaniards sallying forth to hinder the Works were beaten back. But Sir Anthony Wingfield, Sergeant Major of the English, a famous old soldier, having made his will the day before, was slain with a shot of a piece of Ordnance. On the 23rd day of the month with 700 shot of great Ordnance, a small breech was made and the counterscarp thrown down, which Lister, an Englishman seized upon with his men. But whilst the forward young men with firely spirits pressed on further; and the Enemy made stout resistance, several of them were slain, together with Bruder, Jackson and Barker, captains of approved valour; others wounded and many dangerously scorched with gunpowder. Some taxed Norris, as if he were over prodigal of blood, and thrust his men too rashly into dangers. And indeed the Queen, out of her innate tenderness and pity, commanded him by her letters to have more respect to the safety of his men than to his own honour, and not to expose their lives to manifest dangers in a war undertaken for the assistance of others. . . . But this letter came too late. During the heat of the siege D'Aumont and Norris thought good to undermine the Eastern Bulwark on that side where the French were posted, and to blow it up; which took effect, and opened a great breech. Now they fell upon the Fort on all sides, Latham, Smith and others with the English stormed the Western bulwark, while the French set upon the Eastern, and the rest of the wall betwixt both on the South; and this lasted from noon until four of the clock. At last the English made themselves masters of the Western work, and Thomas de Parades, the Commander of the Spaniards, was slain, entered the fort, plucked down the Spanish flags and opened an entrance for the rest, who put the garrison soldiers, in number about 400, to the sword; and laid the Fort level with the ground; and this on the very day that Don John D'Aquila was approaching to relieve them. Neither was this victory gotten by the English without Blood; many valiant soldiers being slain, and Sir Martin Frobisher wounded with a small shot in the hip, who brought back the Fleet to Plymouth, and there died. A Valorous and stout man he was, and to be reckoned among the famousest men of our Age, for Council and Conduct, and Glory gotten by Naval Exploits, as by what I have before spoken of him plainly appeareth. . . .'

II

Extract from 'The Journal of the *Mary Rose*' in the expedition to Cadiz, 1596. Lambeth Codex 250, ff. 352–5; taken from appendix I to S. and E. Usherwood, *The Counter Armada, 1596* (London, 1983).

'Monday [21 July] in the morning after sonne rysing the Lordes Generalls and cownsell mett abord the Arke wheare it was resolved thatt the

L. Thomas Howard Viceadmirall of the fleete in the Nonparylle sr walter Raleigh Rereadmyrall in warspyte, the Lord Martiall in the Raynbow, the mr. of the Ordinance in the Mary Rose, Sr John wingfield in the Vangard Sr. Robert Southwell in the Lyon, Alexander Clyfford in the Dreadnought and Captayn Cross in the Swyftsure, with sertein merchantes and Dutch men of warr should feight with the fleete, the Lordes Generalls wyth the rest of the fleete, to be under sayle, butt not to come in danger or to feight, onles the shypes resysted weare distressed whyle this was in cownsell determining the spanish fleete waighed and came under sale falling further into the bay towardes Port Reall: the marchantes shyppes ronning up the Ryver as far as they could, and the king's shypes with other stayd at Anker over agaynst Puntall garded wyth all the Gallyes except tow left close by Cales Sr walter Raliegh having weighed sooner than the rest, made after them leading our fleete in wyth greate bravery and in passing by the towne, infynyte store of shott was spent betwene our shypes, the towne and the gallyes, much to their damadg and nothing to our los, when we weare come wythin a resonable distance of the enimy whear they weare at Anker, we lykewyse ankered, and roade as conveniently as the strayghtnes of the channell would permytt and imedyately a furyous battery on eyther syde was intertayned. . . . Aboute six a clocke in the morning the feight in our passadge by the towne and gallyes dyd begin, aboute 9 the gallyes rowed to the great shypes to gyve them ayde, but wythin one our after they gallyes shronke for there gard and fell under Puntall whych fort dyd beate us a far of wyth their ordinance aboute one a clock in the after noone the enimy weighed to wythdraw them selves further into the Ryver, whereuppon the generalls resolved to board them, butt so many in there shyppes weare slayne, and every man so much dismayd, as neyther dyd soldyer attend to his pece nor maryner hys service, wherby there shypes ronn a grownd, and before we could come to them there men leaping into the water, weare drowned in greate numbers and those that escaped Ran to Port Reall. The Substance of the enymys fleete was 4: of the kings Armados: to say; the Phylyppo Admyrall: the St Matheo Viceadmirall, the St Andrea, and the St Tomaso, towe great gallyons w[i]ch came from Lysbon 3: greate freighgates of the kinges, the Admyrall vicead: and Rearad: of Nova Hispania, w[i]ch last admyrall was the greatest shyp in all the fleete, thre Raguzcans, in all shypes of warr 21, and of marchantes aboute 40. sale more, besydes 19 gallyes of the best in spayne. . . .

The los that we resaved in this sea service was one flyboote unfortunately fired by negligence [by] some of the same shype; and not above 30: slayne by the enimy; and of them but one gentyllman, sonne to Customer smyth; besides one other pinnas of Sr Rober Soouthwell, whych in layinge the great shyppe abord, whylest she was burning was fired by her, the men all saved. There shypes weare laden rychly and bownd for the Indies, amongst these thatt came agrowned the St Phylippo and the St Tomaso sett themselves presently on fyer, to our exeding glory and joy thereby assured of the victorye, the St Mattew and St Andrew weare left on grownd abandoned by them and taken by us. This don the Lord generall Essex dyd instantly shyp into long boates and Pinnaces aboute 3000 of hys land companyes of every regiment a part, accompaned wyth most of the officers and gentylmen thatt weare for land service, landing them in a lyttle bay betwene Puntall and Cales and from thence m[a]rched dyrectly to the south syde of the Iland, the enymy from the towne beholding our troopes sallyed forth bothe horse and foote to impede our approch unto it, the L. generall thinking by there countenance that they porposed to feight advanced part of hys forces towardes them . . . The Lord Generall being evermore wyth the foremost having now wonne the dytch in gayning whereof some men were lost, and Sir Jhon wingfyld and Captayne merkyrk shott, ascended the Rampire and cawsed his own collors to be first advanced uppon the wall, at sight wherof the enymy flies and dyvers of our men some over the wall some at the corner of the wall entered who opened the port for the generall, in evry streete resistance was mayd wyth los on euther syde even unto the m[a]rkett place where in lyke manner from the toppes of the houses and wyndowes they shott many of our men, and amongst the rest (long after we were posessed of that place) Sir John wyngfyld was slayne, the Lord Marshall in the meane tyme wyth some soldyers led towardes the Pryory, whereunto dyvers men of good qualytie weare fled for succor who uppon honour rendered themselves that nyght, a strong gard was held for as yett the olde towne uperend wherein the castell is seated and whereunto in a manner all the peple of the towne had putt themselves: Towardes sonn setting the L. Admyrall the Lord Thomas Howard Sir Walter Raleigh and others whome we left abord came to us: the castell at Puntall imediately after our landing was by the gard abandoned and entred not by the Hollanders. Captain Samuell Bagnall in this service deserved much honour for he came often to the push of the Pyke and was wounded in sondry places, in regard whereof that night the lord Generall made hym Knight, in wynninge of thys towne above 200 men, Sr Edward Wyngfyld Sr Charles Percy Captain Harvy, captain Hambridg & others weare hurte. . . .'

III

Dispatch by Agustino Nani, Venetian ambassador in Spain, to the Doge and Senate, 15 July 1596 (there was a ten-day difference between the Julian calendar used by the English, and the new Gregorian calendar used by the Spaniards and Venetians; on the Julian calendar, this would be 25 July); taken from the *Calendar of State Papers, Venetian*, vol. IX, no. 470.

'. . . after the slaughter of those who opposed their landing and entry into Cadiz, the English have behaved in accordance with the customs of war. No one has been put to death except the governor of the castle, whose head was cut off because he would not yield at once, and three hundred soldiers of the garrison, who surrendered on terms, were set at liberty. Although the English sacked the city, they have not prophaned the churches, or permitted any violence upon women; and so, to the general surprise, they have won great commendation. There are some, however, who wishing to lessen this merit, declare that the moderation of the English is due to the nature of the population of Cadiz, which, as a commercial city contained for the most part people of other nationalities than Spanish. The English, after sending the women and children out of the town, proceeded to exact ransomes from the rest; it will amount to upwards of one hundred and seventy thousand crowns, they say. The President of the Seville Contracts, who was reported slain, has gained his liberty at the price of ten thousand ducats; he would have escaped with far less had he not been recognised.

There is news that in addition to the first thousand five hundred soldiers who landed alone and without artillery, and entered the city, other six thousand have been landed on the Island. In consequence of this the inhabitants of the forts of Xens and San Lucar, in great alarm, have withdrawn into Seville, though troops have been left in the forts to defend them, in addition to the troops which were placed to guard the bridge, should the English attempt to pass over it to the main land. They say that Don Pedro de Veloso of the Council of War, and captain general of the ordinary guard, will be sent in command of the army which they are raising in Andalusia.

News has come that on the 7th of this month, sixty other ships, the remains of the English fleet, set sail. Destination unknown, though some say Coruna is their object; still the Azores or the Canaries are more likely, with a view to plundering those islands, and to lie in wait for the Indiamen. The Spanish have taken steps to warn the Indiamen, but they are afraid they will fall a prey all the same. It is thought that the English will not leave these waters till they have seen the end of the India navigation. On this point Francesco Idiaquez, in conversation with one, said that though the English know how to conquer, they cannot hold. But if the rumour be true that they are entrenching themselves in several important positions on the island [of Cadiz] that would be a clear proof that they do not mean to withdraw very soon.'

By 1592 the English were operating in a number of different theatres of war. In the Netherlands their record was generally unimpressive, despite some individual heroics, and the Estates General welcomed their continued presence more for symbolic than for military reasons. After the death of the Duke of Parma in that year, and the emergence of William of Orange's son, Maurice of Nassau, as a commander of brilliance, the war turned in favour of the Dutch, and the English contribution became virtually irrelevant.

More important in many ways was the support Elizabeth was giving to Henry IV of France, particularly in Normandy and Brittany. Henry had succeeded to the throne on the death of Henry III in 1589, but because he was a Protestant he was not accepted by the Catholic League. Henry was aided by the Protestants, and by moderate Catholics, but the League, with Spanish backing, prevented him from gaining general control of the kingdom. Elizabeth's help on both fronts was small-scale, but useful. In 1593 the situation in France changed, because the League was unable to find a plausible alternative to Henry as king; and he then announced his conversion to Catholicism. Most of the League support then evaporated, and Elizabeth was able to close down her campaign in Normandy. She wished to end the Brittany operation as well, but there by this time the enemy was less the Catholic League than the Spanish intruders whom they had introduced.

Spanish control of Brest was an intolerable prospect to the queen, and almost equally so to Henry, although for different reasons. Consequently, in 1594, once Henry had been crowned and had secured control of Paris, Brittany rose high on the agenda. The trouble was the Spanish fort of Crozon (Crodon), controlling the entrance to Brest harbour. In September Sir John Norris, who had commanded the forces in Brittany intermittently since 1591, was sent back to his command with reinforcements, and specific instructions to reduce Crozon. After a campaign which brought out many of Norris's best qualities as a commander (whatever reservations the queen may have had), he was completely successful, and the English forces were then withdrawn. In the following year Henry declared war on Spain himself.

The year 1596 was not a good one for the Spanish war effort. The last of the leaguer nobles submitted to Henry IV, depriving Philip of his foothold inside French politics, and in July a combined Anglo-Dutch fleet launched a devastatingly victorious raid on Cadiz. The rather breathless and unpunctuated account quoted here gives a good impression both of the confusion and of the decisiveness of the battle. The damage inflicted was immense, amounting to twenty million ducats according to some Spanish sources, and the psychological damage was even more severe. Apart from two small-scale raids on Cornwall, Spain proved unable to respond to this type of attack, and the English appeared to be able to devastate the Spanish coast at will.

In an attempt to salvage his honour, Philip ordered an immediate response, and 100 ships and 16,000 men were assembled for a counterstroke. This new armada was driven back by the autumn gales, and a second attempt to launch the same fleet in 1597 was also frustrated by the weather. Why the weather hampered Spanish operations so much more often than English ones is not apparent, but it helps to explain why contemporary Englishmen thought that God was on their side. What was almost equally galling was that the English victors at Cadiz behaved like gentlemen and not like heretical barbarians.

The shrewd and objective Nani may be trusted on this point, although he certainly underestimated the size of the ransom demanded for the prisoners. His Spanish informant was right about the English not holding on to their gains, and the Earl of Essex was very angry about not being allowed to remain at Cadiz; but the fact was that England did not have the resources to sustain a presence upon the coast of Spain, or even in the heart of the Spanish Indies. Nani was also right about the English ambition to close down the traffic of the Indies, but in that they were unsuccessful.

The war was not all one way. The Spaniards captured Calais in 1596, which caused something like panic in London, and Amiens in 1597. The English Islands voyage of the same year was a failure bordering on disaster, and both Drake and Hawkins died on an abortive attempt to repeat their swashbuckling exploits in the Caribbean in 1595–6. Spain did not, however, enjoy against England any victories of the significance of Crozon and Cadiz. Philip's main success in the last few years of his life was to keep open his lines of communication with the New World; and that in itself was quite sufficient to ensure against defeat.

FORTY-THREE

Ireland

Notes of the Irish confederates by William Herlle, April 1571; taken from the *Calendar of State Papers Relating to Ireland (1571–75)*, ed. Mary O'Dowd (London, 2000), pp. 16–17.

'In Ireland there are six principal regions of which one is called the English region, which in common parlance is called Meath. Another is Ulster, another Connacht, two Musters, one of which is Desmond, the other Ormond. The other [is] Leinster. Meath is a mountainous land of the king in which live the baron of Slane and the baron of Delvin (note: the greatest, as it will be, in dissimulation), Lord Louth, Lord Bayle, Trimleston, Lord Dunsany, Barnewell, Plunkett, and many other lords and gentlemen (note: although these men are catholics, yet they act as hypocrites and secretly await the opportunity of disturbance).

In Ulster there are two principal and powerful lords, viz. O'Neill and O'Donnell. Those under lord O'Neill are MacMahon, Maguire, Magennis, O'Hanlon, MacCartan, Omeallan, Odunyle and MacDonnell, also O'Cahan and MacQuillan, an exile as I think. Also David Wolfe, priest of great veneration [the] bishop is subject and counsellor to him, although he is for the present detained in gaol in Dublin. To Lord O'Donnell are subject O'Doherty, O'Boyle, O'Gallagher and three other lords MacSweeney and Macoyhn (note: all these most ardent catholics and foremost confederates with force and hatred against the Queen of England).

In Connacht are O'Rourke who is a very good friend and confederate to me, whom I can arrange to be put to the test and is very powerful. O'Reilly, O'Farrell, O'Connor Sligo, O'Connor Roe, O'Connor Don. MacWilliam Burke, chief enemy to the English and partisan of this conspiracy, also a powerful man. O'Kelly. Each of these has under him other lords and gentry. In Connacht besides is Earl Richard [Burke, 2nd Earl of Clanrickarde], who has many subordinates and is most devoted to the catholic religion and our common cause, as it were one of the foremost conspiritors (note: all these catholics and chiefest enemies to the English name and fortune).

In Desmond is the Earl of Desmond whose deputy is James Maurice, brother of the Earl and chiefest enemy of the English, who entered an agreement with the French that reserves be sent to him in that vicinity both of soldiers and ships while they wait for the greater army from the Spanish, so that without any doubt the French will come early this spring to bring support. Under the Earl of Desmond are MacCarthy Mor and MacCarthy Reagh, and in another part of that Desmond is the Earl of Thomond, now a prisoner, who laid the foundations of this conspiracy while he was in France. Also this province has Mac Pieris and Mac Maurice Courcy (note: he is changing his nature into an Englishman). In another part of Munster is Ormond and its earl who has many subject nobles and gentry, whose names I do not know (note: all catholics and sworn to shake off the English yoke).

In Leinster are the Earl of Kildare, O'More, Mac Gillapatrick, O'Carroll, O'Molloy, Mageoghegan and Torelagh, and there was once in the same Leinster a powerful rich proud lord, until he was ejected by the English, viz. O'Connor Faighle (note: these having taken the opportunity are enemies, as it were yielding to the stronger, and are very devoted to the see of Rome).

In Ireland there are four archbishops. Armagh, the primate of all Ireland who has the suffragan bishops of Dromore, Down and Conor, Meath and Clonard, Ardagh, Kilmore, Clogher, Raphoe (note: these catholics and confederates). The Bishop of Derry (note: he is called Redmond O'Gallagher who lately came from Rome with many mandates).[1] The archbishop of Dublin, who has under him the bishops of Kildare, Leighlin, Ossory, Ferns and Contheriewagh (note: these protestants).

The archbishop of Cashel, by name Maurice MacGibbon,[1] who is in Spain with a large payment and is foremost as it were of our conspiracy, and in his province are the bishop of Waterford, the bishop of Ross, the bishop of Achadeo, the bishop of Cork, the bishop of Emly, the bishop of Killaloe, etc. (note: these catholics and confederates).

The archbishop of Tuam, to whom are subordinate the bishop of Clonfert and Elphin, the bishop of Mayo, the bishop of Achonry and the bishop of Killala who is under Mac William Burke (note: these catholics and confederates).'

II

Relation of Thomas Stukeley's proceedings (no date but probably 1573); taken from the *Calendar of State Papers Relating to Ireland*, pp. 18–19.

'Stukeley bought his ship the *Trinity* of Bridgewater in Ireland on 1 February 1570, by means of Alexander Fideli, an Italian and now his servant. He brought the ship to Waterford where he laded it on the

---

1. Neither of these bishops appear in the list recorded in the *Handbook of British Chronology*, because they were papally provided and not recognised by the Crown.

13th March with water wheat and beans. None of his captains understood of his pretence towards Spain, saving one Robert Rene pilot of the ship and Alexander Fideli.

He landed at Vivero in Galicia on 24th April and sent to the court of Spain two messengers, Alexander Fideli and Reynold Digby, who returned on 31st May with 200 ducats from the king. On the 12th August the king called Stukeley to the court, presenting him with 1,000 ducats to bear his charges. The king also asked him to send for his son, William, and gave him 3,000 ducats. Stukeley was lodged and had his diet defrayed by the king for 22 weeks being accompanied by a knight of the order of Calatrava called Don Frances Merles of Catalonia. He was created knight on the 22nd January 1572. He first made an offer to invade Ireland and conquer the kingdom with 1,000 Spaniards. After he demanded only 500 soldiers so long as he might have Julian Romero to govern them. Stukeley has received 1,000 ducats many times from the king. There is now delivered to him, as I am credibly informed, a warrant with the king's hand for 11,000 ducats. Stukeley has as yet had no pension granted to him. Stukeley fell out with the bishop of Cashel because the bishop has two Irishmen who had fled from Stukeley. When Stukeley found the men in the bishop's chamber, he threatended the bishop. The cardinal of Sequenza, Ruy Gomez and Secretary Gayas begin to dislike Stukeley for his evil behaviour towards the bishop.

Stukeley sold his ship to Robert Borne of Vigo, who is bound to pay Stukeley £200 in two years. The Duke of Feryo, Don Antonio de Toledo, the bishop of Quenca are great preferers of Stukeley to the king. Stukeley professes that he has good means to land with a small number in Waterford. Stukeley instructed his servants that if they met with any of my men to answer upon any question made that as I served the Queen of England, so he did serve the pope and King Philip. Before I came to the court at Madrid, Stukeley had taken a house in a village called Arosso near Madrid. Two years ago Stukeley sent one Sutton to Spain about this practice. Stukeley has allowed him of the king 50 ducats for household expenses for the 22 weeks he kept house by the king's appointment. They have an intention in Spain to take the Isles of Scilly to have a harbour for their ships. They plan to take it by stealth, on the sudden. There are twelve great ships and two assaveras in readiness on the coast of Biscay. The king of Portugal prepares an army by sea; 24 sail and 5,000 soldiers to man them. Stukeley's last petition to the king asked that he might have licence to resort to the Pope. The king's answer was that he should not depart without his own contentation. Juan de Castro, a merchant of Burgos in Castile went into Ireland about Spanish wools which Woofall had taken on the seas. Stukeley being then prisoner did practice with this Spaniard for his going into Spain and Baptist St. Victory was made '*prime heneqs*'. Christophero, an Italian and now in England, being nephew to Fideli and servant to Ragasoni was a dealer to the Ambassador of Spain for Stukeley. Pedro de Socibyor, servant to Pedro de

Gurto of Bilbao goes to the ambassador of Spain's house and writes matters concerning the state very maliciously. Robert Jacques, merchant of London, draper, conveys letters for the ambassador of Spain.'

III

Extracts from 'A summary Report made of the estate of the Realm of Ireland . . . debated in Council 5 November 1597'; taken from the *Calendar of the Carew Manuscripts*, eds T.D. Hardy and J.S. Brewer (London, 1864), pp. 271–3.

'Ulster: All the late rebellions in Ireland have had their beginning in Ulster. Like as when Sir William Fitzwilliam surrendered the sword to Sir William Russell, and when Russell delivered up his charge to Lord Burghe, we advertised your Lordships of the bad state of that province, so now we have to report that there is no part freed from the poison of this great rebellion [the Tyrone revolt] and no country or chieftain of a country, being Irish, whom the capital traitor Tyrone hath not corrupted and drawn into combination with him, so as from sea to sea beyond Dundalk, namely from Karrickfergus in Clandeboye to Ballyshanon in Tyrecannell, there is no part that standeth for her Majesty, except Karrickfergus, the Newrie, the fort of Blackwater, and the Cavan in the Breny, which are held with strong and chargeable garrisons to her Majesty, besides three or four petty castles in Clandeboyes and Lecall, namely Belfast, Edendoghe, Carricke, Olderfleet and Dondram, all which are maintained by wards. In Clandenboyes two of the petty lords, Shane McBryon and Neale Oge McHugh McFeolem of the house of O'Neales, made their submission, and are now returned to their countries pardoned, but they are not likely to stand fast longer than may serve their turn.

This bad estate of Ulster is like to grow worse by the late frequent practices of the two great lords of Kantyre in Scotland, Angus McDonnell and McAlane, both labouring vehemently to come into Ulster and bring with them 2,000 or 3,000 Scots; under pretence to make offer to serve her Majesty, they will bend themselves against her, and convert their forces to serve the traitor, with whom it is to be doubted they have contracted underhand. . . .

Leinster and the English Pale: The garboils are greater than ever. It was thought that, by cutting off Feoghe McHugh, they would have come to an end, but the quarrels have been renewed by his two sons. They have been with Tyrone all the last summer, and have wrought him to send forces with them into Leinster, under the conduct of sundry chief lords. . . . These have of late committed sundry burnings in Leax, Offaly, the Ranelaghe, the Byrnes country, Kildare, and in some parts near Dublin, where they have done several hurts upon the subjects, and especially upon the English, as they could come by them; whom principally they sought to expel out of their dwellings in Leinster, as the other rebels in Ulster and Connaught have . . . whereby it is apparent that this great rebellion in Ireland is a mere Irish war followed upon the English of purpose to root them out, and reduce the realm to the old Irish laws and tyrannical customs of Tanistry. . . .

In the English Pale many are suspected of unsoundness, even for that in ordinary warrants . . . for her Majesty's service they are far more backward than good subjects ought to be. . . .

Munster: The best tempered of all the rest at this present. . . . And yet we have intelligence that many are practiced withal from the North, to be of combination with the rest, and to stir coals in Munster, whereby the whole realm might be in a general uproar; a matter which maketh good our former opinion that it is a universal Irish war, intended to shake off all English government.'

IV

Extract from Edmund Spenser, *A View of the Present State of Ireland* (written in 1598, but first published in 1633), ed. W.L. Renwick (Oxford, 1970), pp. 122–5.

'*Ireneus*: I wish that there be a general proclamation made, that whatsoever outlaws will freely come in and submit themselves to Her Majesty's mercy shall have liberty so to do, where they shall either find the grace they desire or return again in safety; upon which it is likely that so many as survive will come in to sue for grace, of which who so as are thought meet for subjection and fit to be brought to good may be received or else all of them, for I think that all will be but a very few, upon condition and assurance that they will submit themselves absolutely to Her majesty's ordinance for them, by which they shall be assured of life and liberty and be only tied to such conditions as shall be thought by her meet, for containing them ever after in due obedience. To the which conditions I nothing doubt but that they will all most readily and upon their knees submit themselves, by the proof of that which I saw in Munster, for upon the like proclamation there they all came in, tag and rag, and when as afterwards many of them were denied to be received, they bade them do with them what they would, for they would by no means return again, nor go forth, for in that case who will not accept almost of any condition, rather than die of hunger and misery?

Eudoxus: It is very likely so, but what then is the ordinance, and what be the conditions which you will propose unto them that shall reserve unto them an assurance of life and liberty?

Ireneus: So soon then as they have given their best assurance of themselves which may be required, which must be, I suppose, some of their principal men to remain in hostage one of another, and some other for the rest (for other surety I reckon of none that may bind them, neither of wife nor of children, since then perhaps they would gladly be rid of both from the famine), I would have them first unarmed utterly, and stripped quite of all their warlike weapons, and then these conditions set down and made known unto them, that they shall be brought and removed with such creet as they have into Leinster, where they shall be placed and have land given them to occupy and live upon in such sort as shall become good subjects to labour thenceforth for their living, and to apply themselves unto honest trades of civility as they shall every one be found meet and able for.

Eudoxus: Where then in God's name will ye place them in Leinster, or will you find out any new land there for them that is yet unknown?

Ireneus: No, I will place them in all the country of the Byrnes and Tooles, which Hugh MacHugh hath, and in all the land of the Cavanaghs which are now in rebellion, and all the lands which will fall to Her majesty thereabouts, which I know to be very spacious and large enough to contain them, being very near twenty or thirty miles wide.

Eudoxus: But what then will ye do with all the Byrnes, the Tooles and the Cavanaghs, and all those that now are joined with them? . . .'

In marked contrast to England, or Wales, Tudor policy in Ireland was consistently unsuccessful. Before 1541 the lordship had been divided into three regions: the Pale, the 'obedient lands', and the tribal territories. Only the Pale was under secure English control; the obedient lands were held by Anglo-Irish lords and their affinities, who paid such attention to the English government as suited them; and the tribal territories were untouched by English influence. Within the Pale, and in some parts of the obedient lands, the Church closely resembled that in England, but in the tribal territories it was in a confused and degenerative state which horrified reformers of all persuasions, not least those who came from Rome.

English political influence had waned in the fifteenth century, but had recovered under Henry VII. Both Wolsey and Cromwell, however, had been deeply dissatisfied with the level of royal control in Ireland, regarding it as a danger to England's security. Ireland was not particularly disturbed by the Royal Supremacy, but a major rebellion in the 1530s convinced both Henry and Cromwell that radical new measures were required. The first (and most positive) idea was to seek to anglicise the Irish chieftains, persuading them to surrender their traditional lands, and receive them back as grants from the Crown; and to take part in the Irish parliaments, which had hitherto been confined to the Pale and the obedient lands. This was a variation on the policy which had worked so well in Wales. However, the starting point was different in Ireland, and much more patience and persistence would have been required than Henry was willing to expend. The elevation of Ireland into a separate kingdom in 1541 had been an aspect of this policy.

A number of circumstances combined to frustrate this initiative. Firstly, the 'new English' who went to Ireland in the king's service quickly came to regard the native Irish as savages, and their own mission as one of civilisation. Not surprisingly, this was bitterly resented, and served to destroy what little trust had ever existed. Secondly, during the reign of Edward VI England became Protestant. Edward made little more than a gesture of imposing English religion on Ireland, but that was sufficient to make the Irish feel a devotion to Rome, which had not been much in evidence in the past. It also further alienated the 'old English' of the Pale, who had resisted the incursions of the new English under Henry, and remained deeply conservative in religion. England's brief return to Rome under Mary did virtually nothing to check this rising tide of hostility, and it was Mary's government which first began the new policy of plantation, in order to protect the Pale from tribal incursions.

Elizabethan Ireland was therefore a mess. England's Protestant settlement after 1559 was the defining factor. As England became Protestant, Ireland became self-consciously Catholic, and that gave the tribes a sense of shared identity which they had never had before. It is meaningless to speak of 'Irish identity' as a positive force before about 1570; insofar as it existed, it was purely negative – a hatred of the English. An Irishman identified himself by his sept, or by his lord, but not by anything more embracing. Even more than in the 1530s, however, by the 1570s the English government had no option but to endeavour to enlarge its authority in Ireland, as the Irish chieftains increasingly looked for continental Catholic aid in order to expel it.

One partial remedy was to expand the policy of plantation. Every time there was a rebellion (and they were endemic, although mostly small-scale) land was confiscated and handed over to English, or loyal Irish, settlers. This worked up to a point, but depended for its viability upon a significant English military presence, which cost money. Elizabeth tried very hard to avoid this dilemma, and the English forces were often surprisingly small, with the result that the groundswell of conspiracy and rebellion continued. It was worst in Ulster, but no part of Ireland was ever 'pacified' for more than a short time, apart from the area immediately around Dublin. This created an ideal situation for England's enemies. Long before war broke out, Philip was supporting adventurers like Thomas Stukeley and, although they failed to deliver anything very substantial, they certainly helped to keep the pot of discontent and rebellion boiling. In 1579, with papal encouragement, FitzMaurice declared a holy war against Elizabeth, and attracted some support, particularly in Leinster; but the small and motley force which landed at Smerwick in September 1580 under a papal banner was hardly the Spanish army that FitzMaurice was expecting. His rebellion was suppressed, and the papal force massacred on the grounds that they were not legitimate belligerents, which was true.

Smerwick, however, was symptomatic of what was to be expected in Ireland, and once war had broken out in 1585, the Privy Council's anxiety intensified. The morass of confusion, double-dealing and hatred which Irish politics had become by that time tended, if anything, to work in favour of the queen. Her forces were limited, but they were relatively efficient and well armed. There was no chance of pacifying the whole of Ireland with such an army, but it was sufficient to suppress the piecemeal risings which occurred.

It was only when Hugh O'Neill, Earl of Tyrone, succeeded in transcending the endemic feuds and divisions of his own people in the 1590s, that something like a war of independence finally developed. Even then the divisions were not always clear-cut, but O'Neill was a formidable leader with a modernising agenda, and he won some significant victories in the field, which his less-effective predecessors had always failed to do. O'Neill was as slippery as he was formidable, and managed to keep Elizabeth's council guessing much of the time about his real agenda. Conversely, in spite of a great deal of communication, and not a little money, he got no military help from Philip II.

The deadlock continued for about seven years, and Elizabeth was forced to commit serious resources to Ireland. After experimenting disastrously with the Earl of Essex (who had no idea how to deal with such an elusive opponent), the queen finally gave the command to Lord Mountjoy, with (just) enough resources to finish the job. O'Neill finally submitted in the last days of Elizabeth's life. Spenser's hopeful plan for 'ethnic cleansing' was not implemented, but there were extensive new plantations. The force which Philip III finally sent to Kinsale in 1601 was defeated without difficulty. As an orthodox military campaign, it lacked all the characteristics which made the Irish themselves so dangerous. The Irish problem was not, of course, solved by these measures, but merely driven underground, to erupt with renewed violence in 1641.

FORTY-FOUR

Money and Hardship

I

Proclamation prohibiting members of the fleet from approaching the court, 22 July 1589; taken from Hughes and Larkin, *Tudor Royal Proclamations* (New Haven/London, 1969), III, no. 712.

'Forasmuch as it found by good proof that many persons which have served of late on the seas in the journey towards Spain and Portugal, in coming from Plymouth and other ports of the realm, have fallen sick by the way and divers died as infected with the plague, and that it is likely that many will of purpose to come from the said navy to the City of London and so consequently to the court, whereby danger of infection may come to her majesty's household and so approach to her sacred person:

Therefore it is commanded by publication hereof, both to the court gate and in all the towns within the verge, that no person that hath served within the said fleet shall come to the court nor within the verge except such as shall be specially sent from those which were the generals of the navy with letters to the court; which persons shall not enter within the court gates until the cause of their coming from the generals with letters of importance be notified to some of her majesty's Privy Council, and thereupon the queen's porters warned to suffer them to enter into the court.

And if any such person shall, contrary to this commandment, from this day, being the 22nd of this month of July, attempt to come either to the court or within the verge, and shall not, immediately upon knowledge hereof, depart with convenient speed, the same shall be apprehended by the knight marshall and his deputies, or by any justice or constable dwelling within the verge, and shall be committed to the Marshalsea without any bail until he shall be dismissed by some two of the Privy Council attending on her majesty's person.

And yet it is not meant but if any shall have necessary cause to come to the court to exhibit any suit or information concerning his service in the said navy, the same person shall cause the same his suit or information to be sent to the court in writing or by message to be brought by a person that hath not been in the said navy and not known to be infected, to be delivered either to one of her majesty's ordinary masters of requests, or to the knight marshall or to some one of the Privy Council, by which means the suit may be duly understood and so a reasonable answer to be made thereto.'

II

> Extract from 'An act for the grant of one entire subsidy and two fifteenth and tenths granted by the temporality'; taken from *Statutes of the Realm*, IV, ii, pp. 778–9, 29 Elizabeth, c. 8 (1586–7).

'Considering with ourselves (most gracious sovereign) what infinite charges your highness hath been driven to sustain, besides your continual princely care to prevent and withstand the sundry most dangerous practices and enterprises of long term devised, and from time to time continually pursued and put in practice, by that capital enemy unto God and your majesty, who for the maintenance of his usurped authority and to suppress the true Christian religion professed within both your majesty's realms of England and Ireland, hath by all means to him possible provoked and stirred up others of great power to do what they can for the utter ruining of the former happy estate of both the said realms, which through the assistance of the Almighty and by your majesty's great care and public foresight hath been hitherto, and by God's grace hereafter still shall be sufficiently and effectually provided for and defended; and understanding also that at this present there are very great preparations made and in making in foreign parts, both for sea and land, of intention to invade your majesty's realms and dominions, to the great danger of all your good faithful subjects; and weighing with ourselves how providently these their like intentions have been hitherto prevented and frustrate, and the inward peace of your realm longer continued than ever was in any time of your progenitours, and how necessarily great quantity of your treasure hath ben expended in maintenance of the said peace, and what dangerous effects would follow if by God's goodness and some politic means the same course should not be continued, and these intended invasions withstood without delay, which we manifestly see can in no wise be done or performed without a continued and inestimable charge.

We therefore your Majesty's most loyal and obedient subjects, having in all duty, for God's honour and your Majesty's safety and our own surety and liberty as it behoveth us [had] due consideration of the premises. . . . Do with all humility present unto your Highness, a subsidy and two fifteenths and tenths towards your Highness great charges. . . .

Your Highness shall have two fifteenths and tenths to be paid, taken and levied of the moveable goods, chattels and other things usual to such fifteenths and tenths to be contributory and chargeable within the shires, cities, boroughs, towns and other places of this your Majesty's realm in manner and form aforetime used. . . . And the said two fifteenths and tenths (the exception and deduction aforesaid thereupon had deducted and allowed) to be paid in manner and form following: that is to say: The first whole fifteen and ten (except before excepted) to be paid to your Highness in the receipt of your Highness Exchequer on and before the 10th day of November next coming; and the said second fifteen and ten . . . to be paid to your Highness in the said receipt of your Exchequer on or before the 10th day of November which shall be in the year of our Lord One thousand, five hundred fourscore and eight. . . .

And the first payment of the said subsidy shall be, by authority aforesaid, taxed cessed and rated according to this act in every Shire, Riding, Lath, Wapentake, Rape, City, Borough, Town & every other place within the realm of England and Wales and other the Queens dominions, before the first day of October next coming [second payment by 1 October 1588]. . . . [The subsidy was rated on all subjects worth more than £3 in lands or goods, at the rate of 1*s* 8*d* in the pound for the first payment, and 1*s* in the pound for the second payment.]'

III

Extract from 'An act against embezzling of Armour Habiliaments of War and Victual', 31 Elizabeth, c. 4 (1589); taken from *Statutes of the Realm*, IV, ii, p. 801.

'Be it enacted by the authority of this present parliament, that if any person or persons having at any time hereafter the charge or custody of any Armour Ordnance Munition Shot Powder or Habiliaments of War, of the Queen's Majesty's, her heirs or successors, or of any victuals provided for the victualling of any Soldiers Gunners Mariners or Pioneers, shall for any lucre or gain, or wittingly, advisedly and of purpose to hinder or impeach her Majesty's service, embezzle, purloin or carry away any of the same Armour Ordnance Munition Shot or Powder Habiliaments of War or Victuals, to the value of twenty shillings at one or several times; that then every such offence shall be judged felony, and the Offender or Offenders therein, be tried and proceeded on and suffer as in cases of felony. . . .'

IV

Extracts from 'An Act for the Relief of Soldiers', 35 Elizabeth, c. 4 (1592–3); taken from *Statutes of the Realm*, IV, ii, p. 847.

'Forasmuch as it is agreeable with Christian charity, policy and the honour of our nation, that such as have since the 25th day of March Anno 1588, adventured their lives and lost their limbs or disabled their bodies, or shall hereafter adventure their lives, lose their limbs or disable their bodies in the defence and service of her Majesty and the State, should at their return be relieved and rewarded, to the end that they may reap the fruits of their good deserving, and others may be encouraged to perform the like endeavours: Be it enacted by the authority of this present Parliament that every Parish within this realm of England and Wales shall be charged to pay weekly such a sum of money towards the relief of such hurt and maimed soldiers and mariners that so have been as afore is said, or shall lose their limbs or disable their bodies, having been prest and in pay for her Majesty's service, as by the Justices of Peace or the more part of them in their general Quarter Sessions, to be holden in the several counties next after the end of two months from the last day of this present session of Parliament, and so from time to time at the like Quarter Sessions to be holden about the feast of St. John Baptist yearly, shall be appointed; so as no parish be rated above the sum of six pence nor under the sum of one penny weekly to be paid, and so as the total sum of such taxation of the Parishes in any county where there shall be above fifty parishes amount not above the rate of two pence for every parish in the same county; which sums so taxed shall be yearly assessed by the agreement of the parishoners within themselves, or in default thereof by the Churchwardens and constables of the same Parish, or the more part of them, or in default of their agreement by order of the Justices of Peace. . . .

And for the true and just distribution and employment of the sums so received according to the true meaning of this act; Be it enacted by the authority aforesaid, that every soldier or mariner, having had his or their limbs lost or disabled in their bodies by this service, being in her majesty's pay as above is mentioned, or such as shall hereafter return into this realm hurt or maimed, or grievously sick, shall repair if he be able to travel and make his complaint to the treasurer of the county out of which he was prest, or if he were no prest man to the treasurer of the county where he was abiding by the more part of three years before his departure to serve. . . .

So that such relief as shall be assigned by such treasurers or Justices of Peace to every such soldier or mariner, having not borne office in the said wars, exceed not the sum in gross nor yearly pension of Ten pounds; nor to any that hath born office under the degree of lieutenant, the sum of Fifteen pounds, nor to any that hath served in the office of lieutenant, the sum of Twenty pounds. . . .'

V

Extracts from 'An Act for the Relief of the Poor', 39 Elizabeth, c. 3 (1597); taken from *Statutes of the Realm*, IV, ii, p. 896.

'Be it enacted by the authority of this present parliament, that the Churchwardens of every parish, and four substantial householders there . . .

who shall be nominated yearly in Easter Week, under the hand and seal of two or more of the Justices of Peace in the same county, whereof one to be of the Quorum, dwelling in or near the same parish, shall be called Overseers of the Poor of the same parish; and they or the greater part of them shall take order from time to time by and with the consent of two or more such Justices of Peace, for setting to work of the children of all such whose parents shall not by the said persons be thought able to keep and maintain their children, And also all such persons married or unmarried as having no means to maintain them use no ordinary and daily trade of life to get their living by; and also to raise weekly or otherwise (by taxation of every inhabitant and every occupier of lands in the said parish in such competent sum and sums of money as they shall think fit) a convenient stock of flax, hemp, wool, thread, iron and other necessary ware and stuff to set the poor on work, and also competent sums of money for and towards the necessary relief of the lame, impotent, old, blind, and such other among them being poor and not able to work, and also for the putting out of such children to be apprentices, to be gathered out of the same parish, according to the ability of the said parish; and to do and execute all other things, as well for disposing of the said stock as otherwise concerning the premises, as to them shall seem convenient. . . .

And be it further enacted, That it shall be lawful for the said Churchwardens and Overseers or the greater part of them, by the assent of any two Justices of Peace, to bind any such children as aforesaid to be apprentices where they shall see convenient, till such man-child shall come to the age of four and twenty years, and such woman-child to the age of one and twenty years; the same to be effectual to all purposes as if such child were of full age and by indenture of covenant bound him or her self

Provided always, That if any person or persons shall find themselves grieved with any cess or tax or other act done by the said Churchwardens and other persons or by the said Justices of Peace, that then it shall be lawful for the Justices of Peace at their general Quarter Sessions, or the greater number of them, to take such order therein as to them shall be thought convenient, and the same to conclude and bind all the said parties. . . .

Provided always, That this Act shall endure no longer than to the end of the next session of Parliament.'

War was messy and expensive. Where the mobilisation of the fleet which went against the Armada had been a model of efficiency and economy, the demobilisation was a shambles. Plague had broken out, and the released seamen died in the streets of the port towns as they came ashore. There was no money available, either to relieve them or to pay them off, and the officers, particularly the Lord Admiral, did the best they could with their own resources. In spite of the anger which this caused, the situation was virtually repeated at the end of the Lisbon expedition in 1589, except that on that occasion there was not even a glow of success to ease the distress. The plague was less serious, but the level of indignation was greater, and it was the anger as much as the infection of these mobs of discharged (but unpaid) soldiers and seamen which was feared. Some of the malcontents expressed the intention of laying siege to the court until their wages were paid, and it was rumours of that intention which provoked the proclamation of July 1589. Under pressure, the council made a major effort to pay off the outstanding wage bill, and a crisis was averted.

The inefficiency of the support services inevitably led to self-help, and the statute of the same year, against embezzlement, reflected the nature of the problem. This was partly aimed against fraudulent contractors, particularly victuallers, who regularly purloined a marketable proportion of what they were supposed to supply to the fleet or the army, making up the deficit with rotten or recycled food from a previous contract. That was not a new problem, but it seems to have become worse after the death of the long-serving Surveyor General of the Victuals, Edward Baeshe, in 1585.

By this time pressed, or conscripted, soldiers were issued with their weapons and other equipment at the point of muster. However, so poor were the arrangements for victuals and pay that it was not unknown for them to sell their equipment to buy food, even when abroad on active service. In theory such an offence carried the death penalty under martial law, but the necessity was often so acute that the law was ignored. If such soldiers still had their equipment when they returned, they were supposed to surrender it to the muster masters at the point of disembarkation; but as usual the practice fell short of the theory. It was not unknown for discharged soldiers to sell their equipment after return, to set against their unpaid wages. By the terms of this act, such action became felony and was punishable by hanging. How many were executed in this way is not known; by 1600 the system of collection (and wage payment) had improved to the point where the temptation had largely disappeared.

As the war continued, and English society became accustomed to the idea of returning soldiers, it also became clear that they represented more than a disciplinary problem. There was indeed a danger that such men, unable or unwilling to reintegrate into civilian life, would go to swell the bands of beggars or 'sturdy vagabonds' who were so much feared. On the other hand, there was the genuine distress of those who returned in some way disabled, and who were unable to work. It was, as the drafters of the 1593 statute recognised, a poor advert for a Christian society if it could not, or would not, make provision for those who had served in its defence. There was no question of the government providing a pension scheme; it simply did not have the money. Parliament was relatively generous with grants of taxation during this long war, but never came anywhere near making adequate provision. In spite of the fulsome language of the acts (of which one is cited here), a subsidy was worth no more than about £120,000, and a tenth and fifteenth about £30,000 – enough to maintain an extremely frugal war effort for about six months.

It is not surprising that Elizabeth made such extensive use of privateers. When it came to providing for the disabled, the money had to come from the parishes, via the county government. The system that was established was reasonably generous, and worked well up to a point. There was provision in the act (not cited) for those who were unable to travel to claim their pensions; and although many no doubt failed to take advantage of their entitlement, that was not the government's fault. The real problem was when particular counties, especially the maritime ones, became unduly burdened with pension claims, and lacked the resources to meet them. Better off (or less burdened) counties were supposed to help out, but they often failed to do so. No doubt some genuine claimants went unsatisfied, but such a scheme was probably the best that could be provided in the circumstances.

Poverty, however, and the need for relief, was not confined to disabled soldiers. The 1590s saw hard times: bad weather, unemployment and harvest failure. Attempts had been made to remedy this by public action as far back as the 1530s; but it was not until the 1570s that a regular national system was put into place, following the municipal schemes already established in such cities as London and Norwich. In 1597 a system of local and discretionary taxation was introduced, perhaps modelled on that already used for disablement pensions. Implementation remained firmly in the hands of the local communities, but the government had laid down a clear policy, which not only recognised the need for relief, but also accepted a level of responsibility for ensuring that it was provided. The statute cited here was the model for the Great Poor Law Act of 1601, which was required by the expiry clause, and which was to form the basis of English Poor Law down to the nineteenth century.

FORTY-FIVE

Roanoake and Imperial Ambition

I

Extract from Holinshed, *Chronicle* (1587 edn), III, p. 1369.

'In this year 1584, even at the prime of the yeare, namelie in Aprill, maister Walter Raleigh esquier, a gentleman from his infancie brought up and trained in martiall discipline, both by land and sea, and well inclined to all vertuous and honorable adventures, having built a ship and a pinesse, set them to the sea, furnished with a provision necessary for a long viage, and committed the charge of them to two gentlemen (his owne servantes), the one called Philip Amadis; the other Arthur Barlow, with direction to discover that land which lay between Norumbega and Florida in the West Indies; who according to their commission, made as sufficient a discoverie thereof as so short a time would permit; for they returned in August next following, and brought with them two savage men of that country, with sundrie other things, that did assure their maister of the goodnesse of the soile, and of great commodities that would arise to the realme of England, by traffique, if that the English had any habitation, and were planted to live there. Whereupon, he immediately prepared for a second viage, which with all expedition (nothing at all regarding the charges that it would amount unto) did presentle set in hand. . . .'

II

Extract from the journal of the *Tiger*: 'The voiage made by Sir Richard Grenville for Sir Walter Raleigh to Virginia, in the yeare 1585'; taken from *The Roanoake Voyages*, ed. D.B. Quinn (Hakluyt Society, 2nd ser., 104, 1955), I, pp. 189–92.

'. . . Iuly. The 3 we sent word of our arriving at Wococon to Wingino at Roanocke.

The 6 Master Iohn Arundell was sent to the mayne, and Monteio with him; and Captayne Aubry, and Captaine Boniten the same day were sent to Croatoan, where they found two of our men left there, with 30 others by Captaine Redmond, some 20 daies before.

The 8 Captaine Aubry and Captaine Boniten returned with two of our men found by them to us at Wococken.

The mature Elizabeth, as much an icon as a portrait.

Sir Francis Drake, the circumnavigator. 'The Queen's pirate'.

William Shakespeare, the symbol of a cultural revolution.

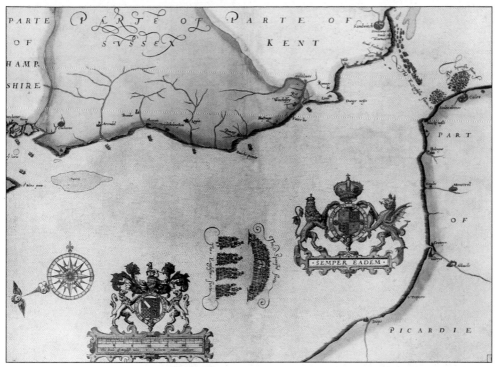

The Armada in defensive formation, off Calais. By Robert Adams.

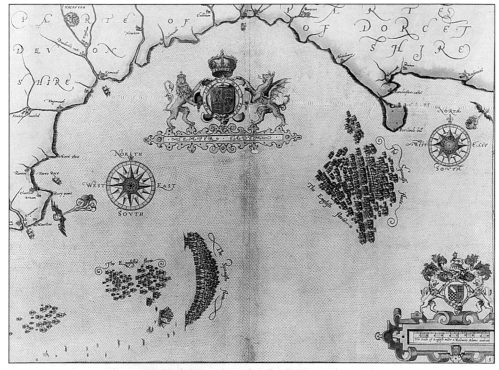

Phases in the 'battle of Portland Bill'. By Robert Adams.

Sir Philip Sidney, the icon of chivalry and letters.

Den VIII february werde onthalst Maria
Stuart Schots Coninginne's tevvende Roomsch Catho-
lyck Hebbende geseost veel onrusten aen te richten Haer scheen
meest ter te maecken van Engelant t dvvelck Haer vanden tact
ofte parlement solemnelyck vvende verstoont, Anno 1587.
Metren XIII fol. XIII. en XIIII.

The execution of Mary, Queen of Scots; from a Dutch manuscript.

The 11 day the Generall [Grenville] accompanied by his Tilt boate with Master John Arundell, Master Stukelye, and divers other gentlemen, Master Lane, Master Candish, Master Harriot and 20 others in the new pinnesse, Captain Amadas, Captaine Clarke with 10 others in a ships boate passed over the water to Ococon to the maine land victualled for eight dayes, in which voyage we first discovered the towns of Pamioke, Acquascoge and Secota and also the great lake called by the savages Paquype, with divers other places and so returned with that discovery to our Fleete. . . .'

III

Extracts from Thomas Hariot, *A Briefe and True Report* . . . (1588); taken from Quinn, *Roanoake Voyages* (1955), I, pp. 333 et seq.

'To all the Adventurers, Favourers and Welwillers of the enterprise for the inhabiting and planting in Virginia.

Since the first undertaking by Sir Walter Raleigh to deale in the action of discovering of that Countrey which is now called and known by the name of Virginia, many voyages having bin thither made at sundrie times to his great charge; as first in the year 1584, and afterwardes in the yeeres 1585, 1586, and now of late this last year of 1587; There have bin divers and variable reportes, with some slaunderous and shamefull speeches bruited abroad by many that returned from thence. Especially of that discovery which was made by the colony transported by Sir Richard Greinvile in the yeare 1585, being of all the others the most principal, and as yet of most effect, the time of their abode in the countrey being a whole yeare, when as in the other voyage before they staied but six weekes, and the others after were onlie for supply and transportation, nothing more being discovered then had been before. Which reports have not done a little wrong to many that otherwise would have also favoured & adventured in the action, to the honour and benefit of our nation, besides the particular profite and credite which would redound to themselves the dealers therein, as I hope by the sequele of events to the shame of those that have avouched the contrary, shalbe manifest; if you the adventurers, favourers and welwillers do but either encrease in number, or in opinion continue, or having bin doubtfull renewe your good liking and furtherance to deale therein according to the worthinesse thereof already found and as you shall understand hereafter to be requisite. . . .

First that some of you which are yet ignorant or doubtfull of the state thereof, may see that there is sufficient cause why the chiefe enterpriser [Sir Walter Raleigh] with the favour of Her Majestie, notwithstanding suche reportes; hath not onelie since continued the action by sending into the countrey againe, and replanting this last yeere a new Colony; but is also readie according as the times and meanes will afforde, to follow and prosecute the same. . . .

The first part of Merchantable commodities

Silke of grasse, or grasse silke. There is a kind of grasse in the countrey upon the blades whereof there groweth very good silke in forme of a thin glittering skin to bee stript of. It groweth two foote and a halfe high or better; the blades are about two foot in length, and half inch broad. The like groweth in Persia, which is in the selfe same climate as Virginia. . . .

Flaxe and Hempe. The trueth is that of Hempe and Flaxe there is no great store in any one place together, by reason it is not planted but as the soile doth yielde of itself; and howsoever the leafe and stemme or stalke doe differ from ours; the stuff by the iudgement of men of skill is altogether as good as ours. . . .

Allum. There is a veine of earth along the sea coast for the space of fourtie or fiftie miles, whereof by the iudgement of some that have made triall heere in England, is made of good Allum, of the kind that is called Roche allum. The richnesse of such a commoditie is so well knowne that I neede not to say anything thereof. . . .

Pearle: Sometimes in feeding on muscles wee found some pearle; but it was our hap to meet with ragges, or of a pide colour; not having yet discovered those places where wee heard of better and more plentie. One of our companie; a man of skill in such matters, had gathered together from among the savage people aboute five thousande; of which number he chose as many as made a fayre chaine, which for their likenesse and uniformitie in roundnesse, orientnesse, and pidenesse of many excellent colours, with equalitie in greatnesse, were very fayre and rare. . . .

Sweet Gummes of divers kinds, and many other Apothecary drugges, of which we will make speciall mention, when we shall recive it from such men of skill in that kynd, that in taking reasonable paines shall discover them more particularly than wee have done. . . .'

IV

Extract from a despatch of Gonzalo Mendes de Canzo to Philip III, 18/28 February 1600 (translated from Seville AGI 54.5.9 (Santo Domingo 224)); taken from Quinn, *Roanoake Voyages* (1955), II, pp. 826–8.

'Another consideration is this; the year that Sir Francis Drake destroyed this fortress [St Augustin, Florida], he dismantled the settlement and carried off the settlers to England, for which he fell out of favour with the Queen.

She immediately went to great trouble to send out new settlers with much valuable aid, as is clear from David's deposition. David asserts that the land is very extensive, that there is much gold and many pearls, in addition to fertile land and its fruits. There are also good harbours for ships and further up still better ones, while the fort is at the latitude which those coming down from New Mexico to this coast must pass. If the settlement is really there, it seems fitting to me that your Majesty should deal with the problem by supplying us with 1000 men, not counting the sailors who man the ships carrying the supplies. . . . In case the English are not settled where it is supposed that they are and this project is abandoned, your Majesty will order what seems fitting to you to be done. . . .'

The English had begun to show interest in the possibility of a transatlantic colony in the 1560s, when there was some discussion about establishing a post in the region of the present North Carolina. The main point of this venture seems to have been to infiltrate the rich trade of the Spanish New World, but it was not thought through, and Elizabeth at that stage preferred John Hawkins's approach. Moreover, the Spanish destruction of a similar French venture in Florida was extremely discouraging (as it was intended to be). However, there were those in England who were looking beyond the Spanish colonies, either as partners or victims, and were advocating a wider idea of colonisation. Both John Dee and the younger Richard Hakluyt argued the positive economic advantages of colonies, not just as markets or strategic posts, but as producers of raw materials and food, and as absorbers of surplus population.

The only field open to English colonisation at that point was Ireland, which was proving both politically difficult and economically problematic. In 1578 Humphrey Gilbert, who had been seriously involved in Irish plantation schemes, was converted to the idea of looking further afield, and obtained a royal patent to explore and settle any lands in North America which were not in the actual occupation of any other Christian prince. After some reconnaissance, he set out in 1583 with about 250 men, mainly artisans, but no declared objective. It has always been supposed that Gilbert intended to build and man a fort or trading post of some kind, because the absence of women and children argues against any vision of a normal civilian settlement. He went first to Newfoundland, which he claimed in the queen's name, but did not attempt to settle, and thence to Cape Cod. At that point, for no known reason, he gave up and sailed for home, perishing with his entire company in a great storm.

Gilbert's plan (and patent) was taken up almost at once by his kinsman Walter Raleigh, and it is at that point that the story outlined in these extracts begins. The reconnaissance carried out in 1584 was brief but efficient and encouraging. There were good harbours, and the land inspected, near Roanoake, appeared to be fertile. Raleigh optimistically named the land Virginia, in honour of the queen, and in 1585 sent out a much larger group, including John White, the painter, Thomas Hariot, the mathematician and cosmographer, and Thomas Cavendish, the future circumnavigator. Again the intention was vague. The first task was clearly exploration, and that was carried out with enthusiasm and some success. A settlement was also established which lasted for about a year, but it is not at all clear what Raleigh (or Grenville) had in mind. The settlers were mostly gentlemen and soldiers, who had neither the desire nor the skill to till the soil. They traded with the local Algonquin Indians, outstayed their welcome and fell out among themselves. As with Gilbert's group in 1583, they lacked the personnel or the motivation to establish themselves permanently, and perhaps there was never any intention of doing so.

When Drake arrived, on his way back from his successful Caribbean raid in 1586, he offered the 'colonists' supplies and a ship, which they accepted. However, while he was still there, and presumably because of a shift in the balance of power among them, the whole company decided to up stakes and return home. According to De Canzo this displeased the queen, who immediately set out to remedy the damage, but according to English sources it was Raleigh who decided to try again in 1587.

This time there is no doubt about the objective, which was the establishment of a viable agrarian colony with a long-term agenda. The party consisted largely of husbandmen, and included some thirty women and children. The intention was to settle in Chesapeake Bay, and if that had been achieved it might well have succeeded. However, either by accident or malign intent the ships arrived again at Roanoake. Not only had this already been shown to be an unsatisfactory site, but the Algonquin Indians were by this time thoroughly hostile.

The plan was to reinforce and resupply the colony in the following year, but the English were otherwise occupied in the summer of 1588, and by the time the relief ships arrived in 1590, the entire colony had disappeared. This was not the work of hostile Spaniards, because the governor of St Augustin in Florida (the nearest Spanish settlement), did not know in 1600 whether the English were still there or not. If they had been, he would happily have wiped them out, but it seems that the Algonquin had saved him the trouble.

There were to be no further attempts as long as Elizabeth lived, and the war continued. The vision was there, and some knowledge and expertise had been painfully acquired, but it was not until ordinary commercial ventures seemed to offer a better return than privateering that serious money again began to seek for an outlet in colonial adventures. A precarious toehold was finally established by the Virginia Company at Jamestown in 1607.

FORTY-SIX

The Cult of Gloriana

I

Sir John Davies's poem 'To the Queen'; taken from Roy Strong, *The Cult of Elizabeth* (London, 1977), p. 6.

'What music shall we make to you?
To whom the strings of all men's hearts
Make music of ten thousand parts:
   In tune and measure true,
   With strains and changes new.

How shall we frame a harmony
Worthy your ears whose princely hands
Keep harmony in sundry lands:
   Whose people divers be,
   In station and degree
     Heaven's tunes may only please,
     And not such airs as these.

For you which down from heaven are sent
Such peace upon the earth to bring,
Have heard the choir of angels sing:
   And all the spheres consent,
   Like a sweet instrument.

How then should these harsh tunes you hear
Created of the troubled air
Breed but distaste – when you repair –
   To your celestial ear?
   So that this centre here
     For you no music finds,
     But harmony of minds.'

II

Queen Elizabeth's speech to the troops assembled at Tilbury, 9 August 1588; taken from Marcus et al., *Elizabeth I: Collected Works* (Chicago, 2000), pp. 325–6.

'My loving people, I have been persuaded by some that are careful of my safety to take heed how I committed myself to armed multitudes, for fear of treachery. But I tell you that I would not desire to live to distrust my faithful and loving people. Let tyrants fear: I have so behaved myself that under God I have placed my chiefest strength and safeguard in the loyal hearts and goodwill of my subjects. Wherefore I am come among you at this time but for my recreation and pleasure, being resolved in the midst and heat of the battle to live and die amongst you all, to lay down for my God and for my kingdom and for my people mine honour and my blood even in the dust. I know I have the body but of a weak and feeble woman, but I have the heart and stomach of a king and of a king of England too – and take foul scorn that Parma [Alexander Farnese, Duke of] or any prince of Europe should dare to invade the borders of my realm. To the which rather than any dishonour shall grow by me, I will my self venture my royal blood; I myself will be your general, judge and rewarder of your vertue in the field. I know that already for your forwardness you have deserved rewards and crowns, and I assure you in the word of a prince you shall not fail of them. In the meantime, my lieutenant general shall be in my stead, than whom never prince commanded a more worthy or noble subject. Not doubting but your concord in the camp and valour in the field and your obedience to myself and my general, we shall shortly have a famous victory over these enemies of my God and of my kingdom.'

III

Extract from Edmund Spenser, *The Faerie Queene* (1590), II, ix, 4.

> 'She is the mighty Queene of Faerie,
> Whose faire retrait I on my shield do beare;
> She is the flowre of grace and chastitie,
> Throughout the world renowned far and neare,
> My liefe, my liege, my Soueraigne, my deare,
> Whose glory shineth as the morning Starre,
> And with her light the earth enlumines cleare;
> Far reach her mercies, and her prayses farre,
> As well in state of peace, as puissance in warre.'

IV

One version of the 'Golden Speech' to parliament, as printed in 1601; taken from Marcus et al., *Elizabeth I: Collected Works* (Chicago, 2000), pp. 342–4.

'Her majesty's most princely answer, delivered by herself at the court of Whitehall, on the last of November, 1601. . . . The same being taken verbatim by A.B., as near as he could possibly set it down. . . .

Mr. Speaker, we perceive by you, whom we did constitute the mouth of our Lower House, how with even consent they are fallen into the due consideration of the precious gift of thankfulness, most usually least esteemed where it is best deserved. And therefore we charge you to tell them how acceptable such sacrifice is, worthily received of a loving king who doubteth much whether the given thanks can be of more poise than the owed is to them. And suppose that they have done more for us than they themselves believe. And this is our reason; who keeps their sovereign from the lapse of error, in which, by ignorance and not by intent they might have fallen, what thank they deserve, we know, though you may guess. And as nothing is more dear to us than the loving conservation of our subjects' hearts, what an undeserved doubt might we have incurred if the abusers of our liberality, the thrallers of our people, the wringers of the poor, had not been told us! Which, ere our heart or hand should agree unto, we wish we had neither, and do thank you the more, supposing that such griefs touch not some amongst you in particular. We trust there resides in their conceits of us no such simple care of their good, whom we so dearly prize, that our hand should pass aught that might injure any, though they doubt not it is lawful for our kingly state to grant gifts of sundry sorts of whom we make election, either for service done or merit to be deserved, as being for a king to make choice on whom to bestow benefits, more to one than another.

You must not beguile yourselves nor wrong us to think that the glosing lustre of a glittering glory of a king's title may so extol us that we think all is lawful that we list, not caring what we do. Lord how far should you be off from our conceits! For our part we vow unto you that we suppose physicians' aromatical savours, which in the top of their potion they deceive the patient with, or gilded drugs that they cover their bitter sweet with, are not more beguilers of senses than the vaulting boast of a kingly name may deceive the ignorant of such an office. I grant that such a prince as cares but for the dignity, nor passes not how the reins be guided, so he rule – to such a one it may seem an easy business. But you are cumbered (I dare assure) with no such prince, but such a one as looks how to give account afore another tribunal seat than this world affords, and that hopes that if we discharge with conscience what He bids, will not lay to our charge the fault that our substitutes (not being our crime) fall in.

We think ourselves most fortunately born under such a star as we have been enabled by God's power to have saved you under our reign from foreign foes, from tyrants' rule, and from your own ruin; and do confess that we pass not so much to be a queen as to be a queen of such subjects, for whom (God is witness without boast or vaunt) we would willingly lose our life ere see such to perish. I bless God, He hath given me never this fault of fear; for He knows best whether ever fear possessed me, for all my dangers. I know it is His gift, and not to hide His glory, I say it. For were it not for conscience and for your sake, I would willingly yield another my place, so great is my pride in reigning as she that wisheth no longer to be than best and most would have me so. You know our presence cannot assist each action, but must distribute in sundry sorts to divers kinds our commands. If they (as the greatest number be commonly the worst) should (as I doubt not but some do) abuse their charge, annoy whom they should help, and dishonour their king whom they should serve, yet we verily believe that all you will (in your best judgement) discharge us from such guilts. Thus we commend us to your constant faith, and yourselves to your best fortunes.'

From the very beginning of her reign, Elizabeth had developed a 'gender specific' style of government. Mary had overcome some of the problems of being a woman ruler by resolute common sense, but she had fallen heavily into the marriage trap, and never seemed sure what kind of an image she should be presenting to her subjects. That it should be royal was clear, but whether it should be saintly or matronly was uncertain. The most effective image, that of mother, was denied her; and the image which has survived is tough, plain and rather grim. Her husband's servants described her as unattractive, saintly, and with a taste for expensive but gaudy clothes.

Elizabeth set out to be as different as possible from her sister. As princess she had affected a plain and simple style, as though to distance herself from the rather flashy world of the court. But as soon as she became queen, she adopted a quite different position. She was much younger than Mary, much better looking, and a practised and consummate actress. All these qualities she called into service at once to set up a relationship with her realm based upon the imagery and traditions of courtly love. The popular ballad 'Come Over the Bourne, Bessy', was the perfect expression of this, with its refrain '. . . give me your hand, my dear lover England, I am thine both with soul and heart'; a relationship which the author prophetically declared, would last as long as her life. This was not the Virgin Queen of later mythology, but the ardent, even flirtatious, lover.

This was a world away from the sober, disadvantaged world of Mary's sexuality. Elizabeth toyed with her baffled courtiers and councillors, who were accustomed to occupy a man's world on their own terms. Alternately charmed, frustrated and infuriated, they soon came to learn (as William Cecil had known from the beginning) that behind this coquettish demeanour lay an extremely shrewd political brain. Elizabeth's style was unique, because it could only have been repeated by another woman with a similar range of accomplishments; and such a one was never to appear.

Had she married she would, of course, have confronted the same problems as her sister. Could she present the faithful wife, and continue to be the flirtatious lover? We do not know, because for a variety of reasons it never happened. Nor can we be sure whether her various marriage negotiations were in earnest, or merely an extension of 'courtship imagery' into foreign policy. Perhaps Elizabeth scarcely knew herself. As her life lengthened, and marriage receded, the imagery began to change. Protestants had always described her as a Deborah, the judge of Israel, and this was a persona that she was reasonably happy with, because it carried the seal of Divine approval. It was, however, quite separate from the courtly love imagery she normally preferred. The Accession Day tilts which Sir Henry Lee began to develop in the late 1570s were built upon the latter: celebrations of beauty, power and mystery; but thereafter the distinctions began to blur. As poets, playwrights and other authors began to extol her as Astraea, Belphoebe and Gloriana, the imagery of classical mythology and the Old Testament merged. Elizabeth was simultaneously the Fairy Queen, the Virgin Queen, and the Lord's Anointed.

Her real appearance became less and less relevant to this process. Even in the 1590s when she was ageing, bewigged and raddled, her peerless beauty remained the courtiers' constant theme – and woe betide them if they forgot it!

How far Elizabeth invented all this apparatus herself, and how far she simply went along with the ideas of her 'spin doctors', we do not know. What we do know is that she revelled in the kind of popularity it generated. In the first months of her reign Philip's representative, the Count of Feria, commented upon the new queen's appetite for public acclaim, remarking that 'she believes all the people are on her side – which is undoubtedly true . . .'. Her skill in exploiting this popularity never deserted her, and was an aspect of her 'love affair' with the realm.

Elizabeth's Tilbury speech (which may not have been given in these words – or at all) was nevertheless published immediately, as representing her intention, or the image she wanted to present. Speeches of a similar kind were certainly delivered in many less momentous circumstances: on progress, when receiving ambassadors or other representatives, or simply when she happened to feel like it. It was a style which was sufficiently honest to carry conviction, and could be used to dig herself out of political holes, as was demonstrated by the so-called 'Golden Speech' of 1601. Elizabeth's political touch to some extent deserted her in the last years of her life, particularly when she felt that war and poverty had left her no option but to allow her courtiers to reward themselves at the expense of her subjects at large. This put their loyalty under severe strain, as the parliament of 1601 had made clear; and the queen chose to redeem herself (up to a point) in this characteristic fashion:

> 'She was and is, what can there more be said,
> In earth the first, in heaven the second maid.'

What more, indeed, can be said, as Sir Roy Strong commented, than that this withered vain old lady of seventy should now reign as a second Queen of Heaven.

FORTY-SEVEN

Music and Theatre

I

Extract from the 'Epistle' by George Whetstone to William Fleetwood, 29 July 1578, prefixed to *Promus and Cassandra*; taken from E.K. Chambers, *The Elizabethan Stage* (Oxford, 1923), IV, p. 201.

'I devided the whole history into two Commedies: for that, Decorum used, it would not be convayde in one. The effects of both are good and bad; vertue intermyxt with vice, unlawful desyres (yf it were possible) quenched with chaste denyals; al nedefull action (I think) for publike vewe. For by the rewarde of the good, the good are encowraged in wel doinge; and with the scowrge of the lewde, the lewde are feared from evil attempts: maintayning this my oppinion with Platoes auctority. "Naughtinesse commes of the corruption of nature, and not by reading or hearinge the lives of the good or lewde (for such publication is necessarye), but goodnesse (sayth he) is beautified by either action." And to these ends Menander, Plautus and Terence, themselves many years since entombed (by their Commedies), in honor live at this daye. The auncient Romanes heald these showes of such prise, that they not only allowede the public exercise of them, but the grave Senators themselves countenaunced the actions with their presence; who from these trifles wonne morallyte, as the Bee suckes the honey from weedes. But the advised devices of auncient Poets, discredyted with the tryfels of yonge, unadvised and rashe witted wryters hath brought this commendable exercise in mislike. For at this day, the Italian is so lascivious in his commedies, that honest hearers are greeved at his actions; the Frenchmen and the Spaniarde follow the Italian humour; the Germaine is too holye; for he presentes on everye common stage, what Preachers should pronounce in Pulpetts. The Englishman in this quallitie is most vaine, undiscreet and out of order; he fyrst groundes his workes on impossibilities; then in three howres roones he throwe the worlde; marryes, gets Children, makes Children men, men to conquer kingdomes, murder monsters, and bringeth Gods from Heaven, and fetcheth Divels from Hel. And (which is worst) their ground is not so imperfect as their workinge indiscreete; not wayinge, so the people laugh, though they laugh them (for their follye) to scorne; Many tymes (to make mirthe) they make a Clowne companion with a king; in their grave counsels, they allowe the advice of fooles; yea they use one order of speeche for all personnes; a gross Indecorum, for a Crowe wyll yll counterfet the Nightingales sweete voyce; even so affected speeche doth misbecome a Clowne. For to work a Commedie kindly, grave olde men should instruct; yonge men should showe the imperfections of youth; Strumpets should be lascivious; Boyes unhappy; and Clownes should be disorderly; entertminglinge all these actions in such sorte as the grave matter may instruct and the pleasant delight; for without this chaunge, the attention would be smale, and the likinge lesse. But leave I this rehersall of the use and abuse of Commedies; least that I check that in others, which I cannot amende in myselfe. But this I am assured, what actions so ever passeth in this History, either merry, or morneful, grave or lascivious; the conclusion showes the confusion of Vice, and cheryshing of Vertue. . . .'

II

Extract from a 'Platt', or staging plan, undated but probably *c.* 1590; taken from W.W. Greg, *Dramatic Documents from the Elizabethan Playhouse* (Oxford, 1931). The original is Dulwich College MS XIX (see p. viii).

'A Platt of the secound Parte of the Seven Deadlie Sinns.

(1) A tent being plast one the stage for Henry the sixt. he in it. A Sleepe to him the Leutenante. A purcevaunt R Cowly Jo Duke and. warden [J Holland] R Pallant: to them Pride. Gluttony. Wrathe and Covetousness at one dore. at an other dore Envie. Sloth and Lechery. The Three put back the foure. and so Exeunt.

(2) Henry Awaking. Enter a Keeper. J Sincler. to him a servant. T Belt. to him Lidgate and the Keeper. Exit then enter againe. Then Envy passeth over the stage. Lidgate speaks.

(3) A senitt. Dumb show. Enter King Gorboduck with ii Counsaillors. R Burbadg. mr Brian. Th Goodale. The Queene with ferrex and Porrex and som attendants follow. Saunder. W Sly. Harry. J Duke. Kitt. Ro Pallant. J Holland. After Gorboducke hath consulted w[i]th his Lords he brings his 2 sonnes to to severall seates. They enving on an other ferrex offers to take Porrex his Corowne. he drawes his weapon. The King Queen and Lords step between them. They Thrust them away and menasing (etc) ech other exit. The Quene and Lo[rd]s depart Heavilie. Lidgate speaks.

(4) Enter ferrex Crowned w[i]th Drum and Coulers and soldiers one way. Harry. Kitt. R Cowly. John duke. to them At an other dore. Porrex drum and Collers and soldie[rs]. W Sly. R. Pollant. John Sincler. J Holland.

(5) Enter Queene w[i]th 2 counsailors. mr Brian. Tho Goodale. to them ferrex and Porrex severall waies w[i]th Drum and powers. Gorboduck entreing in the midst between. Henry speaks.

A Larum with Excurtions After Lidgate speakes. . . .'

III

> Extract from the record of the entertainment offered to the queen at Elvetham, Hampshire, by the Earl of Hertford in 1591; taken from Jean Wilson, *Entertainments for Elizabeth I* (Woodbridge, 1980), pp. 113–14.

'The thirde daies entertainment

On Wednesday morning, about nine of the clock, as her Majesty opened a casement of her gallerie window, there were three excellent Musicians, who, being disguised in auncient countrey attire, did greet her with a pleasant song of Coridon and Phyllida, made in three parts of a purpose. The song, as well for the worth of the dittie, as for the aptnes of the note therto applied, it pleased her Highnesse, after it had been once sung, to command it againe, and highly to grace it with her chearefull acceptance and commendation.

The Three Men's Song, sung the third morning, under hir Majesties Gallerie window.

> In the merrie moneth of May,
> In the morne, by breake of day,
> Forth I walked by the wood side,
> Where as May was in his pride.
> There I spied, all alone,
> Phyllida and Corydon.
> Much adoe there was, God wot,
> He would love and she would not.
> She said, never man was true:
> He said, none was false to you.
> He said, he had loved her long;
> She said love should have no wrong.
> Corridon would kisse her then;
> She said maids must kisse no men,
> Till they did for good and all.
> Then she made the shepheard call
> All the heavens to witnesse truth,
> Never lov'd a truer youth.
> Thus with many a pretie oath,
> Yea and nay, faith and troth,

> Such as silly shepheardes use,
> When they will not love abuse;
> Love, which hath beene long deluded,
> Was with kisses sweet concluded;
> And Phyllida, with garlands gay,
> Was made the Lady of the May.'

IV

Extract from Thomas Morley *A Plaine and Easie Introduction to Practical Musicke* (London, 1597), p. 6; taken from the facsimile edition (New York, 1969).

'[A dialogue between a philosopher and a musician]

Phi. I know not how to beginne.

Ma. Why?

Phi. Because beneath *Gam ut* there is nothing: and the first note standeth beneath *Gam ut*.

Ma. Where as you saie, there is nothing beneath *Gam ut*, you deceive yourselfe: For Musicke is included in no certaine bounds (though the Musicians do include their songes within a certaine compasse). And as you Philosophers say, that no number can be given so great, but that you may give a greater. And no poynt so small but that you may give a smaller. So there can be no note given so high, but that you may give a higher, and none so low but that you may give a lower. And therefore call to minde that which I told you concerninge the keyes and there eightes; for if Mathematically you consider it, it is true as well without the compasse of the Scale, as within; and so may be continued infinitely.

Phi. Why then was your scale devised of xx notes, and no more?

Ma. Because that compass was the reache of most voyces; so that under *Gam ut* the voice seemed as a kind of humminge, and above *E la* a kind of constrained skricking. But we goe from the purpose, and therefore proceede to the singing of your example.

Phi. Then I perceive the first note standeth in *F fa ut* under *Gam ut*, and being the lowest note of the verse I may therefore sing *ut*.

Ma. Right, or *f a* if you will, as you dyd in the eyght above in the other verse before. But goe forward.

Phi. Then though there to be no *re* in *Gam ut*, nor *mi* in *A re*, nor *fa* in *mi*, etc. yet because they be in their eyghts I may sing them there also. But

I pray you why do you set a *b* in *E la mi*? seeing there is neither in it nor in *E la mi* in alte, nor in *E la* any *fa*, and the *b* cliefe is only set to thre keyes wherein their is *fa*?

Ma. Because there is no note of it selfe either flatte or sharpe, but compared with another, is sometimes flatt and sometimes sharpe; so that there is no note in the whole scale which is not both sharpe and flatt: And seeing you might sing *la* in *D fol re*, you might also (altering the tune a litle) sing *fa* in *E la mi*. There be manie other flattes in Musicke, as the *b* in *A la mi re*, whereof I will not speake at this time, because I will not cloy your memorie with unprofitable precepts; and it will be time enough for you to learne them when you come to practice prickesong. . . .'

The reign of Elizabeth saw remarkable developments in English drama, poetry and music, all of which owed a great deal to the culture of the court. In encouraging all these accomplishments, Elizabeth followed her father. Like him, she had a good ear for music, and was an accomplished performer. It was her personal taste and example which maintained the standards of singing in the Chapel Royal, and by that example helped to sustain and expand the tradition of good music in cathedrals and colleges. The fact that so many of the best Elizabethan composers were Catholics is also eloquent of the effective protection she was able to extend to those who pleased her. Because the Queen loved good music, and encouraged innovation, her courtiers followed her example, and their followers in turn imitated them. A gentlemen with any pretensions to social accomplishment, let alone ambition as a courtier, was expected to be able to sight-read a part song and immediately to take his place in an impromptu choir. It was for such people that Thomas Morley was seeking to provide instruction.

In spite of the Chapel Royal, the driving force behind this culture was secular rather than religious; and the most popular mode was the love song – songs of desire, songs of frustration, songs of joy and songs of despair. Quite apart from the fact that these were very basic human emotions, the genre was also encouraged by the premise that Elizabeth's courtiers were expected to play a constant game of courtly love with their mistress. It was the inescapable aura of a court dominated by a woman who had decided that sex could give her unprecedented political advantages. Popular music probably did not change very much, but at a higher social level it was a period of almost unique achievement.

By contrast, the contemporary developments in drama had popular as well as courtly roots. Interludes and burlesques were ancient forms of entertainment, each of which left its mark on the professional theatre of the late sixteenth century; however, the two main influences were the urban morality play, and the masque. The former were loosely based on bible stories, featuring scenes particularly of the nativity and crucifixion, but also included 'Everyman' stories of sin, death and redemption, featuring angels and devils manipulating human destiny. Traces of this sort of play can still be seen in Marlowe's *Dr Faustus*, although by then it was more normal to wrap up theological virtues and vices in human personae. All such plays were broadly didactic in purpose, and in the early days of Protestantism (before about 1570) were often used to pillory what were seen to be the abuses of the traditional Church. The public performance of these play cycles in their traditional form, such as the York and Chester cycles, was banned in the 1570s, and the genre only survived through its influence on the secular public theatre. As can be seen from George Whetstone's letter, the desire to sugar the pill of moral instruction with the 'delights' of entertainment continued to be strong.

The courtly masque was originally chivalric or allegorical in form, and tended to feature nymphs, shepherds, and classical gods and goddesses. Such entertainments continued to be given throughout Elizabeth's reign, and her enthusiasm for them never flagged, not least because they were constant reminders of her own allegorical position as the queen of hearts. The 'Seven Deadly Sins' was a sort of halfway house between allegorical drama and plays which claimed a greater degree of veracity, such as Shakespeare's history cycle. Texts of many such plays survive, but the interest of this 'plat' is not only in the clues it provides to the way in which the play was actually staged, but also in the names of the actors it incorporates, including Richard Burbage.

Mature Elizabethan drama, as represented by Shakespeare, Marlowe, Kidd and others, was only occasionally performed at court. Its normal home was in the public theatres of Thameside, but royal and courtly patronage was still extended to the companies of players, and without that support (and protection) it is very unlikely that they would have been able to experiment in the ways they did. Within a generation English drama advanced from an uneasy mixture of didacticism and knockabout humour to the psychological sophistication of *Hamlet* or *King Lear*. We do not know that the queen's personal taste ever advanced beyond tales of chivalry and bucolic romance (she had once famously wished to play a milkmaid), but she created the culture in which such patronage flourished.

FORTY-EIGHT

Cecil and Essex

I

Minute of a letter from the queen to the Earl of Essex, 24 July 1597; taken from Marcus et al., *Elizabeth I: Collected Works* (Chicago, 2000), p. 388.

'[This letter was prompted by news of the failure of Essex's expedition to the Azores, dispersed by gales.] How irksome long toil, much danger, and heart's care may seem to the feeler's part when they that only hears report of what might be full of evil chance or danger's stroke are so filled with doubts of unfortunate sequel! You may well suppose the weight of these balances, but remember that who doth their best shall never receive the blame that accidents may bring; neither shall you find us so rigorous a judge as to verdict enterprises by events. So the root be sound, what blasts so ever wither the fruits, no condemnation shall light on their share. Make of this fleet, I charge you, a match, which being a fire runs *in extremum*, with good caution of such points as my signed letter gives you. Adieu with many good wishes to yourself, not forgetting good Thomas [Baskerville], [Charles Blount, Lord] Mountjoy with your joined Council [of Ireland], and tell them that no orison shall be made by us of whence they have no part.'

II

Extracts from Lord Burghley's instructions to his son, Robert Cecil, when young; taken from Strype, *Annals of the Reformation* (London, 1725), IV, p. 340.

'Son Robert,

The vertuous Inclinations of thy matchless Mother, by whose tender and godly Care thy Infancy was governed, together with thy Education under so zealous and excellent a Tutor, putteth me rather in Assurance than Hope, that thou art not ignorant of the *summum bonum*; which is only able to make thee happy as well in thy Death as Life. I mean the true knowledge and Worship of thy Creator and Redeemer; without which all other things are vain. . . .

I. When it shall please God to bring thee to Man's Estate, use great Providence and Circumspection in the Choise of a Wife. For from thence will spring thy future Good or Evil. . . . And touching the Government of thy House, let thy Hospitality be moderate, and according to the Measure of thy Estate, rather plentiful than sparing, but not costly. . . .

II. Bring thy Children up in Learning and Obedience, yet without Austerity. Praise them openly, reprehend them secretly. Give them a good Countenance, and a sufficient Maintenance according to thy ability. . . .

IV. Let thy Kindred and Allies be welcome at thy Table. Grace them with thy Countenance, and further them with all other honest actions. . . .

V. Beware of Suretiship for the best Friends. For he that payeth another man's debts seeks his own Decay. . . .

VI. Take no Suit against a poor man, without receiving much Wrong. For besides thou makest him thy Competitor, it is a base Conquest to triumph where there is small Resistance. Neither attempt Law against a Man before thou be thorowly resolved, that thou hast Right on thy side. . . .

VII. Be sure to keep some Great Man thy Friend. But trouble him not for Trifles. Compliment him often. Present him with many, yet small Gifts, and of little Charge. . . .

VIII. Towards thy Superiors be humble, but generous. With thy equals familiar, yet Respective: Towards thy Inferiors show much Humility and some Familiarity. . . .

X. Be not scurrilous in thy Conversation, nor Satyrical in the Jests. The one will make you unwelcome in all Company, and the other will pull on Quarrels, and get thee Hatred of thy best Friends. . . .'

III

> Lord Burghley's last letter to his son, Sir Robert Cecil, Principal Secretary, dated 10 July 1598 (Burghley died on 4 August); taken from Strype, *Annals of the Reformation* (London, 1725), IV, p. 343.

'Tho' I know you count it your Duty in Nature so continually to shew you careful of my State of Health, yet were I also unnatural, if I should not take Comfort thereby; and to beseek Almighty God to bless you with Supply of such Blessings, as I cannot in this Infirmity yield you.

Only I pray you diligently and effectually let her Majesty understand, how her singular Kindness doth overcome my Power to acquit it; who, although she will not be a Mother, yet she sheweth herself, by feeding me with her own Princely Hand, as a careful Nurse. And if I may be weaned to feed myself, I shall be more ready to serve Her on the Earth: if not, I hope to be in Heaven a Servitor for Her, and God's Church. And so I thank you for your Partriches.

Serve God by serving of the Queen. For all other Service is indeed Bondage to the Devil.

Your Languishing Father,

W. Burghley.'

IV

Extract from Camden, *Historie of . . . Elizabeth* (London, 1630), pp. 606 ff.

'All these meeting secretly at Drury House for avoiding suspicion, the Earl of Essex first produced a Catalogue of those Noblemen and Gentlemen which he persuaded himself to be much addicted unto him, wherein were reckoned about 120 Earls, Barons, Knights and Gentlemen of good houses. Then he willed them to consult among themselves, and make report to him, whether it were better to seize first upon the Court, or upon the Tower of London, or both at once; and what should be done concerning the City of London. They all thought it best to seize upon the Court, and that in this manner; Sir Christopher Blount with a select number should seize upon the Court-gate, Davis the Hall, Danvers the Great Chamber (where the guard kept but a careless watch) and the Presence Chamber, and withall Essex himself, from the stable called the Mues, near the court, should with certaine choice men (his hay thus being made) come rushing in, and fall upon his knees before the Queen, and pray her to remove his Adversaries from about her; whom he had determined (as some confessed afterward) to bring to their Trial, and having called a Parliament, to alter the Form of Commonwealth . . . [whereby] . . . suspicions of him grew stronger and stronger, both by reason of a more frequent resort than usual of the Multitude to Essex-House, under pretence of hearing Sermons; as also some words which had dropt from the Preachers Mouths, as of the Superior Magistrates had power to Restrain Kings themselves. Hereupon, or some light discovery of one or other, Robert Sackville, the Lord Treasurer's son gave the earl a visit. . . . The Earl of Essex was shortly after sent for by Sir John Herbert, one of the secretaries, to come to the Lord Treasurer's House, where the Council was met, that he might be admonished to use the Liberty which was granted him soberly; and at the same time there was a Note delivered privately into his hands, whereby he was warned to look to himself. Whereupon, suspecting that somewhat was com to light and fearing that he should be committed again to Custody, he excused his appearing before the Council by his Indisposition of body. . . .

Whilst they were arguing concerning the Affection and Love of the Londoners, and the Uncertain Disposition of the Vulgar, one came in of a set purpose, who as if he had been sent from the citizens made large promises of assistance from them against all his Adversaries. Herewith the earl being somewhat animated, he began to discourse how much he was favoured throughout the city; and persuaded himself, by the former Acclamations of the People, and their Mutterings and Murmurings against his Adversaries, that many of them were devoted to him, to maintain his Credit and Fortune . . . he resolved therefore foreasmuch as delay was now no lesse dangerous than plaine Rashnesse, to enter the next day, which was Sunday, into the city with 200 gentlemen, a little before the end of the Sermon at S. Pauls, there to inform the Aldermen and People of the Reasons of his coming and to crave their aid against his Enemies . . . [his foray having failed]. . . .

In the meanwhile Essex returned to his House; the Lord Keeper with the rest followed him, with intent to have some Discourse with him in Private. Meanwhile they hear some of the Multitude throw out these seditious words, Kill them, Throw away that Great Seal, Shut them up in Custody. When they were come into the Inner Rooms of the House, Essex commanded to bolt the doors and shut them in. Have patience awhile, I must presently go into the City to advise with my Lord Mayor and the Sheriffes, I will return againe by and by. . . .

In the meantime Thomas Lord Burghley and Dethicke Garter King of Arms entering the city proclaimed Essex and his complices traitors. . . .

Essex, wavering in his resolution, began to think presently of yielding, and gave notice upon certeine conditions he would yielde, but when the Lord Admiral [Charles Howard, Earl of Nottingham] would admit no conditions; he said he would not give Conditions but rather take them; yet three things he requested: First that they might be Civilly dealt withall. This the Lord Admiral promised. Secondly that their cause might be justly and duely heard. He answered that there was no reason to doubt thereof. And lastly that Ashton, the Minister of God's Word might be with him in prison for his Soul's comfort. The Lord Admiral answered that for these things he would make intercession to the Queen. When presentlie all the Noblemen falling upon their knees and delivering their swords up to the Lord Admiral, yielded themselves at Ten of the Clock at Night.'

V

Proclamation announcing the arrest of the Earl of Essex, 9 February, 1601; taken from Hughes and Larkin, *Tudor Royal Proclamations* (New Haven/London, 1969), III, no. 808.

'Whereas the Earl of Essex [Robert Devereux], accompanied with the Earls of Rutland [Roger Manners] and Southampton [Henry Wriothesley], and divers others their complices, gentlemen of birth and quality, knowing themselves to be discovered in divers treasonable actions into which they have heretofore entered, as well in our realm of Ireland where some of them had laid plots with the traitor Tyrone as in this our realm of England, did upon Sunday, being the 8th of this month, in the morning not only imprison our Keeper of our Great Seal of England, our Chief Justice of England, and others both of our nobility and Council that were sent in our name to his house to persuade the said Earl to lay open his petitions or complaints, with promise (if he would disperse his disordered company in his house) that all his just requests should be heard and graciously considered; but also did, after straight order given by him to murder our said councillors and others whensoever they should offer to stir out of that place, traiterously issue into our City of London in arms with great numbers, and there breaking out into open action of rebellion, divised and divulged base and foolish lies that their lives were sought; spreading out diverse strange and seditious inventions to have drawn our people to their party, with purpose to attempt traitorous actions both against our person and state and to expose (as it now appeareth) our city and people with their goods to the spoil of a number of needy and desperate persons their adherents; continuing still in arms and killing diverse of our subjects, after many proclamations of rebellion made by our king of heralds.

Forasmuch as notwithstanding (God be thanked) they have found themselves deceived of their expectation, being now all apprehended and within our Tower of London, as well the three principal traitorous Earls of Essex, Rutland and Southampton, as divers others of the principal gentlemen their confederates, our good subjects of our City, and elsewhere, having showed themselves so constant and unmoveable from their duties towards us, as not any one of them of any note (that we can yet hear of) did offer to assist the said Earl and his associates.

We have been contented, in regard of the comfort that we take to know by so notorious evidence the loyal disposition of our people (whereof we never doubted), not only to make known to all our said subjects of our city and elsewhere in how thankful part we do accept both their loyal persisting in their duty and stay from following the false persuasions of the traitors, but to promise on our part that whensoever we shall have cause to show it they shall find us more careful over them than for ourselves.

And hereby also, in regard of our gracious meaning towards our good people, to admonish them that seeing this open act was so sudden as it cannot yet be thoroughly looked into how far it stretched and how many hearts it hath corrupted, but that it is to be presumed by the common example of the manner of proceeding of all rebels in like actions, that it was not without instruments and ministers dispersed in divers places to provoke the minds of our people to like of their attempts, with calumniating our government and our principal servants and ministers thereof; that they shall do well (and so we charge them) to give diligent heed in all places to the conversations of persons not well known for their good behaviour, and to the speeches of any that shall give out slanderous and undutiful words or rumours against us and our government; and they that be in authority to advertise those thereof that have authority to the end that by the apprehension of such dangerous instruments, both the drift and purpose of evil-minded persons may be discovered, their designs prevented, and our people conserved in such peace and tranquility as heretofore, by God's favour, we have maintained and do hope still to continue amongst them.'

The domestic politics of the 1590s were shaped, if they were not dominated, by the rivalry between the Cecils, father and son, and Robert Devereux, Earl of Essex. William Cecil, Lord Burghley, was the queen's long-time confidant. He had outlived virtually all his contemporaries, and his position by this time was unique. Essex was the stepson and successor to the Earl of Leicester, who had died in 1588. He was thirty-four in 1590, a handsome young man and a dashing courtier, who owed much of his favour to feeding the queen's delusions about eternal youth and beauty. He was also a military commander of some ability and overwhelming ambition. As a man high in favour, Essex attracted a following among those who hoped to be able to exploit his influence over patronage. When it came to securing military positions, these expectations were frequently gratified, so he counted many fighting men among his clients. When it came to civilian patronage, however, he usually found himself blocked or countermined by the Lord Treasurer, who did not trust him an inch.

When Sir Francis Walsingham died in April 1590, the Principal Secretaryship became the focus of a prolonged battle. Essex was determined to secure the position for his client, Francis Bacon, and made no secret of the fact. Burghley wanted it for his able second son, Robert Cecil. The queen, not for the first time, refused to make a decision. She did not wish to undermine her favourite's credit, but trusted his judgement in such matters no more than Burghley did. For six years the post remained officially vacant, which saved the earl's face, but in truth Robert Cecil actually did the work, and rapidly acquired an influence in council as great as that of his father. Then in 1596, while Essex was away gaining some genuine renown at the sack of Cadiz, the office was officially conferred on Cecil.

In compensation, Elizabeth probably gave Essex more than his fair share of the credit for the victory in Spain, but he was disappointed and began to grow bitter. He felt that far more could have been achieved at Cadiz if his pusillanimous colleagues had not rejected his advice. He started to see the hand of Lord Burghley behind all his frustrations. He could hardly blame the Lord Treasurer for the gales which ruined his Azores expedition in 1597, and the queen was gracious and consoling, but he felt that he needed a major success in government, and that continued to elude him. He had served in Ireland before, as a military commander and planter, with somewhat mixed fortunes, but in April 1599 he was appointed governor, with the unusually elevated title of Lord Lieutenant. His idea was to bring about the surrender of the long-time rebel the Earl of Tyrone, but he proved no match for the Irishman, either as a politician or a soldier, and was recalled after six months in something very close to disgrace.

By 1600 Essex was becoming paranoid. Burghley had died in 1598, but virtually the full weight of his political influence was now transferred to his son, and the Cecil clientage network was, if anything, more dominant and successful than ever. Essex refused to accept that he had forfeited the queen's confidence over his behaviour in Ireland, and began to cast himself and his friends as the victims of Cecil conspiracies. When he was deprived of his lucrative monopoly for the sale of sweet wines, a move which was probably due to the Principal Secretary, he became desperate. He seems to have convinced himself that Cecil was aiming to have him assassinated, and that he must break through the cordon and confront Elizabeth personally.

He was not the only courtier who hated Cecil's influence. Many who had overstretched their resources in futile bids to attract rich favours and rewards blamed him for their failure. They convinced themselves that not only their personal fortunes, but also the war effort and the honour of the country could only be redeemed by getting rid of Cecil. In February 1601 Essex, accompanied by the Earls of Rutland and Southampton (both young men hopelessly in debt), and a gang of disappointed soldiers and place hunters, tried to raise a rebellion in London, apparently intending to force Elizabeth to gratify their demands by a palace revolution. There was a brief and spectacular alarm, but they attracted virtually no support, and within twenty-four hours were in the Tower. It appears that Cecil had some warning of their intention, and was prepared. Southampton and Essex were attainted, and Essex was executed on 25 February.

The whole episode was symbolic of the state of English politics at the end of the sixteenth century. Three earls, acting together and playing for very high stakes, could do no more than raise a minor disturbance in London. A hundred years before such aristocratic malcontents would have commanded private armies of retainers, and would have mobilised on their estates. They might not have succeeded in achieving anything, but a serious effort would have been required to put them down. By comparison with the Pilgrimage of Grace, or even the rebellion of 1569, Essex's 'revolt' was a trivial event. Both for better and worse, the English peerage was not what it had been.

FORTY-NINE

The Last Years of the Reign

I

Extract from Camden, *Historie of . . . Elizabeth* (London, 1630), p. 657.

'[1603] . . . she granted the Lord Deputy [Charles Blount, Lord Mountjoy] Authoritie to receive him to mercy and favour, in case he would beg the same upon his knees before him with that Humility and Submission which in his Letters he pretended.

No sooner had Tir-Oen Intelligence hereof, but he became an earnest and daily Suitor to obtain the same, employing Arthur MacBaron his brother, and others about it; and after he had been many times rejected, at length upon Promise that he would absolutely submit his Life and Estate to the Queen's Will and Pleasure, the Lord Deputy (who had by some of his friends been acquainted with the Queen's Indisposition, which was the more dangerous because of her great years) permitted him to come to Mellifont; whither he presently hasted with one or two of his company.

Being admitted to the Presence Chamber (where the Lord Deputy sat in his Chair of State, with a great number of Swordsmen about him) he fell on his knees at the very threshold with a dejected countenance, being clad in sordid and careless habit. After he had been in that posture a while, the Lord Deputy beconed him to come nearer him. He arose and having come forward some few steps, prostrated himself again upon his knees and said: I acknowledge my sin against God, and my fault against my most gracious Queen and Sovereign Lady, to whose royal clemency as a sacred Anchor I betake myself, offering up my life and estate to be at her disposing; whose former bounty and present power as I have felt, so I most humbly beseech her, that I may now taste of her mercy, and be made an Eternal Example of her princely Clemency. My Age is not so far spent, nor my body so feeble, nor my mind so broken, but that by my valiant and faithfull service I may yet expiate the sin of this my rebellion.

. . . The Lord Deputy interrupted him . . . [and] commanded him to depart, and the next day brought him with him to Dublin, intending to bring him thence to England to the Queen, that she might dispose of him at her Pleasure.

Thus was Tir-Oen's Rebellion happily brought to an end in the eighth year after it first broke out, by the auspicious fortune of the Queen, and the good conduct of the Lord Mountjoy, Lord Deputy.'

II

Extracts from *A Conference about the Next Succession to the Crowne of Ingland; published by R. Doleman* (Robert Parsons) (Antwerp?, 1594), pp. 141; taken from the Scolar Press facsimile, 1972.

'Cap.VII

Having declared the degrees rights and pretences, which the two noble houses of Scotland and Suffolke, descended of the two daughters of king Henry the seventh, have or may have to the succession of Ingland, with intente afterward to handle the house of Portugal a part, which pretendeth to comprehende in itselfe the whole body, or at least the first and principal branch of the ancient house of Lancaster, it shall not be amisse, perhaps by the way, to treat in this one chapter, so much as appertayneth to the two several houses of Clarence and Bretaine, for that there is less to be said about them than of the other. . . .
. . . Fiftly and lastly, both these and other competitors do allege against the earle of Huntington [Henry Hastings] as an important and sufficient barre against his pretence, the qualitie of his religion, which is (as they say) that he hath bin ever knowne to favour those which commonly in Ingland are called Puritans, and not favoured by the state, but yet this stoppe is alleaged diversely by competitors of diverse religions; for that such as are followers and favourers of the form of religion receaved and defended by publique authoritie in Ingland at this daye, who for distinctions sake men are wont to call by the name of moderate protestants, these (I saye) do urge this exclusion against the earle of Huntington, not upon any certaine law or statute, extant against the same, but *ab aequo & bono.* . . .
. . . This then being so cleere as it is, first that according to the common cause of succession in Ingland, and other countries, and according to the course of all common law, the Infanta of Spaine should inherite the whole kingedom of France, and all other states thereto belonging. She being the daughter and heyre of the eldest daughter of King Henry the second King of France, whose issue male of the direct line is now wholly ended, but yet for that the French do pretend their Law Salik to exclude women (which we Inglish have ever denied to be good until nowe) hereby cometh it to passe that the King of Navarr [Henry IV] pretendeth to enter & to be preferred before the said Infanta or her sisters children, though male, by a colateral line. But yet her favourers say, I mean those of the Infanta, that from the Dukedoms of Bretaine, Acquitaine and the like, that came to the crowne of France by women, and are inheritable by women, she cannot be in right debarred, as neyther from any succession or pretence in Ingland, if either by the blood royal of France, Bretaine, Acquitaine or of Ingland itselfe, it may be proved that she had any interest thereunto, as her said favourers do affirme that she hathe, by these reasons following.

First for that she is of the ancient blood royal of Ingland, even from the conquest, by the elder daughter of William the Conqueror married to Allayne Fergat duke of Bretaine. . . .

. . . and this is in effect as much as I have heard alleaged hetherto in favour of the Infanta of Spayne, but against this pretence, other so produce divers arguments and obiections, as first of all that her claymes be very olde and worne out, and are but co-lateral, by sisters. Secondly that she is a stranger and an alien borne. Thirdly that her religion is contrary to the state. . . .'

III

Extract from Sir John Harrington, *A Tract on the Succession to the Crowne* (London, 1602); taken from the edition by C.R. Markham (Roxburghe Club, 1880), p. 45.

'And therefore to conclude, whatsoever Parsons or Dollman, or Parsons in Dollmans vizor, and so Dollman *personatus* do impute in this kynde of competition to the Lady Arbella and her friendes, I hold myself bound in the dutie of an honest man and of an Englishman thus farre to answere in defence of one of the greatest peers in this lande, against a suspition of disloyaltie and ill affection in a matter of so great consequence to the peace of England. And thus much of your ix section, and of the King of Scots his title by his father, of which lyne the Lady Arbella is also descended.

To the tenth, eleaventh, twelvth and thirteenth passage, wherein he justlie complayneth of some secret Aspirers that broach lyes to her Maiestie, to serve either their owne ambition or others. I add thus much, that notwithstanding all their lyes and false fyers, I mean their false fears, either in my Lord of Leycesters tyme or since, yet to this power they could never perswade her Maiestie in aught I could ever yet learne to goe from that princely worde that she gave at the beginninge of her raigne as is before recited concerning the succession; and though indeed few dare aske her such a question, as who shall be her heire, yet a vertuous and discreet Ladye as any as hath place about hir hath told me that voluntarily some tyme when fewe are present, shee had taken occasion to speake of it her selfe, and then hath not stuck plainely to say that they were fooles that did not knowe that the lyne of Scotland must needes be next heires, but for all that no bodie dares ever sooth her when she saith it.

For the xiiith, where he saith that many perhaps have received the Scottish King in theire heartes alredie, I confesse that my hearte so concurrs with Mr. Wentworths heart in this that I wish Gods blessing on their heartes that have done so, neither doubt I anie danger so muche as treacherie against his noble person. . . .'

IV

Extract from Camden, *Historie of . . . Elizabeth* (London, 1630), p. 658.

'The Queen, who had hitherto enjoyed her health without Impaerment, by reason of her abstinence from wine, and observing a temperate Diet (which she usually said was the noblest part of Physic) now being in her Climacterical year, to wit, the Seventieth year of her Age, began to be sensible of some weakness and indisposition, both of Health and Old Age, which the Badness of the weather increased. . . . And the Courtiers observed that she never before more frequented Prayers and the Service of God than now. Who also report, that she then commanded the Ring wherewith she had been as it were joyned in Marriage to her kingdom at her Inaugeration, and had never since taken off, to be filed off from her finger, because it was so grown into the Flesh, that it could not be drawen off. Which was taken for a sad Omen, as if it portended that her marriage with the kingdom, contracted with that Ring, would now be dissolved. In the beginning of her sickness the Almonds in her throat swelled, and soon Abated again; then her Appetite failed by degrees; and withall she gave herself over wholly to Melancholy. . . .

    . . . They all thought good that he [the Lord Admiral] with the Lord Keeper [Thomas Egerton, Lord Ellesmere] and the Secretary [Sir Robert Cecil] should wait upon her, and put her in mind thereof, and acquaint her that they were come in the name of the rest of the Council to understand her Pleasure touching her successor. The Queen made answer with a gasping breath; I said that my Throne was the throne of Kings, that I would not have any mean person succeed me. The Secretary asked what she meant by these words. I will (said she) that a king succeed me; and who should that be but my nearest kinsman, the King of Scots? . . .

    On the 24 of March, being the Eve of the Annunciation of the Blessed Virgin she (who was born on the Eve of the Nativity of the same Blessed Virgin) was called out of the Prison of her earthly body to enjoy an everlasting Countrey in Heaven, peacefully and quietly leaving this life after that happy manner of Departure, which Augustus wished for, having reigned 44 years, 4 months, and in the seventieth year of her age. . . .'

Mountjoy's ejection of the Spaniards from Kinsale in December 1601 was the beginning of the end for Tyrone. He had achieved more than any former Irish leader in terms of uniting the Catholic Irish against the alien and intrusive English presence, and he was a master of what would later be called guerrilla warfare, but he was no match for the sheer professionalism of Mountjoy. Once the latter was rid of the embarrassment of Essex, and given adequate resources, he was able to defeat the rebels in detail. After Aguila's unsuccessful incursion had been defeated, it was unlikely that any more direct help would come from Spain. The rebels could get money, and some arms, but what they really needed was professional stiffening and discipline, and those things could not be obtained. Moreover, as the tide turned against Tyrone, his support began to crumble.

Maintaining a united front had always been difficult, and by the beginning of 1603 it had become impossible. Bearing in mind the nature of Tyrone's communications with Spanish and papal representatives, to say nothing of his propaganda, the rhetoric of his eventual submission sounds totally hypocritical. However, it echoed earlier half-submissions which he had offered when his cause was not prospering, and it need not be supposed that Mountjoy took it too seriously. What mattered was that this was a real and unconditional surrender, and it was necessary to accept and seal it before the dying queen expired (or at least before Tyrone discovered that she was about to expire). The earl survived for another ten years before he was eventually attainted for renewed activism.

By the time that this surrender was fully accomplished, Elizabeth was dead. In spite of Camden's comment about the robustness of her health, the need to execute Essex in 1601 had hit her hard. For the last time her political instincts had had to defeat her personal feelings, as they had done over her relations with Robert Dudley forty years earlier. However, she was no longer a resilient young woman, and the crisis had brutally exposed flaws in her judgement which she was too honest to deny. That could have been the cause of the melancholy her servants noticed, or that may have resulted from a belated regret that she was the last of her line; it is not known. For a person of her strong religious faith, it is unlikely to have been caused by fear of approaching death, and in political terms she can have had few other things to regret.

The succession had been an issue for more years than anyone could remember, but it had changed its nature. For about twenty years it had been primarily a question of when, or whether, the queen could be persuaded to marry, and if so, who. Since about 1580, though, it had been a question of who had the best claim, in default of such an heir. In spite of 'Doleman's' exhaustive researches, there were not all that many realistic candidates. After the execution of Mary in 1587, her son James was by far the strongest in hereditary terms. The only trouble was that the Stuart claim had been debarred (or at least ignored) by the succession act of 1543, which had steered events from Henry's death until Elizabeth's accession, and had never been repealed. By the terms of that statute, the next heir should have been Edward Seymour, Earl of Hertford, the son of Jane Grey's younger sister Catherine. However, the queen regarded him as illegitimate because she had never sanctioned his parents' marriage, and he had no effective support. The other surviving claimant of the Suffolk line was William Stanley, Earl of Derby, the grandson of Mary Tudor's younger daughter, Eleanor, Countess of Cumberland, but he similarly was almost unconsidered.

'Doleman's' delving into the remoter recesses of royal genealogy produced a claim of a sort for Philip II's eldest daughter, Isabella. Even he was forced to admit that such a claim was remote, and his preference for it was based solely upon the fact that she was a strong Catholic. Only the more extreme wing of the English recusants (especially those who were Spanish pensioners) appear to have accepted his arguments. Like the infanta, the Earl of Huntingdon's claim bypassed the Tudors altogether, and that was a dangerous thing to do; nor is there any sign that he was taken seriously as a candidate (least of all by himself). In spite of 'Doleman's' opinion, it is very unlikely that his religion played any part in this rejection.

The only person, apart from James, for whom there was any identifiable support was the famously obscure Arabella Stuart, the daughter of Charles Stuart, 6th Earl of Lennox, and consequently a great-granddaughter of Henry VIII's elder sister, Margaret, through her second marriage to Archibald Douglas, Earl of Angus. Arabella was married to Lord Beauchamp, heir to the Earl of Hertford, but her claim was preferred (by some) to his. 'Doleman's' *Conference* stirred up enormous controversy, in spite of official attempts to suppress the whole discussion. Harrington was only one of those who responded, but he is cited here because he was persona grata at court and his inside information is likely to have been accurate.

Elizabeth's preference was in fact an open secret, and only those with an axe to grind were determined to ignore it, if possible. The problem was to persuade her to make it publicly known, and thus to silence all contention. That she refused to do, until eventually on her deathbed it became clear that there was nothing further to be gained (and perhaps a lot to lose) by further delay. She must have known that many of her servants and ministers were already in touch with James. They acted secretly, but more out of desire to spare her feelings than because they were engaged in a dangerous intrigue. In spite of a good deal of rhetorical angst, the succession was a foregone conclusion, and was peacefully, even enthusiastically, accomplished. It was the last thing that the old queen got right.

APPENDIX

Maps

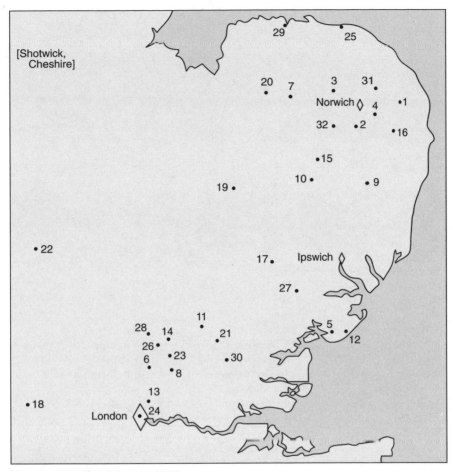

[Shotwick, Cheshire]

29   25

20 7   3 31
Norwich ◊ 4   •1
32 • •2   •16

•15

10 •   •9
19 •

• 22

17 • Ipswich ◊
27 •

11
28 14   21   5
26 •   12
6 •23
•30
•8
13
•18
London ◊ 24

Estates granted to Mary in 1597.

◊ Principal towns

Estates identified by the main seat or manor (many minor lands are not marked):

1 Acle	12 Gt Clacton	23 Roydon
2 Aslacton	13 Highbury	24 St John of Jerusalem
3 Barningham	14 Hunsdon	(Clerkenwell)
4 Brooke	15 Kenninghall	25 Sheringham
5 Chiche St Osyth	16 Loddon	26 Stansted Abbot
6 Copped Hall	17 Long Melford	27 Stoke by Nayland
7 East Bradenham	18 Marlowe	28 Ware
8 Epping	19 Mildenhall	29 Wells
9 Fressingfield	20 Necton	30 Writtle
10 Garboldesham	21 Newhall	31 Wroxham
11 Greenstead	22 Olney	32 Wymondham

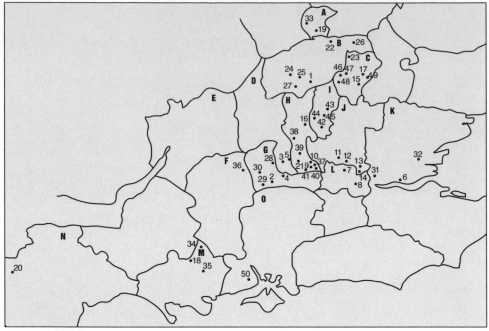

The estates of the Lady Elizabeth.

Properties:

1 Wellingborough
2 Newbury
3 Ewelme
4 Cholsey
5 Watlington
6 Canvey Marsh
7 Enfield
8 Durham Place
9 Amersham
10 Missenden Abbey
11 Berkhampstead
12 Hemel Hempsted
13 Hatfield
14 North Mymms
15 St Neots
16 Newport Pagnell
17 St Ives
18 Sturminster Newton
19 Uppingham
20 Umberleigh
21 Princes Risborough
22 Colleyweston
23 Yaxley

24 Yelvertoft
25 Moulton
26 Maxey
27 Hardingstowe
28 Radley
29 Donnington
30 Hamsted Marshall
31 Cannonberry
32 Woodham Ferrers
33 Barrowghdon (sic)
34 Marnhull
35 Buckland Newton
36 Chilton Folyett
37 Ashridge
38 Hanslop
39 Castlethorpe
40 Langley
41 Farnham Royal
42 Apsley Geyes
43 Old Wardon
44 Evesholt
45 Barton
46 Brampton

47 Brington
48 Bythor
49 Holywell
50 Bulberne Bremer

Counties:

A   Rutland
B   Northamptonshire
C   Huntingdonshire
D   Oxfordshire
E   Gloucestershire
F   Wiltshire
G   Berkshire
H   Buckinghamshire
I   Bedfordshire
J   Hertfordshire
K   Essex
L   Middlesex
M   Dorset
N   Devon
O   Hampshire

NB This list is not exhaustive, nor are the locations precise. County boundaries have moved since the sixteenth century, and several minor properties cannot be identified with certainty.

Reading Suggestions

This is a very selective list from a huge literature. Secondary works only are included, as guidance to primary sources can be found in the selected documents.

GENERAL

Brigden, S., *New Worlds – Lost Worlds* (London, 2000)
Cross, C., *Church and People, 1450–1660* (2nd edn, Oxford, 2000)
Guy, J.A., *Tudor England* (London, 1988)
Haigh, C., *Elizabeth I* (2nd edn, London, 2001)
Loades, D.M., *Politics and the Nation, 1450–1660* (5th edn, Oxford, 2000)
Smith, A.G.R., *The Emergence of a Nation State, 1529–1660* (London, 1984)
Williams, P., *The Tudor Regime* (Oxford, 1979)
——, *The Later Tudors, 1547–1603* (Oxford, 1995)

PART I: QUEEN JANE AND QUEEN MARY

The Suffolk Line

Hoak, D.E., 'Rehabilitating the Duke of Northumberland; politics and political control, 1549–1553', in J. Loach and R. Tittler (eds), *The Mid-Tudor Polity* (London, 1980)
Jordan, W.K., *Edward VI: the Threshold of Power* (London, 1970)
Loach, J., *Edward VI* (London, 1999)
Loades, D.M., *John Dudley, Duke of Northumberland* (Oxford, 1996)
(There is no biography of Henry Grey, Duke of Suffolk.)

The Crisis of July 1553

Alsop, J.D., 'A regime at sea; the navy and the 1553 succession crisis', *Albion*, 24 (1992), 577–90
Harbison, E.H., *Rival Ambassadors at the Court of Queen Mary* (Princeton, 1940)
Loades, D.M., *Mary Tudor: a Life* (Oxford, 1989)
Tittler, R. and Battey, S.L., 'The local community and the Crown in 1553; the accession of Mary Tudor revisited', *Bulletin of the Institute of Historical Research*, 136 (1984), 131–40
(Jordan, *Threshold*; Loades, *Dudley*)

Mary is Received and Established

Hoak, D.E., 'Two revolutions in Tudor government; the formation and organisation of Mary Tudor's privy Council', in D. Coleman and D. Starkey (eds), *Revolution Reassessed* (London, 1986), pp. 87–115
Loades, D.M., *The Reign of Mary Tudor* (London, 1991)
Tittler, R., *Mary I* (2nd edn, London, 1991)
Weikel, A., 'The Marian Council revisited', in Loach and Tittler, *Mid-Tudor Polity*, pp. 52–73
(Harbison, *Rival Ambassadors*; Loades, *Mary Tudor*)

The Old Religion

Carleton, K., *Bishops and Reform in the English Church, 1520–1559* (Woodbridge, 2001)
Duffy, E., *The Stripping of the Altars* (London, 1992)
Hughes, P., *The Reformation in England*, II (London, 1953)
Wooding, L., *Re-thinking Catholicism in Reformation England* (Oxford, 2000)

The First Ruling Queen

Richards, J., 'Mary Tudor as "Sole Quene"? Gendering Tudor Monarchy', *Historical Journal*, 40 (1997), 895–924
——, '"To promote a woman to bear rule"; talking of Queens in Mid-Tudor England', *Sixteenth Century Journal*, 38 (1997), 101–22
(Loades, *Mary Tudor*; *Reign of Mary*; Tittler, *Mary I*)

Negotiations for Marriage

Kamen, H., *Philip II* (London, 1997)
Rodriguez Salgado, M-J., *The Changing Face of Empire, 1551–1559* (Cambridge, 1988)
(Harbison, *Rival Ambassadors*; Loades, *Mary Tudor*; *Reign of Mary*; Tittler, *Mary I*)

Mary and the Papacy

Fenlon, D., *Heresy and Obedience in Tridentine Italy* (Cambridge, 1972)
Mayer, T., *Reginald Pole, Prince and Prophet* (London, 2000)
(Hughes, *Reformation*; Loades, *Mary Tudor*)

The Wyatt Rebellion

Fletcher, A. and MacCulloch, D., *Tudor Rebellions* (London, 1997)
Loades, D.M., *Two Tudor Conspiracies* (Bangor, 1991)
Robinson, W.B., 'The national and local significance of Wyatt's rebellion in Surrey', *Historical Journal*, 30 (1987), 769–90
Thorpe, M.R., 'Religion and the rebellion of Sir Thomas Wyatt', *Church History*, 47 (4) (1978)
(Tittler, *Mary I*)

Elizabeth Imprisoned

Starkey, D., *Elizabeth* (London, 2000)
Wiesener, L., *The Youth of Queen Elizabeth*, trs. C.M. Yonge (London, 1879)
(Loades, *Reign of Mary*; *Conspiracies*)

The Marriage of Philip and Mary

Anglo, S., *Spectacle, Pageantry and Early Tudor Policy* (London, 1966)
Prescott, H.F.M., *Mary Tudor* (London, 1953)
Redworth, G., '"Matters impertinent to women"; male and female monarchy under Philip and Mary', *English Historical Review*, 112 (1997), 597–613
(Harbison, *Rival Ambassadors*; Loades, *Mary Tudor*; *Reign of Mary*; Tittler, *Mary I*)

Anglo-Spanish Entanglements

Russell, E., 'Mary Tudor and Mr. Jorkins', *Historical Research*, 63 (1990), 263–76
(Harbison, *Rival Ambassadors*; Loades, *Mary Tudor*; Mayer, *Reginald Pole*; Rodriguez Salgado, *Changing Face*)

Reconciliation with Rome

Frere, W.H., *The Marian Reaction in its Relation with the English Clergy* (London, 1896)
(Duffy, *Altars*; Hughes, *Reformation*; Loades, *Mary Tudor*; *Reign of Mary*; Mayer, *Reginald Pole*; Wooding, *Catholicism*)

The City of London

Bisson, D.R., *The Merchant Adventurers of England: the Company and the Crown, 1474–1564* (Newark, NJ, 1993)
Brigden, S., *London and the Reformation* (Oxford, 1989)

Foster, Sir William, *England's Quest of Eastern Trade* (London, 1933)
Loades, D.M., *England's Maritime Empire, 1490–1690* (London, 2000)
Pettegree, A., *Foreign Protestant Communities in Sixteenth Century London* (Oxford, 1986)

Religious Persecution
Dickens, A.G., *The English Reformation* (2nd edn, London, 1989)
Haigh, C., *English Reformations* (Oxford, 1993)
Loades, D.M., *The Oxford Martyrs* (London, 1970)
MacCulloch, D., *Thomas Cranmer: a Life* (London, 1996)
Ridley, J., *Bloody Mary's Martyrs* (London, 2001)
(Hughes, *Reformation*)

The Queen's Pregnancy
(Loades, *Mary Tudor*; Prescott, *Mary*; Tittler, *Mary I*)

The Religious Exile
Bartlett, K.R., 'The English exile community in Italy and the political opposition to Mary I', *Albion*, 13 (1981), 223–41
——, 'The role of the Marian exiles', in P.W. Hasler (ed.), *The Commons 1558–1603*, I (London, 1981), pp. 102–10
Garrett, C.H., *The Marian Exiles* (Cambridge, 1938)
Pettegree, A., *Marian Protestantism: Six Studies* (Aldershot, 1996)

The Court of Philip and Mary
Loades, D.M., *The Tudor Court* (London, 1986)
McCoy, R.C., 'From the Tower to the Tiltyard; Robert Dudley's return to glory', *Historical Journal*, 27 (1984), 425–35
Murphy, J., 'The illusion of decline; the Privy Chamber, 1547–1558', in D. Starkey (ed.), *The English Court from the Wars of the Roses to the Civil War* (London, 1987), pp. 119–46
(Starkey, *Elizabeth*)

Queen Mary's Navy
Glasgow, T., 'The navy in Philip and Mary's war', *Mariners' Mirror*, 53 (1967), 321–42
——, 'The maturing of naval administration, 1556–1564', *Mariners' Mirror*, 56 (1970), 3–26
Loades, D.M., *The Tudor Navy* (Aldershot, 1992)
Rodger, N.A.M., *The Safeguard of the Sea, 660–1649* (London, 1997)

The Problem of Elizabeth
(Loades, *Reign of Mary*; Prescott, *Mary*; Starkey, *Elizabeth*; Wiesener, *Youth*)

Plots and Conspiracies
Loach, J., *Parliament and the Crown in the Reign of Mary Tudor* (Oxford, 1986)
——, 'The Marian establishment and the printing press', *English Historical Review*, 101 (1987), 135–48
(Bartlett, 'Exile Community'; Loades, *Conspiracies*; Starkey, *Elizabeth*)

War with France
Davies, C.S.L., 'England and the French war of 1557–9', in Loach and Tittler, *Mid-Tudor Polity*, pp. 159–85

(Glasgow, 'The Navy'; Loades, *Reign of Mary*; Rodger, *Safeguard*; Rodriquez Salgado, *Changing Face*)

The Death of Queen Mary
Froude, J.A., *The Reign of Mary Tudor*, ed. W.L. Williams (London, 1910)
Stone, J.M., *Mary I, Queen of England* (London, 1901)
(Loades, *Mary Tudor*; Mayer, *Reginald Pole*; Prescott, *Mary*)

PART II: QUEEN ELIZABETH

The Accession of a New Queen
Arnold, J., *Queen Elizabeth's Wardrobe Unlock'd* (Leeds, 1988)
Bayne, C.G., 'The coronation of Queen Elizabeth', *English Historical Review*, 22 (1907), 650–73
MacCaffrey, W., *The Shaping of the Elizabethan Regime: Elizabethan Politics 1558–1572* (London, 1969)
Read, Conyers, *Mr. Secretary Cecil and Queen Elizabeth* (London, 1955)

The Settlement of Religion
Bayne, C.G., *Anglo-Roman Relations, 1558–1565* (Oxford, 1968)
Elton, G.R., *The Parliament of England, 1559–81* (Cambridge, 1986)
Haugaard, W.P., *Elizabeth and the English Reformation: the Struggle for a Settlement of Religion* (London, 1970)
Jones, N., *Faith by Statute: Parliament and the Settlement of Religion, 1559* (London, 1982)
MacCullough, P.E., *Sermons at Court* (Cambridge, 1998)
(Bartlett, 'Marian Exiles')

Intervention in Scotland
Dawson, J.E.A., 'William Cecil and the British dimension in early Elizabethan foreign policy', *History*, 74 (1989), 196–216
Donaldson, G., *Scotland: James V–James VII* (Edinburgh, 1965)
Mason, R. (ed.), *Scotland and England, 1286–1815* (London, 1982)
Wernham, R.B., *Before the Armada: the Growth of English Foreign Policy, 1485–1588* (London, 1966)
(MacCaffrey, *Shaping of the Elizabethan Regime*; Read, *Mr. Secretary Cecil*)

Marriage and the Succession
Berry, P., *Of Chastity and Power* (London, 1989)
Black, J.B., *The Reign of Elizabeth* (Oxford, 1959)
Doran, S., *Monarchy and Matrimony: The Courtships of Queen Elizabeth* (London, 1996)
Levine, M., *The Early Elizabethan Succession Question, 1558–1568* (Cambridge, 1966)
(Read, *Mr. Secretary Cecil*)

Intervention in France
Sutherland, N.M., *The Huguenot Struggle for Recognition* (London, 1980)
Wilson, D., *Sweet Robin* (Robert Dudley, Earl of Leicester) (London, 1981)
(Black, *Reign of Elizabeth*; MacCaffrey, *Shaping of the Elizabethan Regime*; Read, *Mr. Secretary Cecil*)

The State of the Nation
Archer, I.W., *The Pursuit of Stability: Social Relations in Elizabethan London* (London, 1991)
Challis, C.E., *The Tudor Coinage* (Manchester, 1978)
Clark, P. and Slack, P. (eds), *English Towns in Transition, 1500–1700* (Oxford, 1976)
Thirsk, Joan (ed.), *The Agrarian History of England and Wales, 1500–1640* (Oxford, 1967)

New Departures
Lewis, M., *The Hawkins Dynasty* (London, 1969)
Ramsey, G.D., *English Overseas Trade during the Centuries of Emergence* (London, 1957)
Scammell, G.V., *The World Encompassed: the First European Maritime Empires*, c. *800–1650* (London, 1981)
Smith, G. Connell, *The Forerunners of Drake* (London, 1954)
(Loades, *Maritime Empire*)

Tragedy in Scotland
Fraser, A., *Mary Queen of Scots* (London, 1969)
Henderson, T.F., *Mary Queen of Scots* (Edinburgh, 1905)
Marshall, R.K., *Mary, Queen of Scots* (Edinburgh, 1986)
(Donaldson, *Scotland*; MacCaffrey, *Shaping of the Elizabethan Regime*)

Dangerous Courses
Read, Conyers, 'Queen Elizabeth's seizure of the Duke of Alva's pay ships', *Journal of Modern History*, 5 (1933), 443–64
Reid, R., 'The rebellion of the earls, 1569', *Transactions of the Royal Historical Society*, 2nd ser., 20 (1906), 171–203
(Black, *Reign of Elizabeth*; Fletcher and MacCulloch, *Rebellions*; MacCaffrey, *Shaping of the Elizabethan Regime*)

French Connections
Levy, F.J., 'A semi-professional diplomatist; Guido Cavalcanti and the marriage negotiations of 1571', *Bulletin of the Institute of Historical Research*, 35 (1962), 211–20
Sutherland, N.M., *The Massacre of St. Bartholomew and the European Conflict* (London, 1973)
(Doran, *Monarchy*; MacCaffrey, *Shaping of the Elizabethan Regime*; Sutherland, *Huguenot Struggle*)

The Problem of the Netherlands
Black, J.B., 'Queen Elizabeth, the sea beggars and the capture of Brill', *English Historical Review*, 46 (1931), 30–47
MacCaffrey, W., *Queen Elizabeth and the Making of Policy, 1572–88* (London, 1981)
Parker, G., *The Dutch Revolt* (London, 1977)
Wilson, C., *Queen Elizabeth and the Revolt of the Netherlands* (Cambridge, 1970)

Elizabeth's Court
Adams, S., 'Eliza enthroned? The court and its politics', in C. Haigh (ed.), *The Reign of Elizabeth I* (2nd edn, London, 2000)
Williams, P., 'Court and polity under Elizabeth I', *Bulletin of the John Rylands Library*, 65 (1983), 259–86
Wright, P., 'A change of direction; the ramifications of a female household', in D. Starkey (ed.), *The English Court* (London, 1987), pp. 147–72

Young, A., *Tudor and Jacobean Tournaments* (London, 1987)
(Loades, *Tudor Court*)

Protestant Nonconformity
Collinson, P., *The Elizabethan Puritan Movement* (London, 1967)
——, *The Religion of Protestants* (Oxford, 1982)
Lake, P., *Moderate Puritans and the Elizabethan Church* (Cambridge, 1982)
Primus, J.H., *The Vestments Controversy* (Leiden, 1960)
Seaver, P.S., *The Puritan Lectureships: the Politics of Religious Dissent, 1560–1662* (London, 1970)

Towards War
Kelsey, H., *Sir Francis Drake: the Queen's Pirate* (New Haven, CT, 1998)
(Black, *Reign of Elizabeth*; Doran, *Monarchy*; MacCaffrey, *Making of Policy*; Wernham, *Before the Armada*; Wilson, *Sweet Robin*)

The Fate of Mary, Queen of Scots
Donaldson, G., *Mary Queen of Scots* (Edinburgh, 1974)
Graves, M.A.R., *Thomas Norton: the Parliament Man* (Oxford, 1994)
Lee, M., 'The daughter of debate; Mary Queen of Scots after 400 years', *Scottish Historical Review*, 68 (1989), 70–9
(Black, *Reign of Elizabeth*; MacCaffrey, *Making of Policy*)

The Presbyterian Challenge
Collinson, P., *Archbishop Grindal, 1519–1583: the Struggle for a Reformed Church* (London, 1979)
Cross, C., *The Royal Supremacy in the Elizabethan Church* (London, 1969)
Lake, P., *Anglican and Puritan? Presbyterianism and English Conformist Thought from Whitgift to Hooker* (London, 1988)
Read, Conyers, *Lord Burghley and Queen Elizabeth* (London, 1960)
Usher, R.G. (ed.), *The Presbyterian Movement in the Reign of Queen Elizabeth*, Camden Society, 3rd ser., 8 (1905)

War, 1585–90
Cruikshank, C.G., *Elizabeth's Army* (2nd edn, Oxford, 1966)
Fernandez Armesto, F., *The Spanish Armada: the Experience of War in 1588* (London, 1988)
Martin, C. and Parker, G., *The Spanish Armada* (London, 1988)
(Kelsey, *Drake*; Loades, *Tudor Navy*; Rodger, *Safeguard*; Wilson, *Sweet Robin*)

Catholic Recusancy
Bossy, J., *The English Catholic Community, 1570–1850* (London, 1975)
Haigh, C., 'The continuity of Catholicism in the English Reformation', *Past and Present*, 93 (1981), 37–69
Holmes, P., *Resistance and Compromise: the Political Thought of the Elizabethan Catholics* (Cambridge, 1982)
McCoog, T.M. (ed.), *The Reckoned Expense: Edmund Campion and the Early English Jesuits* (Woodbridge, 1996)
Morey, A., *The Catholic Subjects of Elizabeth I* (London, 1978)
(Wooding, *Re-thinking Catholicism*)

The Elizabethan Navy and the Privateers

Andrews, K.R., *Elizabethan Privateering* (Cambridge, 1964)

Bovill, E.W., 'The Madre de Dios', *Mariners' Mirror*, 54 (1968), 129–52

French, P.J., *John Dee: the World of an Elizabethan Magus* (London, 1973)

Oppenheim, M., *The History of the Administration of the Royal Navy, 1509–1660* (London, 1896)

Spence, R.T., *The Privateering Earl: George Clifford, 3rd Earl of Cumberland* (Stroud, 1995)

(Loades, *Tudor Navy*; Rodger, *Safeguard*)

The Spanish War, 1590–1604

Corbett, J.S., *The Successors of Drake* (London, 1900)

Lloyd, Howell, *The Rouen Campaign, 1590–92* (Oxford, 1973)

MacCaffrey, W, *Elizabeth I: War and Politics, 1588–1603* (London, 1992)

Nolan, J.S., *Sir John Norreys and the Elizabethan Military World* (Exeter, 1997)

Wernham, R.B., *After the Armada: Elizabethan England and the Struggle for Western Europe* (London, 1984)

(Rodger, *Safeguard*)

Ireland

Andrews, K., Canny, N. and Hair, P., *The Westward Enterprise, 1480–1650* (Liverpool, 1978)

Bradshaw, B. and Morrill, J., *The British Problem, 1534–1707* (London, 1996)

Canny, N.P., *The Elizabethan Conquest of Ireland: a Pattern Established, 1565–1576* (Brighton, 1976)

Ellis, S.G., *Tudor Ireland* (London, 1985)

Falls, C., *Elizabeth's Irish Wars* (London, 1950)

McGurk, J., *The English Conquest of Ireland: the 1590s Crisis* (Manchester, 1997)

Silke, J.J., *Kinsale: the Spanish Intervention in Ireland at the End of the Elizabethan Wars* (Liverpool, 1970)

Money and Hardship

Beir, A.L., *Masterless Men: the Vagrancy Problem in England, 1560–1640* (London, 1985)

Coleman, D.C., *The Economy of England, 1450–1750* (London, 1977)

Dietz, F.C., *English Public Finance, 1558–1641* (New York, 1932)

Sharpe, J.A., *Crime in Early Modern England, 1550–1750* (London, 1984)

Wrightson, K., *English Society, 1580–1680* (London, 1982)

Wrigley, E.A. and Schofield, R.S., *The Population History of England, 1541–1871: a Reconstruction* (London, 1981)

Roanoake and Imperial Ambition

Quinn, D.B. and Ryan, A.N., *England's Sea Empire* (Liverpool, 1983)

Rabb, T.K., *Enterprise and Empire, 1575–1630* (New Haven, 1967)

——, *Jacobean Gentleman: Sir Edwin Sandys, 1561–1629* (London, 1998)

Scammell, G.V., *The First Imperial Age* (London, 1989)

(Andrews, Canny and Hair, *Westward Enterprise*; Loades, *Maritime Empire*)

The Cult of Gloriana

Dovey, Zillah, *An Elizabethan Progress* (Stroud, 1996)

King, J.N., *Tudor Royal Iconography: Literature and Art in an Age of Religious Crisis* (Princeton, 1989)

Strong, R., *The Cult of Elizabeth: Elizabethan Portraits and Pageantry* (London, 1977)
——, *Gloriana: the Portraits of Queen Elizabeth I* (London, 1987)
Worden, B., *The Sound of Virtue: Philip Sidney's Arcadia and Elizabethan Politics* (New Haven, CT, 1996)
Yates, F.A., *Astrea: the Imperial Theme in the Sixteenth Century* (London, 1975)
(Berry, *Chastity*)

Music and Theatre
Ashbee, A. and Lasocki, D., *A Biographical Dictionary of English Court Musicians, 1485–1714* (Aldershot, 1998)
Astington, J., *English Court Theatre, 1558–1642* (Cambridge, 1999)
Boyd, M.C., *Elizabethan Music and Musical Criticism* (London, 1940)
Briggs, J., *The Stage-Play World: English Literature and its Background, 1580–1625* (London, 1983)
Butler, M., *Theatre and Crisis* (Cambridge, 1984)
Pattison, B., *Music and Poetry of the English Renaissance* (London, 1948)

Cecil and Essex
Guy, J.A., *The Reign of Elizabeth I: Court and Culture in the Last Decade* (London, 1995)
Hammer, P.E.J., *The Polarisation of Elizabethan Politics: the Political Career of Robert Devereux, 2nd Earl of Essex, 1585–1597* (London, 1999)
Handover, P.M., *The Second Cecil: the Rise to Power of Sir Robert Cecil, 1563–1604* (London, 1959)
Smith, A.G.R., *Servant of the Cecils: the Life of Sir Michael Hicks, 1543–1612* (London, 1977)
Smith, L.B., *Treason in Tudor England: Politics and Paranoia* (London, 1986)
(MacCaffrey, *War and Politics*; Read, *Lord Burghley*)

The Last Years of the Reign
Collinson, P., 'The monarchical republic of Queen Elizabeth', *Bulletin of the John Rylands Library*, 69 (1987), 394–424
Galloway, B., *The Union of England and Scotland, 1603–1608* (Edinburgh, 1986)
Mason, R.A. (ed.), *Scots and Britons* (East London, 1997)
Stafford, H.G., *James VI of Scotland and the Throne of England* (London, 1940)
(MacCaffrey, *War and Politics*; Nolan, *Sir John Norreys*; Wernham, *After the Armada*)

Index